MW00398907

"Stephen Porges's masterful theory of the nervous system is one of the most detailed, true to life portraits of the embodied nervous system—something we only had glimpses of, because of huge blind spots that Porges has remediated. *Polyvagal Perspectives* extends the range of a theory so important that it is painful to think what our understanding of the nervous system and human behavior would be without it. Hence my excitement, among so many, to see where Porges taken it in this latest volume, *Polyvagal Perspectives*."

—**Norman Doidge, MD,** author of *The Brain That Changes Itself* and *The Brain's Way of Healing*

"Stephen Porges is the exemplar of an outstanding researcher and theorist who has translated his foundational work, Polyvagal Theory, into a transformative perspective on a diverse array of disorders that cause human suffering, as well as developed strategies for dealing with them. In *Polyvagal Perspectives*, Porges elaborates on the mediating role of the autonomic nervous system and how it provides us with a unifying mechanism for understanding psychotherapy, trauma, sociality, regulation, education, and much more. Indeed, his view that the polyvagal system underlies feelings of safety takes us on a journey from neurophysiology to how we experience the world and make meaning of ourselves within it."

—**Ed Tronick, PhD,** professor of psychiatry and pediatrics, University of Massachusetts Chan Medical School, and coauthor with Claudia Gold of *The Power of Discord*

"Just as Copernicus challenged the notion that the sun revolves around the earth, and Darwin helped 'evolve' our view of the origins of mankind, Porges's Polyvagal Theory similarly challenges conventional thinking by extending evolutionary concepts to the vagus nerve. While 'mind–body' medicine has recently become popular, the mechanisms of how the interactions occur were lacking until the conception of Polyvagal Theory. PTSD, inflammatory diseases, cancer, and even disorders such as Alzheimer's disease and autism all have vagal links. Porges's polyvagal heuristic approach gives psychologists and therapists tools to help their patients today, while simultaneously providing a paradigm shift for healthcare professionals across disciplines who are interested in understanding the future of health, stress, and disease."

—**Peter S. Staats, MD, MBA, FIPP, ABIPP,** chair of The Vagus Nerve Society, and founding director of the division of pain medicine, Johns Hopkins University, 1994–2004

POLYVAGAL PERSPECTIVES

The Norton Series on Interpersonal Neurobiology
Louis Cozolino, PhD, Series Editor
Allan N. Schore, PhD, Series Editor, 2007–2014
Daniel J. Siegel, MD, Founding Editor

The field of mental health is in a tremendously exciting period of growth and conceptual reorganization. Independent findings from a variety of scientific endeavors are converging in an interdisciplinary view of the mind and mental well-being. An interpersonal neurobiology of human development enables us to understand that the structure and function of the mind and brain are shaped by experiences, especially those involving emotional relationships.

The Norton Series on Interpersonal Neurobiology provides cutting-edge, multidisciplinary views that further our understanding of the complex neurobiology of the human mind. By drawing on a wide range of traditionally independent fields of research—such as neurobiology, genetics, memory, attachment, complex systems, anthropology, and evolutionary psychology—these texts offer mental health professionals a review and synthesis of scientific findings often inaccessible to clinicians. The books advance our understanding of human experience by finding the unity of knowledge, or consilience, that emerges with the translation of findings from numerous domains of study into a common language and conceptual framework. The series integrates the best of modern science with the healing art of psychotherapy.

POLYVAGAL PERSPECTIVES

Interventions, Practices, and Strategies

STEPHEN W. PORGES

Norton Professional Books

An Imprint of W. W. Norton & Company
Independent Publishers Since 1923

This book is intended as a general information resource for professionals practicing in the field of psychotherapy and mental health. It is not a substitute for appropriate training or clinical supervision. Standards of clinical practice and protocol vary in different practice settings and change over time. No technique or recommendation is guaranteed to be safe or effective in all circumstances, and neither the publisher nor the author(s) can guarantee the complete accuracy, efficacy, or appropriateness of any particular recommendation in every respect or in all settings or circumstances.

 As of press time, the URLs displayed in this book link or refer to existing websites. The publisher is not responsible for, and should not be deemed to endorse or recommend, any website other than its own or any other content available on the Internet or elsewhere, including, without limitation, any app, blog page, or information page, that the publisher did not create. The author, also, is not responsible for any third-party material.

For information about permission to reproduce selections from this book, write to Permissions, W. W. Norton & Company, Inc., 500 Fifth Avenue, New York, NY 10110

For information about special discounts for bulk purchases, please contact W. W. Norton Special Sales at specialsales@wwnorton.com or 800-233-4830

Manufacturing by Lake Book Manufacturing
Production manager: Gwen Cullen

ISBN: 978-1-324-05340-8

W. W. Norton & Company, Inc., 500 Fifth Avenue, New York, NY 10110
www.wwnorton.com

W. W. Norton & Company Ltd., 15 Carlisle Street, London W1D 3BS

1 2 3 4 5 6 7 8 9 0

To my students, mentees, colleagues, friends, and family who have joined me on a shared optimistic journey exploring how a polyvagal perspective demystifies human experience.

Contents

Acknowledgments

Polyvagal Theory has led me on a personal journey of exploration of the core human need to connect and to trust. I have learned that sociality literally nourishes our nervous system and serves as, perhaps, the most potent and relevant "neuromodulator" to calm our nervous systems to optimize and to support the homeostatic functions of health, growth, and restoration. This journey has shifted from a journey of discovery through experimentation to a journey of witnessing the voices of others, especially those whose nervous systems have been retuned through adverse experiences. Thus, the implications of Polyvagal Theory in mental health, education, and society would not have emerged without witnessing those who have shared their experiences with me. They have shared how Polyvagal Theory provided them with a manageable framework to understand, without judgment, the heroic reactions of their nervous systems in their quest for safety and survival. I graciously acknowledge those individuals and especially the power of their personal narratives of recovery. They have taught me that, although behavior and physiological state can be driven by foundational brainstem mechanisms, understanding Polyvagal Theory has enabled their conscious and intentional higher brain circuits to make meaning of their experiences.

Through insightful polyvagal-informed therapists and educators, the theory's applications have expanded into diverse fields such as psychotherapy, medicine, education, and performance. Exploring these broad applications has revealed that Polyvagal Theory transcends its initial scope, leading to a more generalizable *polyvagal perspective*, a perspective that proposes that the principles embedded in the theory can be applied across different disciplines. I want to acknowledge the input from these creative and curious "polyvagal-informed" scientists, scholars, and therapists, to whom I have listened as they explored a more expansive polyvagal perspective, a perspective broader than the initial focus of the theory. Through their insight, the theory is now having an impact in applied areas such as patient care, education, and work environment, areas well outside of the initial defining research questions and hypothesis of the laboratory science from which Polyvagal Theory evolved.

Foremost, I want to acknowledge my wife, Sue Carter. For decades she has listened to, witnessed, and shared ideas that were to become the Polyvagal Theory. Sue's landmark work, discovering the role of oxytocin in social bonds, and her general interest in the neurobiology of social behavior served to focus my thinking on the role the autonomic nervous system and physiological state played in not only health, but also in social behavior. Without Sue's enduring support, love, intellectual curiosity, and collaboration, Polyvagal Theory would not have evolved. Moreover, Sue's loving maternal support in nurturing our sons, Eric and Seth, has contributed to their individual contributions, while allowing me to be a "good enough" father. I am sincerely grateful to Sue's contribution. This book is truly a product of her support and love.

As the reader can surmise, the Porges home has been an intellectual incubator for a neuroscience of sociality that focuses on both the autonomic nervous system (my focus) and the neuropeptides of oxytocin and vasopressin (Sue's focus). Within this culture both our sons have contributed to the expanding realm of Polyvagal Theory. Seth coauthored with me *Our Polyvagal World: How Safety and Trauma Change Us*. Eric elected to follow within the family "business" and is a neuroscientist at the University of Florida. Not surprisingly, he conducts research on vagal stimulation with a focus on how it may reduce PTSD symptoms. He also maintains an interest in neuropeptides and neuroimaging. Thus, I want to acknowledge the welcoming and accessible intellectual culture of exploration and curiosity that has enabled our entire family to find meaning through both our individual as well as collaborative paths of inquiry.

A special thanks to Deborah Malmud, our editor at Norton. Deborah enthusiastically welcomed the idea of *Polyvagal Perspectives* as a collection of recent papers that have expanded the impact of Polyvagal Theory. I am appreciative of her help and support in transforming this collection of papers into an accessible vehicle for the Polyvagal Theory. I am pleased to add *Polyvagal Perspectives* to the expanding polyvagal bookshelf at Norton.

Preface

Polyvagal Theory was first presented in October of 1994 as my presidential address to the Society of Psychophysiological Research. A printed version was published in 1995 that was followed by several publications refining the theory and expanding its application. The theory was presented as an integrated model, encompassing my research excursions over several decades into a variety of disciplines (e.g., neonatology, anesthesiology, neurophysiology, psychophysiology, autism, developmental disabilities, prematurity, signal processing, human factors, ergonomics, child development, education, psychiatry, substance abuse, etc.).

As I developed my presidential address, I became immersed in the literature of several disciplines and literally explored all things vagal. As I read the literature, I attempted to integrate disparate information obtained from several disciplines and hoped to extract organizing principles that would clarify the relationship between autonomic state and both mental and physical processes. Evolution, as an organizing principle, spontaneously emerged when I started to explore comparative neuroanatomy and comparative neurophysiology, especially as I studied the contrast in structure and function of the autonomic nervous system in reptiles and mammals. Suddenly, using evolution as an organizing principle, the disparate information became manageable and interpretable. The result was a narrative of adaptive change in which the vertebrate autonomic nervous system provided a descriptive link between the autonomic nervous system and species-specific behaviors.

In its initial presentation, Polyvagal Theory (Porges, 1995) proposed the use of evolution as an organizing principle to weave a descriptive narrative of the vertebrate phylogenetic journey toward sociality and co-regulation. The journey documented a shift in the anatomical structure of the autonomic nervous system and how these structural changes were involved in the biobehavioral features that support health and are behaviorally observed as sociality and co-regulation in humans and other social mammals. The intent was to use the strong scientific basis of the theory as a bridge to transform the broad mind-brain-body schisms in science and society. The result would be a more unifying perspective, one that incorporated an understanding of autonomic state as a neural platform that could support either sociality and feelings of safety or defensive strategies and feelings of threat.

In 2007, I wrote a paper entitled "The Polyvagal Perspective" that was published in *Biological Psychology* and extracted portions are reprinted in the Appendix. I selected the title to emphasize that the concepts embedded in Polyvagal Theory were beginning to transcend the theoretical framework of a theory. At the time I wrote the paper the theory was gaining traction in the treatment of trauma and had become embedded in several prominent treatment models. However, as reflected in the opening and closing paragraphs of the paper, quoted below, my view of an expansive perspective was conservatively limited to research involving direct measurement of the autonomic nervous system.

> The polyvagal theory (Porges, 1995) introduced a new perspective relating autonomic function to behavior. This perspective includes an appreciation of the autonomic nervous system as a "system," the identification of neural circuits involved in the regulation of autonomic state, and an interpretation of autonomic reactivity as adaptive within the context of the phylogeny of the vertebrate autonomic nervous system. The polyvagal theory encourages a level of inquiry that challenges scientists to incorporate an integrative understanding of the role neural mechanisms play in regulating biobehavioral processes. The polyvagal theory requires an expansive conceptualization of the autonomic nervous system to include target organ afferent and efferent pathways, and a quest to understand the reciprocal influences and bidirectional communication between the heart and the central nervous system. The polyvagal theory provides a "perspective" to frame research questions and is not a static theory. Thus, as knowledge of neurophysiology increases, testable hypotheses will shape and expand the theory. (p. 116)
>
> The polyvagal perspective shifts research from atheoretical strategies toward theory driven paradigms dependent upon explicit neural mechanisms. Foremost, the polyvagal perspective emphasizes the importance of phylogenetic changes in the neural structures regulating the autonomic nervous system. The phylogenetic strategy provides insights into the adaptive function and the neural regulation of the two vagal systems (see Porges, 1995, 2001a). Without having constructs from the polyvagal theory to describe adaptive functions and to determine the measurement specifications of the two vagal systems (one associated with calm states and social engagement behaviors and the other a vestigial defense system that is potentially lethal to mammals), it would not be possible to disentangle the mechanisms and functions of the components of cardiac vagal tone. (p. 140)

During the past 30 years, Polyvagal Theory has been cited in more than 15,000 peer-reviewed articles and revolutionized our understanding of the autonomic nervous system's profound impact on various aspects of life, including sociality, emotional regulation, cognitive functions, and mental and physical well-being. It has reframed our understanding of stress, resilience, and feelings, especially the neurobiological benefits of feeling safe. Although I anticipated that the theory would influence psychophysiological research, I had not anticipated that the theory would impact on other disciplines. Through insightful polyvagal-informed therapists and educators, the theory's applications have expanded into diverse fields such as psychotherapy, medicine, education, and performance.

Exploring these broad applications revealed that Polyvagal Theory transcends its initial scope, leading to a more generalizable **polyvagal perspective,** a perspective that proposes that the principles embedded in the theory could be applied across different disciplines. By focusing on the neurophysiological mechanisms and adaptive functions underlying behavior, the polyvagal perspective triggers new questions, paradigms, explanations, and conclusions regarding the pivotal role of autonomic function in navigating a dynamically challenging world. The theory was not only impacting on defining research questions and testing hypotheses in laboratory science but was impacting in applied areas such as patient care, education, and work environment.

A polyvagal perspective refers to the practical application and broader understanding of the concepts presented in Polyvagal Theory. It encompasses the theoretical framework of Polyvagal Theory but extends beyond the theory to explore the implications of understanding the dynamic adjustment of the autonomic nervous system in various contexts. The perspective emphasizes the practical and clinical applications of Polyvagal Theory, particularly in fields such as psychology, psychotherapy, trauma treatment, education, and interpersonal relationships. It focuses on utilizing the insights from Polyvagal Theory to enhance well-being, regulation, and social connection.

As a perspective it has practical implications in fields such as psychology, psychotherapy, trauma treatment, education, management, parenting, and even politics. In essence, Polyvagal Theory provides the theoretical framework and explanations for the physiological responses of the autonomic nervous system, while the polyvagal perspective takes a broader view, focusing on the practical applications and implications of understanding the autonomic nervous system in relation to human behavior and social interactions. The theory forms the foundation, while the perspective extends beyond it to address the practical aspects and real-world implications of the theory.

This volume is a collection of recent writings that showcase the wide-ranging applications of a polyvagal perspective. The chapters update the theory and delve into sociality, trauma, autism, compassion, functional medicine, vagal nerve stimulation, Ehlers-Danlos syndrome, addiction, management, and dance and movement therapy. Together, these writings demonstrate how adopting a polyvagal perspective enriches our understanding of biobehavioral processes in diverse domains. The volume is a mixture of material that has been peer reviewed, presented in books, published online, and written exclusively for this volume.

The book is organized into five parts. Part I provides new elaborations of the theory that emphasize the three pillars of the theory: neurophysiology, sociality, and safety. Part II provides papers related to trauma and functional medical disorders. Part III provides a glimpse into both my personal journey discovering features of heart rate variability and vagal nerve stimulation through a polyvagal perspective. Part IV is a collection of short papers applying the perspective across disciplines including addiction, autism, Ehlers-Danlos syndrome, and compassion. Part V is a collection of interviews and blog posts relating the theory to societal challenges. In addition, the portions of the paper introducing the term polyvagal perspective is included in the Appendix as a resource to highlight the transformation of the theory into a perspective that is having a positive impact on the lives of many. Similar to my previous edited volumes (Porges, 2011, 2021) the earlier chapters (Parts I, II, and III) are more scientific, while the more accessible chapters are at the end of the book (Parts IV and V). I consider Part I to be resources for Polyvagal Theory. Since each chapter was written as a stand-alone document, there will be a degree of redundancy in outlining the principles embedded in Polyvagal Theory. As you read this volume, I welcome you on my personal journey of how Polyvagal Theory has helped me gain a better understanding of human experience from both a personal and societal level.

POLYVAGAL
PERSPECTIVES

PART I

Theory

1

The Vagal Paradox: A Polyvagal Solution

Stephen W. Porges

INTRODUCTION

The initial presentation of the Polyvagal Theory (PVT; Porges, 1995) proposed the use of evolution as an organizing principle to weave a descriptive narrative of the vertebrate phylogenetic journey toward sociality and co-regulation. This journey documented a shift in the anatomical structure and function of the autonomic nervous system (ANS) and how these changes were involved in the mammalian biobehavioral features that enable co-regulation (e.g., mother–infant interactions) to support health and sociality. The intent was to use the scientific basis of the theory as a bridge to transform the broad mind–brain–body schisms in science into a more unifying perspective that incorporated an understanding of autonomic state as a neural platform that could support either sociality and feelings of safety or defensive strategies and feelings of threat.

As the theory gained traction in the scientific world, crossing several disciplines, and bridging basic science with clinical applications and personal experiences, the task of presenting a succinct statement of the theory became more difficult. Since the theory is dependent on several disparate disciplines, each with its specific literature, research questions, methodology, and theoretical orientation, the pragmatic task of communication has been fraught with complexity. This has created an intellectual challenge to accurately state the tenets of the theory and to convey its scientific foundation into constructs that are accessible and independent of academic background and profession.

The problem is further exacerbated as practitioners representing applied areas (e.g., medicine, education, business, and psychotherapy) have become interested in the theory and frequently convey elements of the theory to their constituencies, many of whom are not educated in the foundational sciences upon which PVT is dependent. The result has been a democratization of information on social media in which individuals may become influencers without having their academic credentials vetted and without the credibility of their claims being determined by the historical process of scholarly review. Unfortunately, given the complexity of the theory, the basics of the theory have not always been accurately transmitted, and misunderstandings can become misinformation within the digital world. This paper is an attempt to clarify the theory and rectify potential misunderstandings by documenting the scientific foundation upon which the theory is based.

BACKGROUND: THE VAGUS
AND THE VAGAL PARADOX

The vagus is a cranial nerve that exits the brainstem and travels to several organs within the human body. It is the primary neural pathway of the parasympathetic nervous system. Functionally, the vagus is a bidirectional conduit between the brainstem and visceral organs. Although we generally focus on the motor functions of the vagus and how the motor pathways regulate the heart and the gut, the vagus is primarily a sensory nerve with approximately 80% of its fibers sending information from the viscera to the brain. The remaining 20% form motor pathways that enable brain circuits to dynamically and, at times, dramatically change our physiology, with some of these changes occurring within seconds. For example, vagal motor pathways can cause our hearts to beat more slowly and can stimulate our gut. Of these 20%, only a small percent is myelinated. Interestingly, the motor fibers dominate discussion of the role of the vagus in the regulation of the heart in biobehavioral and biomedical sciences (see Jänig, 2022; Porges & Kolacz, 2021).

In its tonic state, the vagus functions like a brake on the heart's pacemaker (see Porges et al., 1996). When the brake is removed, the lower vagal tone enables the heart to beat faster. Functionally, the vagal pathways, regardless of brainstem nucleus of origin (i.e., dorsal or ventral) to the heart are inhibitory and slow heart rate. However, vagal cardioinhibitory actions are not solely chronotropic (i.e., influencing heart rate), but may have profound inotropic impact on contractility with consequential influences on heart rate through changes in blood pressure (i.e., baroceptors). Although the influence of inotropic vagal function is complex and not fully understood, recent studies document the important influences of cardioinhibitory inotropic vagal fibers originating from the dorsal motor nucleus of the vagus (Gourine et al., 2016; Machhada et al., 2015; Machhada et al., 2016; Machhada et al., 2017; Machhada et al., 2020).

These studies describe the protective function of these pathways in the calm state as well as interactions with sympathetic inotropic influences. In addition, the literature documents experimental procedures during which the inotropic impact of the vagus, the reduction of contractility, occurs independent of changes in heart rate.

In general, the synergistic effect of slowing heart rate and reducing contractility is experienced as a calm state. Thus, vagal function is frequently assumed to be an anti-stress mechanism. However, there is another literature contradicting the positive attributes of the vagus and linking vagal mechanisms to life-threatening responses, such as bradycardia (and potentially hypotension through diminished contractility) that could lead to sudden neurogenic death (e.g., Richter, 1957). Basically, the same nerve, the vagus, proposed as a health-supporting and anti-stress system, can stop the heart, reduce contractility, and lower blood pressure sufficiently to initiate syncope and, if prolonged, may lead to death (e.g., Meny et al., 1994; Wolf, 1965). Convergent patterns of both positive and negative consequences of vagal excitation that have been observed in the gut have also been described by Burge (1970) as a "vagal paradox." Since the direct vagal input to the gut is primarily through the dorsal vagus, exploration of links between ventral vagal regulation of the heart and gut dysfunction may provide insights into the inotropic influences of the dorsal vagus on the heart.

THE ANS REGULATION: ANTAGONISTIC OR HIERARCHICAL OR BOTH?

In virtually every text on anatomy or physiology, the ANS is described as a paired antagonistic system consisting of two opposing components. The texts generally describe a sympathetic nervous system that supports mobilized reactions to threat (i.e., fight-or-flight) and a parasympathetic nervous system that has the capacity to inhibit these debilitating and metabolically costly processes. The net result of using this model may be described as a balance between these antagonistic systems (e.g., Gellhorn, 1957).

In both clinical and research domains, terms like "autonomic balance" (Wenger, 1966; Porges, 1976) have been used with an expectation that an optimal autonomic balance would be more parasympathetic (i.e., more vagal). This would be expressed as calmer and less reactive behavior. When vagal tone is depressed or withdrawn, we become tense and reactive and experience stress. This concise explanation of the role that the ANS and especially the vagus has in regulating our biobehavioral state is only partially correct. The story of how the vagus influences health and behavior is more complex. However, it is true that most of our visceral organs have neural connections from both the parasympathetic and the sympathetic nervous systems and that most parasympathetic neural fibers travel through the vagus.

The utility of this prevalent model breaks down in clinical investigations of high-risk human newborns in which vagal mechanisms are assumed to both support and compromise health. Insights from the high-risk newborn may further a reconceptualization contrasting the vagal mechanisms that support homeostatic functions with those that support threat physiology, especially during acute, survival-related challenges. There is a large literature documenting that the amplitude of respiratory sinus arrhythmia (RSA), a valid index of cardiac vagal tone (Lewis et al., 2012), is related to positive clinical outcomes (e.g., Porges, 1992). In contrast, massive clinically life-threatening bradycardia also are assumed to be mediated by the vagus. Moreover, the preterm newborns with frequent bradycardia, who were at high risk for serious complications, reliably had low-amplitude RSA (i.e., heart rate patterns with a relatively constant beat-to-beat rate) prior to a bradycardic event (Caldeyro-Barcia et al., 1967; Hon, 1960; Sholapurkar, 2015). This contradiction in interpretation of vagal mechanisms formed the basis of the **vagal paradox** posing the question: How could the vagus be both protective, when it was expressed as RSA, and life-threatening, when it was expressed as bradycardia and apnea?

Identifying the vagal mechanisms underlying the paradox evolved into the Polyvagal Theory. In developing the theory, the anatomy, development, evolutionary history, and function of the two vagal systems were identified: one vagal system mediating bradycardia and apnea and the other vagal system mediating RSA. One system was potentially lethal, while the other system was protective. The two vagal pathways originated in different areas of the brainstem. Through the study of comparative anatomy, it can be inferred that the two vagal circuits evolved sequentially (see Gourine et al., 2016). This sequence was further observed during mammalian development (see Porges & Furman, 2011). Basically, hypotheses driven by PVT are related to the documentation that the mammalian ANS has a built-in **hierarchy of autonomic reactivity** based on phylogeny that is mirrored in embryological development. This fact became a core principle upon which PVT-informed hypotheses could be tested. This emphasis on hierarchy is focused on ANS reactivity and does not preclude the optimal homeostatic states that involved a synergism and functional balance between parasympathetic and sympathetic influences. Thus, depending on the state of the ventral vagus, autonomic regulation may either function hierarchically or antagonistically.

ANS DEPENDENT DISTINCTIONS BETWEEN MAMMALS AND REPTILES

Anatomical clues to PVT, especially those linked to social communication and connectedness, can be identified by investigating the three features that frequently are used to distinguish mammals from reptiles.

First, mammals, as the name implies, have mammary glands, which provide milk to feed their young. This fact informs us that at birth mammalian offspring functionally can suckle (Vogel, 2018). From a polyvagal perspective, nursing is dependent on a functional **ventral vagal complex**, which enables the coordination of the ANS with the striated muscles to suck, swallow, breathe, and vocalize. The ventral vagal complex forms the neuroanatomical foundation of the **social engagement system** proposed in PVT and elaborated in the sections below (see Figure 1.1). The operational definitions for the ventral vagal complex and the social engagement system are specific to PVT. These definitions do not preclude others from using similar terms that may include different anatomical structures supporting other behavioral functions.

The circuit also enables mammals to broadcast their physiological state through vagal efferent fibers that control vocal intonation through pathways regulating laryngeal and pharyngeal muscles. The circuits regulated by the ventral vagal complex not only promote calm autonomic state via the ventral vagus, but also support several features embedded within maternal-infant interactions and sociality.

Second, mammals, unlike reptiles, have small middle ear bones that are detached from the jawbone. These small bones form an ossicle chain that functionally transmits the vibratory stimuli from the eardrum (i.e., tympanic membrane) to the inner ear. The middle ear muscles regulate the stiffness of the ossicle chain, which in turn controls the tension of the eardrum. When the eardrum is tightened the acoustic transfer function of middle ear structures dampens the acoustic energy of low frequencies and optimizes the transmission of frequencies associated with social communication (e.g., vocalizations). This evolutionary adaptation enabled mammals to detect airborne acoustic signals occurring at higher frequencies than those detected by reptiles, whose acoustic processing was dependent on bone conduction. The ventral vagal complex also involves the nerves that regulate the middle ear muscles linking the extraction of prosodic vocalizations with the calming of autonomic state and social accessibility. In contrast, the low-frequency roars of predators can trigger fight-or-flight reactions, while high-pitched screams trigger concern (see Kolacz et al., 2018; Porges & Lewis, 2010).

This understanding of the adaptive function of middle ear muscles links listening to calming. It also provided the neurophysiological basis of an acoustic intervention known as the Safe and Sound Protocol™ (https://integratedlistening .com/products/ssp-safe-sound-protocol/). The Safe and Sound Protocol stimulates the ventral vagal complex to calm autonomic state, improve auditory processing, and stimulate spontaneous social behavior (Heilman et al., 2023; Porges et al., 2013; Porges et al., 2014; Rajabalee et al., 2022).

Third, spontaneous heart rate–respiratory interactions, known as RSA in mammals, are dependent on myelinated vagal fibers originating in the ventral vagal nucleus in a brainstem region known as the nucleus ambiguus. This point distinguishes RSA from observations of heart rate–respiratory interactions in non-mammalian vertebrates and contributes to the maintenance of optimal physiological ventilation/perfusion (Gourine et al., 2016). This function may help explain the frequently noted power of RSA to predict various aspects of health.

EVOLUTION: PARALLELS BETWEEN ONTOGENY AND PHYLOGENY

Evolution is used in PVT to identify the phylogenetic sequence of anatomical appearance and assumed adaptive function in vertebrates of brainstem structures involved in the regulation of autonomic state. The goal of this quest is to gain a better understanding of the structures that are expressed in the adaptive functions of the human ANS. To reach this goal, knowledge is needed of the antecedents of these structures in the vertebrate species that evolved prior to mammals. PVT conveys a deep respect for continuities across vertebrate species. This respect for continuity is coupled with a focus on how repurposing the neural regulation of the ANS in antecedent vertebrates provided humans and other mammals with unique attributes enabling the regulation of the ANS to support sociality and down-regulate threat reactivity.

In mammals, ontogenetic changes in neural regulation of the ANS parallel phylogeny. Comparative anatomy leads the polyvagal-informed scientist to investigate embryology and early development to confirm the maturational sequence in which neural structures regulate the ANS. The order of this sequence is important because the notion of a hierarchy, in which newer circuits inhibit older ones, is a core principle embedded in the history of neurology (e.g., Jackson, 1884). The sequence ordering newer and older circuits is the same when mapped on a phylogenetic or ontogenetic timeline. The simplicity of the ontogenetic timeline is that this perspective is descriptive and does not require a dialogue infused with hypothetical adaptive value or chronological time of emergence. PVT originated from the insights derived from using evolution as an organizing principle and metaphorically investigating the adaptive biobehavioral strategies of vertebrate species. However, PVT is only dependent on the identification of the sequence, a sequence that is also observed in the embryological development of humans and other living mammals (Cerritelli et al., 2021).

PVT does not infer or identify the mechanisms through which evolution works. PVT treats evolution as providing a map of ancestral vertebrate relationships similar to a family tree. Theoretically, PVT is mammal-centric and is focused on the phylogenetic history of social mammals. PVT asks specific human-related questions, such as how does our evolutionary history inform our current understanding of human behavior and health? PVT focuses on the structural and functional changes in the mammalian ANS that relate to human experience. These questions differ from questions relating to modern reptiles. We share a common ancestor with modern reptiles, but we did not evolve from them. This point becomes of particular relevance as we explore the theory and especially how the theory may be misunderstood or misinterpreted.

EVOLUTIONARY TRANSITION FROM REPTILES TO MAMMALS

To understand this evolutionary process, we need to have a better understanding of the timeline in which the transition from reptiles to mammals hypothetically occurred. Acknowledging the evolutionary timeline of mammals is critical in evaluating the relevance to PVT of neurophysiological research conducted with modern reptilian species (which evolved long after the earliest mammals). **Mammals did not evolve from modern reptiles**. Rather, the PVT emphasis on the evolutionary transition from reptiles to mammals refers to ancient and extinct reptiles that served as **common ancestors** for both mammals and modern reptiles. The common ancestor refers to the well-accepted hypothesis that there was a long-extinct reptilian species from which both modern reptiles and mammals evolved (Geggel, 2016). This point is critical, since it informs us that modern reptile species are **not** part of the phylogenetic history of mammals and are, therefore, irrelevant to PVT.

Modern reptiles are a product of an evolutionary journey that has shaped their anatomical structures, physiological functions, and behavioral strategies. This does not preclude consistencies between modern reptiles and mammals but acknowledges that there would have been major (presumably adaptive) changes during the estimated 220 million years since the emergence of both mammals and modern reptiles from the long-extinct common ancestral reptilian species. To put this timeline into perspective, it is estimated that 200 million years is also the period between the earliest bony fish and mammals. Thus, inferences regarding modern reptile-mammal contrasts would need to be based on the hypothetical assumption that modern reptiles provide insights into features of this common, now long-extinct, reptilian ancestor.

Millions of years before the existence of modern reptiles, the earliest mammals already had several features described by PVT. Since there is evidence that the earliest mammals could nurse (Vogel, 2018), we can infer that, similar to modern mammals, they had a functional ventral vagus that was coordinated with the regulation of the structures of ingestion. If it were hypothetically possible to compare the earliest mammals with modern reptiles, these features would still be distinguishable even though 200 million years have elapsed.

COMPARATIVE NEUROANATOMY: LIMITED INFERENCE

Comparative neuroanatomy helps identify the remarkable modifications in the regulation of the ANS in mammals that have resulted in an evolutionary trajectory providing the biobehavioral foundational building blocks of society—the ability to trust, feel safe, and co-regulate with conspecifics. These foundational processes recruit neural pathways that dampen threat reactions leading to emergent features of sociality that characterize most contemporary social mammals (see Porges, 2021, 2022). This does not preclude the importance of the evolutionary journey of modern reptiles, who occupy a niche different from that of social mammals in a complex, dynamically changing and challenging world.

Comparative neuroanatomy does not document evolution but does infer evolutionary transitions from living species on which anatomical studies can be conducted. These extant species vary in their time of origin along the evolutionary timeline of vertebrates. In general, the fossil record has been used to date the time that specific species emerged. However, new molecular techniques, which were not available when the theory was proposed, frequently do not agree with the fossil record (Kumar & Hedges, 1998). Although this contradiction is a challenge within comparative neuroanatomy, it is irrelevant to the basis of PVT, because the phylogenetic sequence relevant to PVT is mirrored in the embryology of contemporary mammals, including humans.

Although a comparative perspective was instrumental in generating the working hypotheses that led to PVT, comparative neuroanatomy is not necessary or sufficiently conclusive to either support or disconfirm attributes of the theory. **Inferences regarding phylogeny can only be validated if the species being studied by comparative anatomists had not changed since their initial emergence.** Optimistically, if the brainstem structures providing the source nuclei for vagal pathways were studied in a reptilian species that did not change during the 200 million years since these lines diverged, then a better understanding of the transition from reptiles to mammals might be described. Of course, because evolution is neither static nor linear, this assumption is too restrictive and impossible to achieve.

When PVT was first developed, the literature was scoured to determine whether it would be possible to study a reptilian species that evolved close to the time that mammals differentiated themselves from their reptilian ancestors. To do this, there is a need to estimate when a specific species evolved. Unfortunately, among reptilian species there is little convergence between methods. For example, using molecular methods, turtle-like species that had been assumed to represent an early reptile appear to be more closely related to the more modern reptiles like crocodilians that evolved about 95 million years ago (Kumar & Hedges, 1998). These inconsistencies disrupted the assumed phylogenetic timeline based on fossils that had been historically incorporated into evolutionary biology. Thus, although we know that mammals and modern reptiles emerged from a common extinct reptilian ancestor, we can only cautiously talk about a timeline of evolution within this group of vertebrates. At this point, the timing is fluid of the exact phylogenetic sequence describing the lineage of reptilian species. This limits the use of comparative neuroanatomy in providing insights into the features of the common ancestor. Beyond the phylogenetic sequence already described, it seems that comparative neuroanatomy and comparative neurophysiology have limited usefulness in refining PVT.

VENTRAL MIGRATION OF CARDIOINHIBITORY NEURONS: THE EMERGENCE OF A SOCIAL ENGAGEMENT SYSTEM

The emergence of two vagal cardioinhibitory brainstem areas is a product of an evolutionary trend in ventral migration of cardioinhibitory neurons from the dorsal motor nucleus of the vagus to the ventral vagal nucleus (nucleus ambiguus). A trend toward ventral migration of vagal cardioinhibitory fibers is present in vertebrate groups that evolved before mammals (Taylor et al., 2022). **However, this research has little value to PVT and the study of mammals, since even with the earliest mammals, this migration was complete before modern reptiles evolved.** Not only does it appear that a ventral cardioinhibitory vagal nucleus is a defining feature of the earliest mammals, but, since it is assumed that the earliest mammals could nurse (Vogel, 2018), the ventral cardioinhibitory vagus appears to have been integrated sufficiently with the regulation of the structures necessary for sucking. More simply put, the earliest mammals, but not reptiles, had already evolved the basic structures that are necessary for the nuanced social engagement system described in PVT based on the neural functions of the ventral vagal complex.

As the function of these two cardioinhibitory brainstem areas in mammals is investigated, an interesting narrative emerges about species differences in the distribution and function of the two cardioinhibitory areas. In certain reptiles, ventral migration of part of the original dorsal efferent cell column is observable in varying extents, from a simple ventral bulging of the cell column to a complete separation (Taylor et al., 2022). Although there is great uncertainty in the precise phylogenetic timeline of this migration in reptiles, we can assume that this migration was minimal within the long-extinct reptilian species that predated the common ancestor. If we are correct, this suggests that a major repurposing of cardioinhibitory wiring occurred in mammals relative to their ancient reptilian ancestors, allowing the integration of social engagement (via special visceral efferent pathways) with cardiovascular and ingestive demands. In fact, it is possible that this was a critical event in mammalian evolution.

The phylogenetic trend in the ventral migration of cardioinhibitory neurons can also be inferred from the study of mammalian development, especially through studies of embryology. This parallel had been acknowledged for decades (see Windle et al., 1933). An interesting interpretation of this developmental process has been reported in rats (Nosaka et al., 1979). This study documented cardioinhibitory cells in three brainstem regions: dorsal motor nucleus of the vagus, ventral nucleus of the vagus, and an area between these two regions. The authors stated that the three locations appear to represent "no" migration, "complete" migration, and "abortive" migration undergone during the embryonal stage. Nosaka and colleagues (1979) speculated that the distribution of the cardioinhibitory neurons in mammals result from a variation in degree of **ventral migration** of these cells specifically determined for each species and potentially determining the autonomic substrate for the adaptive defensive behaviors they express. This speculation potentially explains observations of bradycardia as adaptively supporting immobilization in mammals that are prey species and are consistent with observations of bradycardia following electrical stimulation of the dorsal motor nucleus of the vagus in rabbits (Porges, 1995) and the spontaneous bradycardia that in rats can lead to death in response to life threat (Richter, 1957). However, these chronotropic responses have not been observed in mammals that are predator species (e.g., dogs, cats), although there are reports of electrical stimulation of the dorsal motor nucleus of the vagus producing reduced contractility and lower blood pressure (Calaresu & Pearce, 1965; Geis & Wurster, 1980; Gunn et al., 1968; Hopkins & Armour, 1982). This conclusion suggests that species (and even individual) differences in the function of each cardioinhibitory vagal nucleus might be dependent on the success of ventral migration, which could be influenced during development by various processes (e.g., genetic variation, epigenetic modification, hypoxia, malnutrition, maltreatment, trauma, prematurity, illness, etc.).

As the cardioinhibitory neurons migrated ventrally, regulation of the structures that emerged from the ancient gill arches (facial and head structures in mammals) appear to have developed interneuronal connections with the ventral cardioinhibitory neurons. In mammals, the product of this brainstem neuroanatomical integration links the ventral vagal cardioinhibitory nucleus with nuclei that regulate sucking and social cueing via facial expression and vocalizations. Functionally, this neuronal circuit provided reliable pathways (e.g., vocalizations) to communicate autonomic state to conspecifics. **Developmentally, this is easily observed in humans because the social engagement circuit is active in full-term newborns, creating an adaptive portal for co-regulation between mother and infant.**

Within PVT, this network is called the ventral vagal complex (see Figure 1.1). The ventral vagal complex is proposed as the neurophysiological substrate of an anatomically defined and functionally integrated **social engagement system**. This system is neuroanatomically limited to the cranial nerve source nuclei from which specific special visceral efferent (i.e., branchiomotor) pathways emerge. This system of interneuronal communication among these brainstem nuclei was forged by evolution and serves an important function in mammalian survival through its essential involvement of this system in ingestion and social communication.

The social engagement system, based on a definable neuroanatomical substrate, supports the cooperative behaviors that differentiated the earliest mammals from ancestral reptiles. The social engagement system in modern mammals continues to provide the substrate for co-regulation, attachment, and trust (i.e., processes through which social interactions regulate and optimize autonomic state to support homeostatic functions of health, growth, and restoration). This system, being based on the neuroanatomical structures involved in suck-swallow-breathe-vocalize pathways, has been described as a functional and defining feature of the earliest mammals (Vogel, 2018).

Since the nerves included in the social engagement system are exclusively special visceral efferent, it has been proposed that PVT has inappropriately excluded the hypoglossal nerve. (Neuhuber & Berthoud, 2022). A deeper explanation of PVT notes that although the social engagement system is composed of special visceral efferent pathways, being classified as special visceral efferent is not the sole criterion for inclusion. Given that PVT has its roots in evolution, cranial nerves are viewed from an embryological and not solely from an anatomical perspective. In structuring the functional social engagement system and its anatomical substrate, the ventral vagal complex, the inclusion of specific special visceral efferent nerves was based on two criteria: (1) the nerve arises from pharyngeal arches during embryonic development and (2) there is evidence of interneuronal communication between the nerve and the vagus. Applying these criteria resulted in clustering cranial nerves V, VII, IX, X, and XI, while excluding XII, the hypoglossal nerve. Consistent with these features, the sensory feedback into the motor centers regulating these specific special visceral pathways nerves may, via interneuronal connections, provide additional portals to regulate the ventral vagus and functionally may act as a vagal nerve stimulator.

Consistent with the emergence of a mammalian social engagement system, Theodosius Dobzhansky, a renowned geneticist and evolutionary biologist (1962) rephrased the concept of fitness by emphasizing in his description of mammals that "the fittest may also be the gentlest, because survival often requires mutual help and cooperation." Dobzhansky's insightful statement converges on the emphasis of PVT on the phylogenetic transitions in neuroanatomy and neurophysiology as social mammals evolved from reptiles. Mutual help and cooperation are dependent on a nervous system that has the capacity to down-regulate threat reactions to allow the proximity necessary for cooperative behaviors and co-regulation. In mammals this is neuroanatomically and neurophysiologically observed in the repurposed neural circuits originating in brainstem areas that regulate the ANS. The repurposed system enables feelings of safety to co-occur with sociality, allowing newborn mammals to engage with their mothers immediately following birth. This theme linking the ANS to sociality and feelings of safety has been elaborated in other publications (see Porges, 2021, 2022).

FIGURE 1.1 The social engagement system consists of a somatomotor component (solid blocks) and a visceromotor component (dashed blocks). The somatomotor component involves special visceral efferent pathways that regulate the striated muscles of the face and head, while the visceromotor component involves myelinated ventral vagal pathways that regulate the heart and bronchi.

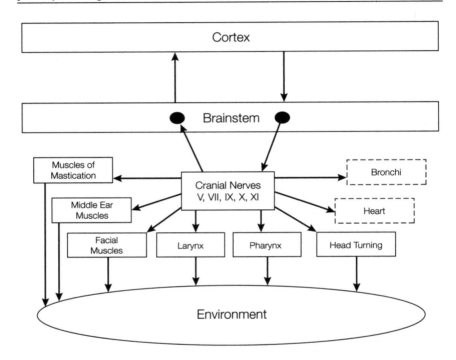

MONITORING DEVELOPMENT OF THE VENTRAL VAGUS VIA RSA

In humans, the embryology literature suggests a maturational progression similar to the phylogenetic trend inferred from comparative neuroanatomy (see Porges & Furman, 2011). Since the preponderance of myelinated cardioinhibitory vagal fibers originate in the ventral vagal nucleus, and not the dorsal motor nucleus of the vagus, there is the opportunity to map the ventral migration through autopsy data detailing the distribution of myelinated and unmyelinated vagal fibers. Autopsy data (Pereyra et al., 1992; Sachis et al., 1982) confirm a developmental increase in the number and ratio of myelinated vagal fibers. Moreover, there seems to be a decrease in the survival rate of infants who have an apparent deficiency in myelinated vagal cardioinhibitory fibers. This deficiency has been reported in infants who have died from sudden infant death syndrome, a disorder assumed to be associated with neurogenic bradycardia (Becker et al., 1993). Thus, although there may be phylogenetic antecedents of a convergent evolution (see Gabora, 2018) of myelinated cardioinhibitory fibers originating from the dorsal motor nucleus of the vagus (Monteiro et al., 2018), the consensus view is that within mammals the predominant cardioinhibitory influence from the ventral vagal nucleus is conveyed through myelinated fibers. The functional output of the ventral vagal nucleus follows a maturational trend. When there is a deficiency in the number of myelinated cardioinhibitory fibers originating in the ventral vagal nucleus there may be a lower threshold (see dissolution below) to neurogenic bradycardia (potentially augmented by inotropic influences) through the unmyelinated cardioinhibitory fibers originating in the dorsal motor nucleus of the vagus (e.g., Becker et al., 1993). The latter point is consistent with PVT.

Since the fibers emerging from the ventral vagal nucleus have a respiratory rhythm (Gourine et al., 2016; Hering, 1910; Richter & Spyer, 1990), it is possible to track the functional impact of these pathways through early development by studying RSA in laboratory mammals (e.g., rats, rabbits) and preterm infants. PVT limits the definition of RSA to the heart rate–respiratory pattern observed in mammals that is a function of myelinated vagal fibers originating in the ventral vagal nucleus (nucleus ambiguus). Historically, the term RSA has been used solely to describe the pattern observed in mammalian species. Describing heart rate–respiratory patterns in other vertebrates does not mean that the neural mechanisms are identical to those observed in mammals. In fact, in vertebrate species other than mammals, except for the report of a myelinated cardioinhibitory pathway emerging from the dorsal motor nucleus of the vagus in the lungfish (Monteiro et al., 2018), all reports document that heart rate–respiratory interactions were mediated via unmyelinated vagal cardioinhibitory pathways originating in the dorsal motor nucleus of the vagus. The identification of the myelinated fibers in the lungfish have been misused to infer a fatal flaw in PVT. However, the identification of myelinated vagal fibers in lungfish is unrelated to PVT and reflects a misunderstanding of PVT. The lungfish appears to be a phylogenetic outlier, having vertebrate ancestry that did not have myelinated cardioinhibitory dorsal vagal fibers; nor has this feature been reliably transmitted to the groups of vertebrates that subsequently evolved (i.e., amphibia, reptiles, mammals).

Larson and Porges (1982) described the development of RSA in rat pups. Rats have a short gestation and are born extremely premature relative to humans. Their study documented a maturational trajectory of increased RSA. At birth and during the first few days of life, postpartum RSA was negligible, although by day 20 it had reached the level of adult rats. A study with fetal sheep (Donchin et al., 1984), documented that as the fetus matured, even in the absence of systematic fetal breathing movements, the pattern of RSA became more sinusoidal, potentially reflecting the maturational increase in the myelination of the ventral vagal cardioinhibitory pathways.

Consistent with the animal research, our human research documented significantly lower amplitude RSA in preterm relative to full-term newborns (Porges, 1992; Portales et al., 1997). In addition, maturational RSA trajectories in high-risk preterm newborns were observed (Doussard-Roosevelt et al., 1997), and RSA was enhanced in preterm newborns through social engagement opportunities with caregivers (Porges et al., 2019). These human infant studies, consistent with PVT, document that the maturation of the ventral vagal cardioinhibitory circuit can be monitored through the measurement of RSA and can be optimized through social engagement opportunities that may function as neural exercises involving the ventral vagal complex.

DISSOLUTION

The identification of this phylogenetic sequence provides the generation of testable PVT-informed hypotheses linked to the Jacksonian principle of dissolution (Jackson, 1884). Embedded in dissolution are the following points: (1) there is a phylogenetic as well as an ontogenetic hierarchy, in which newer circuits inhibit older circuits and (2) during responses to brain illness or damage to the function of brain structures, changes occur in a predictable sequence that has been described as dissolution or evolution in reverse.

PVT broadens the Jacksonian principle to examine its application not only to changes in higher brain structures, but also in foundational survival-based brainstem structures that regulate the ANS. In addition, PVT recognizes the parallel trends expressed in both the ontogeny and phylogeny of the mammalian ANS. Thus, dissolution is expressed as development in reverse, basically hypothesizing that the more ancient (and earliest maturing) autonomic regulatory circuits (i.e., sympathetic nervous system and dorsal vagal) would sequentially be disinhibited during prematurity to optimize survival. With either an ontogenetic or phylogenetic bias defining dissolution, we arrive at the same plausible and testable hypothesis: under challenge there is a progression that could be characterized as either evolution or development in reverse. Thus, the phylogenetic sequence or its equivalent maturation sequence would unfold in reverse in response to life challenges, whether pathogen, physical injury, or anticipation of life threat (e.g., predator). **By focusing on dissolution through a developmental lens, grounded in research from embryology and early postpartum development, we avoid the phylogenetic, and often untestable, distractions that may lead to misunderstandings of PVT.**

A TEST OF PVT: DISSOLUTION IN THE NEONATAL INTENSIVE CARE UNIT

In earlier research Reed, Ohel, et al. (1999) reported a relationship between RSA and a vulnerability to life-threatening bradycardia during delivery. A portion of the abstract follows, which succinctly describes the pattern of dissolution predicted by PVT and supported by the developmental and phylogenetic literature.

> Transitory **heart rate accelerations** and **reduced beat-to-beat variability** reliably preceded heart rate decelerations. The data are interpreted within the context of PVT, which provides a plausible explanation of the neurophysiological mechanisms that mediate fetal heart rate decelerations. Specifically, it is proposed that both the transitory heart rate accelerations and the depression of the respiratory rhythm in the beat-to-beat heart rate pattern reflect a withdrawal of the vagal tone determined by myelinated vagal pathways originating in the nucleus ambiguus. Functionally, withdrawal of vagal tone originating in the nucleus ambiguus results in the cardiac pacemaker becoming vulnerable to sympathetic influences and to the more-primitive unmyelinated vagal pathways originating in the dorsal motor nucleus of the vagus, which may contribute to clinically relevant bradycardia.

Reed, Ohel, and colleagues' explanation of the adaptive functions of the two vagal pathways provides documentation of an empirical solution to the vagal paradox. Whether this sequence is expressed in mature mammals is an empirical question. It is possible that the chronotropic influences via dorsal vagus are minimized with maturation, although inotropic influences may persist and may contribute to neurogenic bradycardia through the ventral vagus. With appropriate research questions and methodologies, this question can be answered.

This does not preclude the special heuristic case of the preterm human newborn, who may be at a point in development during which ventral migration and myelinization of chronotropic vagal neurons are active processes. Thus, the clinical bradycardia observed in the neonatal intensive care unit could be mediated through dorsal vagal pathways. Documentation for this possibility comes from the observation that chronotropic influence through ventral vagal pathways distinctly has a respiratory rhythm (Gourine et al., 2016), while chronotropic influences through the dorsal vagal pathways do not. In the preterm newborn study (Reed, Ohel, et al., 1999), the background heart rate upon which the bradycardia is observed is devoid of a respiratory rhythm. In fact, the prevalence of bradycardic episodes was directly related to periods during which RSA was suppressed.

DORSAL VAGUS THROUGH THE
LENS OF THE PVT: AN UPDATE

Perhaps the focus on vagal chronotropic influences via dorsal vagal pathways, which reliably may be observed in the immature newborn but not the mature adult, has distracted from a potential contribution of the inotropic mechanisms that involve neurons in the dorsal motor nucleus of the vagus. It is possible that during periods of sufficient ventral vagal control to support homeostatic functions (i.e., health, growth, and restoration), the inotropic influence on the ventricles, via the dorsal vagus, would be protective. However, in the absence a strong ventral vagal influence, consistent with dissolution, there may be vulnerability for inotropic influences via the dorsal vagus to be disruptive to blood pressure regulation, which under certain cases might recruit ventral vagal pathways in producing life-threatening bradycardia.

The possibility that myelinated ventral vagal pathways might contribute to bradycardia during conditions of compromise has been suggested as being consistent with PVT (Porges, 2001). Basically, it is possible that dorsal vagal mechanisms may threaten survival by disrupting blood-gas status sufficiently to depress respiration and blunt RSA, while triggering a compensatory bradycardia through ventral vagal pathways. Future research will need to determine whether this is a viable hypothesis.

It is important to note that the dorsal vagus has beneficial functions in humans. During most normal conditions, the dorsal vagus maintains tone to the gut and promotes digestive processes. However, if up-regulated, the dorsal vagus contributes to pathophysiological conditions including the formation of ulcers via excess gastric secretion and colitis. This leads to an important question that might explain the inotropic reactions within a PVT perspective. PVT emphasizes the hierarchical sequence based on evolution and development to develop hypotheses of autonomic regulation in response to challenges. In building the theory, the insights came from the readily observable clinical tachycardia followed by bradycardia in preterm newborns who had depressed RSA. Depressed RSA in preterm newborns is due to the prematurity of their ventral vagal pathways and not a function of illness or stressful contexts, although these factors could further compromise postpartum development. Consistent with PVT, the depressed ventral vagus provides an opportunity for sequential shifts in autonomic regulation involving both sympathetic and dorsal vagal pathways.

PVT proposes that when the ventral vagus is optimally managing a resilient autonomic nervous system both the sympathetic and dorsal vagus are synergistically coordinated to support homeostatic functions including health, growth, and restoration. However, when ventral vagal influences are diminished, as indexed by depressed RSA and overall heart rate variability, then the sympathetic and dorsal vagal pathways are poised to be sequentially recruited for defense. Autonomically, this would be observed initially as increased heart rate and cardiac contractility, while suppressing the inhibitory calming and homeostatic actions of the dorsal vagus on the heart and gut. Since the sympathetic defense strategy is metabolically costly, the dorsal vagal influence on the heart and gut may be triggered as a metabolically conservative, defensive surge expressed as reduced contractility of the heart, a lowering of blood pressure, and a clearing of the bowel. In general, the literature on RSA and heart rate variability suggests that a depressed RSA is a covariate for several health conditions including types of gut dysfunction, which have been assumed to be mediated by dorsal vagal influences.

REPURPOSING THE DORSAL VAGUS: SPECIES SPECIFICITY

The specificity of mammalian species repurposing the function of the dorsal vagus on the heart (minimizing chronotropic functions while maintaining or potentially enhancing inotropic functions) does not appear to modify the roles of the dorsal vagal pathways regulating the subdiaphragmatic organs (e.g., gut), which may contribute to the high prevalence of clinical reports of irritable bowel syndrome in survivors of trauma even if they had not immobilized. Although bradycardia may not be a reliable phenomenon for all who experience life threat, other autonomic changes mediated via the dorsal vagus such as reduction in contractility and gut reactions may be more reliable indicators of a threat reaction. Thus, while species differences accounted for some of the confusion in the literature relating to the chronotropic cardioinhibitory role of the two vagal nuclei (Gunn et al., 1968), the important inotropic role of dorsal vagal pathways may have been neglected.

A full understanding of cardioinhibitory function via vagal pathways in humans is still speculative. However, it may reflect a range of individual differences that could be broadened by potential disturbances to normal development by perinatal challenges, such as prematurity, hypoxia, maltreatment, and malnutrition. Although it has been assumed that in humans the vagal chronotropic fibers traveling from the dorsal motor nucleus of the vagus to the heart are functionally dormant (Grossman & Taylor, 2007), this assumption may not be accurate. Potentially, this system may be sensitive to or reserved for action in response to life-challenging signals such as hypoxia. Alternatively, the dorsal vagal inotropic pathways may trigger, via changes in blood pressure, ventral vagal chronotropic reactions. Thus, hypothetically, this neural circuit may map into a range of individual differences that would parallel the clinical observations of individual variations in the propensity to shut down or even faint in response to threat. Research suggests that in a normal homeostatic state, dorsal vagal pathways have a protective inotropic role on the myocardia (see Gourine et al., 2016; Machhada et al., 2015; Machhada et al., 2016; Machhada et al., 2017; Machhada et al., 2020). However, it is possible that during threat they may cause an acute increase in inotropic influence that would be sufficient to trigger hypotension and syncope.

THE VAGAL BRAKE: A MEASURE OF VENTRAL VAGAL EFFICIENCY

Ventral Vagal Brake

In humans, the ventral vagal efferent pathways to the heart function as a brake. The intrinsic rate of the heart in the healthy human, even without sympathetic excitation, is significantly faster than the resting heart rate. Thus, under most conditions, the vagus, primarily via myelinated vagal fibers originating in the nucleus ambiguus, actively inhibits heart rate. However, when there is a need to engage actively with select elements in the environment, cortical neurons inhibit homeostatic needs, and cardiac output is rapidly increased to match metabolic demands. Under these situations there is a transitory withdrawal of the vagal tone to the heart to increase heart rate, which defines the removal of the vagal brake (Porges et al., 1996).

The vagal brake reflects the inhibitory influence of the myelinated ventral vagal pathways on the heart, which slows the intrinsic rate of the heart's pacemaker. The intrinsic heart rate of healthy adults is about 90 beats per minute. However, baseline heart rate is noticeably slower due to the influence of the ventral vagus, which functions as a brake. When the ventral vagus decreases its influence on the heart, the brake is released, and heart rate spontaneously increases. This is not due solely to an increase in sympathetic excitation; rather, the release of the vagal brake allows the intrinsic rate of the pacemaker to be expressed. The vagal brake represents the actions of engaging and disengaging the ventral vagal influence on the heart's pacemaker. In addition, the release of the vagal brake on the heart also enables tonic underlying sympathetic excitation to exert more influence on the autonomic nervous system. PVT (Porges, 1995; Porges et al., 1996; Porges, 2007b, 2011), specifically assumes that the vagal brake is mediated primarily through the myelinated ventral vagus and can be quantified by the amplitude of RSA. The theory acknowledges other neural (e.g., dorsal vagal pathways) and neurochemical influences that can influence heart rate (e.g., clinical bradycardia), but these mechanisms are not involved in mediating the chronotropic influences of the ventral vagal brake as defined within PVT.

The vagal brake is conceptualized as an adaptive neural physiological mechanism that fosters engagement and disengagement with the environment. When demands require a calm behavioral state, the reengagement of the vagal brake slows heart rate and provides the physiological support for self-soothing behaviors. There is a large literature documenting that baseline or non-challenge level RSA and other metrics of heart rate variability are related to mental health outcomes, with higher values usually being associated with more positive outcomes and greater resilience (see Hage et al., 2017). When the vagal brake efficiently supports the changing metabolic demands, the neural modulation of RSA is paralleled by a monotonic change in heart rate.

Ventral Vagal Efficiency

The efficiency of the vagal brake might be evaluated along several dimensions, including changes in the amplitude of RSA or an index of heart rate change relative to RSA change in response to a defined challenge. The definition of a challenge is arbitrary and often defined within specific experimental paradigms (e.g., mental effort, attention, sleep state, exercise, social interaction, posture shift). Especially during alert or vigilant states, responses to challenges must be rapid and continuous. For example, environmental demands often dynamically change under real-life conditions.

To evaluate the dynamic function of the vagal brake, it is necessary to generate measures of RSA and heart rate for short sequential epochs. Most methods for quantifying RSA, such as spectral analysis, have assumed inappropriately that the amplitude of RSA was a stationary characteristic of the heart rate time series. In general, these methods require periods of several minutes to calculate an average amplitude of RSA. Measurement over longer periods of time assumes that the variations over shorter periods of time are statistically treated as measurement error. However, to evaluate the dynamic function of the vagal brake, the estimates for heart rate and RSA need to be calculated in periods or epochs of short durations.

Epoch-by-epoch shifts in RSA can be evaluated as a measurable manifestation of dynamic changes in the vagal control of the heart and not assumed to be measurement error distributed around a central tendency. Therefore, it would be necessary to quantify RSA over relatively short periods of only a few seconds. Unlike other methods, the Porges-Bohrer method (Lewis et al., 2012; Porges, 1985; Porges & Bohrer, 1990) provides an opportunity to study the dynamically changing amplitude of RSA independently of a potential nonstationary baseline representing dynamic changes in heart rate.

The efficiency of the vagal brake might be evaluated along several dimensions, including an index of heart rate change relative to RSA change in response to a defined challenge. This metric, now labeled vagal efficiency (VE), describes the dynamic relationship between RSA and heart rate. In several papers we have measured VE during a posture challenge, since it reflexively shifts vagal influences on the heart, is independent of cognitive or social demands, and is easily standardized. Moreover, it provides an opportunity to incorporate a manipulation that involves dynamic challenges involving barosensory feedback. VE is calculated as the slope of the linear regression between synchronous pairs of short duration (e.g., 15 seconds) epoch values of RSA and heart period monitored during the posture conditions (e.g., supine, sitting, standing). VE measures the dynamic effect of the vagus on heart rate as the instantaneous coupling between RSA and heart rate. The slope is easily interpreted as the magnitude of heart period (reciprocal of heart rate) change in ms per unit of RSA amplitude. The steeper the slope, the greater the impact or efficiency of the vagal brake on heart rate. In those who have high VE scores, RSA changes produce similar impact on heart rate independent of actual RSA. Low correlations between RSA and VE further support this observed statistical independence.

Previous research demonstrates that VE degrades in response to alcohol (Reed, Porges, et al., 1999); precedes death following surgery in prairie voles (Williamson et al., 2010); differentiates sleep states in healthy newborns (Porges et al., 1999); and exhibits a maturational shift postpartum in high-risk newborns (Porges et al., 2019). Studies evaluating VE during posture challenges documented that it was low in adolescents with joint hypermobility syndrome (Kolacz et al., 2021), low in patients with functional abdominal pain (Kovacic et al., 2020), and was not influenced by partial cholinergic blockade (unpublished analyses of data described in Lewis et al., 2011). The latter finding suggests that VE is reflecting the status of brainstem integrative circuits and may provide information that is not observed in RSA as a measure of cardioinhibitory vagal outflow. Moreover, the data suggest that the metric is useful even when the range of heart rate and RSA are not extended through metabolic or barosensory challenges. Psychometrically, this would be consistent with the report that distributions of regression line slopes are relatively immune to the influence of range (Cohen & Cohen, 1983).

In preliminary research, we explored the relationship between VE and maltreatment history. We investigated whether the atypical patterns of autonomic reactivity and recovery to stressors frequently observed in survivors of trauma is influenced by an inefficient vagal brake (Dale, Kolacz, et al., 2022). The study documented that maltreatment histories were associated with lower VE, which in turn mediated more anxiety and depression symptoms. VE, by reflecting a disruption in feedback between the heart and brainstem that may also lead to body numbness, could index autonomic regulation to stressors and psychiatric symptomatology. Blunted VE may be a mechanism through which maltreatment induces mental health risk; interventions aimed at promoting efficient vagal regulation may be promising for improving resilience and well-being in trauma survivors. In summary, VE may be a powerful, low-cost, easily quantifiable, and scalable measure that would potentially provide rapid throughput screening that would identify a ventral vagal parameter of atypical autonomic regulation. The VE metric might contribute to refined diagnoses of dysautonomia and several functional disorders.

BODY PERCEPTION QUESTIONNAIRE: SELF-REPORTED AUTONOMIC REACTIVITY

PVT emphasizes that autonomic state is an intervening variable mediating individual differences in responding and recovering from challenges. In general, research testing hypotheses produced by the theory have been dependent on monitoring autonomic variables, especially indices of ventral vagal influence such as RSA and VE. However, a dependence on physiological monitoring would limit the ability to test hypotheses outside of well-equipped laboratories. In response to a need to assess autonomic state regulation in survey research, we developed a questionnaire, the Body Perception Questionnaire Short Form (BPQ-SF; Cabrera et al., 2018; Kolacz et al., 2018; Porges, 1993). The BPQ-SF provides a measure of self-reported experiences of reactivity in organs and tissues that are regulated by the ANS. The BPQ-SF has been found to have good psychometric properties, convergent validity with similar measures, and consistent factor structure across samples (Kolacz et al., 2018). In a laboratory validation study (Kolacz et al., 2023) higher scores of autonomic reactivity on the BPQ-SF were associated with destabilized autonomic reactivity patterns (i.e., lower RSA, higher heart rate, poorer recovery to challenge).

In another study using the BPQ-SF, the frequently reported association between sexual function and adversity history was mediated by an ANS biased toward maintaining a physiological state that supports defensive strategies (Kolacz, Hu, et al., 2020). Consistent with the above relationship, we documented that the BPQ-SF measure of autonomic reactivity mediated the relationship between adversity history and mental health symptoms during the early phase of the COVID-19 pandemic (March 29 to May 13, 2020) in individuals who had not been infected (Kolacz, Dale, et al., 2020). These studies confirm that a self-report measure of autonomic regulation can be used in survey research as a reliable intervening variable in mediating the impact of adversity on outcomes (e.g., mental health, sexual function) and provide a tool to inexpensively test polyvagal-informed hypotheses without the burden of physiological monitoring.

NEUROCEPTION

PVT proposes that the neural evaluation of risk and safety reflexively triggers shifts in autonomic state without requiring conscious awareness. Thus, the term **neuroception** was introduced to emphasize a neural process, distinct from perception, capable of detecting and distinguishing environmental and visceral features that are safe, dangerous, or life-threatening (Porges, 2003, 2004). In human and other social mammals, neuroception is conceptualized as reflexive reactions that prepare the organism for defense or inhibit defense to promote homeostatic functions including health, growth, restoration, and sociality. A form of neuroception can be found in virtually all living organisms, regardless of the development of the nervous system. In fact, it could be argued that single-celled organisms and even plants have a primordial form of neuroception that responds to threat. As mammals, we are familiar with reactions to pain, a type of neuroception. We react to pain prior to our ability to identify the source of the stimulus or even of an awareness of the injury. Similarly, the detection of threat appears to be common across all vertebrate species. However, mammals have an expanded capacity for neuroception in which they not only react instantaneously to threat, but also respond instantaneously to cues of safety. It is this latter feature that enables mammals to down-regulate defensive strategies to promote sociality by enabling psychological and physical proximity without an anticipation of potential injury. It is this calming mechanism that adaptively signals the central regulation of autonomic function to dampen the metabolically costly fight-or-flight reactions dependent on sympathetic activation and to protect the oxygen-dependent central nervous system, especially the cortex, from the metabolically conservative defensive reactions of the dorsal vagal complex (e.g., fainting, death feigning).

PVT proposes that neuroception functionally involves both top-down and bottom-up mechanisms. The process of neuroception is assumed to be initiated via top-down pathways involving cortical areas located in or near the temporal cortex, components of the central nervous system that reflexively interpret cues of threat and safety. These areas of the cortex are sensitive to the intentionality of biological movements including voices, faces, gestures, and hand movements. Embedded in the construct of neuroception is the capacity of the nervous system to react to the intention of these movements. Neuroception functionally decodes and interprets the assumed goal of movements and sounds of inanimate and living objects. Thus, the neuroception of familiar individuals and individuals with appropriately prosodic voices and warm, expressive faces frequently translates into a positive social interaction, promoting a sense of safety. For example, safety cues in mothers' voices reduce infant heart rate and behavioral distress (Kolacz, daSilva, et al., 2022).

Autonomic state responds to the top-down detection of risk or safety. Autonomic reactions send sensory information regarding bodily feelings to the brain, where they are interpreted and consciously felt. The bottom-up limb of the neuroception is functionally equivalent to interoception. Thus, although we are often unaware of the specific features of the stimuli that trigger neuroception, we are generally aware of our body's reactions (i.e., visceral feelings) embodied in autonomic signatures that support adaptive behaviors (i.e., social engagement, fight-or-flight, shutdown).

POLYVAGAL THEORY: PRINCIPLES

As listed in Table 1.1, PVT can be summarized in five primary principles. Although the principles are succinctly stated, they reflect an extraction of the complex interdisciplinary material presented in the preceding sections as well as the wealth of information that has accumulated since the theory's initial presentation in 1994. During that period, PVT has been cited in more than 15,000 peer-reviewed journals. Unexpectedly, thousands of therapists currently self-identify as being polyvagal informed.

TABLE 1.1   Polyvagal Theory Principles

Principle 1	Autonomic state functions as an intervening variable.
Principle 2	Three neural circuits form a phylogenetically ordered response hierarchy that regulates autonomic state adaptation to safe, dangerous, and life-threatening environments.
Principle 3	In response to a challenge, the ANS shifts to states regulated by circuits that evolved earlier, consistent with the Jacksonian principle of dissolution (Jackson, 1884), a guiding principle in neurology.
Principle 4	Ventral migration of cardioinhibitory neurons leads to an integrated brainstem circuit (ventral vagal complex) that enables the coordination of suck-swallow-breathe-vocalize, a circuit that forms the neurophysiological substrate for an integrated social engagement system.
Principle 5	Neuroception: Reflexive detection of risk triggers adaptive autonomic state to optimize survival.

The principles form an interdependent hierarchical model in which each principle needs to be acknowledged sequentially. Feedback from both the research and clinical communities has helped provide clarity in articulating these principles as the theory evolved during the three decades since its initial presentation. In its original form the theory had a speculative, hypothetical focus derived through extracting principles from the literature. Literally, the initial presentation was structured as a challenge to colleagues to expand, refine, or refute features of the presentation with an optimistic and collaborative goal of gaining a better understanding of how autonomic state was related to human experience.

When I introduced the theory in 1994, as a laboratory scientist, I had limited experience in the realm of mental health and especially in the now burgeoning field of trauma. By the late 1990s, I was presenting the theory at meetings for mental health providers, often with a focus on trauma. To my surprise, at these meetings I was informed by survivors of severe adversity that PVT provided them with a narrative to explain their personal experiences. I was also being informed by several therapists that the first thing they did with their trauma patients was to explain PVT. Through these experiences in the clinical world, I witnessed an intuitive validity and utility of PVT as a scientific biobehavioral narrative that was consistent with the experiences of trauma survivors. Moreover, both therapists and survivors personally informed me about the therapeutic power of understanding that their reactions were neurobiological reflexive scripts of survival outside the realm of intentional behavior. This shifted their understanding of their own experiences from shame and blame (e.g., why didn't they run or fight?) to a deep respect for their body's foundational survival mechanisms that were dependent on brainstem circuits regulating the ANS.

Overview: PVT as an Algorithm

Given the background of having approximately 30 years of feedback from both the research and the clinical communities, the challenge is whether the principles of PVT can be succinctly refined to be sufficiently accessible in a manner that is respectful of both its scientific basis and the experiences reported in the clinic. To do this, we need to delve into the roots of the theory and the fundamental questions that it addresses.

PVT proposes that specific features of autonomic function in mammals are recruited to optimize survival. This is far from an innovative proposition. However, PVT proposes that this hypothetical optimal survival is the product of a functional neural algorithm through which the nervous system makes survival-related decisions based on a variety of factors. Like any decision-making entity, there is an acknowledgment of three sources of information (i.e., input, output, internal processing). In this model, input is the challenge, output is the response, and internal processing is conducted by the nervous system.

Historically, in its dedicated search for laws of nature, science primarily focused on only two of these sources (cause and effect or stimulus-response), while treating the internal resources of the entity (i.e., organism) as random error. This is the case in the application of Randomized Control Trials (RCT), the gold standard in medical research. However, if we include features of autonomic resilience, such as its individual or situational capacity to efficiently recover from disruptive challenges to support homeostatic functions, then the model expands from testing cause-and-effect hypotheses to questions of how neural regulation of ANS mediates reactivity and recovery to challenges. In today's data-oriented world, this neural algorithm would be conceptualized as a mediational model; it would generate ANS signatures (i.e., profiles) to optimize processes across a wide range of adaptive adjustments, from those supporting the body's homeostatic processes (i.e., health, growth, and restoration) to the metabolically costly survival processes demanding efficient fight-or-flight actions. This mediational algorithm contrasts with the cause-and-effect inference extracted from a RCT model or epidemiology's reliance on linear models to infer cause-and-effect relationships.

PVT explores the implication of this mediational algorithm. The algorithm would provide autonomic signatures useful for a variety of disciplines (i.e., monitoring accessibility to learn; to socialize; to support homeostatic processes of health, growth, and restoration). Perhaps the most informative aspect of such an algorithm would be to identify the autonomic pathways that would support the ability to down-regulate threat to enable mobilization and immobilization to occur with trusted others and not trigger defense. For example, the algorithm could be applied to confirm whether specific autonomic pathways are recruited to support apparently contradictory demands that require mobilization, such as play in contrast to fight-or-flight behaviors, or immobilization, such as intimacy in contrast to death feigning. **It is this process of functionally liberating mobilization and immobilization from defensive, threat-driven strategies that PVT hypothesizes to have supported the emergence of social behavior and cooperation in species of social mammals** (Porges, 2021, 2022).

Principle 1. Autonomic state functions as an intervening variable.

Within this concept of an algorithm, how do the theory's principles fit? Principle 1 focuses on the resource and flexibility of the system—the capacity to respond, process, and recover. Functionally, this principle emphasizes that autonomic state serves as a neural platform that limits and fosters broad domains of behaviors and psychological experiences during contexts of safety, danger, and life threat.

PVT expands and diverges from the neuroscience disciplines, studying parallels between autonomic state and mental, physical, social, affective, and health processes. PVT encourages researchers to go beyond conducting studies to confirm these correlations. PVT emphasizes the limitations of correlational research as an imprecise research strategy that obfuscates the critical mediating mechanisms of the correlated phenomena. PVT views correlational research as focusing on the phenomena that covary and not the underlying neural pathways that would explain how autonomic mechanisms would be integrated within the actual processes being studied. PVT emphasizes an important perspective missed by correlational research: how the ANS is part of an integrated response and not a covariate. This might reframe the current use of comorbidities within mental and physical health diagnostic systems from correlative relationships to being an attribute of a disrupted system that could be expressed in several outputs, including features of both mental and physical health.

PVT is historically consistent with the work of Ernst Gellhorn (1957), who emphasized the integration of autonomic, cortical, and somatic systems. In contrast, correlation-based sciences such as epidemiology provide probabilities that are frequently interpreted as insights into causal mechanisms and often, due to faulty inference, lead to inappropriate treatments with poor outcomes.

Once the research target shifts from a focus on correlations to the identification and quantification of parameters mediating the integration, then the diverse components of the nervous system (e.g., somatic, cortical, autonomic, endocrine, histamine, and immune systems) may be viewed as interdependently functioning circuits that through dynamic bidirectional dialogue continually inform and adjust output. This point was eloquently stated in 1949 by Walter Hess in the opening few sentences of his Nobel Prize speech. Mediational models shift the research agenda from correlation and the tendency to generate faulty causality inferences when correlations are high (e.g., epidemiology) and to miss important mediating variables when correlations are low.

Acknowledging that autonomic state functions as an intervening variable is the first principle of PVT. This principle transforms research questions and hypotheses, which had previously focused on exploring correlational data to an algorithm that would have predictive utility in explaining the dynamic adaptive adjustment of autonomic state. An algorithm, through extensive scientific investigation, could lead to a better understanding of conditions and individual differences that would document the impact of enhanced or dysfunctional autonomic support on homeostatic processes including health, growth, restoration, and sociality.

Principle 2. Three neural circuits form a phylogenetically ordered response hierarchy that regulates autonomic state adaptation to safe, dangerous, and life-threatening environments.

Principle 2 has been thoroughly described in the sections above. PVT emphasizes that three neural circuits regulating autonomic state are important determinants of the biobehavioral algorithm that enables autonomic state variations to predictably support different adaptive functions. A careful literature review documents that brainstem nuclei regulating the ANS follow a phylogenetically ordered sequence that was initiated within ancient vertebrates and through the process of evolution was modified and repurposed in mammals. PVT is mammalian-centric and focused on identifying and describing the biobehavioral scripts produced by a hypothetical brainstem algorithm that would optimize survival in humans. The phylogenetic sequence, initiated by a dorsal vagus, is followed by a spinal sympathetic system, and the ventral vagus. By identifying the biobehavioral scripts of each of these circuits, we become appreciative of the efficiency of the three neural circuits in an attempt to optimize survival in response to signals of safety, danger, and life threat.

The scripts are helpful in identifying when the ANS is in a state that supports homeostatic functions (health, growth, restoration, and sociality), when it supports the metabolically costly states requiring fight-or-flight behaviors, and when it supports threat reactions of immobilization (death feigning). Identification of the three circuits provides a neurophysiological basis to explain the mechanisms through which each ANS state supports different behaviors and experiences. As emphasized in Principle 4, the biobehavioral consequences of this ventral migration of cardioinhibitory neurons in the brainstem provide an organizing principle to understand that the neural regulation of the ANS in humans is an enabler of sociality (Porges, 2021, 2022).

Principle 3. In response to a challenge, the ANS shifts to states regulated by circuits that evolved earlier, consistent with the Jacksonian principle of dissolution, a guiding principle in neurology (Jackson, 1884).

There are hundreds, if not thousands, of peer-reviewed publications documenting the involvement of ventral vagal regulation of the heart in response to behavioral and psychological challenges. In these studies, the ventral vagal contribution is monitored through metrics of heart rate variability (HRV) and especially RSA. The research reliably documents a systematic withdrawal of the phylogenetically newer ventral vagal calming pro-homeostatic actions during contexts requiring the recruitment of metabolic resources to deal with a vast array of challenges including adversaries (e.g., fight-or-flight behaviors), mental and physical illness, psychological challenges (e.g., mental effort, sustained attention), and the anticipation to move when feelings of threat are experienced. In contrast, feelings of safety seem to parallel an ANS in a more flexible state that enables movement to be integrated with other forms of co-regulation involving attributes of the social engagement system, thus providing the autonomic substrate that would discriminate play from defense.

Although a much smaller literature, there appears to be documentation of an immobilization defense response to signals of life threat that trigger a death feigning response (e.g., mouse in the jaws of a cat, rats; Richter, 1957). The response would include a reduction in neuromuscular tone and an associated reduction in autonomic activation that has been hypothetically linked to dorsal vagal influences on heart rate, contractility, and gut motility. It should not be a surprise that individuals whose nervous systems have responded as if they were under life threat frequently have a retuned ANS with features of autonomic dysregulation, especially gut problems. Potentially, gut symptoms may be a product of a dampened ventral vagal circuit that resulted in a vulnerability to the dorsal vagal circuit being recruited in defense (Kolacz, 2019, 2021; Kolacz, Kovacic, et al., 2022).

Principle 3 is helpful in redefining psychological constructs of stress and anxiety as physiological states that support defense. Succinctly, PVT would define stress, anxiety, or any threat-related experience as a disruption in homeostatic function. Although PVT was initially focused on transitory, acute challenge-related changes in autonomic state, the theory provides insights into chronic states and illnesses. It proposes that the resilience of the ANS may be dampened or retuned to be chronically locked into states of defense. Hypothetically this may be the consequence of a life-threatening experience with symptoms that would persist even when the body was not physically injured or even after the body healed. This sequence appears to reflect a nervous system that is adaptively reluctant to relinquish its defenses. Examples of this have been reported as a consequence of severe adversity history in which the regulation of the ANS has transitioned from an algorithm supporting homeostatic functions to one that supports defense at all costs. Trauma therapists are familiar with these observations in which patients react defensively when socially engaged through proximity and even eye contact. In these cases, the nervous system is optimizing defense at the expense of supporting the homeostatic processes of health, growth, restoration, and sociality.

Principle 4. Ventral migration of cardioinhibitory neurons leads to an integrated brainstem circuit (ventral vagal complex) that enables the coordination of suck-swallow-breathe-vocalize, a circuit that forms the neurophysiological substrate for an integrated social engagement system.

PVT describes the process through which ventral migration of cardioinhibitory neurons became integrated in the regulation of the striated muscles of the face and head. This is a critical event, enabling mammals to nurse and to signal the caregiver. Interestingly, this system seems to have provided the core mechanisms that enabled mammals to co-regulate and to communicate with conspecifics. PVT speculates that the ventral migration paved the path for mammalian sociality, which enabled co-regulation and trust to be a highlight of human behavior as well as the system that is most challenged when the ANS shifts into a state of defense. It is a system that literally can be monitored in real time by studying heart rate patterns during delivery (Reed, Ohel, & Porges, 1999) and in preterm human newborns (Doussard-Roosevelt et al., 1997; Suess et al., 2000). The social engagement system, through the expression of autonomic state calmness in vocalizations and facial expressions, is a potent stimulus through neuroception (see Principle 5) for mammals to down-regulate threat reactions and can become a portal to signal safety to conspecifics. This intuition is frequently understood by therapists, parents, teachers, friends, and pet owners as they use their voice and gestures—projecting their own calm state to calm others.

Principle 5. Neuroception: Reflexive detection of risk triggers adaptive autonomic state to optimize survival.

The construct of an algorithm was selected to emphasize that the autonomic signatures related to navigating in contexts that are safe, dangerous, or life-threatening are basically reflexive brainstem scripts. Neuroception is the hypothetical process through which these scripts are triggered. According to PVT these scripts reside in the brainstem area that regulates foundational survival mechanisms. In humans and other social mammals, these scripts are triggered by higher brain structures that process information outside of awareness. By being reflexive, these processes are unimpeded by intentionality and cognitive appraisal. Adaptively, if they were, decisions would be slow and potentially tentative, and survival might be compromised. To emphasize the independence of these processes distinct from awareness and intention, PVT introduced the construct of neuroception, which detects and triggers foundational survival mechanisms. Since neuroception does not involve perception or appraisal of causality, neuroception is difficult to modify through cognitive channels.

CURRENT STATUS OF PVT

The foundation of PVT is based on the listed principles (see Table 1.1) extracted from an accepted scientific literature. The validity of the theory should be based on the utility of these principles to provide plausible explanations in clarifying human experience. The theory is informed by several disciplines (e.g., evolution, comparative neuroanatomy, cardiopulmonary neurophysiology), although PVT was not structured to answer questions or test hypotheses relevant to these disciplines. The theory should be evaluated based on the scientific questions that stimulated the quest to understand the vagal paradox as framed in the presentation of the theory and the scientific foundation from which the above five principles have been extracted. The theory focuses on the role of the ANS as an intervening variable and explores the impact of disruptive challenges on homeostatic functions. The model embedded in the theory, by emphasizing the ANS as an intervening variable, expands clinically relevant research questions from testing cause-and-effect hypotheses to questions of how the neural regulation of ANS mediates reactivity and recovery to challenges. Thus, this mediational model could be conceptualized as a functional neural algorithm.

Given the strong scientific foundation, there have been few criticisms in the scientific literature. As stated above, almost 30 years ago the initial presentation of the theory was structured as a challenge to colleagues to expand, refine, or refute features of the presentation, with an optimistic and collaborative goal of gaining a better understanding of how autonomic state was related to human experience. In general, the scientific and clinical community welcomed PVT with almost universal acceptance as an innovative perspective linking the ANS with human health and experience. Consistent with this acceptance, during this period several peer-reviewed grants from the National Institutes of Health supported my research exploring the clinical relevance of PVT. However, there were and are a few scientists (e.g., Grossman & Taylor, 2007; Grossman, 2023; Taylor, 2022) who have criticized PVT on the basis of inaccurate misrepresentations of the theory.

Their criticisms evolved into a classic straw man argument: first they have articulated inaccurate versions of the theory, and then they have argued that

those inaccurate versions of PVT do not have a scientific basis, and that, therefore PVT itself is false. Investigation of the criticisms has identified two important points: (1) the criticisms were based on inaccurate representations of the
theory and (2) the criticisms were irrelevant to the theory and the questions that
stimulated the structuring of the theory. Then, consistent with the classic structure of a straw man argument, the misrepresentations were repeatedly presented
as evidence that the theory was untenable.

These arguments were initially seeded about 20 years ago (Grossman &
Taylor, 2007). Despite my own repeated detailed responses to their claims and
despite decades of research that supports PVT, they continue to misrepresent
the theory and to argue points unrelated to the principles embedded in PVT
(Grossman, 2023; Taylor et al., 2022).

Now, approximately 30 years after the initial presentation of the theory,
this chapter attempts to clarify PVT by providing accessible principles and an
updated review of the supporting scientific literature. It is hoped that future scientific dialogue and debate will more accurately represent PVT and challenge
it through more traditional strategies such as hypothesis testing and alternative
explanations of the literature, rather than through arguments that mischaracter-
ize PVT's underlying principles and are beside the point.

**Misrepresentation #1: RSA is a mammalian form of cardio-respiratory
coupling.** In 2005, a paper titled "Does Respiratory Sinus Arrhythmia Occur in
Fishes?" was published (Campbell et al., 2005) that stated:

> In addition to these data on fish, it has been observed that many amphibians
> and reptiles, characterized as breathing discontinuously, show close correlations
> between the onset of a bout of breathing and an instantaneous tachycardia, imply-
> ing overriding central nervous integration of their cardio-respiratory systems
> (Burggren 1987). However, Porges (1995) proposed that cardio-respiratory cou-
> pling is restricted to mammals. (p. 484)

This statement was factually inaccurate: **I have never proposed, and PVT
does not assume, that cardio-respiratory coupling is restricted to mammals**.
But these critics continued to repeat that inaccurate assumption, including in
an article (Grossman & Taylor, 2007) to which I responded (see quote below
from [Porges, 2007a]):

> This statement is perplexing, since the specific restriction of cardiorespiratory cou-
> pling to mammals was not stated in the Polyvagal Theory. Moreover, as discussed
> in the commentary, from the Polyvagal perspective, RSA is a uniquely mamma-
> lian cardiorespiratory interaction because it is dependent on the outflow of the
> myelinated vagus originating in the nucleus ambiguus. This does not preclude
> cardiorespiratory interactions involving the unmyelinated vagus originating in the
> dorsal motor nucleus of the vagus in other vertebrates.

Nevertheless, these critics continue to insist on this misrepresentation of PVT. For example, a 2019 paper reporting the observation of a respiratory heart rate interaction in rattlesnakes (Sanches et al., 2019) stated that "the conclusion that RSA does not exist in non-mammalian vertebrates and forms the basis of the polyvagal theory (Porges, 2003)" (p. 2635).

The reason this mischaracterization of PVT is so important is that if one accepts it, one can then claim that any the existence of any form of non-mammalian heart rate–respiratory interaction proves that PVT is inaccurate. For example, in the same 2019 paper, the same critics stated, "This [the observation of a respiratory pattern in the heart rate pattern in a rattlesnake] data refutes the proposition that centrally controlled cardiorespiratory coupling is restricted to mammals, as propounded by the polyvagal theory of Porges (Porges, 1995; Porges, 2003)" (p. 2635).

Following this logic, observations of heart rate–respiratory coupling in other vertebrate species also would be inconsistent with PVT. That convoluted logic works well *only* if the term RSA is redefined to include all forms of heart rate–respiratory coupling observed in vertebrates. Then, since PVT uses the construct of RSA, one could argue, as they do (see Taylor et al., 2022), that any statement regarding RSA as being uniquely mammalian would be false. That argument, however, misses two important points about the relationship between RSA and PVT: **(1) the specific vagal pathways mediating RSA in mammals, unlike their ancestral vertebrates, originate in the ventral vagus, and (2) RSA is a portal to the function of the ventral vagus, enabling the testing of polyvagal-informed hypotheses, but is not a foundational construct of the theory.**

Despite my having pointed out the flaws in their characterization of RSA in relation to PVT, Taylor's group has continued using their distorted redefinition of RSA in inaccurate representations of the theory:

> Several authors have shown that HRV related to respiration is present in species of amphibians, reptiles [for example, rattlesnakes], and birds [ducks and shearwaters]. Thus, the repeated contention, central to the polyvagal theory, that the structural and functional bases of RSA are solely mammalian is clearly fallacious. (Monteiro et al., 2018, p. 8)
>
> These findings do not provide support for Porges' so-called "polyvagal theory," in which the author claims respiratory sinus arrhythmia and its basis in parasympathetic control of the heart is solely mammalian. (Sanches et al., 2019)
>
> Nevertheless, the promoter of the polyvagal theory recently stated that: "only mammals have a myelinated vagus." (Sanches et al., 2019)

Misrepresentation #2: Myelinated cardioinhibitory vagal fibers originating in the nucleus ambiguus is a defining feature of the phylogenetic transition from ancient, long-extinct reptiles to mammals. Although Taylor's research group acknowledges that in mammals myelinated cardioinhibitory vagal fibers predominantly originate from the nucleus ambiguus, the group argues that the identification of myelinated cardioinhibitory vagal pathways in non-mammalian species disproves PVT. In a paper entitled "Cardiorespiratory Interactions Previously Identified as Mammalian Are Present in the Primitive Lungfish" (Monteiro et al., 2018), they stated,

> He [Porges] identifies a phylogenetic progression from the regulation of the heart by endocrine communication, to unmyelinated nerves, and finally to myelinated nerves found exclusively in mammals and persists in stating that "only mammals have a myelinated vagus," linking this to the evolution of the NA [nucleus ambiguus]. The present study reveals that the mechanisms he identifies as solely mammalian are undeniably present in the lungfish that sits at the evolutionary base of the air-breathing vertebrates. (p. 7)

Recently, a similar argument was used by citing a study documenting a myelinated vagal pathway originating in the dorsal motor nucleus of the vagus in sheep (Grossman, 2023), although the study did not identify the function of these fibers or document that the functional output was coupled with respiration.

In other words, they maintain, since PVT presupposes that only mammals have a myelinated vagus, the presence of such mechanisms in lungfish and sheep proves that PVT is wrong. In the discussion above, we saw how the concept of RSA has been generalized as a term for heart rate–respiratory coupling across vertebrate species. Here, the word "myelinated" is being recharacterized from referring only to mammals with cardioinhibitory pathways originating in the ventral vagal nucleus, to a general feature of cardiorespiratory interaction that is independent of nucleus of origin (i.e., either ventral or dorsal motor nucleus of the vagus) and independent of function.

What Taylor's group seems not to comprehend is that just stating descriptively that RSA in mammals is dependent on myelinated cardioinhibitory vagal pathways originating in the ventral vagus and *not* on unmyelinated (or potentially myelinated) cardioinhibitory vagal pathways originating in the dorsal vagus does not preclude the identification of myelinated cardioinhibitory vagal fibers in vertebrate species. PVT simply emphasizes the distribution *in mammals* of myelinated cardioinhibitory vagal fibers that predominantly originate in the ventral vagal nucleus and *not* the dorsal motor nucleus of the vagus. The ventral migration of cardioinhibitory vagal neurons culminating in the clustering of these neurons in the ventral vagus that is mapped out in phylogeny has been documented since the late 1970s (Nosaka et al., 1979).

Even in the original PVT paper there is a strong emphasis that the primary source of myelinated cardioinhibitory vagal pathways in mammals originate in the ventral vagal nucleus.

> The Polyvagal Theory argues that [in mammals] the vagal fibers from the DMNX and NA are distinguishable in structure and function. Specifically, it has been argued that the vagal efferent fibers from the NA [nucleus ambiguus is the ventral vagal nucleus] are myelinated and contain a respiratory rhythm and the vagal efferent fibers from the DMNX [dorsal motor nucleus of the vagus] are unmyelinated and do not express a respiratory rhythm. (Porges, 1995, pp. 307–308)

This statement is consistent with current neurophysiological research (Gourine et al., 2016) and does not contradict reports of a myelinated vagal pathway from the dorsal vagus in lungfish or the citation of one occurring in sheep. Although interesting, these findings are irrelevant to the theory and not a test of it.

Taylor and colleagues have also questioned the assumption that the dorsal motor nucleus of the vagus is an evolutionarily older structure than the ventral vagus. It has been reliably documented that prior to mammals the prominent cardioinhibitory vagal neurons in vertebrates originated in the dorsal motor nucleus of the vagus. Thus, it is indisputable that estimating an evolutionary timeline through phylogeny, cardioinhibitory neurons originated first in the dorsal motor nucleus of the vagus and then, consistent with Taylor's own work migrated ventrally (Taylor et al., 2022). In the earliest (now extinct) mammals this ventral migration was sufficiently complete to embed cardioinhibitory functions with activities of branchiomotor neurons (i.e., special visceral efferent pathways) that regulate the striated muscles of the face and head promoting ingestion (e.g., nursing) and social communication via facial expression and vocalizations.

Grossman has argued that a repurposing of the ANS that would support sociality is inconsistent with the critical role of nursing in mammals as a social behavior, and its dependence on the ventral migration of cardioinhibitory neurons (Grossman, 2023). Or, more generally, how feeding is used to tame and calm (i.e., socialize) domesticated mammals of several species. Grossman argues the point that the mammalian repurposing of the autonomic nervous system was not necessary for social behavior since from his perspective reptiles are social. He supports this point by citing a paper that appeared in a special issue of *Biological Psychology*, which he edited, which argues that PVT is unappreciative of the social behavior of non-mammalian vertebrates (Doody et al., 2023). The authors argue that PVT inappropriately describes reptiles as being asocial, since reptiles have social behaviors. These criticisms are irrelevant to PVT, however, because PVT is solely mammal-centric and focuses on the transformative qualities of social behavior expressed in mammals (i.e., co-regulation to calm and optimize homeostatic functions) that are highlighted in PVT. So, not only does this argument purport to apply PVT to questions in another discipline, but it purports to apply PVT to social behavior in reptiles, a subject that has been explicitly stated to be outside the scope of PVT.

In fact, Taylor and his group have acknowledged that PVT defines mammalian RSA as restricted to the ventral vagus and myelinated cardioinhibitory fibers (Campbell et al., 2006). But even when they do appear to acknowledge that anatomical fact, they blur the anatomical and functional distinctions of the dorsal and ventral vagal nuclei that have occurred through evolution, by postulating a primitive ventral vagus without acknowledging functional limitations of this hypothetical anatomical structure. See Taylor and colleagues (2006):

> The "polyvagal theory" has suggested that the beat-to-beat control of fH [heart rate frequency] that generates RSA is restricted to mammals, which have evolved myelinated vagal pathways that originate in the NA [nucleus ambiguus] (Porges 2003; Porges et al. 2003). However, CRS [cardiorespiratory synchrony] has been reported in both resting dogfish (Taylor 1992) and hypoxic trout (Randall and Smith 1967), and both species have CVPN [cardiac-specific preganglionic neurons] located both in the DVN [dorsal motor nucleus of the vagus] and in a ventrolateral location outside the DVN that may constitute a primitive NA [nucleus ambiguus]. (Taylor, 1992)

The generalization of common mechanisms underlying heart rate-respiration interactions across vertebrate species has its limitations. Evolution repurposed and modified both how the mammalian autonomic nervous system is structured and how it functions. If we do not acknowledge the evolutionary repurposing of structures, we in essence will appear to be accepting "recapitulation" theory—a disproven theory that assumes that evolution preserves not only structure, but also function.

In fact, RSA has historically been used to describe a mammalian heart rate rhythm. It has a history of use that has been agnostic of the heart rate–respiratory interactions of other vertebrates. Even Taylor, in his earlier papers (i.e., prior to 2000), uses the term RSA only when discussing mammals. Althoug heart rate–respiratory interactions are highly conserved during evolution and even evidenced in mammals, the underlying mechanisms have been modified through evolution (e.g., Richter & Spyer, 1990). The foundation of PVT focuses on the structural and functional consequences of mammalian modifications of this highly conserved system, a point that was unambiguously stated in the title of my 1995 paper introducing PVT (Porges, 1995): *Orienting in a Defensive World: Mammalian Modifications of Our Evolutionary Heritage. A Polyvagal Theory.*

To sum up, the arguments of Taylor and colleagues that purport to undermine PVT are based on or arise from factual misrepresentations of PVT itself. They are not scientific challenges to the hypotheses and inferences generated by the theory. Reading the articles mentioned above, one might conclude that PVT was developed to answer questions in those authors' areas of interest—such as whether HRV is present in rattlesnakes or fish—even though PVT focuses solely on mammals. All of these authors are well-credentialed scientists who certainly are qualified to raise questions about PVT that actually might generate some useful debate about PVT. But applying PVT to areas of scientific study that PVT was never meant to affect will not make that happen.

What makes these authors' relentless criticism of PVT especially perplexing to me is the fact that they use PVT as an explanatory vehicle to interpret their own work. Much of Grossman's own research on RSA can be explained by PVT. Indeed, as I pointed out in my own 2007 paper (Porges, 2007), one paper by Grossman and Taylor (2007) paraphrases aspects of PVT and presents them as novel.

- Grossman and Taylor (2007) propose, as an alternative to the Polyvagal Theory, several points stated previously in the Polyvagal Theory (Porges, 1995). They state, "What we measure with any heart rate index of vagal tone are only the final functional vagal effects on cardiac activity." This statement is consistent with summary point four in the Polyvagal Theory (Porges, 1995): "The functional output of the NA vagus on the heart may be monitored by RSA (p. 314)."
- They state that "variations in RSA magnitude currently provide an unreliable index of central vagal outflow or tone." This statement is implicit in the first and third summary points of the Polyvagal Theory: "The vagal system does not represent a unitary dimension," and, "In mammals the concept that vagal tone represents a single or summed system may have limited physiological or heuristic value (p. 314)."
- They state that RSA serves an active biological function in enhancing "the efficiency of pulmonary gas exchange by matching blood perfusion to air flow in the lung through each breathing cycle." A similar statement is made in Porges (1995): "The covariation of the bronchi with heart rate oscillations (e.g., RSA), mediated by NA [nucleus ambiguus], may have a functional influence on the oxygenation of blood (p. 311)."
- They state that resting RSA reflects a "functional energy reserve capacity from which the organism can draw during more active states." This statement is consistent with the functional impact of the myelinated vagal efferent activity on behavior described in the Polyvagal Theory (1995): "The high NA vagal tone [observed as high amplitude RSA] keeps mammals from, literally, bouncing off the walls. Thus, in contrast to that observed in reptiles, in mammals vagal tone is highest during unchallenged situations such as sleep, and vagal tone is actively withdrawn in response to external demands, including metabolically demanding states such as exercise, stress, attention, and information processing (p. 306)." These points were subsequently formalized as the vagal brake construct and introduced in Porges et al. (1996), which states that "the theory [Polyvagal Theory] proposes that the successful adaptation of mammals is dependent on systematic and reliable withdrawal and reengagement of the vagal brake [quantified by the amplitude of RSA] as a mechanism to

rapidly regulate metabolic output in response to environmental demands (p. 700)." (Porges, 2007, pp. 305–306)

It is important to deconstruct these arguments because these arguments in turn have encouraged others to assert that PVT is speculative and not supported by science. Such statements are inconsistent with an immense and expanding literature supporting attributes of PVT. On the surface, the theory has been cited thousands of times as support for research conducted by independent researchers. However, this is a gross underestimation of the explanatory value of the theory. By investigating the literature on autonomic reactivity through a polyvagal lens, we can explore whether the results of studies can be explained by the principles embedded in PVT, even if PVT was not cited in a particular study. This strategy was implemented in a systematic review documenting the impact of contemplative practices on ventral vagal tone, which was evaluated from a polyvagal perspective (Poli et al., 2021).

As emphasized in the principles, the succinctly outlined phylogenetically ordered hierarchy involving brainstem structures regulating autonomic state provides a plausible road map of human autonomic reactivity by providing examples of biobehavioral features associated with each of the three major autonomic pathways. The simplicity of embedding in PVT this unchallengeable hierarchy with the Jacksonian principle of dissolution has been transformative in explaining biobehavioral consequences of adversity in the treatment of mental health challenges. Moreover, these principles are permeating the treatment of patients in medicine and students in education.

From a polyvagal perspective, the numerous studies that document or test hypotheses related to autonomic state as an intervening, a response, or an individual difference variable are implicitly testing attributes of PVT. Reviewing the literature through the lens of PVT provides plausible explanations and neurophysiological pathways mediating outcomes. For example, PVT provides plausible explanations of studies that structure protocols to evaluate the following processes:

1. Autonomic state functions as an intervening (mediational) variable (Principle 1).
2. Changes in heart rate and RSA during challenge (Principles 2 & 3).
3. The efficiency of the vagal brake is related to clinical symptoms (Principles 3 & 4).
4. The impact of vagal nerve stimulation on autonomic state regulation and social behavior (Principle 4).
5. Autonomic state biases reactions (neuroception) along a continuum of risk (Principle 5).

CONCLUSION

The scientific method seeks to distinguish valid points from conjectures. Theories flourish only if they are useful in describing phenomena that can inform future investigations. Of course, theories must be modified and informed by empirical research and when necessary, replaced by alternative theories that are more effective in explaining naturally occurring phenomena. If we use this as an acceptable standard, then PVT provides a testable model describing how the mammalian autonomic nervous system reacts to threat and safety. The theory specifically provides an understanding of the core features of the mammalian ANS needed to co-regulate and trust others. It also provides insights into the consequences of autonomic state for mental and physical health. Perhaps, most important the theory gives a voice to the personal experiences of individuals who have experienced chronic threat (i.e., trauma and abuse) or illness and structures an optimistic journey toward more optimal mental and physical health. It is this core, described by PVT, that links our biological imperative to connect with others to neural pathways, via neuroception, that calm our ANS. These systems, in the context of mammalian physiology, are foundational processes through which behavioral experiences can lead to sociality and optimal health, growth, and restoration. In the future, without the distractions of the misleading arguments described above, there is an optimistic possibility of a more informed level of scientific discourse that would further explore the important relationships between the ANS and human experience that have been highlighted by PVT.

2

Polyvagal Theory: A Biobehavioral Journey to Sociality

Stephen W. Porges

THE TRANSDISCIPLINARY ORIGINS OF POLYVAGAL THEORY

A polyvagal perspective clarifies the evolutionary transition that enabled mammals to be social and to use sociality as a mechanism to regulate and optimize physiological state and homeostatic processes. This journey is highlighted by the phylogenetic transition from reptiles to mammals, during which the autonomic nervous system was repurposed to suppress defensive strategies in order to support and express sociality. The product of this transition was an autonomic nervous system with capacities to self-calm, to spontaneously socially engage others, and to mitigate threat reactions in ourselves and others through social cues. Thus, social behavior became embedded with specific neurobiological processes that had capabilities to support homeostatic functions that would lead to optimized health, growth, and restoration. Succinctly, Polyvagal Theory (PVT) emphasizes sociality as a core process in mitigating threat and supporting mental and physical health.

To understand the origins of PVT, visualize a Rubik's cube with surfaces representing different disciplines moving in time as each field is selectively updated by new information. Metaphorically, PVT is the solution of a Rubik's puzzle, a solution to how evolution repurposed the mammalian autonomic nervous system to contain defensive reactions and enable sociality to thrive. This metaphor is helpful, since PVT is a product of an extraction of principles derived from the integration of several disciplines each with its own history, research paradigms, literature, methodology, and theoretical context. PVT evolved to ask new questions and was not conceptualized to replace the predominant theories associated with these foundational disciplines. Thus, the solution to the puzzle produced a transdisciplinary theory that had a foundational basis but was not limited or biased by any specific discipline.

This chapter is structured to explain how evolution and development of neuroanatomical structures and neurophysiological processes contribute to PVT. The initial assumptions of PVT provide insights into deconstructing autonomic and behavioral reactions to threat consistent with the Jacksonian principle of dissolution or evolution in reverse (Jackson, 1884). Thus, evolution became the initial organizing principle for the theory. As the theory developed, other disciplines provided convergent support of the hierarchy of autonomic states introduced in the initial publication of PVT (Porges, 1995). The study of development and maturation paralleled the insights extracted from evolutionary biology (see Porges & Furman, 2011). In addition, dissolution of autonomic state converged with the personal narratives of survivors of trauma (see van der Kolk, 2015). The theory validated the immobilization shutdown responses reported by survivors.

All three pathways (i.e., evolution, development, clinical observation) help us understand the dependence of sociality on the neural regulation of the autonomic nervous system. From evolutionary biology, we see shifts in structure and function of the autonomic nervous system as asocial vertebrates evolved into social mammals with a biological imperative to connect, nurse, cooperate, and trust select others (e.g., Dobzhansky, 1962). From developmental biology, we observe shifts in neural regulation of the autonomic nervous system starting during the last trimester that prepare the newborn to suckle, to breathe, and to co-regulate. From the study of trauma, we see the dissolution of many of these social systems with profound consequences for mental and physical health (see van der Kolk, 2015). Similarly, during difficult deliveries, the neonate follows a predictable pattern of dissolution that is characterized by a sequence of depressed heart rate variability, metabolically costly tachycardia, and finally the shutting down of vital systems as indexed by life-threatening bradycardia (Reed, Ohel, et al., 1999).

HISTORICAL CONTEXT

The early conceptualization of the vagus in mammals focused on an undifferentiated efferent (motor) pathway that was assumed to modulate tone concurrently to several target organs. Little attention was directed to the afferent (sensory) limb of the vagus that provides dynamic feedback to the brainstem structures regulating the efferent outflow. Thus, neural circuits regulating the supradiaphragmatic (e.g., myelinated vagal pathways originating in the nucleus ambiguus and terminating primarily above the diaphragm) were not functionally distinguished from the subdiaphragmatic (e.g., unmyelinated vagal pathways originating in the dorsal motor nucleus of the vagus and terminating primarily below the diaphragm). Without this distinction, research and theory in psychophysiology and psychosomatic medicine focused on the paired antagonism between the parasympathetic and sympathetic innervation to target organs. The consequence of an emphasis on paired antagonism in physiology was an acceptance and use of global constructs (e.g., autonomic balance, sympathetic arousal, vagal tone) without documenting the specific neural pathways and feedback circuits involved in dynamically regulating the autonomic nervous system. Missing was an understanding of how areas of the brain communicated with and regulated the visceral end organs of the autonomic nervous system.

More than 50 years ago, Walter Hess (1954) proposed that the "autonomic" nervous system was not solely "vegetative" and automatic but was an integrated system with both peripheral and central neurons. Hess demonstrated the influence of the hypothalamus on the autonomic nervous system. By emphasizing the central mechanisms that mediate the dynamic regulation of peripheral organs, Hess anticipated the need for methodologies and technologies to continuously monitor the neural circuits involving both defined brain structures and peripheral nerves in the regulation of visceral function and state. Consistent with these insights, PVT was proposed and methods were suggested to extract the time course of the influence of two vagal circuits on the beat-to-beat heart rate pattern (Porges, 1995, 2007).

PVT was introduced as an attempt to shift the science of psychophysiology from a descriptive science conducting empirical studies and describing correlations between psychological and physiological processes to an inferential science generating and testing hypotheses related to common neural pathways involving both mental and physiological processes. It was the first volley in a conceptual dialogue challenging the questions and methods involved in psychophysiological research and especially in the subdomain of cardiovascular psychophysiology.

Psychophysiology emerged in the 1960s, a relatively atheoretical empirical period of science in which a simplistic arousal theory dominated research. Basically, arousal theory emphasized that arousal was a linear construct indexing a dimension from low to high levels of activation that could be measured or inferred from observing behavior or physiology. The relationship between arousal and performance was often portrayed as an inverted U-shaped function in which optimal performance occurred within a mid-level range, while poor performance was observed at low and high levels of arousal. This relationship was already known as the Yerkes-Dodson law (Yerkes & Dodson, 1908). Metaphorically, arousal represented the energy of the human nervous system. Arousal was easily understood, since when it was reflected behaviorally it could be quantified as greater activity and when reflected autonomically it could be observed as increases in sweating and heart rate.

Early psychophysiological research assumed that peripheral autonomic measures provided sensitive indicators of arousal. This view was based on a rudimentary understanding of the autonomic nervous system in which changes in electrodermal activity (e.g., sweating) and heart rate were assumed to be accurate indicators of sympathetic activity. As the activation arousal theory developed, a continuity between peripheral autonomic responses and central mechanisms was assumed (see Darrow et al., 1942), and sympathetic activity was assumed to parallel activation of the brain. According to this assumption, organs influenced by sympathetic efferent fibers, such as the sweat glands, blood vessels, or the heart, were potential indicators of limbic or cortical activity (Duffy, 1957; Lindsley, 1951; Malmo, 1959).

Although the specific pathways relating these various levels were never outlined and are still sketchy, electrodermal activity (often known as galvanic skin response or GSR) and heart rate became the primary focus of research during the early history of the Society for Psychophysiological Research. This was due to their presumed sympathetic innervation and, in part, to their measurement availability. By default, this emphasis created a research environment that neglected several important factors: (a) parasympathetic (e.g., vagal) influences, (b) interactions between sympathetic and parasympathetic processes, (c) peripheral autonomic afferents, (d) central regulatory structures, (e) the adaptive and dynamic nature of the autonomic nervous system, and (f) phylogenetic and ontogenetic differences in structural organization and function. In the initial presentation, PVT was an attempt to provide an integrated theory (Porges, 1995) based on the literatures of several disciplines that would be the basis for testable hypotheses relating autonomic function to sociality and health in humans and nonhuman mammals.

EVOLUTION REPURPOSES THE NEURAL REGULATION OF THE AUTONOMIC NERVOUS SYSTEM TO SUPPORT SOCIALITY

Evolution informed the development of PVT. Through the lens of evolution, the theory focused on how mammals adapted many of the phylogenetical ancestral structures that evolved to support survival in a hostile world. Note that the title of the initial publication presenting the theory (Porges, 1995) is actually a synopsis of the theory: *Orienting in a Defensive World: Mammalian Modifications of Our Evolutionary Heritage. A Polyvagal Theory.* The title summarizes a phylogenetic narrative in which the survival of mammals was dependent on an ability to down-regulate and modify the innate defensive systems that were inherited from their reptilian ancestors. These embedded vestigial circuits with their emergent adaptive strategies are embedded in genes of mammals. For mammals, whose survival is dependent on their sociality to cooperate, to connect, and to co-regulate (e.g., Dobzhansky, 1962), the ancient defense programs had to be harnessed and repurposed to enable the expression of several defining features including signals of safety and calmness in proximity to another trusted mammal.

PVT's emphasis on investigating mammalian autonomic regulation from a phylogenetic perspective does not focus on the obvious similarities with more ancient vertebrates. Rather, it focuses on the unique modifications that enabled mammals to optimize their survival. Consistent with this theme, PVT focuses on the evolved neural circuits that enabled mammals to down-regulate the sympathetic activation that could support mobilization to fight or flee, to reduce psychological and physical distance with conspecifics, and to functionally co-regulate physiological and behavioral state. The theory focuses on the transition from reptiles to mammals and emphasizes the neural adaptations that enable cues of safety to down-regulate states of defense. Within PVT the evolutionary trend has led to a conceptualization of an emergent and uniquely mammalian social engagement system in which a modified branch of the vagus is integral. Neuroanatomically, this system is dependent on a brainstem area known as the ventral vagal complex. This area not only regulates the mammalian ventral cardioinhibitory vagal pathway, but also regulates the special visceral efferent pathways controlling the striated muscles of the face and head. This does not preclude other structures being involved in mammalian social engagement behaviors or homologous structures in other vertebrates who do not share our phylogenetic history being involved in social engagement behaviors.

The relationship between mothers and their nursing offspring illustrates the social engagement system in action. To survive, mammalian offspring must initially nurse as the primary mode of ingesting food. To nurse, the infant must suck, a process dependent on a brainstem circuit involving the ventral vagal complex. Survival is dependent on the infant's nervous system efficiently and effectively coordinating suck-swallow-breathe-vocalize behaviors with vagal regulation of the heart through the ventral vagal pathways originating in the nucleus ambiguus. Through maturation and socialization, this ingestive circuit provides the structural neural platform for sociality and co-regulation as major mediators to optimize homeostatic function leading to health, growth, and restoration (see Porges & Furman, 2011). For mammals there is a dependency between reactions to contextual cues and the function of this circuit. Cues of threat may disrupt function, while cues of safety may enhance function. The sensory branches of the facial and trigeminal nerves provide major input into the ventral vagal complex. Functionally, changes in the state of this circuit through the process of dissolution will either disinhibit phylogenetically older autonomic circuits to support defense (e.g., predator, disease, physical injury, etc.) or inform all aspects of the autonomic nervous system, including the enteric system (e.g., Kolacz & Porges, 2018; Kolacz et al., 2019), to optimize homeostatic function.

Mammals uniquely have detached middle ear bones, which distinguish mammals from reptiles in the fossil record. Detached middle ear bones expand the frequency band that mammals can hear and provide safe frequency bands on which they can socially communicate that will not be detected by reptiles.

Middle ear bones are small bones that separate from the jawbone during gestational development and form an ossicle chain that connects the eardrum to the inner ear. Small muscles regulated by branches of the trigeminal and facial nerves regulate the transfer function of the middle ear and determine the frequencies of sounds transduced through middle ear structures by controlling the stiffness of the ossicle chain. When the chain is stiff, the eardrum is tighter and low-frequency sounds are attenuated; when the muscles relax, lower frequency sounds pass into the inner ear. In all mammalian species, based on the physics of their middle ear structures, there is a frequency band of perceptual advantage that is expressed when the middle ear muscles contract (see Kolacz et al., 2018). It is within this frequency band that social communication occurs. The low frequencies that through evolution have been associated with predators are attenuated (Porges & Lewis, 2010).

Interestingly, the coordination of the contraction and relaxation of these small muscles is frequently co-regulated with autonomic state, and thus the muscles contract when there is strong ventral vagal tone to promote social communication and co-regulation. In contrast, when the autonomic nervous system shifts to a state of defense, the muscles relax to detect low-frequency predator sounds, which support defense strategies with auditory cues. The link between behavioral and autonomic state and listening is obvious in the study of language delays and auditory processing problems in children. Many children with problems in auditory processing also have behavioral-state regulation limitations. This neurophysiological link provides a portal to regulate autonomic state through acoustic stimulation, which is easily observable when a mother calms her infant using prosodic vocalization. Similarly, we can observe the potent calming influences when a pet is calmed by the voice of a human. In addition, clinicians frequently report that survivors of trauma experience an auditory hypersensitivity to background sounds and an auditory hyposensitivity to human voices.

Through the evolution of vertebrates there are strong trends in the structures involved in regulating autonomic function. These trends may be summarized as moving from chemical to neural and then evolving greater specificity, efficiency, and speed through feedback circuits involving myelinated pathways. Evolution is a process of modification in which existing structures and circuits are modified to serve adaptive functions. In mammals, three primary autonomic states with specific neural circuits are observable and emerge at different times within the evolutionary history of vertebrates. In PVT terms, the newest is labeled the **ventral vagal complex**, the oldest is the **dorsal vagal complex**, and in between a spinal **sympathetic nervous system** evolved. Thus, evolution informs us of the sequence through which three circuits regulate autonomic function.

DISSOLUTION EXPLAINS RESPONSES TO THREAT, CHRONIC STRESS, AND ILLNESS

PVT, following the work of John Hughlings Jackson (1884), assumes a phylogenetic hierarchy in which the newer circuits inhibit the older. Thus, when the ventral vagus and the social engagement system are dampened or go offline, the autonomic nervous systems move into a sympathetic state that supports mobilization. If this functional shift in state does not lead to a positive survival outcome, the autonomic nervous system may abruptly shut down via the dorsal vagal circuit. Jackson described this process of sequentially disinhibiting older structures as "dissolution" or evolution in reverse. Jackson used dissolution to explain the consequence of brain damage and disease, while PVT applies the principle of dissolution to adaptive autonomic reactions to cues of threat, which optimistically are reversible by cues of safety.

Convergent parallels with the phylogenetic evidence come from anatomical studies investigating human embryological origins and development of the autonomic nervous system through anatomical research via human autopsy studies (see Wozćiak & O'Rahilly, 1981). The autopsy studies provided an opportunity to link maturational landmarks from anatomical studies with research monitoring fetal and preterm heart rate patterns. The neuroanatomical literature documents a maturational trend of myelination of the ventral vagus during the last trimester, with notable changes occurring after 30 weeks gestational age (see Porges & Furman, 2011). In our research we have been able to infer the maturation of the ventral vagal circuit by monitoring respiratory sinus arrhythmia in high-risk preterm newborns (Doussard-Roosevelt et al., 1997; Porges, 1992; Porges et al., 2019; Portales et al., 1997).

In full-term newborns it is possible to observe a predictable dissolution sequence during challenging deliveries. This sequence is initiated by a withdrawal of ventral vagal tone (i.e., depressed respiratory sinus arrhythmia) leading to tachycardia and finally to potentially lethal bradycardia (see Reed, Ohel, et al., 1999). The literature supporting this maturational trend is summarized in Porges and Furman (2011). This literature documents that high-risk preterm newborns enter the postpartum world unprepared to cope with environmental challenges. By entering the world with an immature ventral vagal circuit, the neural circuits regulating the high-risk newborn are prone to recruit the threat reactions of the functionally available sympathetic nervous system that would produce the metabolically costly tachycardia (i.e., increases in heart rate) or the dorsal vagal circuit that would produce a potentially lethal bradycardia (i.e., rapid and massive decreases in heart rate). Both reactions disrupt homeostatic function and compromise the preterm neonate's viability.

The survival challenges of the high-risk preterm infant provide a real-life example validating several features of PVT. First, we observe the hierarchical organization of the mammalian autonomic nervous system in the support of basic homeostatic processes that lead to optimized health, growth, and restoration. Juxtaposed to the traditional paired-antagonism model of the autonomic nervous system that would focus on a hypothetical autonomic balance, we are informed that homeostasis requires the ventral vagus to functionally calm the autonomic nervous system to enable metabolic resources to be diverted from defense and directed toward health, growth, and restoration. Second, under challenge we observe the process of dissolution. Third, we observe the development and coordination of the social engagement system as the preterm develops the capacity to coordinate suck-swallow-breathe, which is followed by directed vocalizations and facial expressivity leading to sending cues of calmness and distress. These examples provide an understanding that stress or threat reactions may be operationally defined as the shifting of neural regulation of the autonomic nervous system (i.e., withdrawal of ventral vagal tone) into a state that does not support homeostatic processes.

Metaphorically, the high-risk preterm neonate comes into the world with an autonomic nervous system that is more reptilian than mammalian. During the last trimester, the ventral vagus develops. Preterm neonates are frequently born prior to the development of a functional ventral vagus (see Porges, 1992; Porges et al., 2019). Without a functioning ventral vagus, the preterm neonate is predisposed to react with a reptilian defensive response via the dorsal vagal pathway to the stressors and challenges of birth. When recruited for defense, the dorsal vagal system may produce bradycardia and apnea. For reptiles, who are not as oxygen needy as mammals, this reaction supports survival by minimizing detection by predators by appearing not to be living. However, for the oxygen-needy mammals this response pattern is potentially lethal.

A preterm infant's depressed social engagement system will have a negative impact on caregivers, who are anticipating reciprocal cues of social connection via facial expressivity and prosodic vocalizations. The result may be a parent who feels they love their child, but their child does not love them. Similar disconnects have been felt, if not voiced, by parents who have children with dampened social engagement systems, such as children on the spectrum of autism. In addition, children of depressed parents may interpret their parents' dampened emotionality as reflecting lack of interest or lack of love.

POLYVAGAL THEORY: A TESTABLE
SOLUTION OF THE VAGAL PARADOX

PVT emerged from my research studying heart rate patterns in human fetuses and newborns. In obstetrics and neonatology, the massive slowing of heart rate known as bradycardia is a clinical index of risk and assumed to be mediated by the vagus. During bradycardia, heart rate is so slow that it no longer provides sufficient oxygenated blood to the brain. This type of vagal influence on the fetal and neonatal heart could potentially be lethal. However, with the same clinical populations, a different index of vagal function was assumed to be a measure of resilience (Porges, 1992). This measure was the respiratory oscillation in beat-to-beat heart rate variability (i.e., respiratory sinus arrhythmia), which was the focus of my research for several decades. Animal research demonstrated that both signals could be disrupted by severing the vagal pathways to the heart or via pharmacological blockade (i.e., atropine), interfering with the inhibitory action of the vagus on the sinoatrial node (for review, see Porges, 1995). These observations posed a paradox. How could cardiac vagal tone be both a positive indicator of health when monitored with heart rate variability and a negative indicator of health when it manifests as bradycardia?

The resolution to the paradox came from understanding how the neural regulation of the autonomic nervous system changed during evolution and that the sequence of these phylogenetic shifts in global autonomic regulation was mirrored in prenatal development. The study of comparative neuroanatomy identified a structural change in vagal regulation occurring during the transition from primitive extinct reptiles to mammals. During this transition, mammals evolved a functional diaphragm (also observed in some reptiles) and a second cardioinhibitory vagal motor pathway that originated in the ventral vagal nucleus (i.e., nucleus ambiguus). This vagal pathway provides the primary cardioinhibitory influences on the heart. The circuit originating in the ventral vagal complex selectively services organs above the diaphragm (e.g., heart, bronchi) and interacts with the regulation of the striated muscles of the face and head via special visceral efferent pathways. This uniquely mammalian ventral vagal pathway is myelinated and conveys a respiratory rhythm to the heart's pacemaker, resulting in a rhythmic oscillation in heart rate at the frequency of spontaneous breathing known as **respiratory sinus arrhythmia**.

PVT uses evolution to highlight neuroanatomical and functional changes in how the brainstem regulates physiological state in mammals. These changes resulted in two vagal pathways operating in a hierarchal manner, with one pathway being protective and supporting homeostasis, while the other evolutionarily older pathway supports homeostasis only when the more evolutionarily modern vagus is functional (Kolacz & Porges, 2018). Other than this coordinating role, this more modern vagal pathway has other attributes that functionally constrain, inhibit, and dampen other components of the autonomic nervous system that can be recruited in defense—the sympathetic nervous system that supports fight-or-flight behaviors and the older vagal circuit that triggers immobilization, behavioral shutdown, diarrhea, and potentially lethal bradycardia. Thus, when the newer circuit is withdrawn (i.e., dissolution) there is a shift in physiological state (i.e., loss of ventral vagal tone) with major survival-related consequences as the neural regulation of the autonomic nervous system shifts to defensive strategies from coordinating other attributes of the autonomic nervous system that optimize health, growth, restoration, and social behavior.

PVT extracts from contemporary neuroanatomy, neurophysiology, and evolutionary biology two basic uncontroversial conclusions: (1) mammals have two vagal pathways (i.e., supradiaphragmatic, subdiaphragmatic) and (2) evolution and development provide insight into the changes in brainstem structures that enable mammals to be physiologically calm and socially interact. Functionally, mammals have neural attributes that act efficiently via rapidly responding cardioinhibitory fibers (e.g., ventral vagal pathways), capable of calming to promote social communication. The ventral vagal pathways also coordinate and repurpose circuits that evolved to support defense in socially relevant processes, such as play (i.e., ventral vagal influences constrain sympathetic reactivity) and intimacy (i.e., ventral vagal influences constrain dorsal vagal reactivity).

POLYVAGAL THEORY LINKS THE MAMMALIAN AUTONOMIC NERVOUS SYSTEM TO SOCIALITY

The polyvagal model emphasizes the evolutionary transition from the extinct reptiles to primitive mammals to modern mammals and humans. This transition resulted in the capacity to functionally retune the autonomic nervous system, thus fostering social engagement behaviors and permitting physiological state co-regulation through social interactions. The theory also provides an understanding of increased metabolic demands of mammals as compared to reptiles. The theory emphasizes the need for social interactions in regulating the human autonomic nervous system and in fostering homeostatic functions. The theory further emphasizes that there are unique attributes of the mammalian autonomic nervous system that differ from reptiles and other earlier vertebrates. Focal to PVT is the integration of brainstem structures (i.e., ventral vagal complex) to coordinate the regulation of the ventral vagal nucleus (i.e., nucleus ambiguus) with special visceral efferent pathways emerging from cranial nerves V, VII, IX, X, and XI. This integration forms the neural circuit that fosters survival by enabling the coordination of suck-swallow-breathe-vocalize processes. As proposed by PVT, as these pathways mature they form a spontaneous social engagement system that supports homeostasis and co-regulation.

This link between vagal activity and social engagement behaviors potentially can be monitored through the output of ventral vagal pathways on the heart, providing a diagnostic and prognostic index of cardiac vagal tone (i.e., respiratory sinus arrhythmia). It is important to emphasize that respiratory sinus arrhythmia, by providing a quantifiable portal of the vagal contribution to the social engagement system, enables the structuring of testable hypotheses related to PVT. However, the theory is not dependent on the attributes or even the evolutionary history of respiratory sinus arrhythmia. The theory links mental and physical health and well-being through the co-regulation of autonomic state via social behavior. Since the model is based on a detailed literature review, the reader is encouraged to read the initial presentation of the theory (see Porges, 1995, and the subsequent updates: Porges, 1998, 2007, and Chapter 1).

AUTONOMIC STATE AS AN INTERVENING VARIABLE

Central to PVT is the role that the autonomic nervous system plays as an intervening variable influencing mammalian behavioral and physiological reactions to challenges both in the body (e.g., illness and distress) and in the environment (e.g., cues of threat and safety). The theory encourages us to think of autonomic state as a functional neural platform from which different adaptive behaviors and reactions may spontaneously emerge. The theory embraces a stimulus-organism-response (S-O-R), with autonomic state being a measurable intervening variable, rather than the deterministic S-R model that has been prevalent in both behaviorally oriented psychology and mechanistic models of physiology. The theory proposes that there are three global autonomic states that functioned, in general, as a hierarchy that is phylogenetically ordered. In this model, the evolutionarily newest vertebrate autonomic modification is a mammalian ventral vagal circuit with features that support the mammalian dependence on transporting oxygenated blood to the brain and visceral organs and the regulation of physiological state through sociality and ingestion.

POLYVAGAL THEORY LEADS TO TESTABLE HYPOTHESES AND POTENTIAL INTERVENTIONS

Once the conceptualization of the vagal brake was introduced within PVT (Porges, 1996), the commonly observed changes in global measures of heart rate variability and the more specific vagal component of respiratory sinus arrhythmia during psychological and physical challenges could be understood from a neurobiological perspective. This perspective has embraced technologies to quantify specific neural signals such as respiratory sinus arrhythmia as an accurate index of ventral vagal tone (Lewis et al., 2012). Similarly, once the integrated social engagement system (Porges, 1998) was introduced into the theory, then the cues of safety and trust that are features of social support could be mechanistically understood as supporting greater vagal regulation and healthful homeostatic functions.

We live in a culture that honors technologies as potential interventions to optimize mental and physical health. A proliferation of various noninvasive trigeminal and vagal nerve stimulators work through feedback mechanisms described in PVT. Consistent with polyvagal principles, these devices stimulate afferent pathways that go to the brainstem area that communicates with the ventral vagus to increase vagal outflow, resulting in calming and optimized homeostatic function. As we are informed by neuroanatomy and the phylogenetic development of an integrated social engagement system, we learn that listening is an alternative portal to regulate ventral vagal tone and the entire social engagement system.

Recently I developed an intervention called the Safe and Sound Protocol™ that uses computer-altered, modulated vocal music to amplify the prosodic cues of social communication (see Porges et al., 2013, 2014). These are similar to the acoustic cues that human and other mammalian nervous systems interpret as cues of safety and trust. For example, a mother's vocal cues have the capacity to signal safety and calm her child (e.g., infant-directed speech), and vocal cues by adults can calm their children and pets. These acoustic cues increase neural tone to middle ear muscles, which are regulated by brainstem structures (see Kolacz et al., 2018; Porges & Lewis, 2010) involved in responding to threat and safety similar to the vagal brake. Under threat, the middle ear muscles relax and the eardrums become sensitive to low-frequency sounds to detect movements that could be potentially dangerous. In this state, the ability to detect human speech may be compromised. When there are cues of safety, the body calms and the autonomic nervous system is in a state predominantly regulated by the ventral vagus. This ventral vagal state is also reflected in a more melodic or prosodic human voice via a noncardiac branch of the vagus, the recurrent laryngeal nerve. Thus, the auditory system is an important portal to our autonomic nervous system. Functionally, the intervention leverages an understanding of neuroception (see Chapter 1) and the cues that trigger a state of increased ventral vagal tone observed in behaviors of calmness, accessibility, and spontaneous social engagement. When the initial patent (Porges, 2018) was awarded for the technologies embedded in the Safe and Sound Protocol, the specific claim that acoustic stimulation functioned as an acoustic vagal nerve stimulator was accepted.

WHAT IS POLYVAGAL THEORY?

PVT focuses on differences rather than similarities between vertebrate species and especially the neuroanatomical and functional phylogenetic changes that we observed as a product of the transition from asocial reptiles to social mammals. For example, we see profound distinctions between the mammalian respiratory sinus arrhythmia and heart rate–respiratory interactions in other vertebrates. In mammals there is a well-defined common central respiratory oscillator that sends a respiratory rhythm from the brainstem to both the heart and the bronchi. This information flows through the vagal neurons originating in the nucleus ambiguus. In fact, the oscillator can be conceptualized as an emergent property of the interactions among structures regulated by the nucleus ambiguus including the larynx and pharynx (Richter & Spyer, 1990). This, of course, is not consistent with the features of a primitive nucleus ambiguus that might be seen in vertebrates that preceded mammals. The observation of a common central oscillator is functionally unique to mammals and is the neurophysiological foundation enabling the quantification of respiratory sinus arrhythmia to act as a portal to measure ventral vagal tone.

As a theory, PVT has two components: (1) a descriptive model and (2) a series of hypotheses related to explanations and applications. The first component is a model of the mammalian autonomic nervous system. The second component is hypothesis driven and future oriented, which could potentially lead to enhancements of mental and physical health. This chapter was written to help researchers distinguish between the interdisciplinary literature that supports the principles of the theory and the testing of hypotheses derived from the theory. The interdisciplinary literature supports a convergence among sources of evidence including the literatures describing: (1) the development of the neural structures regulating the autonomic nervous system, (2) the insights derived from studying the phylogeny of the autonomic nervous system, (3) research evaluating autonomic reactions to chronic stress and threat, and (4) clinical observations illustrating the principle of dissolution in physical and mental illness especially in studying both high-risk preterm infants and the personal histories of individuals who have survived trauma.

As our science evolves, we hope new technologies will be developed to measure the dynamic regulation of the dorsal vagus. When this is accomplished, then a polyvagal-informed autonomic mapping of an individual could potentially evaluate the function of each pathway. Currently, although dependent on an accurate metric of the ventral vagal tone, we have discovered a new dimension of this system that reflects **vagal efficiency**. Vagal efficiency is a metric that evaluates the effectiveness of dynamic change in the vagal brake (i.e., changes in the amplitude of respiratory sinus arrhythmia) on dynamic heart rate. Over time, we identified sleep-state differences in vagal efficiency in newborns (Porges et al., 1999), a maturational influence on vagal efficiency in high-risk preterm infants (Porges et al., 2019), a sensitivity to alcohol (Reed, Porges, et al., 1999), and the utility of vagal efficiency in predicting pain reduction during noninvasive vagal stimulation in adolescents with functional abdominal pain disorders (Kovacic et al., 2020). In our ongoing research, we are observing that individuals with features of dysautonomia had noticeable low vagal efficiency when compared to healthy controls (Kolacz et al., 2021). In addition, in another study we noted low vagal efficiency in survivors of trauma and maltreatment. Within the concept of dissolution, a reduction in vagal efficiency may reflect a dampening of feedback involved in regulating autonomic function that may precede end-organ dysfunction.

HOW WOULD RESEARCH TEST ATTRIBUTES
OF THE POLYVAGAL THEORY?

PVT emphasizes the role of autonomic state as an intervening variable in how we respond to internal and external cues. The theory changes the personal narrative from a documentary of events to a personalized narrative of feelings (i.e., autonomic state). Applications of PVT in the clinical world focus on autonomic state as a mediator of mental and physical health problems. For example, trauma retunes the autonomic nervous system from calmness and spontaneous social engagement to defense, thus interfering with the ability to socially engage, communicate, and connect. By placing autonomic state in the model as an intervening variable, neural regulation of the autonomic nervous system becomes both an assessment of neural state that would promote safety or defense and a portal for intervention. Functionally, **calm physiological states become more common and aberrant behaviors become less prevalent.**

My personal goal in proposing the theory was not for the theory to be either proven or disproven, but rather for the theory to be informed by research and modified. Arguing that the scientific foundations for the theory were false is a precarious strategy for a critic, since the foundational principles of theory such as evolution, phylogeny of the autonomic nervous system, and dissolution are well established. If we speculate on the consequence of these foundational principles being false, then the evolved changes in the autonomic nervous system would not support a social engagement system and the socially delivered cues of safety would not calm the autonomic nervous system and consequentially social behavior and trusted relationships would not spontaneously emerge. The theory is dependent on evolution and development to structure a hierarchical model of autonomic function inclusive of the Jacksonian principle of dissolution. This model could explain how co-regulatory social interactions are not merely social behaviors but neuromodulators of autonomic state via an integrated social engagement system that is capable of either supporting or disrupting homeostatic functions. Thus, aspects of social behavior can functionally support or disrupt health.

The theory uses evolution to extract a phylogenetic sequence of autonomic regulation. This sequence identifies stages during vertebrate evolution when a spinal sympathetic nervous system and the two vagal pathways emerge and become functional via maturation in mammals. It would be difficult to argue that the sequence does not occur, although it would be possible to identify antecedent similarities in most vertebrates regardless of class or group. **The question is not whether there are similarities in ancestral vertebrates, but rather how these circuits have been adapted to provide a unique mammalian autonomic nervous system that is intimately intertwined with co-regulatory social behavior.**

There are many examples of the unique type of sociality expressed in mammals that differentiates mammals from their reptilian ancestors. Since PVT is focused on the phylogenetic transition from reptiles to mammals, it does not focus on the sociality of other vertebrate species that evolved from reptiles (e.g., birds) following the divergence of mammals. PVT is dependent on the processes that evolutionary theorists describe as ex-adaptation and co-opting. These processes involve modifications that shift in the function of a structure during evolution. For example, a structure can evolve because it served one particular function, but subsequently it may come to serve another. Ex-adaptation and co-opting are common strategies of repurposing vestigial structures in both anatomy and behavior. PVT is agnostic about the evolutionary pressures that result in the selection of specific changes. In contrast, the theory is phylogenetically descriptive and focused on the functional outcome of repurposing. More specifically, the theory explains how the structures regulated by the ventral vagal complex were repurposed to provide the regulation of an integrated social engagement system that provides the primary portal to socially engage and communicate, ingest, and calm. Current neuroanatomical knowledge documents the refinement of the ventral vagal complex in mammals. Thus, although the ventral vagus (i.e., originating in the nucleus ambiguus) may have an origin in reptiles (Taylor et al., 2014), it appears that it is only in mammals that this pathway has been repurposed to convey and respond to social cues, via neuroception, as a potent mediator of autonomic state.

CONCLUSION

Evolution transformed attributes of the autonomic nervous system into an integrated social engagement system that incorporated a brainstem communication area (i.e., the ventral vagal complex) that regulated, via special visceral efferent pathways, the striated muscles of the face and head and coordinated these processes with the vagal regulation of the heart and the bronchi. In mammals the ventral vagal complex enables the coordination of a suck-swallow-breathe-vocalize system with the vagal regulation of the heart. As the neuroanatomy of this ingestive circuit matures, the circuit becomes a functional social engagement system that enables physiological state to be communicated to conspecifics via facial expression and vocalizations. This does not preclude the validity of observations that document in earlier vertebrates links between the brainstem regulation of the special visceral efferent and the source nuclei of the vagus. For example, in more primitive vertebrates the special visceral efferent pathways regulate structures that evolved from ancient gill arches. Thus, in fish there is often a synchrony between gill movements and heart rate, although the regulation of heart rate is mediated through the dorsal vagal nucleus. However, in mammals these structures and their neural regulation have been modified via evolution to support functions unique to the survival of mammals such as nursing and social communication via an integrated social engagement system dependent on the ventral vagal complex. This transition in neuroanatomy and function provides the basis to understand that for humans, similar to other mammals, connectedness and trusting relationships are direct expressions of our biological imperative and are integrated into our biology.

3

Polyvagal Theory:
A Science of Safety

Stephen W. Porges

INTRODUCTION

Contemporary strategies for health and well-being fail our biological needs by not acknowledging that feelings of safety emerge from inside the body. This chapter focuses on feelings of safety, an elusive construct that has historically been dependent upon subjectivity. It is proposed that feelings of safety have a measurable underlying neurophysiological substrate. Acknowledging that feelings of safety are an emergent property of autonomic state would shift investigations of feelings of safety from a subjective to an objective science.

In writing this, I have considered several personal questions: What principle can be extracted from conducting empirical research for more than 5 decades? What principle has captivated my passion and intellectual curiosity? What theme would I use to organize the information from my papers, books, and talks? Or, simply phrased, what have I learned?

After reflecting on these questions, I arrived at a concise and intuitive principle that humans, as social mammals, are on an enduring lifelong quest to feel safe. This quest appears to be embedded in our DNA and serves as a profound motivator throughout our life. The need to feel safe is functionally our body speaking through our autonomic nervous system—influencing our mental and physical health, social relationships, cognitive processes, and behavioral repertoire and serving as a neurophysiological substrate upon which societal institutions dependent on cooperation and trust function are based.

Feeling safe functions as a subjective index of a neural platform that supports both sociality and the homeostatic processes optimizing health, growth, and restoration. Operationally, feeling safe is our subjective interpretation of internal bodily feelings that are being conveyed via bidirectional neural pathways between our bodily organs and our brain. Feelings of safety are not equivalent to an objective measurement of safety, which may pragmatically be defined as the removal of threat. Feeling safe is more akin to a felt sense as described by Eugene Gendlin (2017). Although Gendlin, as a philosopher and psychologist, was not physiologically oriented, he described a "felt sense" not as a mental experience but as a physical one.

In understanding the motivation to feel safe, feelings of safety may be conceptualized from the Polyvagal Theory (PVT). PVT provides an innovative scientific perspective that incorporates an understanding of phylogenetic shifts in vertebrate neuroanatomy and neurophysiology; this perspective identifies neural circuits that down-regulate neural regulation of threat reactions and functionally neutralize defensive strategies via neural circuits communicating cues of safety. Feelings of safety are operationally the product of cues of safety, via neuroception (see Chapter 1), down-regulating autonomic states that support threat reactions and up-regulating autonomic states that support interpersonal accessibility and homeostatic functions. Basically, when humans feel safe, their nervous systems support the homeostatic functions of health, growth, and restoration, while they simultaneously become accessible to others without feeling or expressing threat and vulnerability.

In explaining the profound importance of feeling safe, we are immersed in the ambiguity of our language when it comes to describing feelings and linking feelings to underlying neurophysiological states. This problem dates to the earliest psychologists such as Wilhelm Wundt (1896/1902), who adopted and standardized introspection techniques to explore sensations that were essentially limited to external stimuli. PVT leads toward a hierarchical conceptualization of feelings as higher brain interpretations of the neural signals conveying information regarding visceral organs (e.g., heart, gut, etc.) to the brainstem. This psychophysiological perspective emphasizes the foundational function of autonomic state in the subjective experiences of global feelings and specific emotions. Within this hierarchical conceptualization, feelings of safety are preeminent and form the core of an enduring motivational system that shifts autonomic state, which in turn drives behaviors, emotions, and thoughts. The resulting model suggests that feelings of safety reflect the foundational autonomic state supporting maturation, health, and sociality.

In an earlier paper (Porges, 1996), a hierarchical model of self-regulation was proposed to provide insights into optimizing intervention strategies for high-risk infants. The model reflects maturational competencies in neural regulation that provide a substrate for the more complex co-regulatory social behaviors. The main point of the model is that higher behavioral functions, which are frequently intentional, are dependent on the functioning of the more survival-focused foundational systems embedded in the brainstem. The levels are described in Table 3.1. Level I is focused on the function of brainstem structures in optimizing physiological homeostasis through neural and neurochemical bidirectional communication between visceral organs and brainstem structures, which regulate the autonomic nervous system. The neural pathways involved in Level I are functional at birth in healthy full-term infants. An index of Level I can be derived from quantifying respiratory sinus arrhythmia, a periodic component of beat-to-beat heart rate variability that is synchronous with spontaneous breathing and a valid index of cardiac vagal tone via ventral vagal pathways (Lewis et al., 2012). However, in the preterm infant the system is not sufficiently mature, and the amplitude of respiratory sinus arrhythmia is notably low (Porges, 1992). Porges and Furman (2011) provide a more detailed description of the maturational changes in the neural regulation of the autonomic nervous system as a "neural platform" for social behavior.

Level II emphasizes connections between higher brain structures and the brainstem in regulating autonomic state. Success in Level II is achieved when the suck-breathe-vocalize circuit is integrated with the ventral vagal pathway (Porges & Lipsitt, 1993). This circuit enables nursing and soothing to occur and is dependent on the neural pathways that define the ventral vagal complex (Porges, 1998). Higher brain structures regulate the brainstem nuclei of the ventral vagal complex via corticobulbar pathways; the pathways are subsequently repurposed as an integrated social engagement system, which fosters social communication and co-regulation. It is through these connections that safety cues can recruit metabolically efficient states of calmness (e.g., slow heart rate) to optimize health, growth, and restoration. Or alternatively, threat cues can down-regulate the social engagement system to optimize metabolically costly defensive strategies.

The metabolic requirements for fight-or-flight behaviors require resources to be diverted from homeostatic functions. Autonomically this is observed through the disengagement of the vagal brake (Porges et al., 1996). In safe social settings the vagal brake is dynamically adjusting heart rate to match the metabolic needs of the behavior. The ability to disengage the vagal brake is related to competencies in social behavior, since physical movement is frequently a component of social interactions. Recently, a new metric, vagal efficiency, was introduced to describe the dynamic efficiency of the vagal brake (i.e., cardio-inhibitory pathways to the heart monitored by quantifying the amplitude of respiratory sinus arrhythmia) in regulating heart rate. This metric evaluates the slope of the regression line between short time periods (e.g., 15 seconds) of synchronous measures of heart rate and respiratory sinus arrhythmia. Functionally, the slope is providing an estimate of how much heart rate would change with a standardized unit change in the amplitude of respiratory sinus arrhythmia. This metric has been useful in evaluating sleep state in full-term newborns (Porges et al., 1999) and the maturational trajectory in preterm infants (Porges et al., 2019). It is also sensitive to alcohol (Reed, Porges, et al., 1999) and may serve as a potential indicator of dysautonomia, since it is greatly depressed in individuals with an adversity history (Dale, Kolacz, et al., 2022) and in those diagnosed with the hypermotility subtype of Ehlers-Danlos syndrome (Kolacz et al., 2021). In the context of this chapter, Level II provides the foundational neural platform for feelings of safety and access to the circuits that would enable a neuroception of safety.

Table 3.1 emphasizes the hierarchical nature of specific autonomic states and accessibility of behaviors that we cluster as self-regulation skills. The optimal function of each level is contingent on each of the preceding levels adequately functioning. Observers of developing children are aware of the strong maturational influence that pushes the child through the sequence. However, few are aware of the parallels between development and evolution and how this information informs us regarding the adaptive functions of specific autonomic states. It is not that a specific autonomic state is good or bad, but rather what adaptive functions ancestral vertebrates accessed while being in a specific autonomic state.

DISSOLUTION

Consistent with PVT (Porges, 2021a, 2021b), the sequencing of the hierarchy of neural maturation mirrors features of vertebrate evolution. The theory emphasizes the modifications in the neural regulation of the autonomic nervous system that is highlighted through phylogenetic transitions, especially the transition from asocial reptiles to the sociality and co-regulation features of social mammals. Operationally defining feelings of safety as dependent on an autonomic state provides an opportunity to study the potential emergent properties that are dependent on access to this state. Thus, it is proposed that the consequence of feeling safe provides the neural platform for cooperative behaviors, both supporting physiological systems and enabling accessibility to higher brain structures for learning, creativity, appreciation of aesthetics, and even spirituality.

An acknowledgment of this hierarchy results in questions about the sequential unfolding of responses to challenges orienting within the body (e.g., fever and illness) and outside the body (e.g., threat). Disease and injury to the brain have been observed to disinhibit phylogenetically ancient evolutionary structures that in the healthy individual are regulated (e.g., inhibited) by newer brain structures. This was described by John Hughlings Jackson (1884), who stated that "the higher nervous arrangements inhibit (or control) the lower, and thus, when the higher are suddenly rendered functionless, the lower rise in activity." Jackson labeled this process dissolution to emphasize that it is evolution in reverse.

While Jackson emphasized a dissolution process that mirrors the reverse of evolution in brain structures (i.e., moving from neocortex to lower brain structures), PVT emphasizes the reverse of evolution in the neural structures and pathways that regulate the mammalian autonomic nervous system. In this hierarchy of adaptive responses, the newest social engagement circuit is used first; if that circuit fails to provide safety, the older circuits are recruited sequentially. The elements of the social engagement system are functional at birth in the full-term infant (see Porges & Furman, 2011) and serve to enable infant and mother to co-regulate autonomic states via reciprocal cues of safety. The product of this co-regulation is the optimization of homeostatic functions enabling the infant to mature and the mother to recover from the metabolically demanding delivery process. Early in life this co-regulation provides the neurophysiological platform for mother–infant interactions and attachment (Bowlby, 1988) and the establishment of social bonds, which can be conceptualized as being dependent on associations with feelings of safety.

TABLE 3.1: Hierarchical Model of Self-Regulation   (Porges, 1996)

Level I	Neurophysiological processes characterized by bidirectional communication between the brainstem and peripheral organs to maintain physiological homeostasis.
Level II	Physiological processes reflecting the input of higher nervous system influences on the brainstem regulation of homeostasis. These processes are associated with modulating metabolic output and energy resources to support adaptive responses to environmental demands.
Level III	Measurable and often observable motor processes including body movements and facial expressions. These processes can be evaluated in terms of quantity, quality, and appropriateness.
Level IV	Processes that reflect the coordination of motor behavior, emotional tone, and bodily state to successfully negotiate social interactions. Unlike those of Level III, these processes are contingent with prioritized cues and feedback from the external environment.

Focusing on Levels I and II we see that optimal behavior is dependent the neural regulation of the autonomic nervous system and the connectivity between cortical areas, allowing the accurate interpretation of cues of safety and threat, and the brainstem areas regulating the autonomic nervous system. The quantification of respiratory sinus arrhythmia provides a quantitative portal into Level I, while the vagal efficiency metric would reflect Level II competency.

AUTONOMIC STATE AS AN INTERVENING VARIABLE

By placing autonomic state at the core of feelings of safety or threat, the pragmatic survival behaviors of fight-or-flight, as well as complex problem-solving strategies that would lead to escape, are consequential and dependent on the facilitatory function of the autonomic nervous system in optimizing these strategies. Similarly, turning off threat reactions and calming autonomic state via the ventral cardioinhibitory vagal pathway will promote interpersonal accessibility, while simultaneously supporting the co-regulation of autonomic state. This model positions autonomic state as an intervening variable mediating the interpretation of contextual cues and shaping our reactions. Within this conceptualization, depending on the individual's autonomic state, the same contextual cues and challenges may result in different behavioral, cognitive, and physiological reactions. For example, recent research documents that indices of autonomic state influenced the impact of the COVID-19 pandemic on mental health (see Kolacz, Dale, et al., 2020), perceived stress in college students (Fanning et al., 2020), effectiveness of neurostimulation on abdominal pain (Kovacic, Kolacz, et al., 2020), calming behavior in infants following the still-face procedure (Kolacz et al., 2022), and protest behaviors in infants in day care settings (Ahrnet et al., 2021). This would be true both within and between individuals (see Porges et al., 2013). Thus, there may be a range of reactions among individuals who share the same environmental context, but who are in different autonomic states. In addition, the same individual may also have a range of reactions to repeated exposures to the same environmental context that would be mediated by variations in autonomic state. PTSD symptoms may be the product of a retuned autonomic nervous system following extreme and/or repeated exposures to threat. Research supports the conceptualization that the mental and physical health consequences of adversity are reflected in a retuned autonomic nervous system locked into states of defense that limit access to the calming pathways through the ventral vagus associated with sociality (Kolacz, Hu, et al., 2020; Williamson et al., 2013, 2015).

Acknowledging the important role of autonomic state as an intervening variable would have profound consequences on our understanding of behavior and the often faulty assumption that a behavior is always intentional and reliably regulated by rewards and punishments. The model proposes that our cognitive intent and our bodily state can promote competing behavioral outcomes. As an observer of both behavior and autonomic state, my bet is on the potency of autonomic state. This conclusion is supported by the link between autonomic state and feelings of threat and our embedded biobehavioral program to survive. Since these states of defense are regulated by primitive neural circuits, circuits that are shared with many ancient vertebrates, intentional self-regulation efforts originating in the cortex are frequently ineffective in down-regulating survival-driven reactions to threat, which are dependent on lower brain structures. The survival program is evolutionarily old, while the program that turns off threat reactions with cues of safety to promote calmness, sociality, and homeostatic functions is a mammalian innovation of a repurposed autonomic nervous system that may be influenced by higher brain structures. Although the calming system is effective in down-regulating threat reactions in response to mild threats, the calming system is difficult to access when the defensive systems are in a highly activated survival mode.

Functionally, we need to conceptualize the model as having both bottom-up and top-down pathways with the bottom-up pathways being a combination of being both reflexive and derivative of early evolutionary survival processes. The foundational survival circuits in the brainstem are functionally hardwired via neuroception. Thus, although cues of safety or threat will trigger top-down reflexive changes in autonomic state, the states become associated with thoughts and behaviors. This process is initiated through interoception and then bottom-up feelings of autonomic state are interpreted by higher brain structures, which in turn may initiate intentional behaviors. This linkage between feelings (i.e., autonomic state) and behaviors and thoughts forms the neurophysiological basis for aspects of associative learning.

The premise of many therapeutic strategies is to separate feelings from associative thoughts and behaviors. Strategies that are polyvagal informed focus on enabling the client to experience the feelings without linking the feelings to thoughts or behaviors (see Dana, 2018; Porges & Dana, 2018). Basically, the client learns that the feelings are not intentional or under voluntary control but are part of an adaptive reflexive system that is wired into our nervous system. Thus, although attributes of the sequence are initially reflexive, there are effective portals to modify the association. For example, acknowledging the hierarchy of organization of the autonomic nervous system would suggest that the introduction of cues of safety would be a functional antidote to threat reactions by reducing the associative links between feelings of threat and thoughts and actions. These speculations are consistent with dissolution (Jackson, 1884), a process in which the cortical influence on regulating (i.e., calming) autonomic state becomes less effective. Functionally, the repurposed neural system that emerged during the transition from ancient reptiles to early mammals allowed sociality to function as a neuromodulator, calming physiology and optimizing bodily functions. In addition to sociality, positive memories and visualizations associated with positive experiences enable humans to access positive feelings (i.e., autonomic state) to actively inhibit threat reactions.

Access to sociality as a neuromodulator is influenced by both autonomic state and the flexibility or resilience that an individual's autonomic state has in returning from a state of threat to a state that supports homeostasis. We also learn that this accessibility is in part dependent on a personal history during which autonomic state may have been retuned to optimize defense.

This is frequently observed in individuals with a severe adversity history, whose traumatic experiences have retuned the autonomic nervous system to be locked in states of defense. This is reported by foster parents of children who have been abused and for safety concerns have been removed from their biological parents.

CULTURAL AND PHILOSOPHICAL INFLUENCES DIVERT INTEREST IN FEELINGS OF SAFETY

Within our educational institutions we have been acculturalized to accept the dictum coined by philosopher Rene Descartes (1637/1986) "I think, therefore I am" (cogito, ergo sum). This view has led to a cultural expectation that the rational mind defines us and that feelings distort this expectation and need to be constrained.

PVT provides an alternative perspective to this historical proposition. First, the theory would lead to a perspective that rather than thinking defining our existence, feeling does. Specifically, a revised polyvagal-informed statement would suggest that I feel myself, therefore I am. I frequently use this example in my talks, although I use the French and not the Latin presentation of the dictum. Reflexive verbs are more commonly used in French than in English. Reflexive verbs are actions that the subject is performing upon itself. Thus, using the reflexive form of the verb to feel will unambiguously convey internal feelings and not the sensations of feeling (touching) an object. In English when we use the word feel, it is ambiguous and may reflect either situation. By using *je pense, donc je suis*, it is easily rephrased with the reflexive form of the verb to feel. The modified statement *je me sens, donc je suis* emphasizes that if I feel myself, I exist. This statement is consistent with the current interest in embodiment and reports from trauma survivors of being disembodied and experiencing a bodily numbness.

Descartes's philosophy led to a partitioning of human experience into separate domains dependent on mind (mental activities) and body (physical structure). Descartes states that mental states or processes cannot exist outside of the body and the body cannot think. The separation between mind and body, often labeled as Cartesian dualism, has been consistent with our contemporary cognitive-centric world view that is mirrored in a cortico-centric brain-body separation that dominates much of medical and mental health treatment models. This preeminence of brain over body is even embedded the brain focus of contemporary neuroscience. Descartes argued that rational decision making can only be developed when judgments are not based on passion (i.e., bodily feelings). This dualism is still prevalent in current medical practices, especially when illness cannot be linked to a specific organ dysfunction. When objective clinical assessments of bodily fluids and/or tissues do not provide a positive clinical indicator leading to an understood disorder, physicians often assume that the disorder is psychiatric or psychosomatic and the patient should get psychiatric consultation and care.

According to Damasio (2005), Descartes's perspective had a fatal error in not acknowledging the interaction of feelings (i.e., body) with the mental activities (i.e., brain). Consistent with the PVT, Damasio emphasizes that bodily feelings can have a powerful influence on mental processes. Thus, rational thought espoused by Descartes would be a special case of mental processing in which the autonomic nervous system is not disrupting cognitive function. Perhaps this special case is dependent on an autonomic state associated with feelings of safety.

Culturally, we have also been influenced by the concept of **survival of the fittest**. This concept was first introduced by Herbert Spencer (1851). Spencer proposed that individual self-preservation is the most important moral principle. The term was then used by Charles Darwin (1859) in *On the Origin of Species*. Darwin suggested that the organisms best adjusted to their environment were the most successful in surviving and reproducing. Over the decades, survival of the fittest has frequently been interpreted as the strongest and most aggressive, which would suggest that control of resources and access to mating partners could be an objective metric of fitness and eventually the product of natural selection.

In the mid-20th century, a more integrated model emerged that began to reconcile the findings of genetics and inheritance with Darwin's theory and its emphasis on natural selection. The resolution was called the evolutionary synthesis or modern synthesis, and one of its architects was Russian population geneticist Theodosius Dobzhansky. The key revelation was that mutation, by creating genetic diversity, supplied the raw material for natural selection to act on. Instead of mutation and natural selection being alternative explanations, they were joined in this new synthesis. This synthesis led to an alternative perspective of fitness. Dobzhansky's insights led to the following frequently quoted statement that "the fittest may also be the gentlest, because survival often requires mutual help and cooperation" (Dobzhansky, 1962). According to Dobzhansky, it is this capacity to cooperate that enabled the earliest mammalian species to survive in a hostile world dominated by physically larger and potentially aggressive reptiles.

Dobzhansky's insightful statement converges on the emphasis of PVT on the phylogenetic transitions in neuroanatomy and neurophysiology as social mammals evolved from asocial reptiles. Mutual help and cooperation are dependent on a nervous system that has the capacity to down-regulate threat reactions to allow the proximity necessary for cooperative behaviors and co-regulation. In mammals this is neuroanatomically and neurophysiologically observed in the repurposed neural circuits originating in brainstem areas that regulate the autonomic nervous system. The repurposed system enables feelings of safety to co-occur with sociality.

THE PHYLOGENETIC JOURNEY

Feelings of safety form the foundational neural platform for sociality. Through the lens of evolution, PVT focuses on how mammals adapted many of the phylogenetical ancestral structures that evolved to support survival in a hostile world. Note that the title of the initial publication presenting the theory (Porges, 1995) is a synopsis of the theory: *Orienting in a Defensive World: Mammalian Modifications of Our Evolutionary Heritage. A Polyvagal Theory.* The title summarizes a phylogenetic narrative in which the survival of mammals was dependent on their ability to down-regulate and modify the innate defensive systems that were inherited from their reptilian ancestors. These embedded vestigial circuits with their emergent adaptive strategies are embedded in genes of mammals. For mammals, whose survival is dependent on their sociality to cooperate, to connect, and to co-regulate (Dobzhansky, 1962), the ancient defense programs had to be harnessed and repurposed to enable the expression of several defining features including signals of safety and calmness in proximity to another trusted mammal.

PVT's investigation into mammalian autonomic regulation from a phylogenetic perspective does not focus on the obvious similarities with more ancient vertebrates. Rather, it focuses on the unique modifications that enabled mammals to optimize their survival. Consistent with this theme, PVT focuses on the evolved neural circuits that enabled mammals to down-regulate the sympathetic activation that could support mobilization to fight or flee, to reduce psychological and physical distance with conspecifics, and to functionally co-regulate physiological and behavioral state.

The theory focuses on the transition from reptiles to mammals and emphasizes the neural adaptations that enable cues of safety to down-regulate states of defense. Within PVT the evolutionary trend has led to a conceptualization of an emergent and uniquely mammalian social engagement system in which a modified branch of the vagus is integral. Neuroanatomically, this system is dependent on a brainstem area known as the ventral vagal complex. This area not only regulates the mammalian ventral cardioinhibitory vagal pathway, but also regulates the special visceral efferent pathways controlling the striated muscles of the face and head. This does not preclude other structures being involved in mammalian social engagement behaviors or homologous structures in other vertebrates who do not share our phylogenetic history being involved in social engagement behaviors.

The relationship between mothers and their nursing offspring illustrates the social engagement system in action. To survive, mammalian offspring must initially nurse as the primary mode of ingesting food. To nurse, the infant must suck, a process dependent on a brainstem circuit involving the ventral vagal complex. Survival is dependent on the infant's nervous system efficiently and effectively coordinating suck-swallow-breathe-vocalize behaviors with vagal regulation of the heart through the ventral vagal pathways originating in the nucleus ambiguus. Through maturation and socialization, this ingestive circuit provides the structural neural platform for sociality and co-regulation, as major mediators, to optimize homeostatic function leading to health, growth, and restoration (see Porges & Furman, 2011). For mammals there is a dependency between reactions to contextual cues and the function of this circuit. Cues of threat may disrupt, while cues of safety may support or enhance function. The sensory branches of the facial and trigeminal nerves provide major input into the ventral vagal complex. Functionally, changes in the state of this circuit through the process of dissolution will either disinhibit phylogenetically older autonomic circuits to support defense (e.g., predator, disease, physical injury, etc.) or inform all aspects of the autonomic nervous system, including the enteric system to optimize homeostatic function (Kolacz & Porges, 2018; Kolacz, Kovacic, et al., 2019).

Mammals uniquely have detached middle ear bones, which distinguish mammals from reptiles in the fossil record. Detached middle ear bones delineate the frequency band that mammals can hear, which allows species-specific vocalizations associated with social communication and provides a safe frequency band on which they can socially communicate without detection by reptiles. Middle ear bones are small bones that separate from the jawbone during gestational development and form an ossicle chain that connects the eardrum to the inner ear. Small muscles regulated by branches of the trigeminal and facial nerves regulate the transfer function of the middle ear and determine the acoustic properties of the sounds transduced through middle ear structures by controlling the stiffness of the ossicle chain. When the chain is stiff, the eardrum is tighter and low-frequency sounds are attenuated; when the muscles relax, lower frequency sounds pass into the inner ear. In all mammalian species, based on the physics of their middle ear structures, there is a frequency band of perceptual advantage that is expressed when the middle ear muscles contract (see Kolacz, Lewis, et al., 2018). It is within this frequency band that social communication occurs, while the low frequencies that through evolution have been associated with predators are attenuated (see Porges & Lewis, 2010).

Interestingly, the coordination of the contraction and relaxation of these small muscles is frequently co-regulated with autonomic state and contract when there is strong ventral vagal tone to promote social communication and co-regulation. This coordination between listening to specific sounds and autonomic regulation provides the neurophysiological basis for sound to communicate cues of safety and trust. In contrast, when the autonomic nervous system shifts to a state of defense, the middle ear muscles relax to support defense strategies with auditory cues and allow detection of low-frequency predator sounds. In this state, the acoustic perception is biased toward detecting cues of threat.

The link between behavioral and autonomic state and listening is obvious in the study of language delays and auditory processing problems in children.

Many children with problems in auditory processing also have behavioral-state regulation limitations. This neurophysiological link provides a portal to regulate autonomic state through acoustic stimulation, which is easily observable when a mother calms her infant using prosodic vocalization. Similarly, we can observe the potent calming influences when a pet is calmed by the voice of a human. In addition, clinicians frequently report that survivors of trauma experience an auditory hypersensitivity to background sounds and an auditory hyposensitivity to human voices, which could be related to middle ear muscle tone (Borg & Counter, 1989). These points further support the frequently observed link between hypersensitivity and poor autonomic regulation reflected in hyperarousal.

In a recent study (Kolacz et al., 2022), our research group documented that the acoustic parameters of maternal vocalization had differential influences on calming their infants, following an experimental manipulation known as the "still face" procedure (Tronick et al., 1978). More prosodic maternal vocalizations were more effective in calming behavior and reducing heart rate following the social disruption of the still face procedure. Of course, parents and pet owners are familiar with the impact of their voices on calming their children and mammalian pets.

Based on this link between prosodic vocalizations and calming, a listening intervention known as the Safe and Sound Protocol™ (SSP) was developed to reduce auditory hypersensitivities, improve auditory processing, and calm the autonomic nervous system. The SSP functionally amplifies the embedded prosody in music by applying dynamic filters to prerecorded music. Preliminary publications document the effectiveness of this strategy (Porges et al., 2013; Porges et al., 2014). The technology embedded in the SSP has received three patents and is marketed by Unyte/Integrated Listening Systems (https://integratedlistening.com/porges/). One of the awarded claims on the patents is for the application of technology as an acoustic vagal nerve stimulator.

Through the evolution of vertebrates there were strong trends in the structures involved in regulating autonomic function. These trends may be summarized as moving from chemical to neural and then evolving greater specificity, efficiency, and speed through feedback circuits that relied on myelinated pathways. Evolution is a process of modification in which existing structures and circuits are modified to serve adaptive functions. In mammals, three primary autonomic states with specific neural circuits are observable and emerge at different times within the evolutionary history of vertebrates. In polyvagal terms, the newest is labeled the ventral vagal complex, the oldest is the dorsal vagal complex, and in between is the spinal sympathetic nervous system. Thus, evolution informs us of the sequence through which the three phylogenetic-dependent circuits regulate autonomic function in response to survival-driven threat reactions.

SOCIAL CONNECTEDNESS:
A BIOLOGICAL IMPERATIVE

A biological imperative identifies a need that must be fulfilled for a living organism to perpetuate existence and survival. PVT suggests that social connectedness is a core biological imperative for humans, since human survival is dependent on trusted others, is wired into our genetics, and is expressed throughout the life span starting from the moment of birth.

PVT proposes that social connectedness is tantamount to stating that our body feels safe in proximity with another. The theory elaborates that the neural structures involved in the social engagement system (Porges, 2009) orchestrate the autonomic states of the interacting dyad to both broadcast and receive cues of safety that down-regulate threat reactions of defense and promote accessibility and co-regulation.

To be socially connected via a functional social engagement system (Porges, 2009), common brainstem structures must appropriately coordinate the striated muscles of the face and head with the vagal regulation of the viscera originating in a brainstem region known as the nucleus ambiguus. Interestingly, neuroanatomically the special visceral efferent pathways regulating the striated muscles of the face and head originate and communicate with the brainstem area (i.e., ventral vagal complex) that regulates the ventral vagal cardioinhibitory pathway. The ventral vagal cardioinhibitory pathway provides the neural pathways that are expressed as the vagal brake and can be monitored by quantifying the amplitude of respiratory sinus arrhythmia.

An optimally resilient individual has opportunities to co-regulate physiological state with a safe and trusted other. Ideally, the other person projects positive cues regarding their autonomic state through prosodic voice, warm and welcoming facial expressions, and gestures of accessibility. From an evolutionary perspective the integration of the neural regulation of the viscera with the regulations of the striated muscles of the face and head enable the visceral state to be projected in vocalizations and facial expressions. Modulated by autonomic states, this also allows vocalizations and facial expressions to serve as cues of safety or threat to others. Together these pathways connect behavior to the nervous system and form the basis for social communication, cooperation, and connectedness. This system also produces, via a ventral vagal cardioinhibitory pathway, an autonomic state that produces feelings of safety and reflects an adaptive mastery of Level II processes (see Table 3.1).

PVT, by articulating an evolutionary hierarchy (i.e., based on Jacksonian dissolution; 1884) in the function of the autonomic nervous system to challenges, provides a guide to dynamically monitor adaptive autonomic responses. The autonomic state of an individual serves as a functional map of the foundation for emergent behavioral, emotional, and physiological reactivity that an individual may have in response to threat or alternatively to positive experiences. The state of the autonomic nervous system provides a neural platform for an expanded range of feelings from threat to safety that engenders a neurophysiological substrate for higher brain structures to elaborate these feelings. If the feelings are negative and dependent on autonomic states supporting defense, the feelings may evolve into diffuse states of anxiety or specific emotions such as fear or anger. Alternatively, if the feelings are positive and dependent on an autonomic state of calmness, thus enabling interpersonal accessibility and co-regulation, then these feelings may be associated with trust, love, and intimacy.

CLINICAL IMPLICATIONS

From a polyvagal perspective it may be helpful to investigate how challenges move us into physiological states of threat that would disrupt our connectedness and place our mental and physical health at risk. But, more relevant to both to clients and personal survival, therapists need to identify and emphasize the innate resources their clients have available to mitigate the potentially devasting reactions to threat that in turn can destabilize the autonomic nervous system, sometimes resulting in visceral organ dysfunction and compromised mental health.

Awareness of the neural systems underlying PVT informs both therapists and clients regarding the threats to survival that can shift autonomic state, moving it through sequential neural platforms or states that mimic evolution in reverse or dissolution (Jackson, 1884). Functionally, to inhibit the trajectory of dissolution to calm, we must first use the competence of our social engagement system (a uniquely mammalian myelinated ventral vagal pathway involving brainstem structures regulating vocal intonation and facial expressions) to connect with others and calm our physiology. Without these resources, we are vulnerable to move into adaptive defensive states.

Our defense repertoire is first expressed as chronic mobilization requiring activation of the sympathetic nervous system and then expressed as immobilization, which is controlled by an evolutionarily older unmyelinated vagal pathway. In the absence of an active social engagement system, the mobilized state provides an efficient neural platform for fight-or-flight behaviors. For many individuals this state will reflect chronic anxiety or irritability. When mobilization does not successfully move the individual into a safe context, there is the possibility that the nervous system will shift into an immobilized state. Immobilization with fear can be associated with features of death feigning, syncope, dissociation, withdrawal, loss of purpose, social isolation, despair, and depression.

Although both defensive strategies have adaptive values in protecting the individual, they are dependent on different neural pathways (i.e., sympathetic or dorsal vagal). Activation of these systems, independently or simultaneously, will interfere with interpersonal interactions, co-regulation, accessibility, trust, and feeling safe with another person. Thus, defensive states emerge from neural platforms that evolved to defend, while simultaneously compromising capacities to down-regulate our defenses through the co-regulation with a safe and trusted individual. Basically, the theory emphasizes that in the presence of cues of safety, which we associate with positive social interactions, the mammalian social engagement system can down-regulate our innate reactions to threat, whether the threat is tangible and observable or imagined and invisible.

STRESS AND THREAT HAVE A COMMON NEUROPHYSIOLOGICAL FOUNDATION

Years ago, I wrote a paper on stress and tried to unravel the ambiguity of the term, especially the circularity of using stress as both a stimulus and as a response. Now after almost 30 years seeing the world through a polyvagal perspective, as I write about safety and threat, I am reminded about my earlier approach to operationally define stress (Porges, 1985). It is easy to understand that the use of stress as a construct is ambiguous since stress has been operationalized to be a response as well as the contextual trigger producing the response. As this circularity is disentangled, note that the concept of threat has had a scientific history similar to stress in which removal of stress is conceptualized as optimal and removal of threat is assumed to produce feelings of safety. Both constructs focus on the negative attribution of potentially observable and quantifiable features influencing biobehavioral processes, while originating outside of the body. Moreover, neither construct elaborates on the mechanisms that would optimize function following the removal of stress or threat, while implicitly assuming that removal is sufficient.

A polyvagal perspective shifts the discussion from stress and threat to the nervous system's ability to support or disrupt homeostatic function (i.e., processes supporting health, growth, and restoration). This new conceptualization would redefine stress as a measurable state during which homeostatic functions are disrupted. A redefinition would be consistent with the distinction between stress and coping by emphasizing that coping would have an autonomic dimension of a return to homeostatic function. It would also refine the dialogue distinguishing between good and bad stress from the stimulus to the response. Thus, similar to threat, stress results in a retuned autonomic nervous system to support defense, while disrupting optimal bodily processes. If we assume that feelings of safety are dependent on a return to an autonomic state that would support homeostatic function, then feelings of safety would be incompatible with autonomic states associated with stress and threat. Potentially, the ability to move into an autonomic state that supports feelings of safety could also operationally define resilience.

Consistent with Cartesian dualism, there is an inherent acceptance that the external disruptor (i.e., stressor) can be operationalized and reliably result in a measurable stress response. In the 1985 paper I challenged the prevalent S-R model, which had been fundamental to experimental science, with an S-O-R model in which the O or organismic state measured by autonomic nervous system indices would function as an intervening variable mediating or moderating the influence of S on the R. Note that the S-R model is a behavioral restatement of the cause-and-effect relationship that has served as the basis of empirical science's quest for laws of nature.

Because the intervening variable is assumed to be a source of response variability, researchers within the experimental, laboratory-based disciplines are often uncomfortable and seek reassurance in comparatively simple interventions that are independent of the individual differences associated with organismic variables. Among many examples of this approach are manipulations of neural blockades (powerful drugs that block specific neural pathways), surgical severing of neural pathways, or brain lesions ablating specific areas of the brain. These manipulations are powerful and the impact on all participants is relatively similar. In the analyses of manipulation studies statistical significance is driven by the relative change to the manipulation versus the individual variations in response parameters among subjects. With powerful interventions, strong relations are easily observed and statistically confirmed. In contrast, using the S-O-R model, consistent with a polyvagal perspective, we are looking for an interaction that will inform us about the features that distinguish between those who have strong or weak responses to the same manipulation.

In interpreting interactions with autonomic state (i.e., O) on the parameters of the R there is often a discomfort within the experimental laboratory-based sciences; this can provoke criticism that response variations are due to poor experimental control and design and may be overlooking yet-to-be-identified variable(s) influencing the gradation of reactivity. Basically, many scientists are more comfortable with large reliable effects versus more nuanced studies describing intervening variables and interactions. Weak cause-and-effect relationships are frequently assumed to reflect poor experimental control. Frequently an alternative plausible explanation that the response (i.e., effect) is not deterministically related to the stimulus (i.e., cause) is not entertained. Fortunately, with the advent of robust multivariate statistical models, now there are accepted techniques that enable researchers to evaluate how other variables may indirectly via intervening variables mediate and moderate cause-and-effect relationships. These quantitative techniques were not commonly available during the early part of my research career. Below is the introductory segment of the 1985 paper.

> The construct of stress has a variety of definitions. Often the definitions appear circular, since stress has been defined in terms of environmental stimuli (i.e., a stressing environment), as an organismic vulnerability (i.e., a stress-prone organism), and as a response to the environment (i.e., a stress response). The inherent circularity of the definition has limited the succinct articulation of what stress is and what causes it.

Even if stress was operationally defined by labeling the stressing stimulus as the stressor and the behavioral and physiological response or adaptation to the stressor as stress, at least two problems would remain: 1) the definitions of stress and stressor would be circular, and 2) there would be situations in which individual and state variables mediate and modulate the degree of responsivity and adaptability (i.e., stress) of an organism to constant environmental manipulations (i.e., stressor). For example, the same environmental conditions that may result in physiological debilitation for one subject may not produce a discernible behavioral or physiological response in another subject or even in the same subject tested a second time. Thus, stress must be conceptualized not only in terms of the stressor and the observed response but also in terms of the physiological state or vulnerability of the organism at the time of exposure to the stressor.

. . .

One approach to the complex problems associated with stress research would he to reformulate the research strategy. Research is generally conducted within the framework of a mechanistic stimulus-response (S-R) model. In this model the response variance is assumed to be determined by stimulus variance. Thus, stress responses would be determined primarily by the stressor. As noted above, however, the characteristics of the organism at the time of experimental manipulation would contribute to the manifestation of the stress response. Therefore, it would be expedient to use research designs that would enable the examination of the stress response not solely as the product of the stressor but also in terms of the state or condition of the organism prior to the stressor. The research would be formulated within the framework of a stimulus-organism-response (S-O-R) model. Thus, the changing characteristics of the organism might index vulnerability to the stressor and determine the degree to which the individual would experience stress.

As we discuss stress, we note that experiences of stress and threat appear to reflect a common neurophysiological platform. Substituting threat for stress in the above paragraphs would result in similar conclusions. Stress, similar to threat, could objectively be defined as a disruption in homeostatic function. Basically, stress is triggering a bodily state of threat and reorganizing the autonomic nervous system to promote survival. Using this definition, we would be able to decouple good and bad stress (e.g., McEwen, 2013) as being defined by the durations and consequences of the disruptions. Short disruptions or acute stress followed by rapid recoveries would function as neural exercises promoting resilience, while more chronic disruptions without periods of recovery would lead to disease and tissue or organ damage. Research on perceived stress and coping (e.g., Folkman & Lazarus, 1984) that focuses on coping and the link between coping and positive emotions is consistent with Polyvagal Theory's emphasis on an operational definition of a stress response as prolonged disruption of homeostatic function and the powerful influence of cues of safety in down-regulating threat.

A problem with using either threat or stress is that both constructs lead to binary models in which removal of threat is sufficient to feel safe and removal of stress is sufficient to optimize recovery (i.e., homeostatic functions) and relaxation. Missing is an acknowledgment of the nervous system's need for cues of safety and connectedness. These models could be reconceptualized to incorporate an understanding of safety and optimal homeostatic function, which might lead to operationally define neurophysiologically based measures of recovery and resilience.

Others have proposed relationships between safety and stress (Bond et al., 2010; Brosschot et al., 2017; Dollard & McTeman, 2011; Slavich, 2020) that focus on constructs previously explained by PVT (Porges 1995, 1998, 2001, 2003, 2007). For example, the relationship between safety and stress forms the basis for the Generalized Unsafety Theory of Stress (GUTS) proposed by Brosschot and colleagues (2017). Although the two theories use different terms and constructs, the two theories can be contrasted if we assume that stress and threat responses are equivalent. The initial principle proposed in GUTS emphasizes that "the stress response is a default response." In contrast, PVT argues that stress is due to a disinhibition of a safety state and is not a default state. In fact, PVT would propose that stress (i.e., threat reactivity) rather than being a default state, can be reflected in two defensive states that would compromise homeostatic functions. The defensive states adaptively require foundational survival-oriented autonomic states that differ from the safe state that supports homeostasis. To shift states, PVT proposes a process of dissolution, triggered by a neuroception of threat, that results in the disinhibition of evolutionarily older neural pathways that compromise homeostatic functions to serve foundational survival needs. By invoking the Jacksonian (1884) principle of dissolution, PVT proposes that stress is an adaptive product of the disinhibition of a safety circuit that supports homeostatic functions. This disinhibition will occur when survival is challenged by cues of danger, which trigger, via neuroception, the autonomic nervous system into states of defense. By acknowledging a hierarchy of autonomic states that parallel vertebrate evolution, the theory proposes a dissolution sequence in which ancient autonomic circuits become available for defense. The critical points are: (1) stress is not a default state but a disinhibition of older survival circuits resulting in shifting the autonomic nervous system into states of defense, (2) autonomic state mediates the behavioral and physiological features of stress and safety, and (3) autonomic reactivity follows a predictable hierarchical sequence of disinhibiting evolutionarily newer circuits in the service of survival. Two of the GUTS principles (i.e., 2 and 3) deal with the relationship between perceived safety and autonomic state. From a polyvagal perspective, the use of the term perceived safety is a problem. PVT emphasizes and contrasts neural detection (i.e., neuroception) with the psychological process of perception, since perception is often interpreted as having a conscious intentional dimension. Rather, PVT introduced the term neuroception (Porges, 2003, 2004) to emphasize that the detection of the entire continuum of contextual cues from safety to life threat is a reflexive process that does not require awareness. We are familiar with a neuroception of risk, since virtually all living organisms have a reflexive response to pain and injury. However, with the evolution of mammals, there is a repurposing of the regulation of the autonomic nervous system to reflexively calm through cues of safety that enable co-regulation, trust, and sociality. Principles 5, 6, and 7 link the autonomic component of stress to higher brain structures. PVT acknowledges the role of interoception in conveying bodily feelings to higher brain structures and the involvements of these top-down mechanisms, through associative learning, linking thoughts and behaviors to the autonomic states that we associate with threat and stress (see Porges, 2021a, 2021b).

RESILIENCE: AN EMERGENT PROPERTY OF CONNECTEDNESS AND FEELINGS OF SAFETY

Recently, I was interviewed for a documentary on resilience. The documentary was structured to define resilience through the personal narratives of three survivors of severe adversity. My role in the documentary was to provide a common theme capturing the essence of resilience from a polyvagal perspective. The personal stories were emotionally penetrating and reflected very different experiences. One interviewee survived a suicide attempt of jumping off the Golden Gate Bridge. He related that at the moment he jumped, he knew he had made a mistake and knew he was loved and connected. He survived and has become an active suicide prevention speaker. Another interviewee was an award-winning chef with an incurable inflammatory disease that has impacted her eyes, skin, heart, liver, and kidneys. During the pandemic, she continued to pay her staff and used the remaining food in her restaurant to feed those in need. The third interviewee when a 19-year-old college student contracted a flesh-eating bacterium. Twice during the initial treatments, his heart stopped, and he needed to be resuscitated. The consequence of the infection was that both legs and his fingers were amputated. Following his recovery he returned and graduated from college, climbed the highest mountain peak in Australia, played golf, and started a foundation to help people like himself.

As I listened to their narratives, I felt humbled. How would I translate their courageous actions of survival and generosity into basic principles that were embedded in our biology? Two consistent principles emerged from their stories. First, they had a heightened degree of connectedness with others (e.g., family, community, and humanity). Second, this connectedness shifted them from a self-focused survival orientation to a concern for others with a sincere need to support others through actions of compassion, benevolence, and generosity.

Even during their health challenges, they were signaling concern for their caregivers' well-being.

Consistent with a polyvagal perspective, their survival stories were narratives of individuals who had effectively fulfilled their biological imperative of connectedness. By intuitively connecting, they had tapped into a powerful resource, the social engagement system with its neurophysiological substrate, the ventral vagal complex. Even during the profound challenges of their illnesses, injuries, and personal losses, their nervous systems maintained a capacity to connect and to calm. This still leaves the important question of how some individuals efficiently recruit top-down mechanisms, effectively accessing cues of safety from context and memories, while others do not. PVT would propose that this access is mediated by autonomic state and the efficiency of top-down mechanisms in regulating autonomic state. Potentially, this might be indexed by the vagal efficiency metric (see Dale, Kolacz, et al., 2022).

PVT informs us that sociality is a neuromodulator and functionally supports homeostatic functions that serve as a neurophysiological foundation for the positive emergent emotional and social consequences. In this paper, several related processes have been associated with feelings of safety or threat. In a sense, we could say that PVT emphasizes that resilience reflects a physiological state, a state that is sufficiently flexible and resourced to recover from disruptions, support feelings of safety, and connect with others via an active social engagement system. Moving into this state has positive outcomes that are not solely reflected in sociality and trust, but also are seen in prosocial actions of compassion, benevolence, and generosity that enable humans to actualize their biological imperative of connectedness. The narratives highlighted that possibility that resiliency might be a product of a nervous system with sufficient resources to move out of the self-oriented focus of threat and stress to an other-oriented focus of feelings of safety that naturally emerge in actions of sociality and compassion.

Resilience is a complex construct that appears to embody the successful integration of several skills and underlying neurophysiological mechanisms to recover from severe survival-related challenges. Considering the focus and organization of this paper, resilience and feelings of safety share a common neurophysiological substrate. On its most foundational level, resilience reflects behavioral, physiological, emotional, and social processes that are dependent on the recovery of autonomic function to a state that supports social engagement as an adaptive strategy to co-regulate with others and to mutually support health, growth, and restoration. The antithesis of resilience might be thought of as being locked in an autonomic state that would support threat reactions within the body (e.g., injury and infection) and from others. This foundational level would be reflected in the descriptions of Levels I and II in Table 3.1. When these foundational levels are functional, the nervous system can support coordinated goal-directed behaviors (Level III) and social interactions (Level IV).

An optimally regulated autonomic nervous system would support homeostasis and appropriately respond to challenges with an efficient vagal brake (i.e., enhanced vagal efficiency) by reacting and recovering to transitory challenges. But these narratives of resilience emphasize that there is a more integrative mechanism involved that is linked to fulfilling the biological imperative of social connectedness. This capacity for connectedness requires an active social engagement system, which broadcasts the individual's accessibility through voice and facial expressivity. In a simplistic manner, the face and voice, via brainstem pathways in the ventral vagal complex, provide a mechanism through which the autonomic state of two individuals can be shared and functionally transmit feelings of safety, trust, and accessibility that lead to an effective co-regulation. The ability to co-regulate is not simply a collection of voluntary operant behaviors involving facial expressions and vocalizations but seems to require the transmission of veridical cues of safety that are sufficient to elicit a neuroception of safety. It is hard to calibrate these cues, although we subjectively know through our personal reactions that with some people we feel safe and accessible, while with others we feel uncomfortable. I have come to label people whose presence triggers a smile with feelings of accessibility and connection as super co-regulators. Perhaps resilience, as a process, reflects the successful biobehavioral navigation of the four levels described in Table 3.1 and could succinctly be summarized as the capacity to spontaneously foster feelings of safety in both self and other.

CONCLUSION: CLAIMING OUR PHYLOGENETIC HERITAGE

Feelings of safety play a fundamental role enabling humans not only to survive, but to thrive. This supposition poses the important scientific question of how a feeling could be so critical to the survival of our species. To answer this question, it is first necessary to understand the relationship between feelings of safety and the specific neurophysiological architecture that underlies this specific category of feelings. Unfortunately, historical attempts to answer these types of questions have been elusive. Attempts to identify neurophysiological signatures of specific feelings, emotions, thoughts, or even global processes such as sociality have produced, at best, confusing and ambiguous results (e.g., Cacioppo et al., 2000; Levinson, 2003).

Central to the solution of this problem is how terms and constructs are used in different disciplines. In general, attempts to translate from psychological to physiological phenomena have focused on a strategy that could be succinctly labeled as **psychophysiological parallelism**. Psychophysiological parallelism is an intriguing strategy with a strong assumption that it is possible to identify unique neurophysiological signatures of specific mental processes (e.g., feelings, emotions, thoughts, etc.). In the 1960s, psychophysiology emerged as an interdisciplinary science with historic roots embedded in this assumption.

Although PVT (Porges, 1995) emerged from traditional psychophysiology, it provided a theoretical demarcation from parallelism. In a sense, psychophysiological parallelism implicitly assumed that of the constructs employed in different domains were valid (e.g., subjective, observable, physiological) and focused on establishing correlations across domains that optimistically would lead to an objectively quantifiable physiological signature of the construct explored in the psychological domain. In contrast, PVT emphasizes the interactive and integrative aspect of different levels of the nervous system. The theory emphasizes a hierarchical organization that mirrors phylogenetic shifts among vertebrates. The evolutionary changes are also reflected in maturational trends. Thus, what appears to be more complex and related to higher brain structures, such as language and sensitivities to another's physiological state via intonation of voice and gesture, is reflecting the functional and structural changes mapped into the evolutionary history of vertebrates. Frequently missed with our cortico-centric and cognitive-centric orientation is the importance of lower brain mechanisms in managing our basic survival-oriented reactions. Although the less complex earlier evolved systems are often repurposed in mammals, they remain survival oriented and are efficiently available to support states of defense when survival is challenged.

Psychophysiological parallelism is functionally a scientific strategy that assumes an isomorphic representation of a process with the gradations being mapped with equivalent precision on all levels. An alternate and more parsimonious strategy would be to organize the nervous system into a hierarchical format in which neurophysiological processes related to basic biologically determined survival needs are required to be managed successfully before higher brain structures are functionally given access to be activated for problem solving, creativity, and even sociality. PVT postulates that our biology is hierarchically organized with the basic survival needs, such as managing homeostatic functions, residing in foundational brainstem structures and optimal access and utilization of higher neural circuits being dependent on success at the foundational level. PVT provides insights into what the hierarchy is and how it can be identified and potentially monitored. According to the theory, the hierarchy reflects the phylogenetic shifts in the nervous system.

To reduce the intellectual burden of visualizing the evolutionary changes in the nervous system, PVT focused on the phylogenetic transitions of the autonomic nervous system. Specifically, the theory focused on the functional consequences of how the autonomic nervous system was repurposed during the transition from asocial reptiles to social mammals. This focus had a serendipitous benefit, since the brainstem area is relatively small and there was sufficient comparative neuroanatomy conducted to map the changes in the brainstem pathways and their potential adaptive functions. The theory focused on how phylogenetic changes in the neural regulation of the heart provided the foundational properties for feelings of safety and emergent sociality. This chapter emphasized that these two psychological constructs have a dependence on an evolved link between social engagement behaviors and vagal regulation. However, there are convergent evolutionary changes in how the neuropeptides of vasopressin and oxytocin function to support the advent of sociality in mammals (Carter, 2022; Porges, 2001). Specifically, oxytocin plays an important convergent role with the autonomic nervous system in enabling mammals to immobilize without fear, give birth, and experience intimacy without recruiting physiological defensive reactions through dorsal vagal pathways (e.g., bradycardia, syncope, and diarrhea).

Information from three scientific strategies leads to an understanding of the critical role that feelings of safety play in human survival. Complementing the evolutionary and developmental trends introduced above there is a third strategy, an unfolding or de-evolution of the hierarchy in response to threat. This third strategy represents the study of pathology and adaptive reactions to challenges including threat and illness. Jackson (1884) formally introduced de-evolution as dissolution to emphasize the functional impact of disease or damage to the brain. He noted that as evolutionarily newer circuits became dysfunctional, they no longer inhibited the actions of older circuits, and the older circuits became active. Threat is a generalized response that can occur in response to a physical challenge, a pathogen, or even an inaccurate interpretation of context. The elements resulting in a threat response do not have to be valid from an objective interpretation of threat. Rather, threat responses reflect the nervous system's interpretation of risk. In polyvagal terminology, threat responses are due to a neuroception of danger or life threat in which the nervous system determines risk outside of conscious awareness. From a polyvagal perspective, threat reactions represent a disruption of homeostatic function regardless of the validity of threat. Conversely, a neuroception of safety results in an autonomic state that supports homeostatic function with emergent feelings of safety.

Feelings of safety and threat recruit different autonomic resources to optimize survival. However, survival as a construct is overly broad and confusing. Survival can initially be deconstructed into two domains of competence: one within the body and the other outside of the body. Although adequately responding to both challenges is necessary, **internal competence needs to precede external competence**. The internal processes focus on how the nervous system manages the regulation of bodily organs and supports the basic homeostatic processes of health, growth, and restoration. This is obvious when observing the challenge to survival of being born premature, basically born too soon for the nervous system to effectively manage homeostatic demands. The external processes focus on how the nervous system supports responses to challenges. For humans this starts with mastering the coordination of suck-swallow-breathe-vocalize behaviors that enable ingestion and social signally.

On the most basic level feelings of safety are a direct reflection of autonomic state when it is efficiently supporting homeostatic functions. But there is a consequential factor. Being in a calm autonomic state provides neural access to the regulation of the muscles of the face and head that form an integrated social engagement system. This system utilizes the same neural network that coordinates sucking, swallowing, vocalizing, and breathing at birth. Interestingly, access to this system is also a portal to calm as evidenced by the overlap between social behavior and ingestion. Thus, feelings of safety not only reflect a calm autonomic state supporting homeostatic functions that is effectively regulated via the ventral vagus, but also provide access to the special visceral efferent pathways that also originate in the ventral vagal complex that enable social communication.

Frequently missed is the understanding that the brainstem area regulating the autonomic state that supports feelings of safety also regulates the muscles of the face and head that we use for ingestion, social communication, and signaling that we can be trusted and are safe to approach. For example, the intonation of voice reflects our autonomic state. If we are calm and our heart rate is slow and rhythmically variable, our voice is prosodic. The intonation of voice reflected in prosody is the product of vagal pathways regulating laryngeal and pharyngeal muscles. When we are frightened or angry our voice loses prosody, and our heart rate is fast and loses rhythmic variability. Feeling safe, by being in an autonomic state, provides access to efficiently use the social engagement system and to convey the feelings of safety to another. This is universally observed as a mother calms her infant with melodic vocalizations, gentle reassuring gestures, and warm facial expressions. Underlying the effectiveness of the mother's vocalizations and facial expressions in calming the infant is the fact that these cues of safety are actively both reflecting the mother's autonomic state and directly impacting on the nerves that regulate the infant's autonomic nervous system and are being regulated by the same brainstem structures located in the ventral vagal complex. However, access to the structures involved in ingestion and social engagement behaviors are limited by autonomic state. These structures are efficiently accessible when the autonomic nervous system is calm, not in a state of defense, and under the regulation of the ventral vagal pathway.

This chapter has emphasized the common theme that feelings of safety reflect a core fundamental process that has enabled humans to survive through the opportunistic features of trusting social engagements that have co-regulatory capacities to mitigate the metabolically costly defense reactions. The short-term outcome of having trusted co-regulatory relationships is obvious, since it provides opportunities to down-regulate defenses and to support homeostatic functions. However, there is also a long-term consequence of feelings of safety that are reflected in the emergence of communities of trusted individuals in which feelings of safety expand through spontaneous social engagement. Prosocial behaviors in a collective become the norm. Thus, our sociality enables an expansion of those with whom we feel safe and trust. This, of course, is the underlying premise of communities—including legal systems, business transactions, political negotiations, and international treaties.

Through the study of neural development and phylogeny, we can extract foundational principles and their underlying mechanisms through which the autonomic nervous system leads to feelings of safety and opportunities to co-regulate. The study of mental and physical illnesses provides a convergent research strategy to confirm these principles, since illness is a trigger of dissolution, which functionally disrupts autonomic regulation and compromises social engagement behaviors.

In Table 3.2, the foundational principles are outlined. The principles succinctly form a hierarchy that leads to an optimization of health as well as mental, social, and behavioral processes. An acknowledgment of these principles in daily interactions and societal institutions would reinstate processes that would support the qualities of human experience, in which feelings of safety form the foundation of a healthier and more productive society. These principles highlight the validity of a science of safety that when implemented in societal institutions, ranging from health care to education, would enhance health and sociality and lead to greater productivity, creativity, and sense of well-being. In a way, by respecting our need to feel safe, we respect our phylogenetic heritage and elevate sociality as a neuromodulator and functionally provide the scientific validation for a societal focus on promoting opportunities to experience feelings of safety and co-regulation.

In summary, feelings of safety and threat are subjective interpretations of the autonomic nervous system communicating via interoception with higher brain structures. As humans, we are on a lifelong quest to feel safe. PVT deconstructs this intuitive truth into a plausible neuroscience with testable hypotheses and objective neurophysiological indices. Functionally, this quest to feel safe is the product of respecting the important functions of neuroception and the powerful role of co-regulation and other attributes of sociality as a neuromodulator that can optimize health, growth, and restoration.

TABLE 3.2   Principles of a Science of Safety

Principle 1	Feelings of safety are a subjective interpretation of a calm autonomic state regulated by the ventral vagal pathway that supports homeostatic functions (i.e., health, growth, and restoration).
Principle 2	Feelings of threat, stress, or anxiety are subjective interpretations of a shared defensive autonomic state that disrupts homeostatic function.
Principle 3	Feelings of safety provide access to the social engagement system.
Principle 4	When recruited, the social engagement system sends signals of safety (e.g., intonation of voice, facial expressions) to others that functionally down-regulate (via neuroception) autonomic states of defense to states of calmness and accessibility mitigating the metabolically costly threat reactions through co-regulation.
Principle 5	Co-regulation provides the neural state that supports the establishment of trusting relationships.
Principle 6	Autonomic states of calmness (e.g., feelings of safety) enable efficient access to the higher brain structures involved in problem solving and creativity.
Principle 7	The reciprocal benefits of co-regulation form the basis of sociality and support the neural systems optimizing health and performance.

4

A Transdisciplinary Theory of Sociality: Polyvagal Theory

Stephen W. Porges

While preparing this talk as the keynote speech of an international conference (see Sources), I concluded that my approach as a scientist is transdisciplinary. My world has always been focused on bridging disciplines. I just didn't realize how much my scientific perspective was bridging disciplines until I prepared this talk. This is a new type of talk for me to give. My normal audiences are generally faculty at medical schools and universities and scientists affiliated with specific organizations. Prior to this talk, my experience bridging disciplines has been to translate my science into a language that can be understood by clinicians, administrators, and educators.

My talk is about the human quest to be embodied, a process in which our mind and our body function in collaboration as an integrated system. One thing we need to know, as we start talking about this journey to embodiment, is that we're really talking about an evolutionary journey of mammals—and we are mammals—into a social world, where we have to interact with each other to enable our body to, in a sense, be embodied. And as we detail the alternative discipline-dependent perspectives, we will need to acknowledge how our physiological state can distort or bias our acceptance of information from other perspectives. Thus, underlying our personal ability to be truly transdisciplinary is our nervous system and how it influences our mental and behavioral capacities to be informed.

THE TWO CULTURES

Many years ago, as an undergraduate student, I read C. P. Snow's lecture, *The Two Cultures* (1959). I never forgot it. I recall, at the time I read it, it seemed to be a pessimistic prediction of the intellectual future in Western cultures. It described an academic future in which the gap between foundational sciences and the humanities would expand and become separate intellectual cultures. The following quote summarizes his prediction:

> I believe the intellectual life of the whole of western society is increasingly being split into two polar groups . . . Literary intellectuals at one pole—at the other scientists, and as the most representative, the physical scientists. Between the two, a gulf of mutual incomprehension—sometimes (particularly among the young) hostility and dislike, but most of all lack of understanding.

Since, as a developing scientist, I was also interested in the arts and humanities, I interpreted this premise as a personal challenge. As an undergraduate I wondered how an intellectually curious student would be able to navigate through this complex world of discrete disciplines. Today, I'm going to tell you that it's much worse than he saw it in 1959. I recently found a quote from a position paper I wrote in the 1990s. The quote from a personal communication (1998) below expresses my personal feeling as an established full professor:

> I have spent my entire professional life in the academic scientific community, a community that takes a Tower of Babel approach to scientific inquiry. Often, I felt I was talking to illiterate primitives although these individuals had doctorates from the major research-oriented universities. At times, I've struggled to understand the research questions about their disciplines. And, at other times, I have attempted to convey the most basic concepts of my research. I've struggled with communication and have searched for a common vocabulary and scientific metaphor.

Over the years, I realized that if I could develop a language to convey the passion and intuitions of my work, then my ideas would be more acceptable to those who were within or outside my discipline. The acceptability of novel ideas is biased by the knowledge and orientation of the audience. Currently, within universities there is a bias away from a broad liberal arts education and a bias toward STEM disciplines and applied programs. STEM is shorthand for science, technology, engineering, and mathematics. Its interdisciplinary and applied approach is not transdisciplinary or reflective of the integration of shared disciplines. Rather it is structured on the common core knowledge of the STEM disciplines and a separation from the arts and humanities.

Even in the biomedical or mental health areas, we learn that when stakeholders encourage interdisciplinary research, they are basically arguing for a place at the table. They're not arguing about sharing underlying principles or solving problems. They're arguing for resources to fund their programs. Over the past 75 years, the disciplines that were fortunate to be funded by government agencies and foundations have flourished, as have applied areas such as business schools that attract students focused on obtaining jobs and not discovery or creativity. In universities this trend translates into the shrinkage of academic departments in the arts and humanities.

In university settings we are aware of the consequence of this strategy. For those of us who have been faculty members for several decades, we have observed the impact of a bias toward technology, science, and application and what it has done to the humanities and arts. It has basically diverted resources. Now, in most universities, the academic departments representing the humanities and the arts are literally starving. Since these departments rarely receive grants from foundations and government institutes, the disciplines tend to be solely dependent on university resources. Moreover, the humanities and arts are attracting fewer students and thus receive less funding from their universities. As universities continue to lose federal and state funding, the business plan of universities has focused on faculty generating funds and offering high-demand undergraduate courses. In both these domains, the humanities and the arts have lagged behind the STEM sciences and applied areas such as business. On an individual level, faculty in the humanities and arts receive lower salaries than faculty in the STEM disciplines or business. In fact, faculty in highly rated schools of business may be receiving salaries as high as surgeons.

WESTERN PHILOSOPHY AND SCIENCE CARTESIAN DUALISM: UNDERSTANDING OUR BIOLOGY

Is this lack of interest in linking disparate intellectual strategies a reflection of a culturally deficient link between an awareness and a respect for mind and body? Missing in our institutions is a deep understanding or even an appreciation of mind–body and brain–body relationships that would enable a convergence between objective neural measurements and subjective feelings and thoughts resulting in a truly transdisciplinary approach to the construct of embodiment. However, what happens when disembodiment is the cultural norm? When it is, we actualize C. P. Snow's vision. And, if we affiliate in our thinking with the objective and mechanistic sciences, we literally, reflexively become uninterested in the humanities. Missing in the narrative of how institutions have become disciplined is an understanding of biology and the role of the nervous system in our objective and subjective experiences. Missing is an awareness of how biology biases emotional, mental, and behavioral processes, including boldness, insight, creativity, aesthetic expression, and even spirituality.

Our biology influences our capacity to accept and process novel information and alternative perspectives and models. Functionally, our biology determines or limits whether we can accept a transdisciplinary perspective. On a personal level, it determines whether transdisciplinary is a viable concept that we welcome, because our capacity to incorporate a transdisciplinary perspective into our world view is dependent on our biology as expressed in our physiological state. This functionally means that when our bodies are in states of threat, we limit our intellectual and emotional access to novel information. For those of us who are bonded to university communities, we realize through our experiences that universities are not safe places. Since the day-to-day experiences within universities are framed through continuous evaluation, our nervous systems are bathed in cues of constant threat. The nervous system unambiguously interprets evaluation as threat.

Through the process of creating intellectual domains or disciplines, we have lost the knowledge and insights that are not discipline defined. As a product of this process, we have lost the tools and strategies to fulfill our basic need to connect and truly cooperate with others. This need to connect is not merely an intentional behavioral action, it is a profound expression of our biological imperative—our need to survive through connection and cooperation with others. This biological need to connect and cooperate is a major theme of this talk. If we don't have access to this process of connection, we will fail to appreciate the biases we experience when we are either feeling safe or threatened. Thus, as a threatened species, we focus on the predictable and the familiar. We gravitate away from novelty and curiosity. However, when we feel safe, we spontaneously become curious, bold, and creative.

ESTABLISHING DISCIPLINES AS INTELLECTUAL SANCTUARIES COMES WITH A GREAT COST TO SOCIETY

Academic disciplines provide a platform to un-educate the educated. If we look at the prevalence or percentage of bachelor's degrees in the United States by discipline major, we are informed that the most popular major is business, which accounts for about three times the total majors in the humanities and liberal arts. In fact, more than 50% of the majors are focused on professions (e.g., business, education, journalism, etc.). In contrast, in the 1960s and 1970s, most majors were included within liberal arts, which represented a broader educational experience including courses in both the humanities and sciences. At the time, this composite of educational material helped form the concept of a well-rounded educational experience producing a culturally embodied, educated person. In today's academic institutions, majors in liberal arts have become a much smaller segment as students move toward applied areas that fit targeted professions. In a historic way, university students are no longer being educated, but being trained similar to the traditions of technical schools. However, as a by-product of this strategy, is the creation of an educated population in which many have lost the history of their own humanity.

Disciplines functionally limit understanding and creativity beyond the defined boundaries of the discipline. A discipline-oriented education functionally imprisons the creative mind. I have frequently used the concept of being imprisoned to describe my experiences as a university professor. This doesn't mean that my experiences as a professor were negative and that I did not enjoy or experience benefits of exploration and discovery. But, in retrospect, I realize that my experiences were primarily limited by the administrative structures within a university of colleges, departments, institutes, and divisions. The structures form ecological niches, since they have responsibilities for delivering education (i.e., teaching), conducting and obtaining resources for research, and the hiring and evaluation of faculty. Similar to most business models, finances limit the vision.

As a professor, I certainly did not have the time or resources to venture too far from my unit and build bridges across disciplines that might foster the defining of new problems and creative problem-solving techniques. Thus, intellectually, we were functionally imprisoned and now need to reflect on these administrative and self-imposed limitations. We need to break the chains that restrain scholars from a true commitment to transdisciplinary research.

In my quest for transdisciplinary solutions, I use the Rubik's cube as a metaphor. The metaphor is useful in understanding my work in developing the Polyvagal Theory (PVT). To understand the origins of PVT, visualize a Rubik's cube with the surfaces representing different scientific disciplines moving in time as each science is selectively updated by new information. Metaphorically, PVT is the solution of a Rubik's puzzle, a solution to how evolution repurposed the mammalian autonomic nervous system to contain defensive reactions and enable sociality to thrive. This metaphor is helpful, since PVT is an extraction of principles derived from the integration of several disciplines each with its own history, research paradigms, literature, methodology, and theoretical context. PVT provides both an example of a transdisciplinary theory and an explanation of strategies that would encourage or discourage transdisciplinary work.

If we are interested in identifying principles that are not discipline-based but may underlie several disciplines, we would compare and contrast information as if we were playing with a Rubik's cube. We're twisting and translating discipline-dependent constructs as we try to find common themes and principles across disciplines. When we solve the puzzle, we identify relatively simple common themes in which human experience is limited by biology. Some of these principles bridge the arts and sciences. For example, pointillism pioneered by Seurat in art could be studied from sciences dedicated to the study of both perception and brain processes.

When we appreciate that we are a biological system, we acknowledge that our biology limits and biases our experiences. Our intellectual accessibility to a transdisciplinary perspective is vested in our biology. When we are threatened, our biology changes our accessibility and flexibility becomes limited as we shift our resources to deal with threat and survival. As we bring our biology and physiological state into the discussion of transdisciplinary work, we start to acknowledge general themes about our own biology and how our biology can impact our understandings from other disciplines.

I believe, in our journey to become rational and objective, we have neglected our biological roots and assumed that we are a simple input-output machine governed by the laws of learning and personal intentions. However, we are an adaptive biological system with a flexibility to shift physiological states based upon threats or conditions in the environment or in our health. PVT emphasizes that physiological state influences how we process and evaluate information. Creativity and productivity in both the sciences and the humanities are dependent on the evolutionary history of human biology and the adaptive features of the human nervous system, especially how we relate to each other.

OUR BIOLOGICAL IMPERATIVE: CONNECT, COOPERATE, AND COLLABORATE

I now want to emphasize that a powerful motivator for human behavior is our biological imperative to connect, to cooperate, and to collaborate. Mammals evolved from ancient, now extinct, reptiles. They survived through their ability to cooperate and to share, and to be safe in the presence of others. We need to rectify a common misunderstanding of the survival of the fittest. We frequently are led to believe that survival of the fittest is related to those who are the strongest, who have the most personal resources and not those who can co-regulate with others and cooperate. Through a different lens we can twist the Rubik's cube and start to extract principles of a science of sociality. We can look at the newborn baby's reaction to the mother and see a common theme—the ability of maternal behavior to trigger in the nervous system of the infant a unique ability to give up all defenses. As these threat reactions are resolved by vocal and behavioral gestures, the infant's nervous system can now regulate internal organs to efficiently support health, growth, and restoration. This behavior is reciprocal and co-regulatory. The mother's potent cues are enabling the infant to relax on the chest of the mother, while synchronously enabling the mother to relax as well. This co-regulatory interdependence among individuals is shared with different mammalian species.

EVOLUTIONARY PERSPECTIVE: A COHERENT TRANSDISCIPLINARY NARRATIVE

Theodosius Dobzhansky, an evolutionary biologist (1900–1975), stated that: "Nothing in Biology makes sense except in the light of Evolution" (1973). I want to extrapolate from that statement and move it to other areas of the human experience that would include a transdisciplinary perspective and state that intellectual products in the sciences, arts, and humanities make sense only in light of evolution. Generalizing from this statement, we might conclude that the totality of human experience is bounded and at times biased by our biology. By acknowledging our biological basis, we can create organizing principles that initially appear to be oblique or unrelated to our biology. But if we understand our biology as the foundation of our experiences, we see commonality across disciplines, and it may help us create a more coherent transdisciplinary narrative. Dobzhansky (1962) also stated that: "The fittest may also be the gentlest because survival often requires mutual help and cooperation." When we see this statement as a hint about how knowledge of the human experience might be shared, it leads us into a transdisciplinary perspective.

CONNECTEDNESS: A BIOLOGICAL IMPERATIVE

What is a biological imperative? It defines what living organisms need to perpetuate their existence. It's survival of the fittest, not the strongest. It's the survival of those who cooperate, help each other to mitigate threat responses, and co-regulate and collectively solve problems. Connectedness is this process, which we as humans express as our biological imperative. It's the body's need to co-regulate our biobehavioral state through engagement with others. Connectedness is the ability to mutually, synchronously, and reciprocally regulate physiological and behavioral state to optimize social interactions.

When we reflect on the terms synchronous and reciprocal, we realize that in our current digital and asynchronous culture our nervous system is not getting the contingent signals that support our biological imperative of connectedness. Without an efficient access to social connectedness, we experience chronic stress due to our inability to efficiently down-regulate defenses. It is only when we down-regulate our defenses that we can enjoy the benefits of sociality. These precious attributes that we experience as trust and safety with others reflect the underlying biological principles that allowed mammals to survive in a hostile world. Connectedness is an evolutionary biobehavioral process that linked social behavior with both mental and physical health. Connectedness leads to cooperation and collaboration, which fosters creative, intellectual expansiveness in us and even spirituality. The basic underlying transdisciplinary principle is that human sociality is not solely a social behavior, but rather a biobehavioral process that enables behavior to regulate our biology to promote calmness and to optimize not only social behavior, but also collaboration in all forms of problem solving and in understanding and expanding human experience.

As a metaphor, we can use the protective functions of the energy shields employed on the Starship *Enterprise*. In the Star Trek movies and television series, we realize employing protective shields utilizes energy and compromises the mobility and function of the starship. In contrast, when the shields were not necessary, the energy of the starship could be directed to increase speed and provide greater mobility to support the mission of exploration. Similarly, when we as humans feel safe, we are more likely to explore, to create, and to cooperate and collaborate. However, if we have to use our defenses, we use our resources to protect rather than integrate or problem solve. Similar to the starship's defenses in Star Trek, human defensives are metabolically costly. It takes energy to defend, and defenses compromise function by diverting energy away from intellectual pursuits and our accessibility to interact with others, to learn from others, to exhibit a type of intellectual flexibility, to be respectful, and to be compassionate about others. In other words, we have the capacity to be transdisciplinary only when we are not in a physiological state of defense.

POLYVAGAL THEORY

The word polyvagal comes from poly, meaning many, and vagus, the name of the tenth cranial nerve. During the evolutionary transition from reptiles to mammals, mammals developed a unique vagal pathway that enabled them to down-regulate defenses, which enabled mammals to come in close proximity and create social relationships. This evolutionary change in neurophysiology enabled mammals to engage in a journey to sociality. As PVT developed, it provided a theoretical basis for a neuroscience of safety and explained how safety promotes spontaneous social engagement behaviors and optimizes health, growth, and restoration. The theory provides insights regarding the role that feeling safe plays in education, medical care, and social relationships.

If you're involved or interested in education, reflect on the school experiences of many young children. Going to school is frequently a trigger of painful somatic symptoms such as gut pains. For these children, the school environment provides triggers to their autonomic nervous system indicating that they're under states of threat. Typically, how do educators and parents respond to these situations? They frequently demand and even force the child to attend school. They tell the child to get over these responses and assume that the child is feigning distress. In making these appraisals, the parents and educators are not respecting that the child's nervous system is detecting threat.

We need to acknowledge and respect that only when our body (i.e., nervous system) feels safe will our minds expand our mental capacities to be creative and to develop bold new ideas. In acknowledging this dependency, we also acknowledge that the chronic evaluation in our educational systems triggers threat reactions that limit our productivity. As we visualize the educational experience on all levels, including universities, evaluation emerges as the powerful primary principle and evaluation procedures are potent triggers of threat. A focus on this process impacts and compromises intellectual resources. Are our respective roles supporting intellectual growth and creativity, or are we compromising it?

The models that we use for evaluation compromise how our nervous system works in intellectual pursuits. We can apply the same model to medicine. Medicine has become a discipline of evaluation and assessment. How does our body react to evaluation and assessment? Our responses are reflexively and adaptively dependent on recruiting neural circuits that support defense and efficiently express threat reactions. However, threat reactions interfere with accessing the higher brain circuits that support creativity and problem solving.

Can a new transdisciplinary model be developed for disciplines such as medicine and education that appreciate the dependence of learning, creativity, and collaboration on a physiological state reflecting feelings of safety instead of feelings of threat? Do we go to a physician to learn about our body and develop a strategy for health? Or are our appointments with physicians cloaked with feelings of uncertainty and fear, reflecting our personalized physiological state of defense? Do we leave the physician's office in a state of anxiety and fear, not knowing what the tests will uncover while assuming that the tests may detect a potentially fatal disorder?

In 1994, I introduced the basic principles of the PVT in my *Presidential Address to the Society for Psychophysiological Research*. The address was published in 1995 (Porges, 1995) with a title that succinctly abstracts the core of the theory—*Orienting in a Defensive World: Mammalian Modifications of Our Evolutionary Heritage. A Polyvagal Theory*. The title emphasizes the importance for mammals to be able to direct their attention, while actively inhibiting their defensive reactions. To implement these functions reliably and efficiently, mammals had to repurpose their evolutionary heritage. Through evolutionary processes, the transition from asocial reptiles to social mammals required changes in how the nervous systems regulated physiological state. Our intellectual creativity and problem-solving capacity are dependent on these changes. In retrospect, PVT is transdisciplinary, since it provides identifiable and quantifiable links among physiological state, social behavior, and cognitive function. At its core, the theory explains the emergent products of our evolutionary journey to sociality. Thus, the theory elevates sociality and feelings of safety and threat to discussions of all aspects of the human experience.

THE AUTONOMIC NERVOUS SYSTEM

All vertebrates have a nervous system that detects threat and reflexively defines and responds defensively. However, unlike our reptilian ancestors, mammals have a nervous system that detects safety and reflexively calms. This distinction is important and provides information in how a polyvagal-informed culture would structure social and educational institutions. Respecting this knowledge means that we can send potent cues to our family, our colleagues, our students, and our children with neurally informed contextual cues capable of shifting the body from states of defense, transforming these individuals into states in which they are more emotionally, physiologically, and intellectually accessible.

Depending on the physiological state we are in, we are either socially and intellectually accessible or defensive. Our physiological state influences our accessibility to new perspectives and information. The transdisciplinary approach requires a physiological state in which our nervous system supports accessibility and intellectual flexibility. Understanding this dependence on physiological state needs to be an underlying theme within strategies that encourage transdisciplinary approaches. Our physiological state determines whether we can even think within a transdisciplinary perspective or whether it's viable for us to encourage others to think in a transdisciplinary way.

Some of you may be familiar with the primary components of the autonomic nervous system, the sympathetic and parasympathetic nervous systems. The sympathetic nervous system is a set of pathways coming off our spine, which functionally act like an accelerator. It tends to activate the visceral organs within our body to promote movement. Juxtaposed to the sympathetic nervous system is the parasympathetic nervous system that acts as a braking system. The primary parasympathetic influences are transmitted through a large nerve called the vagus. The vagus is a cranial nerve that originates in the brainstem. The vagus is the longest nerve in the body and travels through the viscera providing a bidirectional communication highway between the brain and the visceral organs. In general, the vagus and the sympathetic nervous system send signals to the same organs. This observation leads to a paired antagonistic model in which the sympathetic nervous system functions as an accelerator and the vagus functions as a brake.

PVT challenges this model, while acknowledging that under specific conditions it may be true. The theory emphasizes that we react to the environment in a different way. We react with two different vagal pathways, because mammals have a second vagal pathway that goes primarily to the heart and lungs. It is connected in the brainstem to the nerves that regulate our facial expressions, our vocalizations, and even whether we can extract human voice from background sounds. This second vagal pathway originates in an area of the brainstem ventral to the evolutionarily earlier dorsal vagal pathway that is shared with most vertebrates and in mammals provides the primary vagal regulation to organs below the diaphragm.

When the ventral vagus is working appropriately, it down-regulates the sympathetic nervous system that supports defensive behaviors such as fight-or-flight activities. However, the more ancient vagal circuit that goes primarily below the diaphragm can be recruited in defense. When this occurs, it disrupts our digestive system and provides the neural mechanism through which threat reactions are manifest in gut problems. Many people who experience severe abuse and trauma have severe problems in their subdiaphragmatic organs including gut and genitals.

This provides some of the background of the evolutionary journey of the autonomic nervous system and how in mammals, social behavior is dependent on autonomic nervous system state. With the evolutionary emergence of a brainstem area known as the ventral vagal complex, the mammalian ventral vagus becomes involved in social communication and social communication becomes a regulator of autonomic state. Specifically, the ventral vagal complex identifies the neuroanatomical structures that link the ventral vagus with the nerves regulating the muscles in the face and the head, producing an integrated social engagement system that enables us to calm. This system also enables those with whom we interact to be calmed by us through the facial, vocal, and gestural cues of our engagement behaviors. The evolutionarily more primitive systems, the sympathetic nervous system and the older dorsal vagus, have critical roles in our survival, but only during states of safety are those roles related to sociality, trust, connectedness, collaboration, and co-regulation. When under threat the sympathetic nervous system and dorsal vagus promote defensive reactions respectively characterized by flight-or-flight behaviors and immobilization (e.g., death feigning, fainting).

What happens when the social engagement system is ineffective in moving us into a state of safety or helping us survive? We use evolutionarily more primitive adaptive circuits in our quest to survive. In the absence of an effective social engagement system, we recruit the sympathetic nervous system as an efficient system to mobilize to fight or flee. And if mobilization doesn't effectively serve to move us into a safe place, we recruit the dorsal vagal complex. This ancient neural circuit conserves metabolic research and is observed as immobilization with lower heart rate, cessation of breathing, and at times, fainting, defecation, or appearing to be dead. This reaction mirrors the reptilian reaction to threat. When reptiles are threatened, they frequently immobilize. However, since mammals have large brains and great needs for oxygen, when they immobilize under threat the slowing of heart and the cessation of breathing is potentially lethal.

Neuroception and the Quest for Safety

We live in an environment where we are bombarded with cues from inside the body and outside the body. Our nervous system evaluates this information through a process linked to PVT called neuroception. Neuroception is the process that evaluates risk without awareness. Neuroception interprets cues as safe, dangerous, or life-threatening. It's not perception, which may have a cognitive component. Neuroception is reflexive and rapid. It happens before we can consciously interpret it. For example, if you step into the street and you hear a car horn or brakes squealing, your body reacts; you don't know what the stimulus was until after you already reacted. This is a neuroception of danger. Similarly, if someone talks to you with a warm smile and melodic voice, suddenly you feel calm and trust the person, even if the person is a stranger. This is a neuroception of safety.

Neuroception occurs rapidly to save us and to put our bodies into different physiological states without a conscious evaluation. It's not perception. When we receive cues of safety, our faces become more animated. We make eye contact. Our voices become more melodic. As faces beam and social interactions occur, the same neural pathways defining the social engagement system are supporting homeostatic regulation of our visceral organs including our gut.

When we are under threat, we mitigate our threat reactions through social interactions with others. When we detect via neuroception cues of danger, the social engagement system is reflexively down-regulated to enable efficient mobilization that would optimize fight-or-flight behaviors. If a child is intimidated and overwhelmed by a large adult, the child's neuroception of potential life threat gets triggered and the child may totally shut down. This shutting down reflects a primitive reptilian defense reaction.

If we visualize the reaction of a mouse in the jaws of the cat, we will see that the body of the mouse has lost muscle tone. This dorsal vagal state illustrates the loss of sympathetic activation that muscle tone requires. In the absence of sympathetic tone, the body collapses and literally motorically shuts down. Children can be so scared that they can pass out, urinate, or defecate—processes being mediated by the dorsal vagus. Survivors of severe trauma and abuse may describe similar personal experiences.

Although immobilization as a defense strategy is infrequently discussed within psychology or psychiatry, mobilization reactions such as fight-or-flight are. This focus on fight-or-flight is in part due to a relatively greater understanding of mechanisms that support fight-or-flight than the mechanisms supporting shutdown reactions. However, PVT basically explained shutdown as a defense system regulated by an evolutionarily older vagal pathway. Prior to the PVT, the vagus had been viewed in the literature as a system that supported health, growth, and restoration. This led to the question of how could that same nerve be used in defense? PVT clarified this apparent contradiction by documenting the evolutionary history of the vagus and identifying the different adaptive roles that the ventral and dorsal vagal branches have in supporting the disparate functions of sociality and behavioral shutdown.

When we visualize a mother playing with her infant, we can see how the social engagement system is working. As we focus on the upper part of the faces of the mother and child, we see the liveliness and animation of the upper part of the face, especially the orbital muscle around the eye. The muscle is called the orbicularis oculi and is regulated by a branch of the facial nerve that also is regulated by the anatomical structures in the ventral vagal complex. The orbicularis oculi sends cues between the mother and child reflecting their mutual feelings of safety, trust, and joy in the interaction. Underlying these observable facial expressions is a physiology that is also supporting health, growth, and restoration. In our visualizations we become aware that face-to-face interactions provide a portal to co-regulate physiology that supports homeostatic processes. When face-to-face interactions degrade into arguments, physiological processes also become disrupted.

Conceptually, face-to-face interactions function as neural exercises of the social engagement system. These neural exercises become features of therapy, which can also be applied in the workplace or in education. Physiological processes are supported by face-to-face interactions including facial expressivity, vocalizations, and gestures. When cued by these features, immobilization becomes an opportunity to feel safe in the presence of another; we can visualize the infant relaxed in the arms of the mother in a state of immobilization without fear, a state that does not require metabolically costly muscle tone.

Immobilization without fear is the optimal state to rest, relax, sleep, digest, and perform bodily processes. When immobilized without fear in the presence of a trusting partner or friend, the state promotes intimacy and enables feelings of trust, safety, and love. However, it is a challenge for mammals to experience this state because it requires down-regulating defenses. If a person has a severe trauma history, their brain may detect proximity of another as threat and a gesture of engagement or casual embrace may trigger an autonomic state change that would support severe defensive behaviors.

Vagal Brake

Social behaviors are neural exercises of the ventral vagal circuit, which function as a vagal brake inhibiting sympathetic activation that potentially could lead to fight-or-flight behaviors. These neural exercises are calming and promote neurophysiological states that support mental and physical health. Thus, positive supporting social interactions lead to physiological states of safety and enhance homeostatic functions with the emergent benefits of improved health, optimal maturation, and restoration. In contrast, histories of trauma and abuse lead to a retuning of the autonomic nervous system, in turn lowering the threshold to trigger defensive behaviors that disrupt connectedness and the ability to co-regulate.

With this knowledge that threat disrupts the neurophysiology of health and social behavior, we may reflect on the experience students have within academic institutions. Is the student's experience traumatic? For those who have higher education degrees, did they feel safe and enjoy the educational experience? Was the educational experience co-regulatory or was the experience traumatic?

Moving Toward Embodiment

Our body is on a mission. It's on a quest to be safe. We evolved with the tools to detect cues of safety such as intonation of voice, gesture, and facial expression.

Our neuroception is our personal threat-detection system. If we have a severe trauma history, the nervous system is potentially retuned into chronic states of defense, with a very low threshold to detect threat. If our nervous system is more buffered, we are more resilient to transitory challenges. If we have safety in our lives and good relationships with opportunities to co-regulate, the threshold to react is elevated and we become more resilient.

In the world of transdisciplinary studies, this may mean that if our body is in a sense safer, we're interested in alternative models and views. We are basically interested in becoming transdisciplinary. If our bodies are in states of threat, we are not accessible to any idea that violates our expectations of what we already know, and this violation of expectancy can trigger a threat reaction.

If our social engagement system works, we may be more accessible not only to others, but also to new ideas. However, under chronic threat, social engagement can become dormant. Retraction of the social engagement system is an adaptive response to chronic stress or threat. What happens when we experience chronic threat? We lack intonation or voice. We have poor eye contact with others, difficulties in social communication, blunted facial expressivity, and difficulties regulating our behavioral state. We may become hypervigilant, anxious, distractable, or impulsive. Some individuals become irritable and have tantrums and panic attacks. Others become totally hypoaroused and socially withdraw and may even dissociate. We might have a compromised visceral regulation that could manifest in cardiac arrhythmias or digestive problems. We often have difficulties listening to oral commands.

The profile of symptoms expands and crosses several domains and disciplines of health care. An individual with a dormant social engagement system might also express a vast portfolio of disorders including speech and language delays, sound hypersensitivities, oral motor defensiveness, selective eating, digestive problems, limited co-regulation and cooperation with other people, and limited creativity and intellectual integration.

In response to these problems, what does our society do? Does it do a good job creating access to our social engagement system? Do we have sufficient opportunities to exercise the social engagement system by socially communicating? Are we replacing the opportunities our nervous system needs to regulate through social interactions with email, texting, or other diversions? The bottom line is that we are wasting our creative intellectual resources by supporting states with defense and not states of safety and connectedness.

Even in the realm of spirituality, we have to evaluate whether we are sufficiently embodied. Are we safe enough within our body to promote the bidirectional communication between our brain and visceral organs through the vagus? Are we safe enough to connect and trust others? Are we safe enough to have a pathway to spirituality through connectedness with others versus a pathway to spirituality through detachment and dissociation? These two paths lead to different conclusions about our own personal spiritual experience. PVT, by emphasizing the biological roots of safety and sociality, offers a perspective that transforms the human narrative from a documentary emphasizing events and objects to a pragmatic and often heroic quest for safety with the implicit bodily drive to survive emphasizing feelings.

Polyvagal Theory: Information from Several Disciplines

PVT is transdisciplinary and integrates information from several disparate disciplines including themes common within the transdisciplinary worldview such as pathology, ontogeny, adaptation, and phylogeny. As the theory is becoming recognized, interest and applications have broadened beyond psychology and medicine to neuroanatomy, evolutionary biology, and comparative and developmental physiology. Applications of Polyvagal Theory are moving into mental health therapies, speech and hearing sciences, institutional organization, education, health-related assessments, musical composition to enhance healing, architectural design of healing spaces including schools and hospitals and treatments for auditory processing deficits, language development, and chronic pain. In practice, PVT is truly transdisciplinary, both in its foundational background and in its applications.

The theory informs us that our nervous system craves safety and, when safe, is accessible for collaboration and creativity. We need to rethink our conceptualization of collaboration and how it leads to creativity. Safety is the foundational substrate for collaboration and collaboration is a form of the connectedness that promotes safety. These are essentials in our biological imperative to survive.

Much of the information about the integration of brain and body systems has been available for decades but was not integrated into medicine. For example, Walter Hess received the Nobel Prize in 1949 for an integrated perspective of the brain-body system. A quote from the first sentence of Hess's Nobel speech is truly transdisciplinary. He says:

> A recognized fact, which goes back to the earliest times is that every living organism is not the sum of a multitude of unitary processes, but is, by its virtue of interrelationships of higher and lower levels of control, an unbroken unity.

Hess's transdisciplinary conceptualization has not been embedded in contemporary medicine. It is conceptually incompatible with the mechanistic, machine model that contemporary physicians frequently apply, which focuses on external fixes such as pharmaceuticals and surgery. Hess's perspective includes a respect for the body's own resources to heal. This point is consistent with PVT, which would emphasize that when feeling safe (i.e., being in a physiological state that supports feeling safe) the nervous system promotes homeostatic functions that lead to optimized health, growth, and restoration. Basically, feeling safe allows the body to repair and heal itself.

Once we respect our biological nature, we can begin to adaptively incorporate a transdisciplinary approach. Being in a physiological state of threat or chronic evaluation limits acceptance of other discipline-defined knowledge and insights. Being in a physiological state of safety promotes accessibility, cooperation, and connectedness and opens portals to other discipline-defined knowledge and insights. Being transdisciplinary is not solely about accumulation or integration of information from disparate disciplines, but about the interactions and connectedness with thought leaders independent of discipline.

In closing I ask you to join me in speculating what our contemporary world would be like if Descartes had been polyvagal informed and, instead of stating "I think, therefore I am," stated "I feel myself, therefore I am."

PART II

Clinical Implications

5

Appeasement: Replacing Stockholm Syndrome as a Definition of a Survival Strategy

Rebecca Bailey, Jaycee Dugard,
Stefanie F. Smith, and Stephen W. Porges

CRITIQUE OF STOCKHOLM SYNDROME

Words can carry strong messages about intentionality, motivation, and healing. Consider the recent awareness around the use of victim versus survivor. Some people choose to use the word victim when describing life-threatening traumatic experiences, while others prefer the word survivor, warrior, or victor. What is important is that individuals who have experienced these traumas have a voice in how they refer to themselves and that the words we use accurately reflect their lived experiences.

One particularly problematic term for survivors of kidnapping, as well as trafficking, interpersonal violence, and sexual abuse is Stockholm syndrome. Stockholm syndrome was originally proposed when trying to explain why some survivors of hostage-type situations do not, to the outside observer, appear to react to their situation with fight-or-flight behaviors, and furthermore seem to sympathize with their perpetrator as supposedly evidenced by lack of cooperation with police and expression of understanding or lack of expression of hostility toward their perpetrator. The term has since been used in other traumatic situations in which there are power imbalances, such as kidnapping and abusive relationships. The term Stockholm syndrome postulates a positive emotional relationship between victims and abusers that developed because of the trauma (Jülich, 2005). This term persists despite several critiques.

First, Stockholm syndrome has been interpreted to assume that there is a relationship between perpetrator and victim that reflects mutual care and affection between them, but that mutuality does not exist in cases of abduction, abuse, and perceived life threat (Graham et al., 1988). Furthermore, Stockholm syndrome attempts to explain survival from captivity as a formula derived from the perpetrator or observer's perspective (Namnyak et al., 2008). The variables include: the perceived threat to survival, the belief that the threat will be carried out, the captive's perception of some small kindness from the captor, and the hostage's experience of a perceived inability to escape. Each of these perspectives requires a level of conscious processing that contradicts what occurs physiologically during a terror state. These conceptual difficulties with Stockholm syndrome may explain why a review of the professional literature on survival techniques utilized during violent crimes (Jordan, 2013) demonstrates a lack of validated criteria for Stockholm syndrome as a psychiatric diagnosis along with a limited empirical research base (Geisler et al., 2013). The concept's origin in the media rather than research or clinical practice and its application to various crimes, ages, and interpersonal contexts raise questions about its meaning, validity, and continued relevance to theory building and research (Namnyak et al., 2008).

Although past theorists have suggested that the concept of Stockholm syndrome may help normalize survivors' behavior (Graham et al., 1988), it can be argued that the term does not reflect survivor experience, a critique not yet reported in the professional literature. A more accurate term would be **appeasement** because the word and overall description of appeasement emphasize the asymmetry in the relationship and the adaptive strategy to regulate and calm the captor, thus minimizing potential injury and abuse to the victim (Treisman, 2004).

Using Polyvagal Theory's (PVT) (Porges, 2011) assertion of the fundamental drive to internalize a sense of safety through sociality (Porges, 2022), we propose that the term appeasement may be operationally defined to more accurately describe a powerful instinctual strategy to survive and thrive regardless of the circumstances that can be separated from the concept of mutual affection and bonding with the perpetrator. This perspective can be applied to a variety of populations in which the power differential and basic survival needs perpetuate abuse and victimization regardless of the previous relationship with the perpetrator.

A BRIEF HISTORY OF APPEASEMENT AS A RESPONSE TO THREAT

Cantor and Price (2007) introduced the concept of appeasement, proposing that it is a natural mammalian response to entrapment or confinement. They suggested that appeasement could contribute to a better understanding of PTSD, Stockholm syndrome, and hostage dynamics. They proposed a step in articulating the normalization of a shutdown process and suggested implications for further understanding of victim dynamics. From their perspective, appeasement was a pacification and submission response. Since appeasement may serve to de-escalate a situation, it was suggested that the resulting pacification could contribute to survival. Although we reject the definition of Stockholm syndrome, Cantor and Price's appeasement concept helps operationalize dynamics present in circumstances in which a victim perceives and experiences threat to physical and psychological survival, especially when there is social isolation.

However, the Cantor and Price formulation of appeasement misses the two-way functional interaction, with the beneficial neurobiological impact of co-regulation, between perpetrator and victim that is better understood in defining appeasement through PVT. PVT (Porges, 2004, 2021, 2022) suggests that when faced with a life threat the foundational survival circuits originating in the brainstem, which regulate bodily organs via the autonomic nervous system, take over, moving the nervous system into a defensive state that supplants intentional behavior and social interactions. This process is observed as a variation of the cascade of fight-flight-freeze and potentially collapse and shutdown. This defensive cascade is dependent on autonomic states that functionally divert neural activity from higher brain structure; the result is reduced problem-solving capacity, limited cognitive processing, and displaced intentionality. Authentic forms of sociality are replaced with defensive strategies. Basic survival needs can determine and impact an individual's definition of life threat. For example, a parent facing housing and food insecurity can experience a lack of resources as a life threat, while social connection with the perpetrator may be experienced as a type of lifeline for an abductee.

Dissociation is a product of these foundational survival-oriented brainstem circuits and may serve as a buffer to the realization that one's life is at risk. From the polyvagal perspective, dissociation is viewed as an unconscious process that serves as a protective buffer when a threat is imminent. When an individual dissociates, their higher level of thinking is disrupted and the autonomic functions of the nervous system take over to optimize the regulation of bodily systems via the autonomic nervous system, even during life-challenging situations. Heart rate is slowed, digestion is interfered with, and awareness is impacted. Individuals who have suffered a traumatic (life-threatening) experience may internalize a feeling of extreme vulnerability and may have difficulty moving out of the dissociative state (Cantor & Price, 2007). From a pure survival stance, the slowing of heart rate, digestion interference, and impaired reality perception serve to save resources and protect from panic. Although these strategies of conservation are evolutionarily effective in asocial reptiles, they compromise homeostatic functions and sociality for humans. It is later, after the imminent threat has passed, that continued dissociation can become problematic, resulting in an array of mental and physical health comorbidities. By accepting the preeminent need to survive as a biological imperative, then disassociation could be studied as an adaptive survival-related physiological buffer in response to overwhelming circumstances. In extended periods of captivity or when under threat, an individual may function in a disassociated state, allowing for a tolerance of the intolerable.

A SCIENCE OF SAFETY LEADS TO AN UNDERSTANDING OF THE INTERNAL PROCESSES SUPPORTING SURVIVAL

The motivation to feel safe is a primary goal of the nervous system (Porges, 2022). PVT (Porges, 2021) provides an innovative scientific perspective that includes the neurophysiological description of the neural circuit that downregulates threat reactions. This physiological adjustment occurred during the evolutionary shift from asocial reptiles to social mammals (Porges, 2021). From the perspective of evolution, the shift in the autonomic nervous system is at the core of our ability to connect socially with others. When we apply and refine the concept of appeasement to PVT's assertion of the fundamental drive to internalize a sense of safety, we can more accurately describe the powerful instinctual desire to survive and thrive, regardless of the circumstances. In this context, the concept of appeasement eliminates most suggestions of mutual affection and bonding when in survival mode. The importance of feeling safe as an objective feeling has been debated going back to the earliest psychologists, such as Wilhelm Wundt (Ogden, 1907).

The ambiguous language used to describe emotions and feelings adds to the challenge of operationalizing a "felt sense of safety" (Porges, 2022). PVT suggests a definition of resilience in victims or survivors that conceptualizes a hierarchical explanation of feelings as higher brain interpretations of the neural signals conveying information regarding visceral organs (e.g., heart, gut, etc.) to the brainstem (Geisler et al., 2013). This biopsychological-evolutionary perspective emphasizes the foundational function of the autonomic state in the subjective experiences of global feelings and specific emotions. Within this hierarchical conceptualization, feelings of safety are preeminent and form the core of an enduring motivational system that shifts autonomic state, which in turn drives behaviors, emotions, and thoughts.

When faced with a physical threat, the natural response is to revert to a defensive stance, including fight-or-flight or a complete shutdown of emotional responses (Porges, 2022). Faced with a situation where no escape is immediately possible, some survivors may have the resource to express a type of *super social engagement* that may enable them to engage and effectively co-regulate and calm their perpetrator. We operationally define this capacity to co-regulate and calm the perpetrator as appeasement. The ability to access the appeasement process requires the neural capacity to manage a hybrid state that enables access to the calming and social cuing of the social engagement system (Porges, 2011, 2021, 2022), while simultaneously maintaining access to the energetic mobilization sympathetic system to engage fight-or-flight behaviors if necessary (Porges, 2011). Firsthand accounts from survivors of abduction underscore their awareness of the importance of establishing some type of social connection with the perpetrator. Repeated themes of awareness of the need for the establishment of connection are brought into therapeutic settings and are described by these survivors. In the terms used within PVT, this process of connection between the survivor and the perpetrator is considered co-regulation, a process through which there is a mutually beneficial bidirectional expression of cues of safety that functionally calm the autonomic nervous system and observable behavior (Mohandie, 2002).

Not only does social engagement help calm the autonomic nervous system, but also the withdrawal of this social engagement can dysregulate the system. This may necessitate a continued need for social engagement in order for the survivor to stay safe. In a study on co-regulation between mothers and infants, the caregiver of young children provides cues to calm infants. Specifically, prosodic tone was demonstrated to help regulate a baby who is having behavioral distress. Furthermore, the infants appeared distressed after social engagement was withdrawn from their caregiver. This particular study not only focused on the impact of prosodic tone on the infants' internal stress, it also presents the dysregularity impact of social withdrawal, suggesting the biodirectional impact between two autonomic nervous systems (Sarrate-Costa et al., 2022).

The ability to appease when in an activated state requires sufficient regulation to appear to the perpetrator as being calm. This form of regulation is not easily accessed or universally available but requires innate abilities to resources to inhibit the sympathetic arousal that would trigger the perpetrator's defense. Appearing calm and sending cues of engagement when faced with a predator provides an opportunity for co-regulation to occur. The visceral response to threat is a foundational survival circuit located in the brainstem and shared by several vertebrate species that preceded the evolution of social mammals. These circuits coordinate sympathetic arousal or dorsal vagal shutdown to support survival via defensive behaviors. The ability to be in the proximity of a life-threatening individual or event without shutting down, fleeing, or fighting, requires the ability to access the social engagement system with its neurophysiological dependence on the ventral vagal complex that regulates primary structures (e.g., facial expression, the intonation of voice) upon which social connection and co-regulation are dependent (Porges, 2022). Activating the neural substrate to appease is a challenge to the nervous system and is not an easily accessible intentional behavior. Rather, it requires a retuning of the autonomic state that opportunistically maintains sufficient inhibition over the adaptive threat reactions of the sympathetic nervous system (i.e., fight-or-flight) or the dorsal vagal system (i.e., shutdown, collapse, fainting, defecation). By placing an autonomic state at the core of feelings of safety or threat, the pragmatic survival behaviors of fight-or-flight and complex problem-solving strategies that would lead to escape are consequential and dependent on the facilitatory function of the autonomic nervous system in optimizing these strategies. Similarly, turning off the threat reactions and calming the autonomic state via the ventral vagal pathway will promote interpersonal accessibility, while simultaneously supporting the co-regulation of the autonomic states of both the survivor and the perpetrator. This model positions the autonomic state as an intervening variable, mediating the interpretation of contextual cues and shaping the reactions of both predator and captive. Within this conceptualization, depending on the individual's autonomic state, the same contextual cues and challenges may result in different behavioral, cognitive, and physiological reactions. This would be true both within and between individuals.

APPEASEMENT IS A POWERFUL UTILITY FOR SURVIVAL, ADAPTABILITY, AND RESILIENCE

There is a range of responses among individuals who share the same traumatic environmental context. Studies on hostages indicate that a calm, regulated state may increase survival rates (Jaeger et al., 2014). Furthermore, the adaptive utility of appeasement in the experiences of survivors of abuse may functionally neutralize defensive strategies in the victim as well as the perpetrator via neural circuits communicating cues of safety. Thus, if the perpetrator starts to feel safe with the victim, then there is the possibility of the perpetrator's nervous system calming and receiving cues of safety emitted by the victim, resulting in less violence, anger, and injury. This is not to be confused with the notion of fawning. Fawning is the use of people-pleasing to diffuse conflict and earn the approval of others (see Owca, 2020). It's a maladaptive way of creating safety in our connections with others by essentially mirroring the imagined expectations and desires of other people. Reid and colleagues (2013) discuss fawning:

> We propose that the victim is not using fawning techniques, but is indeed influencing the perpetrator by an internal process of co-regulation (Porges, 2004). Co-regulation encourages regulation of both captor and abductee. It is a feature that enables all mammals to down-regulate defensive strategies like yelling and screaming and instead promotes sociality by enabling psychological and physical proximity without the consequences of injury, even in survival situations. It is this calming mechanism that adaptively adjusts to protect us when in fight-or-flight mode (Geisler et al., 2013). This message has been confused by some as Stockholm syndrome or as a type of affection instead of a powerful adaptive survival reaction. In fact, fawning does not use the powerful biological forces of co-regulation. Fawning involves less attunement and is more one sided. In addition, from a polyvagal perspective, fawning may have the opposite effect of appeasement because it could be perceived by the aggressor as a highly vulnerable state, inciting more aggression.

Bonanno and Burton' s research (2013) builds on the growing body of literature that underscores the acceptance that the fluid process of the nervous system and self-regulation has become an important variable for understanding resiliency (Bonanno, 2021; Chen & Bonanno, 2020; Jiang et al., 2021). In summary, the first step of self-regulation is an assessment of what is required in the specific scenario. The second step, according to Bonanno's theory, is the choice of what they describe as a regulatory response. The question becomes, "What can I do?" Lastly, the question becomes, "Is it working?" The last question requires a conscious assessment of the strategy. It may be assumed that in a life-or-death situation, the question becomes, "How likely am I to be kept alive?" This research supports the notion that the nervous system, especially brain structures involved in regulating intentional behavior, plays an important role in survival. However, from a biological perspective, what is missing is the understanding of the role that foundational brainstem survival mechanisms play in response to imminent danger. It is also unclear how one develops a resilient enough autonomic state to be able to have an appeasement response in the face of that threat.

It is well documented that conscious thought is impacted by the biological response to terror (Pyszczynski et al., 1999). In times of life threat, the foundational survival circuits in our nervous system take over and interfere with executive functioning, suggesting that logical thought and strategy development are dependent on these unconscious foundational survival processes. All mammals operate from the perspective of safety versus vulnerability. A flexible nervous system provides options for survival and resilience, although these actions may be the result of unconscious processes. Animal models have also presented data to support that all mammals reach a level of saturation in which the threshold is too high for one nervous system to influence the other without rest and deactivation (Chemtob et al., 1992). This is important when understanding resilience because, in many situations, the fate of the victim is, of course, predicated by the pathology or motivation of the perpetrator.

CLINICAL IMPLICATIONS

Treating trauma victims or survivors is not a one-size-fits-all process. There are numerous treatment approaches, many supported by robust evidence-based research (Etchison & Kleist, 2020; Han et al., 2021; MacFarlane & Kaplan, 2012; Warshaw et al., 2013; Williamson et al., 2010). The common variable across modalities is the adaptive nervous system of the individual trying to make sense of the horrific past. The question initially is "Why didn't you leave?" but a more important question is "How did you survive?" The clinical focus should support the natural instinctual process that kept the individual alive. Post recovery, the challenge becomes how to help support the internalization and the realization that there is no longer danger and life threat. There lies the dilemma; victims or survivors of long-term and isolative abuse seen in kidnapping and interpersonal violence are often led to believe there will always be danger and life threat even when the perpetrator is not present. Fear immobilizes and compromises higher level processing, reinforcing dependency.

The belief that one fell in love with the perpetrator can be confusing and frightening to an individual who has experienced captivity. The concern can lead to fears of further vulnerability and may connote the message that the individual is capable of being easily fooled. Another factor is the message given to family members that the individual intentionally did not escape out of a twisted allegiance to the perpetrator. This message is also confusing and dysregulating to family members and supporters, which can prevent the family members from being actively supportive of the survivor. Perception of support is important to the healing and well-being of the whole family system (Bailey et al., 2020). To begin to receive and give this support, it is important for survivors and their families to understand that kidnapping, trafficking, and intimate partner violence by definition occur in contexts of differentials. Captivity in these circumstances can be easily confused with love as survival needs shape dependency in the same way a small child is forced to depend on the caregiver.

Finally, shame has been identified as one of the key factors underlying many trauma symptoms (López-Castro et al., 2019; Saraiya & Lopez-Castro, 2016). Ideas such as Stockholm syndrome can increase shame. Providing survivors with the appeasement framework normalizes and commends the survival mechanism given the rare capacity to engage the social network when under threat. Appeasement can and should be framed as an alternate explanation for what may be a strong survival tactic, a tactic not solely intentional, but dependent on the capacities of a resilient autonomic state as a resource.

PURPOSE AND HOPEFUL
OUTCOME OF THIS ARTICLE

In the field of trauma research, recognizing resiliency as the norm has grown from being considered rare to being viewed as a majority outcome (Bonanno, 2021). What is not so clear is what variables constitute resilience. A large body of research has looked at personality variables, supportive resources, financial and educational assets, minimal searching for meaning and experience, and expression of positive emotions (Bonanno, 2004; Bonanno et al., 2015). Another important variable cited is emotion-regulation strategies. This poses the question of how or what makes one individual more able to handle adverse events more positively than others. Research has not been able to accurately assess the future coping ability of individuals perceived to be resilient at the time of traumatic stress.

As Bonnano's research presents a picture of modest outcomes for isolating and categorizing individual variables found in the resiliency literature (Bonanno, 2021), we postulate that operationalizing a singular explanation for survival and achieving resiliency cannot be condensed down to a singular or multivariable recipe. Logically, a state preserving resources and altering the reality of circumstances would be optimum for preventing overwhelming anxiety and, in some cases, what Walter Cannon and Barbara Lex referred to as "voodoo death" (Cannon, 1942; Lex, 1974).

The goal of our proposed model of appeasement is to provide an alternative to the Stockholm syndrome in understanding how a survivor may have navigated and functionally adaptively negotiated with the perpetrator's nervous system. Additionally, we propose the introduction of a powerful unconscious survival response. Appeasement is not guaranteed to achieve survival, but we propose appeasement to be one possible unconscious reflexive process when faced with a life threat in the context of interpersonal violence. This life threat is the key factor for appeasement to occur. The understanding that one person's nervous system can unconsciously impact another nervous system has been identified in research looking at therapeutic presence and variables contributing to effective therapeutic interventions (Geller & Porges, 2014; Porges & Dana, 2018). When this theory is applied to circumstances involving captivity and life threat, it provides a plausible explanation of how we can understand and honor the survivors who have had a regulated nervous system that when confronted with life threats enabled them to express features of calmness, interest, and social engagement, thus possibly diffusing or altering the agitated state of the perpetrator. As a caveat, the model is solely explanatory to honor the capacity of the survivors who have had the resource to access appeasement during life-threatening situations. The model does not infer that this capacity can be learned or trained. Further research should include the impact of operationalizing this concept in a manner that supports the healing and well-being of survivors of a variety of crimes. An important research question should be: If the survivors' behaviors are interpreted as unconscious processes dependent on their nervous system, will it impact the recovery process, especially if their behaviors are conceptualized from their perspective and not that of the perpetrator?

6

The Sensitive Patient Through the Lens of the Polyvagal Theory: A Neuroscience of Threat and Safety

Stephen W. Porges

INTRODUCTION

Contemporary medical treatments frequently fail our biological needs by not acknowledging the foundational neural platform that mediates the clinical expression of patients who report a variety of hypersensitivities through the basic exteroceptive pathways (i.e., touch, hearing, sight, smell, and taste) often involving reactions to chemicals, pollutants, foods, medications, and background stimulation as well as through interoceptive pathways related to visceral and skeletal motor pain. This chapter proposes that several of the clinical features of sensitive patients are not determined solely by a sensitivity to the specific form of stimulation but represent a coordinated adaptive neural reaction by an autonomic nervous system (ANS) and other systems involved in supporting homeostatic functions (e.g., endocrine, immune, neuropeptide, etc.) being locked in a coordinated state of defense. Within this chapter, the ANS is broadly defined to include interdependent systems involved in supporting homeostatic functions. From a polyvagal perspective, the focus is whether the structures and system within the body are supporting safety and enhance homeostasis or are supporting reactions to threat that disrupt homeostatic functions. Hypothetically, once the ANS and related systems are in a state of defense, thresholds to detect threat are lowered, resulting in a generalized hypersensitivity syndrome amplifying reactivity via multiple sensory channels. Thus, the frequently described symptoms by sensitive patients are functional reactions to cues of threat emanating from both within and outside the body.

Often the sensitive patient reports clinical symptoms associated with chronic pain and a subjective discomfort without an identifiable metric documenting a bodily reaction. This has led to the labeling of many of these patients with the ambiguous and potentially demeaning diagnosis of having **medically unexplained symptoms** (MUS). MUS is a term liberally used to describe persistent bodily complaints for which adequate examination does not reveal sufficiently explanatory structural or other specified pathology (Henningsen et al., 2007). The term is commonly used to describe people with pain and discomfort in general practice and secondary care and includes noncardiac chest pain, irritable bowel syndrome, and fibromyalgia (Marks & Hunter, 2015). More recently there has been a shift toward an acknowledgment that although neural or physiological markers may not be detected under examination or through available assessments, these disorders represent measurable shifts in function. This acknowledgment of functional disorders such as functional somatic disorders (Burton et al., 2020), functional neurological disorders (Rajabalee et al., 2022; Stone, 2016), and functional gastrointestinal disorders (Hyams, 2016) including functional abdominal pain disorders (Kovacic et al., 2020) has resulted in a heightened interest in identifying potential underlying neurobiological mechanisms that may lead to more objective diagnoses.

There is an overlap in the conceptualizations of functional disorders and dysautonomia. Although many functional disorders have an autonomic feature of dysregulation, dysautonomia as a diagnostic category tends to be used to describe disorders of the ANS that have an organic etiology. Along these lines, postural orthostatic tachycardia syndrome (POTS) caused by dysregulation of the autonomic system falls under the umbrella of functional disorders, while POTS caused by autoimmune autonomic neuropathy falls under the umbrella of dysautonomia. A polyvagal perspective would lead to a more expansive use of the term dysautonomia, which would include features of autonomic dysregulation in functional disorders independent of an assumed etiology.

This chapter will elaborate on the premise that functional symptoms experienced by the sensitive patient share a neurophysiological substrate of being locked in a state of defense. This chronic state of defense often includes a disruption of the systems involved in managing and maintaining homeostatic function (e.g., autonomic, endocrine, neuropeptide, and immune systems). When the autonomic nervous system's role in health and distress is discussed, it is assumed that the function of the ANS is not independent of endocrine, immune, neuropeptide, and psychological processes. The perspective emphasized is that the nervous system is integrated with other systems facilitating bidirectional communication between the brain and bodily organs to foster health and survival. Consistent with this perspective, these clinical symptoms would be functional parallels, via interoceptive pathways, to the exteroceptive hypersensitivities often reported as a psychological or sensory comorbidity. It is hoped that this perspective will lead to both a better understanding of the neurobiological substrate of hypersensitivities and more effective treatments.

ARE SENSITIVE PATIENTS LOCKED IN AN AUTONOMIC STATE OF DEFENSE?

Defensive reactions evolved to acutely, but not chronically, deal with threat. In the healthy individual acute reactions temporarily disrupt the homeostatic functions that support bodily health, growth, and restoration. Optimistically, once the threat has passed, the nervous system returns to a state that would support homeostatic function. This recovery phase is characteristic of a resilient and flexible system that recovers to optimize function both within the physical body (e.g., homeostatic functions) and with the behavioral and psychological interactions with others in the environment that we conceptualize as mental health and sociality. However, if the disruption is chronic, then the nervous system adapts by retuning to a defensive state in which the threshold to internal and external cues to threat are lowered. The result is a greater sensitivity to cues of threat, which is frequently characterized by the diffuse symptoms of hypersensitivity clinically observed in the sensitive patient. The premise of the chapter is that hypersensitivities are the product of a nervous system maintaining hypervigilance to detect threat even when there is no longer a threat, a predator, an injury, or an illness due to a pathogen. Embedded in this neurophysiologically informed understanding of symptoms is a path to positive outcomes. Due to the hierarchical function of our nervous system, cues of safety are instrumental in inhibiting threat reactions and fostering recovery.

The history of modern medicine lacks insights into our phylogenetic history of humans as social mammals. In contrast to being informed from our evolutionary history, contemporary medicine focuses on a mechanistic cause-and-effect model of disease, illness, and injury. Moreover, it makes little distinction between acute and chronic disruptions. By not acknowledging that feelings of threat and safety support or disrupt homeostatic functions, the medical community has marginalized its most important ally, the body's innate ability to heal when not in a state of threat.

Simply stated, there is a bidirectional link between our ANS and our conscious brain. When our ANS is supporting homeostatic functions, we have the capacity to feel safe. When our ANS supports defense, our feelings are biased toward threat. This link is bidirectional: top-down when the brain influences our ANS and bottom-up when the ANS influences our thoughts and feelings. Functionally, feelings of safety and threat are our brain's interpretations of whether our ANS is in a state supporting homeostasis or defense.

A NEUROBIOLOGY OF SAFETY

Although neuroscience has established the impact of threat on the nervous system, with consequential degrading impact on mental and physical health, research on the neurobiology of safety has been minimal. Acknowledging that feelings of safety are an emergent property of autonomic state would shift investigations of feelings of safety from a subjective to an objective science.

The need to feel safe is functionally our body speaking through our ANS— influencing our mental and physical health, social relationships, cognitive processes, and behavioral repertoire and serving as a neurophysiological substrate upon which societal institutions dependent on cooperation and trust function are based. Feeling safe functions as a subjective index of a neural platform that supports both sociality and the homeostatic processes optimizing health, growth, and restoration. Feelings of safety are not equivalent to an objective measurement of safety, which may pragmatically be defined as the removal of threat. Feeling safe is more akin to a felt sense as described by Eugene Gendlin (2017). This is consistent with important work by Craig (2002, 2003), who emphasized the pathways involved in interoception and Critchley and colleagues (2004), who have applied imaging techniques to document the representation of interoceptive processes in the brain.

To understand the motivation to feel safe, feelings of safety may be conceptualized from the perspective of the Polyvagal Theory (PVT). PVT provides an innovative scientific perspective that incorporates an understanding of phylogenetic shifts in vertebrate neuroanatomy and neurophysiology; this perspective identifies neural circuits that down-regulate neural regulation of threat reactions and functionally neutralize defensive strategies via neural circuits communicating cues of safety. Feelings of safety are operationally the product of cues of safety, via neuroception (Porges, 2004), down-regulating autonomic states that support threat reactions and up-regulating autonomic states that support interpersonal accessibility and homeostatic functions. Basically, when humans feel safe, their nervous systems support the homeostatic functions of health, growth, and restoration, while they simultaneously become accessible to others without feeling or expressing threat and vulnerability.

The clinical profile of a sensitive patient tends to define a diffuse phenotypic diagnosis in search of a diagnostic metric that would optimistically lead to an effective treatment model. This perspective is confronted with the reality of the training of physicians and their available tools. In the clinic, patients frequently describe feelings, while physicians seek tests and assessments to document a neurophysiology or a neurochemistry substrate and to infer mechanisms of dysfunction that would support the patient's subjective experiences. In clinical settings sensitive patients are often on a frustrating journey to get confirmation that their symptoms represent a disorder that has a physiological substrate and can be effectively treated. Without metrics of dysfunction, the patient often is treated as feigning symptoms or told that the symptoms are of psychiatric origin—the uninformed view that mental and physical health are disparate domains. The patient on this journey believes that once the physiological substrate can be confirmed, the information will lead to efficient and effective treatments. In general, this is wishful thinking, due in part to a cause-and-effect orientation within medicine that focuses on causes initially being external to the body and effects reflecting reliable and predictable dysfunction to bodily organs. Similarly, this simplistic cause-and-effect model is assumed on the treatment side of illness and injury. If there is an identifiable cause, then there is an identifiable treatment. This logical thinking follows the basic principles of science in the search of laws of nature. However, what if this principle is too limiting in dealing with the myriad of individual differences and even temporal intraindividual variations to effectively understand and optimize physical and mental health? What if dysfunction is initially reflected not in the chemistry of blood, but in how the nervous system communicates with visceral organs? Do physicians have tools to evaluate the functional status of neurophysiological feedback circuits that shift resources from homeostatic functions to metabolically costly defense and finally to metabolically conservative shutdown strategies that would lead to end-organ damage? The pessimistic answer is no. However, there is a scientific literature that if incorporated into health care would have the potential of reducing the dysfunctional impact of symptoms and optimizing function.

WALTER HESS: A UNIFIED MODEL OF THE NERVOUS SYSTEM

The contemporary conceptualization of bidirectional communication between visceral organs and the brain is rooted in the work of Walter Hess. In 1949, Hess was awarded the Nobel Prize in Physiology or Medicine for his paradigm-shifting research on the central control of visceral organs. As documented in Chapter 4, his Nobel lecture discussing brain control of visceral organs provides the context upon which development, application, and acceptance of neuro-visceral disciplines such as neuro-cardiology or neuro-gastroenterology have emerged. This integrative one-nervous-system perspective encourages a better understanding of the dynamics of neural regulation of an integrated nervous system, while being constrained by the limited paradigms that are frequently used in the contemporary training of physicians with an emphasis on end-organ defined specialties within internal medicine.

By emphasizing the central mechanisms that mediate the dynamic regulation of peripheral organs, Hess anticipated the need for methodologies and technologies to continuously monitor the neural circuits involving both defined brain structures and peripheral nerves in the regulation of visceral function and state. His lecture provides a framework for evaluating subsequent progress in developing theory, describing neural circuits, providing measurement technologies, and understanding clinical conditions. The lecture provides a succinct statement: (1) to emphasize the importance of feedback circuits linking peripheral organs to brain structures and the bidirectionality of these feedback circuits; and (2) to acknowledge that, although much can be learned about neural structures and functions via traditional experimental paradigms (e.g., neural blockade, surgery, electrical stimulation), the dynamic feedback circuits cannot be adequately studied through these paradigms. This limits our understanding of how these circuits function in real time to support survival challenges, a limitation that still characterizes much of the research in contemporary neurophysiology.

THE LEGACY OF LANGLEY

In his Nobel lecture, Hess paid respects to Langley (1921), who contributed to the understanding of the paired antagonistic innervations of the internal organs and the definition of sympathetic and parasympathetic functions. Prior to Hess, the prevailing conceptualization of the neural regulation of visceral organs focused on vegetative and autonomic features. Hess (1949) notes, however, "In contrast to the exploration of the vegetative nervous system, which is very far-reaching (even if it is not still without certain inner contradictions), stands a relatively limited understanding of the central organization of the whole mechanism of control."

Hess was aware that, although the components of a feedback circuit might be identified and studied independently, the functioning of independent parts did not explain how the system as a whole functioned dynamically during the moment-to-moment challenges of life. This limitation was in part dependent on the methodologies of the day that required pharmacological, surgical, or electrical manipulations to block or stimulate global branches of the ANS that shared either a specific neurotransmitter (e.g., acetylcholine) or an easily identifiable nerve (e.g., vagus) that could be cut or stimulated. Needed was a technology that would enable real-time dynamic monitoring of various limbs of the ANS.

Hess's view of an integrated nervous system involving the mutual and dynamic bidirectional interactions between the brain and visceral organs did not receive traction within traditional medical education. In contrast, medical education confirmed Hess's view that advances in specialization resulting in medical subdisciplines threaten the ability to appreciate the organization from an organ to the integrated organism. Few physicians are familiar with Hess's landmark research and his warning against partitioning the body into central and peripheral nervous systems. From Hess's perspective there is only one integrated nervous system. Instead of incorporating Hess's prescient view, medical education remained dependent on an earlier and more limited view of the ANS proposed by Langley (1921), which has remained the predominant model taught in medical schools. If you doubt this, ask a cardiologist, a nephrologist, a hepatologist, a gastroenterologist, or even a more eclectic internist, if specific neural pathways could contribute to symptoms of dysfunction. If they agree, ask them what neural test would confirm this speculation. In addition, ask the specialist if anxiety, depression, or chronic stress could be a function of or the cause of an organ dysfunction. Also inquire about the possibility that medical treatments to peripheral organs could, via afferent feedback from the organ to the brain, contribute to the specific symptoms experienced. These inquiries will provide an understanding of the massive gaps in our knowledge involving the role of the nervous system in health and illness.

Langley was a distinguished professor of physiology at the University of Cambridge. In 1898 he proposed the term ANS "to describe the sympathetic system and the allied nervous system of the cranial and sacral nerves, and for the local nervous system of the gut" (p. 270). Collectively, the autonomic function of the cranial and sacral nerves defined the parasympathetic nervous system, and the nervous system of the gut became known as the enteric nervous system. In the first paragraph of his classic text, *The Autonomic Nervous System, Part I*, he clearly provided his definition of the autonomic nervous system (Langley, 1921). He stated that "the autonomic nervous system consists of the nerve cells and nerve fibers, by means of which efferent impulses pass to tissues other than multi-nuclear striated muscle."

Langley's view of the ANS consists of efferent pathways and target organs in the viscera, a top-down model excluding both the brain structures involved in regulation and the afferent pathways communicating peripheral organ status back to the brain. In fact, the Langley model does not include the requisite components of a system capable of regulation through feedback. Such a system would require a central regulator connected to a target structure via both motor and sensory pathways. The Langley model disrupted the expanding view of an integrated whole-body nervous system proposed by Bernard (1865) and described by Darwin (1872) that was characterized by bidirectional communication between the brain and the visceral organs. A naive treatment of autonomic responses without the consequential influence of afferent feedback is consistent with Langley's (1921) definition of a limited ANS excluding the influence of the sensory fibers that accompany most visceral motor fibers. Although the definition is often expanded to include both visceral afferents and central structures (e.g., medulla, hypothalamus), contemporary textbooks focus on the motor components, minimizing in their description the important role of afferent and central contributions to the regulation of the peripheral autonomic organs. This bias, by ignoring the importance of the afferent pathways, neglects the feedback and central regulatory features of a functional system. Moreover, it limits the study of the dynamic regulatory function of the ANS, since the regulation of visceral state and the maintenance of homeostasis implicitly assume a feedback system with the necessary constituent components of motor, sensory, and regulatory structures. Thus, from a systems perspective, the ANS includes afferent pathways conveying information regarding the visceral organs and the brain areas that interpret the afferent feedback and exert control over the motor output back to the visceral organs.

Walter Cannon (1927), another iconic physiologist, proposed that the autonomic responses associated with emotions were driven primarily by brain structures and transmitted through sympathetic-adrenal pathways to support fight-or-flight behaviors. Cannon's view contradicted William James's (1884), who proposed that it was the afferent feedback from the body that framed the emotional experience. Cannon's view was readily accepted and merged with the views of Hans Selye (1936, 1956) to dominate contemporary views of stress physiology. Perhaps James's lack of physiological sophistication and an inability to describe the neural pathways through which the afferent feedback traveled from the periphery to the brain contributed to this bias.

The generalized stress responses described by Cannon and Selye emphasized the sympathetic nervous system and the adrenals. These views minimized the role of the vagus and did not acknowledge the primary role of afferent vagal pathways as a surveillance system in physiological and emotional regulation, communicating organ status to brain structures. As researchers attempt to communicate and translate findings and conceptualizations into clinical practice, they continue to be confronted with the products of a medical education that conceptualized the ANS within the limitations of the Langley definition. This restricted model influenced physicians' general understanding and conceptualization of the communication between the brain and visceral organs. At best, physicians acknowledge the top-down communication from brain to organ, although virtually all physicians have limited knowledge about the afferents monitoring visceral organs and informing the brain centers that regulate the organs. The Langley model, in part, has been misunderstood, since its contribution represented important progress by providing an organizing principle to the efferent regulation of visceral organs. It was not proposed as an alternative to the more integrative features of visceral regulation proposed approximately 50 years earlier by Bernard (1865). From a historical perspective, it is important to reconcile these discontinuities as the science and clinical practice become reintegrated into neuro-visceral disciplines. It was in search of a more integrative model of the neural regulation of the ANS that PVT emerged (Porges, 1995, 1998, 2001, 2007, 2009, 2011, 2021a, 2021b, 2022, 2023).

PVT was introduced as an attempt to shift the science of psychophysiology from a descriptive science conducting empirical studies and describing correlations between psychological and physiological processes to an inferential science generating and testing hypotheses related to common neural pathways involving both mental and physiological processes (i.e., a science of brain-body communication). It was the first volley in a conceptual dialogue challenging the questions and methods involved in psychophysiological research and especially in the subdomain of cardiovascular psychophysiology.

POLYVAGAL THEORY: EMPHASIZING
AUTONOMIC FUNCTION AS A CORE PROCESS
UNDERLYING MENTAL AND PHYSICAL HEALTH

In the initial presentation PVT was an attempt to provide an integrated theory (Porges, 1995) based on the literatures of several disciplines that would provide the basis for testable hypotheses relating autonomic function to sociality and health in humans and nonhuman mammals. By acknowledging the important role of autonomic state as an intervening variable, the theory has profound consequences on our understanding of behavior and clinical symptoms. Attending to the clinical histories of sensitive patients will confirm that many have a severe trauma history, which may include medical trauma as well as abuse. These survivors often have myriad clinical symptoms that have been inappropriately diagnosed as comorbidities. Collectively, the symptoms usually reflect a disruption in the homeostatic processes that would support health, growth, and restoration. These symptoms reflect a nervous system under threat. Sequentially, as threat is processed by the nervous system it initiates a familiar clinical cascade in which nonneural pathways (e.g., endocrine, histamine, cytokine, etc.) support a physiology that has shifted from supporting health to a chronic state of defense that may result in organ damage and subsequently organ failure and death.

As we investigate the autonomic regulation of those who present clinical hypersensitivities, there is frequently a dysfunctional neural regulation substrate (see Kozlowska et al., 2020). Unfortunately, the observation does not necessarily lead to a reliable treatment model. However, we can learn from patients with these symptoms. The patients are reflecting symptoms of a disruption in the internal regulation of their bodily organs. The primary message is that the feedback systems that in a healthy individual would ensure end-organ health is well managed and healthy are compromised in the hypersensitive individual. By using the term homeostasis and the support of homeostatic functions as shorthand for the processes that manage the health of our organs, we can operationalize and potentially quantify what is functionally happening to these patients. By listening to the patients, we may find other important clues including that the feedback from their body (i.e., bodily feelings) may have a degree of numbness or insensitivity to internal feelings. This illustrates that the dampened feedback circuits that evolve to maintain health are disrupted and expressed as blunted visceral feelings. Rather than positive feelings, patients experience the consequences of a disruption in homeostatic function: pain, disrupted social relationships, and symptoms of mental and physical illness.

Often, survivors of adversity have been confronted with therapists, colleagues, friends, and family who have assumed that intentionality was a major contributor to their asociality and clinical symptoms. In fact, many well-intentioned supporters may have expressed the faulty assumption that their behavior was intentional and could be reliably modified by incentives. During the past decade trauma-informed therapies have incorporated a somatic orientation that respects the powerful influence that bodily states can have in resisting intentional behaviors and insights. The work of Bessel van der Kolk highlights the acceptance of this trend (2015).

Clinical symptoms through the lens of PVT emphasize that our cognitive intent and our bodily state can promote competing behavioral outcomes. As an observer of both behavior and autonomic state, my bet is on the potency of autonomic state. This conclusion is supported by the link between autonomic state and feelings of threat and our embedded biobehavioral program to survive. Since these states of defense are regulated by primitive neural circuits, circuits shared with many more ancient vertebrates, intentional self-regulation efforts originating in the cortex are frequently ineffective in down-regulating survival-driven reactions to threat, which are dependent on lower brain structures. The survival program is evolutionarily old, while the program that turns off threat reactions with cues of safety to promote calmness, sociality, and homeostatic functions is a mammalian innovation of a repurposed ANS that may be influenced by higher brain structures. Although the calming system is effective in down-regulating threat reactions in response to mild threats and effectively enabling feelings of safety, the calming system is difficult to access when the defensive systems are in a highly activated survival mode.

Functionally, we need to conceptualize the model as having both bottom-up and top-down pathways with the bottom-up pathways being a combination of being both reflexive and derivative of early evolutionary survival processes (Kleckner et al., 2017). The foundational brainstem survival circuits are functionally hardwired via neuroception. Thus, although cues of safety or threat will trigger top-down reflexive changes in autonomic state, the states become associated with thoughts and behaviors. This process is initiated through interoception (Craig, 2002, 2003; Critchley et al., 2004; Porges, 1993); bottom-up feelings of autonomic state are interpreted by higher brain structures, which in turn may initiate intentional behaviors. Interoception is the perception of sensations from inside the body and includes the perception of physical sensations related to internal-organ function such as heartbeat, respiration, satiety, and needs to urinate and defecate. This linkage between feelings (i.e., autonomic state) and behaviors and thoughts forms the neurophysiological basis for aspects of associative learning. The premise of many trauma-informed therapeutic strategies is to separate the feelings from the associative thoughts and behaviors.

CONCLUSION: CLAIMING OUR PHYLOGENETIC HERITAGE

Awareness of the neural systems underlying PVT informs both health-care professionals and their patients regarding the threats to survival that can shift autonomic state, moving it through sequential neural platforms or states that mimic evolution in reverse or dissolution (Jackson, 1884). Functionally, to inhibit the trajectory of dissolution to calm, we must first use the competence of our social engagement system (a uniquely mammalian myelinated vagal pathway involving brainstem structures regulating vocal intonation and facial expressions) to connect with others and calm our physiology. Without these resources, we are vulnerable to move into adaptive defensive states, which would include lowering thresholds to detect threat and to potentially present the symptom profile of a sensitive patient.

PVT focuses on the phylogenetic transitions of the ANS. Specifically, the theory focuses on the functional consequences through which the ANS was repurposed during the transition from asocial reptiles to social mammals. This focus has had a serendipitous benefit to the scientific documentation of the structures and mechanisms outlined in the theory, since the brainstem area is relatively small and there is sufficient comparative neuroanatomy conducted to map the changes in the brainstem pathways and their potential adaptive functions. The theory focuses on how phylogenetic changes in the neural regulation of the heart provided the foundational properties for feelings of safety and emergent sociality. This chapter emphasizes that these two psychological constructs have a dependence on an evolved link between social engagement behaviors and vagal regulation. However, there are convergent evolutionary changes in how the neuropeptides of vasopressin and oxytocin function to support the advent of sociality in mammals (Carter et al., 2020; Carter, 2022; Porges, 2001). Specifically, oxytocin plays an important convergent role with the ANS in enabling mammals to immobilize without fear, give birth, and experience intimacy without recruiting physiological defensive reactions through dorsal vagal pathways (e.g., bradycardia, syncope, and diarrhea).

This chapter has emphasized that an autonomic nervous system locked in a state of defense may be a common underlying neurophysiological feature of the sensitive patient. This may influence both mental and physical health, which through a disruption of optimal autonomic function has become sensitive (i.e., biased) to the detection of threat cues, both from the internal and external environment, that preclude feelings of safety that are manifest in health and sociality. It is this fundamental process of feeling safe that has enabled humans to survive through the opportunistic features of trusting social engagements, which have the co-regulatory capacity to mitigate the metabolically costly defense reactions. The short-term benefits of safety are obvious since they support homeostatic functions. However, there are also long-term consequences of feelings of safety that are reflected in the emergence of communities in which feelings of safety expand through spontaneous social engagement and prosocial behaviors within the community become the norm. Thus, our sociality enables an expansion of those with whom we feel safe and trust. This, of course, is the underlying premise of societies and their institutions including legal systems, business transactions, political negotiations, and international treaties.

Neuromodulation Using Computer-Altered Music to Treat a Ten-Year-Old Child Unresponsive to Standard Interventions for Functional Neurological Disorder

Nadia Rajabalee, Kasia Kozlowska, Seung Yeon Lee,
Blanche Savage, Clare Hawkes, Daniella Siciliano, Stephen
W. Porges, Susannah Pick, and Souraya Torbey

CASE HISTORY

Anna (not her real name) was a 10-year-old girl in Year 5 of primary school referred to the Mind–Body Program by a pediatrician for treatment of functional somatic symptoms—unsteady gait, blurry vision, periods of confusion or appearing dazed, and persisting headache—that had been triggered in the context of a viral illness. Anna lived with her parents and a younger sibling. Both parents worked full time in professional positions. The family history included rheumatoid arthritis (mother), epilepsy (uncle), and Type 2 diabetes (grandfather) on the mother's side of the family, and colorectal cancer (grandfather) on the father's side. Anna had been diagnosed with celiac disease at age 6, which was being managed with a gluten-free diet.

Presentation

In the 3 weeks prior to referral, Anna had been ill with a viral infection: a runny nose, sneezing, nasal congestion, and frontal headaches. In the second week of this illness, she developed blurriness in the right eye, neck stiffness, pain on eye movement, facial pain, lethargy, and anorexia. With a working diagnosis of partially treated meningitis, she was admitted to hospital for intravenous antibiotics (5-day course). A swab returned rhinovirus positive. In the third week of this illness, her headache persisted, the blurred vision spread to both eyes, and she developed additional neurological symptoms: unsteady gait and difficulty speaking (mumbling). Some days later she became confused, appeared dazed and slow to respond to the pediatrician's questions, and developed slurred speech, right-hand weakness with an occasional tremor, right-jaw twitching, and ongoing unsteadiness that required a walker for mobility. Routine bloods—full blood count, electrolytes, inflammatory markers, and thyroid function tests—were normal. A contrast-enhanced CT scan and an MRI were also normal, with an incidental finding of Chiari malformation (4 mm). A lumbar puncture was deemed potentially unsafe and therefore was not performed. A review by a neurologist yielded the diagnosis of functional neurological disorder (FND) and comorbid complex/chronic pain (see Box 7.1). (For details about the neurology examination for children with FND, see Kozlowska and Mohammad [2023]).

Psychological Medicine Assessment with Anna and Her Family

The family assessment with our team—a child and adolescent psychiatrist, a clinical psychologist, and two pediatric trainees on their psychological medicine rotation—took place via telehealth in the midst of the COVID-19 pandemic. The family was seated in one clinic room, and each member of the team was in a separate room.

Developmental History: Summary of Key Issues

Anna's early developmental history—in utero, delivery, developmental milestones in the first 5 years—were all unremarkable. Anna had been an outgoing and happy preschooler. She underwent tonsillectomy and adenoidectomy when she was 3 years old and had been diagnosed with celiac disease at 6 years of age (Year 1 at school) after she had experienced persistent abdominal pain and was found to be anemic. Anna also began to experience recurring headaches.

Anna showed an aptitude for learning, and her school reports described her as a conscientious and bright student. There was a history of school stress, beginning in Year 1 of school and continuing into Year 5. Anna reported that

BOX 7.1
Summary of Anna's Positive Rule-In Signs for Functional Neurological Disorder in the Neurology Examination

Repeated neurology examinations with Anna yielded positive rule-in signs—listed below—consistent with FND:

- A very dramatic, sudden onset of symptoms, occurring spontaneously or in the context of an identifiable stressor—in this case rhinovirus infection and incidental finding of a Chiari malformation on CT.
- Mixed neurological signs that were not clinically congruent in their origin. For example, Anna's unsteady gait was subsequently complicated by right-hand weakness, which became a right-hand tremor, which then reverted back to right-hand weakness (back and forth, back and forth).
- Anna's leg and right-arm weakness varied with distraction.
- Anna's tremor could be entrained (made to follow a particular frequency), and it increased with attention and decreased with distractibility.
- Anna's symptoms varied with distractibility. They were better when she was engaged in an activity she liked—for example, coloring—and worse when her parents focused on the symptoms

her years at school had been made very stressful because her class had been ongoingly disrupted by children with behavioral problems (confirmed by Anna's school teacher). In this context Anna also described her distress pertaining to a variety of issues: failing to receive acknowledgment from her teacher for working well (Year 1); the stress of a strict teacher constantly yelling at the class, making Anna's ears hurt (Year 2); loss of a close friend (who left that school), feelings of loneliness and exclusion, and experiences of being bullied (Year 3); the loss of her teacher, who left due to stress and was followed by multiple substitute teachers (Year 4); and teasing and bullying by a group of girls (Year 5). Anna and her parents described how her stress level had dropped substantially (from 9/10 to 4/10) during the two months—during the pandemic—that she did schoolwork from home and engaged in extra tuition in preparation for selective school tests. Her stress level rose again (to 8/10) on returning to school. She became more withdrawn and had stopped talking to her parents—in particular, her mother—about her difficulties relating to school. Her headaches became severe, and she was admitted to hospital for review by a neurologist (including an MRI).

In a parallel process, the family themselves had been stressed following the birth of Anna's sibling (for Anna, Year 3) because the sibling suffered from severe colic followed by night terrors.

Formulation

The psychiatrist shared the team's formulation at the end of the family assessment. She highlighted that in 50% of cases, FND was triggered by a physical stressor—such as a viral illness—and that Anna's presentation fit this pattern. She also acknowledged that Anna had a long history of stress at school and that she had experienced stress-related headaches. Using a visual metaphor the psychiatrist explained the current medical understanding of FND and comorbid pain (see Figure 7.1; Kozlowska et al., 2020; Perez, Aybek, et al., 2021), adding that changes in cognitive function were seen in approximately 10% of pediatric cases and were understood to be related to the release of brain stress hormones and to hyperventilation (Kozlowska et al., 2017). The psychiatrist noted that throughout the assessment, Anna's breathing rate had ranged from 30–50 breaths per minute, ≥99th percentile (Fleming et al., 2011; Kozlowska et al., 2017). She also noted that Anna had appeared very flat during the assessment (flat affect and slumped posture), and indicated that the team would further assess her mood and mental state more generally since comorbid depression and anxiety were common in FND (Perez, Aybek, et al., 2021). The psychiatrist told the family that with treatment, most young children achieved a full recovery (Kozlowska et al., 2021). Finally, she discussed the treatment program in detail (see Box 7.2; Kozlowska et al., 2012). Anna was offered admission into the Mind–Body Program following the two-week break for school holidays.

Managing Parental Anxiety About the FND Diagnosis

Anna made no improvement at home during the holiday break. Her headaches got worse as she tried to mobilize, and she had developed the new symptom of dizziness. In this context her parents and the family doctor became increasingly anxious that the diagnosis of FND was incorrect. Because the Mind–Body Program does not accept children whose diagnosis has not been clarified or whose parents do not accept the diagnosis—everyone has to be on the same page (Kozlowska et al., 2020)—our team put the mind–body admission on hold and supported the family to seek re-review from the neurologist and second opinions from a second neurologist and a neurosurgeon. During the resulting 4-week period—which included two additional presentations to the ER because of Anna's symptoms of worsening gait, back pain, nausea, difficulty swallowing, and difficulties talking (Visit 1) and a 40-minute functional seizure (Visit 2)—the diagnosis of FND was reaffirmed at all consultations. Additional investigations included MRI of the spine, video electroencephalogram, and nerve conduction studies.

FIGURE 7.1   Visual representation of the formulation. In explaining the neurobiology of FND to Anna and her parents, we used this visual metaphor alongside the following language: "The dark gray ball represents the brain regions that underpin salience detection, arousal, and emotional states—the *brain stress systems*, for short. The light gray ball represents brain areas involved in motor processing—*motor-processing regions*, for short. The white ball represents brain areas involved in sensory processing—*sensory-processing regions*, for short. The spikey ball represents pain-processing regions—*pain maps*, for short. When all is well, the brain stress systems get on with their job, as do the motor-, sensory-, and pain-processing regions, and they interact together in a balanced way. In FND the relationship between the brain stress systems and motor-, sensory-, and pain-processing regions changes and becomes unbalanced. The brain stress systems become larger and stronger, and they disrupt motor and sensory processing and amplify pain." © Kozlowska, 2019

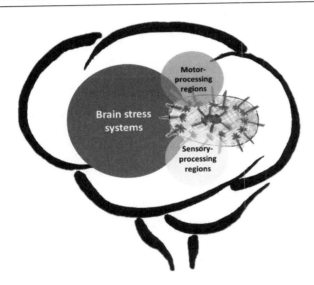

Mind–Body Rehabilitation Program

Six weeks after the family assessment interview, Anna was admitted into the Mind–Body Program (see Table 7.1). Anna was now very unwell (see Figure 7.2). The process of the admission was difficult for Anna, her parents, and the team.

Unlike most children her age, Anna struggled to engage in all components of the program. Individual therapy sessions were difficult for her. She was unable to talk (though sometimes spoke in a whisper), generally had to communicate in writing, intermittently lost her hearing or use of her hands, or was unable to open her eyes. By the same token, the therapist found it difficult to

TABLE 7.1 Key Components of the Inpatient Mind–Body Program for FND

Treatment component	Interventions embedded in the daily timetable
Physical therapy (daily)	Broad range of physical interventions to normalize motor function and prevent secondary complications
Psychological therapy (daily, including art therapy sessions)	Broad range of mind–body interventions to help the child identify states of high arousal and distress, and to use strategies—including a change in the focus of attention—to down-regulate arousal and manage distress Interventions to help the child build up her emotional capacity to manage pain and future stress Interventions promoting a playful, relaxed body-brain state
Pharmacotherapy	Use of medication to regulate sleep, help with pain, switch off the brain-stress systems, and manage comorbid anxiety and depression
Family work (weekly, with additional meetings if needed)	Identifying problems in family system that may be contributing to the activation and maintenance of the child's stress response (and therefore the FND) Supporting the family in managing their anxiety and focus of attention, and in building parental capacity so that at discharge, parents are able to run the program independently Addressing any other pertinent family issues
Hospital school (daily)	Maintaining normal daily function and normal age-appropriate activities

communicate with Anna, to use visual representations, and to engage in regulation work. The therapist's attempts to help Anna track her body state (including escalations of arousal that precede functional seizures) (Kozlowska et al., 2018a), to use hypnosis, to engage in slow-breath training using biofeedback (Chudleigh et al., 2019), and to use visualization and relaxation exercises, as well as grounding (weighted blanket) and sensory (clay, stress ball) strategies, all failed. Anna remained in a state of high arousal that was reflected in an elevated respiratory rate and an inability, using any of the above-described regulation strategies, to achieve any increase in heart rate variability (restorative parasympathetic function) on the biofeedback device. Her high levels of anxiety and low mood became apparent to her psychologist (in session, where her tendency to ruminate and catastrophize was identified) and to the physiotherapist

FIGURE 7.2 Visual representation of the time frame of Anna's constantly changing functional symptoms during the 6 months of her illness. PNES, psychogenic non-epileptic seizures (current term: functional seizures).

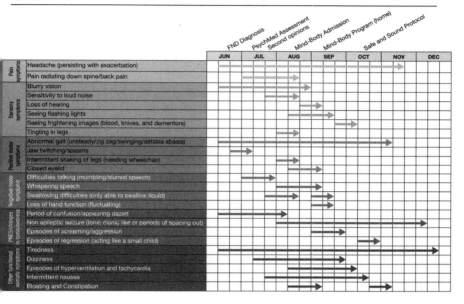

(in session, where the anxiety emerged as reluctance to play and to try new activities and games). Anna functioned best in the setting of the school classroom—completing her work as requested—where the teacher, who was used to dealing with functional somatic symptoms, kept the focus away from the symptoms. The only therapeutic spaces that Anna enjoyed were the art therapy sessions, where no demands were placed on her.

Anna's parents found the process stressful. During the admission Anna's symptoms continued to shift and change (see Figure 7.2), and with each new metamorphosis, the parents experienced a new wave of panic and were unable to shift their focus of attention away from the new symptom(s). For example, when Anna's blurry vision and swallowing difficulties resolved, they were replaced by increased nausea, loss of hearing, and a fluctuating inability to open her eyes. In the same way, Anna's symptom of blurred vision morphed into seeing flashing lights, and then morphed into images of knives, blood, and dementors (spirit-like creatures in the Harry Potter books). Anna's parents also struggled to tolerate her distress during exacerbations of headache, and they experienced anguish and disbelief when the team expected Anna to continue on with the scheduled activities of the Mind–Body Program even with ongoing pain (headache).

It proved to be a challenge for the team to trial pharmacotherapy for arousal, pain, anxiety, and low mood. Anna's parents were inclined toward natural therapies (e.g., herbal medicines, Chinese cupping, acupuncture) and disliked the idea of using medications, and it was difficult (for everyone) to distinguish new functional symptoms from potential medication side effects. During the admission a trial of quetiapine (6.25 mg before physiotherapy sessions to decrease arousal) was discontinued because Anna's parents thought that it made Anna more flat. A trial of gabapentin (300 mg a day) for headache was discontinued after two days when Anna experienced an increase in nausea. A trial of fluvoxamine (titrating to 25 mg morning, 50 mg at night) for Anna's ruminating, catastrophizing, anxiety, and mood was withdrawn—with no change in mental state—when Anna's ruminations began to have suicidal content (see Box 7.2). Eventually, Anna was stabilized on a regimen of amitriptyline (10 mg at bedtime), which resulted in substantial improvement in her headaches, and guanfacine (1 mg in the morning), which helped decrease her arousal and led to a decrease in the frequency and number of her functional seizures. Her other symptoms persisted unabated (see Figure 7.2).

Despite the challenging nature of the admission, six important goals were achieved: (1) Anna's parents came to the realization that their anxious responses to Anna's morphing symptoms were unhelpful. They began the hard task of working to stay calm and to manage their focus of attention away from symptoms and toward activities that promoted normal function. (2) When Anna filled out the Depression, Anxiety, and Stress Scales (DASS) with her mother—and scored 48 of the possible score of 63 (very high)—her mother understood that

---

BOX 7.2
Examples of Anna's Suicidal Ideation, Drawn from Texts to Her Mother

---

"I hate life. I want to stab myself."

"Nothing helps. I try and try to distract myself and I do breathing but I still felt like dying."

"It is just that I keep on getting so so much BLUE AND RED [code for bad thoughts] that it is out of control, so feel like dying and going on the road and getting killed."

"Just I felt too bad."

"Why is life horrid? I kept on trying to calm down but it doesn't help. I want to die because there is so so so so much RED AND BLUE that is so unbearable that I want to go on a road and die and stab my left nostril right nostril. I am trying to do, trying to play with clay but doesn't work."

"I hate life. I hate you. I hate everyone."

"But I am such a horrible horrid person. I can't control myself."

"RED headache I just want to stab myself."

"I am too horrible. I can't calm myself down but I am trying trying a lot."

Anna perceived the cumulative stressors that she had experienced as very substantial. (The total DASS score just prior to commencement of the Safe and Sound Protocol seven weeks later was even higher.) (3) Anna's parents—and the team—realized that Anna's recovery process would take longer than was typical for young children and that they needed to prepare for the long haul. (4) By the end of the 2-week admission, Anna's parents felt capable of running the program from home, with Anna attending physiotherapy and psychotherapy sessions as an outpatient and returning to her home school with a safety plan and in a wheelchair. (5) The therapeutic relationship now established between Anna's parents and the team would enable the team to support the parents via weekly telehealth meetings. And (6) it was clear that Anna was unable to benefit from any of the active regulation interventions, whether bottom-up and top-down (Cristea et al., 2021; Kozlowska et al., 2020; Myers et al., 2021; Velani & Gledhill, 2021) that helped most children.

The Quest for a Passive Regulation Strategy

Our team had come across difficult-to-treat cases before where the children seemed to be unable to use any of our standard interventions and where their state of arousal remained elevated despite all our efforts. Six years previously, we had unsuccessfully tried to obtain a topical (via the tongue) noninvasive neuromodulation device that had been safely used in children with posterior fossa syndrome—the Portable Neuromodulation Stimulator (PoNS)—which was reported both to induce a relaxation response and to facilitate motor rehabilitation (Harbourne et al., 2014; Wildenberg et al., 2013). Subsequently, other neurostimulation methodologies—which used the ear, rather than the tongue, as a portal to the brain—had been developed. For example, in 2014, Stephen Porges developed a 5-hour modified-music intervention, the Safe and Sound Protocol, whose aim was to decrease auditory hypersensitivity and chronic autonomic arousal in children with autism (Patriquin et al., 2019; Porges et al., 2014). More recently, Kovacic and colleagues (2017) used Neuro-Stim, a means of auricular neurostimulation developed by Innovative Health Solutions, which delivers percutaneous electrical nerve field stimulation in the external ear, to treat children with functional abdominal pain. They found that the intervention improved pain scores and overall well-being (Kovacic et al., 2017; Krasaelap et al., 2020) and that children with more substantial autonomic dysregulation as measured by vagal efficiency experienced better responses to the auricular neurostimulation (Kovacic et al., 2020). Our team trained in the Safe and Sound Protocol because it was available in Australia and because we thought that a passive music intervention would be a good addition to our Mind–Body Program (Kozlowska et al., 2017, 2020).

Safe and Sound Protocol with Anna

The Safe and Sound Protocol was added to Anna's outpatient treatment program 7 weeks after her discharge. During the intervening period her symptoms had persisted (see Figure 7.2). The 5-hour intervention was delivered in nine sessions over 6 weeks, starting with a 15-minute block and building up to 30 minutes.

During her first session, Anna reported that the music made her ears feel funny. She settled after a 5-minute break.

In the next six sessions (resulting in a total of 3 hours of music), Anna became chatty during the sessions, engaged in "mindfulness coloring-in" exercises (Carsley & Heath, 2018), but would move restlessly in her wheelchair toward the end of the sessions. At this point in the treatment, Anna's parents reported that she had started walking around the house utilizing the walls as support, something that she had previously been too anxious to try. Her physical therapist, outside psychologist, and schoolteacher all reported that she had become more engaged in her therapies and in school. Anna also begun to actively use the regulation strategies she had previously learned (e.g., slow breathing and managing catastrophic thoughts) to settle herself when she felt her body activating.

During the period of the next two sessions (the 4th hour of music, overall), Anna showed substantial improvement in her gait: she was now able to walk without the support of a parent or a wall; she began to climb onto play equipment; and she came to her session pushing her wheelchair (rather than sitting in it). During the sessions themselves, her previously ceaseless chatter abated, and she was now content to sink into a soft chair to listen to the music. She appeared deeply relaxed while she did so.

During the period of the next two sessions (the 5th hour of music, overall) Anna began to walk normally, her suicidal thoughts settled, and her functional seizures decreased to once a day for seconds at a time. She and her parents were now able to identify the warning signs of an impending functional seizure, which enabled Anna, in turn, to practice implementing active strategies to avert it (Kozlowska et al., 2018b). Physiotherapy was replaced by engagement in exercise appropriate to Anna's age. Anna continued therapy sessions with her outside psychologist. The amitriptyline for headache was ceased 1 week after completion of Safe and Sound. She remained on the guanfacine because her parents had noticed that when she missed a dose, Anna's functional seizures increased.

Autonomic measures on the biofeedback device (HeartMath) were taken before, during, and at the completion of the Safe and Sound intervention. While HeartMath is promoted as delivering research-level heart rate variability data, it was unable to handle signals from the highly dysregulated Anna, even though she was compliant and still during testing. The situation may have been complicated by the bronze tone of Anna's skin, which, a HeartMath scientist later informed us, might have affected the acquisition of data. In any case, because HeartMath failed to give reliable, valid heart rate variability metrics, they are not included in the current report.

The self-reported data (see Table 7.2) of decreases in the DASS and Body Perception Questionnaire were consistent with Anna's observed functional improvement.

Follow-Up and Outcome

Following the 2-month summer break, Anna returned to school full time with no functional symptoms (see Figure 7.2). A year and a half later, her sense of well-being was ongoing.

QUESTIONS TO THE CONSULTANTS

1. What is the potential value of neuromodulation for treating functional neurological symptoms? (Pick)
2. Children and teenagers with severe functional neurological symptoms often struggle with maintaining emotional and behavioral regulation to allow for participation in treatment. Against that background, what are the rationale and underlying mechanisms for the use of modulated music in the care of this patient? (Porges)
3. Complex FND presentations in a young child can often be a challenge requiring multimodal treatment approaches. Against that background, what is the role of behavioral and pharmacological approaches in treating children and teenagers with FND and overlapping pain? (Torbey)

CONSULTANTS' ANSWERS

1. Susannah Pick

Neuromodulation broadly refers to the use of external (i.e., electrical, magnetic, chemical) stimuli to modulate functioning in targeted regions or circuits in the peripheral or central nervous system. Depending on the stimulation device and protocol used, neuromodulation can inhibit or facilitate neural activity in a given region, with effects that last from seconds to months.

Well-established neuromodulation approaches with reasonable evidence bases for treatment efficacy include surgical (invasive) approaches such as deep brain and vagus nerve stimulation, and noninvasive techniques such as transcranial magnetic stimulation (TMS), transcutaneous direct current stimulation (tDCS), and transcranial focused ultrasound (Lewis et al., 2016). Existing neuromodulatory treatments have been applied in a range of neurological, psychiatric, and neurodevelopmental disorders, including chronic pain, Parkinson's disease, epilepsy, multiple sclerosis, obsessive-compulsive disorder, major

TABLE 7.2   Pre- and Posttreatment Measures on the Depression, Anxiety, and Stress Scales (DASS) and on the Body Perception Questionnaire (BPQ)[a]

Measure and domain	Pretreatment with Safe and Sound Protocol (baseline)	Posttreatment with Safe and Sound Protocol (1 month after completion of protocol)	Health control comparison (n = 155)
Depression, Anxiety, and Stress Scales[b]			
Depression scale	18	2	Mean = 6.25 (range, 0–12)
Anxiety scale	21	1	Mean = 1.38 (range, 0–12)
Stress scale	17	8	Mean = 2.84 (range, 0–7)
Total DASS score[c]	56 (clinical range)	11 (normative range)	Mean = 5.63 (range, 0–37)
Body Perception Questionnaire			
Body awareness (percentile)	91.0% (clinical range)	21.3% (normative range)	
Body awareness (T-Score)	63.4 (clinical range)	42 (normative range)	
Supradiaphragmatic (heart/chest/throat) reactivity (percentile)	98.0% (clinical range)	26.3% (normative range)	
Supradiaphragmatic reactivity (T-Score)	70.6 (clinical range)	43.7 (normative range)	
Subdiaphragmatic (gut) reactivity (percentile)	98.9% (clinical range)	9.0% (normative range)	
Subdiaphragmatic (gut) reactivity (T-Score)	72.8 (clinical range)	36.6 (normative range)	

[a] The Body Perception Questionnaire is a measure of autonomic activation.
[b] For comparison, DASS scores for 155 healthy children who had taken part in a research program for FND are reported for the DASS 21 (as reported in Hilton et al., 2022).
[c] The maximum total DASS score is 63.

depression, and autism (Lefaucheur et al., 2014; Lewis et al., 2016; Slotema et al., 2010; Sullivan et al., 2021).

Emerging noninvasive topical approaches include the following: Portable Neuromodulation Stimulator (PONs), delivering low-grade rhythmic electrical signals to the mucosa of the tongue (FDA, 2021; Hou et al., 2020; Kaczmarek, 2017; Leonard et al., 2017); Safe and Sound Protocol, delivering sound waves to the middle ear in the form of modified music (Porges, 2018); IB-STIM (previously Neuro-Stim), delivering percutaneous electrical nerve field stimulation via the external ear (IB-Stim; Kovacic et al., 2017, 2020; Krasaelap et al., 2020); NeuroSigma, delivering low-level electrical pulses to the forehead region innervated by the trigeminal nerve (Loo et al., 2021; McGough et al., 2015, 2019; NeuroSigma); and other forms of transcutaneous vagus nerve stimulation (tVNS; Yap et al., 2020). Topical approaches aim to stimulate homeostatic afferents, including the afferent component of the vagal nerve (Craig, 2005, 2016), to modulate neural networks and facilitate induction of neuroplastic changes (Frangos et al., 2015; Wildenberg et al., 2011a, 2011b, 2013). Evidence pertaining to topical approaches is in the process of being established (Hou et al., 2020; Kaczmarek, 2017; Kovacic et al., 2017; Kovacic et al., 2020; Krasaelap et al., 2020; Leonard et al., 2017; Porges et al., 2013, 2014; Yap et al., 2020). Kaczmarek (2017) summarizes all preliminary studies using the PONs published prior to 2017. The present case report highlights the potential value of auricular neurostimulation as a treatment for comorbid chronic pain and functional neurological symptoms.

Functional neurological symptoms (FNS) refer to any types of neurological symptoms that are not explained by, or consistent with, identifiable neurological disease. They include seizures, motor disturbances (weakness, tremor, dystonia, jerks), and sensory disturbances. FNS cause significant disability and are often associated with additional physical symptoms (e.g., pain, fatigue, swallowing or speech dysfunction, etc.) and psychological distress (e.g., anxiety, depression, dissociation, post-traumatic symptoms; Nicholson et al., 2020) that further exacerbate impairments in functioning and quality of life.

Contemporary explanations of FNS suggest that they are manifestations of disturbed motor and cognitive control, elevated affective reactivity and autonomic arousal, and impaired awareness of the bodily self (Kozlowska, 2017; Pick et al., 2019). Neuromodulatory treatments have considerable potential for modifying these disordered processes by targeting underlying neurocircuitry, possibly resulting in improvements in both FNS and associated symptoms (e.g., depression, pain, anxiety).

Several randomized, controlled trials have tested the feasibility or efficacy of TMS for treating functional motor symptoms in adults. Most studies thus far have targeted the primary motor cortex with TMS, showing some benefits in subjective or objective functional motor symptom measures. Potential mechanisms of action include the following: changes in the patient's higher level beliefs (effecting top-down modulation via expectations because TMS has demonstrated the limb's capacity for function) (Garcin et al., 2017; Pick et al., 2020; Pollak et al., 2014), motor retraining, and modulation of motor cortex excitability (Broersma et al., 2015; Taib et al., 2019). In addition to treating functional motor symptoms, neuromodulation could potentially be harnessed to target other FNS or, indeed, disturbed neurocognitive processes that cut across FNS presentations. For example, stimulation of sensory cortical regions may be a valuable approach for treating functional sensory deficits (e.g., functional numbness, visual or auditory impairments). Neuromodulation could also be used to facilitate improvements in emotion regulation and cognitive control, and to regulate autonomic arousal. The dorsolateral prefrontal cortex may be an optimal target for excitatory neuromodulation in patients with FNS, given its known involvement in these core processes and existing evidence that repetitive TMS (rTMS) to the dorsolateral prefrontal cortex can successfully treat mood disturbance.

The current case report, however, suggests that a minimal, auricular, neuromodulatory treatment may be of value in treating FNS. The Safe and Sound Protocol was developed to noninvasively stimulate parasympathetic nervous system activation via the vagus nerve, thus promoting regulation of autonomic arousal. As suggested above, it has been proposed that a key mechanism underlying FNS symptoms is excessive autonomic responsivity combined with diminished bodily awareness (interoception) and dissociation (Pick et al., 2019). The Safe and Sound Protocol and other similar treatments might therefore be valuable tools for regulating autonomic reactivity, enhancing bodily awareness, and self-regulating affect in people with FNS.

A key advantage of the Safe and Sound Protocol is that, rather than targeting a specific symptom, it has potential to act on core mechanisms that span the full range of FNS presentations (e.g., functional seizures, motor symptoms, sensory symptoms). The approach is also likely to be acceptable to patients with FND for several reasons. First, it assumes a brain-based mechanism, which minimizes the stigma that can be associated with purely psychological explanations and treatments. Second, the Safe and Sound Protocol can potentially be delivered in a wide range of settings, thus maximizing convenience for patients and their caregivers. Nevertheless, because the protocol is designed to modulate the autonomic nervous system, it can, in the short term, be associated with various low-grade (and usually temporary) adverse events. These include the following: increased auditory or other sensory sensitivities, ear discomfort or pressure, ringing in the ears, emotion dysregulation (changes in arousal), gastrointestinal discomfort, fatigue, and headache (personal communication, 1 March 2022, from Rebecca Knowles). (Rebecca Knowles, OTD, OTR/L, RYT, training and research manager at Unyte Health, reviewed data on adverse events through the Unyte Health case consultation process and put together a risk statement on the Safe and Sound Protocol. The statement was reviewed by the Clinical Advisory Board for Unyte Health.)

The adverse side effects with the Safe and Sound Protocol (headaches and discomfort are also common side effects with other neuromodulatory treatments) are managed by titrating sessions according to what the patient's nervous system can manage (e.g., Anna's sessions began with a 15-minute block) and by implementing regulation strategies (e.g., Anna used mindfulness coloring exercises) or activities that involve co-regulation with the therapist (e.g., a joint activity that helps to regulate the child).

Larger controlled studies, as well as feedback from patients, families, and others, are needed to determine the extent of the Safe and Sound Protocol's adverse effects, patient and caregiver views on tolerability, and whether the adverse effects result in withdrawal from treatment. It should also be noted that the efficacy and acceptability of the Safe and Sound Protocol for treating FND is not yet established and that, more broadly, the evidence base for Polyvagal Theory (PVT)—the approach's scientific rationale—is still limited and emerging. Larger trials are therefore also needed to test more stringently this novel but promising treatment, ideally alongside investigations of its mechanism(s) of action.

2. Stephen Porges

As a consultant in this clinical challenge, I see my role as twofold: (1) to explain the core mechanisms that would manifest in a subset of symptoms experienced by Anna and (2) to explain how modulated vocalizations and music would function as a neuromodulator to optimize neurophysiological regulation and reduce Anna's symptoms.

This case study of a child with FND, complicated by other functional somatic symptoms, documents that the child's clinical course improved following the use of computer-altered music as a neuromodulator. The neuromodulator in question, the Safe and Sound Protocol, is one that I developed as part of a long-term research and clinical endeavor to understand the workings of the vagal nerve and how that knowledge may be used to improve clinical care. PVT, which I first articulated in the mid-1990s, continues to serve as the main intellectual framework for my research and clinical efforts (Porges, 1995, 2011, 2023).

My work is consistent with important advances in neuroscience—in particular, those of A. D. (Bud) Craig—pertaining to the neuroanatomy of homeostatic afferents (including vagal afferents) and their major role in modulating important neural networks (Craig, 2005, 2016). The work is also consistent with advances in the field of medicine, where a range of surgically implanted devices—and transcutaneous devices in the more recent past—were developed to modulate spinal cord afferents or the vagal nerve itself in cases of intractable pain, refractory epilepsy, or depression (Yap et al., 2020). Likewise, recent advances in neuroscience have confirmed that breathing interventions used for up-regulating vagal function and for promoting states of well-being rest on a solid evidence base (Brown & Gerbarg, 2005; Gevirtz, 2000; McCraty &

Childre, 2010). That is, although the history and effective use within Eastern traditions date back thousands of years, it is only very recently that the neuro-anatomy, including the close anatomical proximity of the respiratory rhythm generator and vagal nuclei in the brainstem, which facilitates the functional coupling between them, has been clearly delineated (Benarroch, 2007). Prior to that, research identifying a common cardiopulmonary oscillator was published in 1990 (Richter & Spyer), which was then incorporated into the original 1995 description of PVT. The upshot has been a burgeoning range of portable bio-feedback devices (Peake et al., 2018; Yu et al., 2018).

Regarding the Safe and Sound Protocol, preliminary research using an ear-lier version (Listening Project Protocol) with children with autism spectrum disorders showed that the intervention improved sociality, vagal regulation of the heart, and auditory processing, while reducing hyperacusis (Porges et al., 2013, 2014). Studies currently in progress with other clinical populations of chil-dren (e.g., autism spectrum, Ehlers-Danlos syndrome, Prader-Willi syndrome) are expected to provide a further evidence base.

The use of modulated vocalizations and music as a neuromodulator may appear distinct to both the clinical features and the neurophysiological mecha-nisms assumed to underlie the patient's clinical status. However, if the clinical features are viewed through a different theoretical perspective, then the fea-tures and the clinical success of neuromodulation through an acoustic portal are explainable. PVT provides a science-based theoretical orientation to reor-ganize expressed symptoms and succinctly explain why and how the interven-tion would be helpful (Porges 1995, 2007, 2011, 2023). On that theory, several of Anna's symptoms can be understood as the product of a destabilized auto-nomic nervous system—in particular, a disruption in the ventral vagal circuit involving a brainstem area known as the ventral vagal complex. This brainstem area provides the neuroanatomical and neurophysiological substrate for both spontaneous social engagement behaviors and the vagal regulation necessary to promote calmness and optimize homeostatic function.

An inspection of Anna's symptom profile (see Figure 7.2) suggests common neural mechanisms involving the ventral vagal complex. Specifically, damp-ening vagal influences from this area would result in tachycardia and atypical breathing, a general feeling of threat reflected in anxiety, and gastrointestinal issues including nausea, bloating, and constipation. In concert with this auto-nomic backdrop, decreased neural tone via special visceral efferent pathways to the striated muscles of the face and head (taken together, the substrate of the social engagement system) would result in hyperacusis and hyposensitivity to voice, eyelid dropping, flat facial affect, atypical intonation of speech, and dys-regulation of the coordination of sucking, swallowing, and breathing.

Passive listening to modulated vocalizations and music within a specific fre-quency band associated with positive social communication (e.g., a mother's pro-sodic voice or lullaby) is an efficient portal to the ventral vagal complex and becomes the basis for how music can be composed to calm the autonomic nervous system. All social mammals have a frequency band on which modulation of vocalizations serves to signal safety. This frequency band is determined by the physics of the middle ear structures of the species and forms a mechanism through which mammals communicate that they are safe enough to approach or to be approached (Kolacz et al., 2018; Porges & Lewis, 2010). A recent study has documented that the degree of vocal intonation of the mother has an almost linear impact on calming her infant following a stressing disruption. The more prosodic the mother's voice, the more effective she was in reducing behavioral features of distress and in lowering heart rate (Kolacz et al., 2022). In essence, the mother's voice was functioning as a neuromodulator increasing both vagal regulation of the heart and calming behavior.

Listening to modulated vocalizations and music is potentially an efficient strategy for neuromodulation of the autonomic nervous system. Passive listening may enhance vagal regulation and reduce symptoms. Consistent with this explanation, the technology embedded in the Safe and Sound Protocol received a patent that included a claim for its application as an acoustic vagal nerve stimulator (Porges, 2018). In addition, as noted earlier, two previous studies documented beneficial effects of the protocol with children on the autism spectrum (Porges et al., 2013, 2014).

Since PVT is based on a complex literature at the interface of several disciplines (e.g., evolutionary biology, comparative neuroanatomy, developmental neurophysiology, psychophysiology, speech and hearing sciences, etc.), specific features of the theory as it relates to this clinical case are summarized below.

- Autonomic state influences behavior and mental process by functioning as an intervening variable influencing behavioral and physiological reactivity (e.g., calming or arousing) to environmental cues.
- Ventral vagal pathways enable mammals to experience physiological calmness and sociality while also supporting homeostatic processes leading to optimized health, growth, and restoration.
- The ventral vagal pathways originate in a brainstem area known as the ventral vagal complex, which includes the origin of both ventral vagal efferent pathways regulating the heart and bronchi and special visceral efferent pathways regulating the striated muscles of the face and head traveling through several cranial nerves (i.e., CN V, VII, IX, X, XI) (Porges 2009).
- Acoustic cues of safety (e.g., prosodic vocalizations) influence the ventral vagal complex and function like an acoustic vagal nerve stimulator that potentially can down-regulate threat reactions by slowing heart rate, signaling safety to the enteric nervous system (Frangos et al., 2015; Kolacz & Porges, 2018; Kolacz et al., 2022; Porges, 2017) and hypothetically increasing neural tone to the muscles of the middle ear (reducing hyperacusis and improving auditory processing), face (increasing facial expressivity), and larynx and pharynx (enhancing intonation of voice).

If we look at Anna's symptoms, do they converge with a disrupted social engagement system? When we look at the clinical trajectory following the Safe and Sound Protocol, is the outcome profile consistent with a reinstatement of that system? The organizing principles of PVT provide the rationale to cluster many of Anna's symptoms as a depressed or dysfunctional social engagement system. This system becomes dormant when the autonomic nervous system is retuned to support defense. When that occurs, it compromises sociality and accessibility, which would require a down-regulation of defenses to enable proximity. An autonomic pattern of chronic defense is frequently observed in several psychiatric disorders (e.g., anxiety, autism, depression, post-traumatic stress disorder; Jung et al., 2019).

A review of the clinical material suggests that Anna's feedback is consistent with the model. For example, Anna reported during the first session that her "ears feel funny." This is a frequently reported response to the Safe and Sound Protocol and appears to reflect a tensing of the eardrum as the middle ear muscles become more active and the ossicle chain becomes more rigid. Similarly, "her previously ceaseless chatter abated" reflects a calmer autonomic state. In addition, her self-report on the Body Perception Questionnaire (see Table 7.1) emphasizes that her subjective feelings of autonomic state have profoundly moved from an autonomic state of defense to a state of calmness. These subjective responses are convergent with a more regulated autonomic nervous system.

PVT identifies the hypothetical mechanisms through which modulated music works as a neuromodulator. Intuitively, we know the calming power of a mother's lullaby, which is supported by a recent study documenting the potency of prosodic features in calming distress and shifting autonomic state (Kolacz et al., 2022). Similarly, we are aware of the calming effect of melodic music. There is a science beneath these familiar observations (Vuilleumier & Trost, 2015). Our own research has documented that prosodic maternal voices are effective in calming their infants' heart rate following a social disruptor (Kolacz et al., 2019), and computer-modulated vocal music, similar to the Safe and Sound Protocol, has been documented to improve sociality, vagal regulation of the heart, and auditory processing, while reducing hyperacusis in children with autism spectrum disorders (Porges et al., 2013, 2014). With this knowledge we can reconceptualize the calming effect of the prosodic voice and modulated music as an efficient and effective neuromodulator to retune the autonomic nervous system—an intervention that can potentially be used broadly in the clinical treatment of extreme states of anxiety and, in this case, FND.

When we understand the role of the bidirectional communication between specific brainstem structures (i.e., ventral vagal complex) and the autonomic nervous system, as well as the role of vagal afferents in the modulation of brain systems mediating arousal (Craig, 2005; Frangos et al., 2015), then we are in a position to understand, too, the link between Anna's symptoms and the effectiveness of the intervention. Functionally, this neurally informed understanding links several of the symptoms expressed by Anna to a destabilized autonomic nervous system coupled with the neural network changes that characterize FND (Perez, Nicholson, et al., 2021). This understanding also directs the clinician to an effective intervention strategy.

3. Souraya Torbey

Patients with FND have unique presentations and needs that are affected by distinctive biological, psychological, and social factors: predisposing, precipitating, and perpetuating. Given the range of possible co-occurring factors, however, any single modality of treatment is unlikely to be effective for all patients. For example, upon presentation, Anna was unable to communicate verbally and had heightened levels of arousal, difficulty with her vision, and chronic pain. Her parents' behaviors also reinforced Anna's FND. Given her presenting symptoms, traditional therapeutic modalities such as cognitive-behavioral therapy (CBT) could not be successfully implemented at that initial stage. The team therefore devised an individualized plan involving pharmacotherapy and other treatment modalities to target her needs. Given the unique challenges of every FND case, the gold standard is to conceptualize a patient's presentation through a biopsychosocial approach and to provide holistic, integrated, multidisciplinary treatment involving a diverse range of professionals focused on developing different skill sets and coping strategies.

It is common for patients with FND to have comorbid neurological and medical conditions, chronic pain, a history of trauma, and comorbid psychiatric disorders. Notably, patients with FND are at risk of being misdiagnosed as having an organic condition, with data showing that accurate diagnosis may be delayed by more than 7 years and that patients are often treated with unnecessary interventions (Reuber, 2009). This is especially concerning because early diagnosis and treatment are associated with positive prognoses, especially in youth (such as Anna), who have higher rates of remission than adults. Early diagnosis can also help prevent overmedicalization, excessive health care utilization, and the functional deconditioning often seen in this patient population.

As noted above, the biopsychosocial approach is commonly used to describe predisposing, precipitating, and perpetuating factors for FND and chronic pain (Ezra et al., 2019). Anna's case presents a good example of the importance of identifying these factors, which play a critical role in guiding medical decision making and creating an individualized behavioral approach and treatment plan. Anna presented with several predisposing risk factors for FND, including female sex, history of bullying, loss of friendships, chronic pain, celiac disease, and family history of epilepsy and chronic medical illness (rheumatoid arthritis). Common predisposing factors for FND also include genetics, temperament, illness exposure, early childhood trauma, dissociative symptoms, and neurological illness.

The onset of FND symptoms is often precipitated by multiple factors, and in this case the triggers included recent viral illness, return to school, and loss of friends and supportive teacher, along with worsening anxious distress and mood.

Functional seizures can be maintained and perpetuated by multiple biological factors, including destabilization of the autonomic nervous system, neural network deficits in limbic sensorimotor and prefrontal areas, and psychological factors. The latter include maladaptive coping skills, catastrophizing (Janet, 1907), increased attention to physical symptoms, loss of sense of agency (Fobian & Elliott, 2018), and secondary gains (Carson et al., 2016). Secondary gains are maintained by operant conditioning through both positive and negative reinforcement, such as avoidance of stress associated with school or increased attention from family or friends (Bouton, 2002). These psychological factors are best addressed through behavior modification and parent-training interventions (often one of the most challenging aspects of addressing FND). In the initial process, parents often become distressed when asked to refrain from attending to their child during an episode; consistent support is therefore required early on. As expected, Anna's symptoms improved when parents and teachers minimized attention to her symptoms.

The multidisciplinary approach involves intervening in patients' illness beliefs, reducing maladaptive behaviors (Nielsen et al., 2015), minimizing and normalizing functional symptoms, addressing problematic family dynamics, and emphasizing the importance of restoring functioning, along with psychoeducation (Weiss et al., 2021). This approach was paramount in achieving a positive outcome in Anna's case. Once the diagnosis of FND is made, the first step is to communicate effectively and provide psychoeducation about the disorder, thus promoting a constructive relationship between the patient and the treatment team. The second step is to develop a plan to reassess the need for certain medications and to discontinue certain unnecessary medications, such as anti-epileptic medications for functional seizures and opiates for chronic pain (Gasparini et al., 2019). Given the paucity of research on pharmacological treatment of FND in youth, the recommended approach is to minimize medication administration except in cases where comorbid psychiatric disorders or other medical problems are present (Gasparini et al., 2019). For patients with comorbid anxiety, depression, ruminative thoughts, or obsessive-compulsive disorder, antidepressants such as selective serotonin and serotonin-norepinephrine reuptake inhibitors may be helpful in select cases. In Anna's case, guanfacine was used to curb arousal and facilitate her capacity to engage in treatment.

If antidepressants are prescribed, close monitoring for response and tolerability is warranted, especially given the low, but existing, risk of suicidal ideation—as happened with Anna when fluvoxamine was trialed. One randomized, clinical trial demonstrated a significant 59% reduction of functional seizure frequency for patients treated with both CBT and sertraline, and a 51% reduction with CBT alone (LaFrance et al., 2014). The sertraline-only group did not significantly reduce seizure frequency, whereas the CBT-only group experienced a greater improvement of secondary outcomes such as quality of life, depression, and anxiety. In an open-label, uncontrolled, prospective study of the effect of venlafaxine on patients with functional seizures and comorbid depression or anxiety, the frequency and intensity of episodes decreased over 5 months (Pintor et al., 2010). Generally, serotonin-norepinephrine reuptake inhibitors are rarely used in young school-age children such as Anna. They can be considered in older youth who have failed trials with selective serotonin reuptake inhibitors or have comorbid chronic pain. Their use should also be considered carefully as they can worsen arousal and consequently functional seizures. Tricyclic antidepressants such as amitriptyline have been showed to be beneficial for pain and sleep and are often used for headaches, as was the case with Anna. It is important to note, however, that analgesia is achieved at lower doses than those needed to address depression (Dale & Stacey, 2016) and that tricyclics are ineffective for depression in youth (Sutherland et al., 2018).

As was evident in Anna's case, patients with functional seizures often present in a high state of physiological arousal (Kozlowska et al., 2015). Given that alpha agonist medications, such as the guanfacine used with Anna, often decrease sympathetic arousal, they may be helpful with FND symptoms (Rice et al., 2018; Stahl, 2021). Anticonvulsants are also often prescribed for patients with FND. Some studies have found that anticonvulsants can potentially reduce the frequency of episodes, but this finding is thought to reflect a placebo or antianxiety effect (Bowman & Markland, 2005). Unless the patients have comorbid conditions (e.g., chronic pain) for which anticonvulsants may be helpful, it is generally recommended to discontinue these medications once the diagnosis is confirmed.

Similarly, patients with FND are often prescribed benzodiazepines, but no research supports their use except in the presence of comorbid acute anxiety.

Anna had several medication trials. Eventually, her hyperarousal symptoms responded favorably to quetiapine (which is supported by the literature) and subsequently to guanfacine (after Anna's parents perceived that the quetiapine left her feeling too flat). Nevertheless, the use of neuroleptics should be carefully considered, especially in younger youth, and the benefits should outweigh the nonnegligible risk of extrapyramidal symptoms and metabolic syndrome (Ahearn et al., 2011).

Larger clinical trials are needed to fully assess the clinical impact of pharmacological treatment on functional symptoms, particularly in youth. At present, the use of pharmacological treatments for FND in youth is mostly extrapolated from adult data. Psychotherapeutic approaches are also critical. These can be classified into two groups: bottom-up and top-down modalities. Bottom-up approaches are body-based interventions that work with the felt sense of the body (homeostatic feelings) and that use interventions that target the body: mindful attention to the body, slow-paced breathing, grounding techniques, regulating movement, therapeutic touch, and biofeedback approaches. These interventions facilitate the individual's capacity to track body state, tolerate states of activation, and facilitate states of calm (Kozlowska et al., 2020; Myers et al., 2021; Velani & Gledhill, 2021).

Top-down approaches, CBT in particular, have been shown to have a high level of efficacy, with the majority of the data from adults. To facilitate behavioral modifications in older patients with FND, motivational interviewing may reduce ambivalence about treatment (Lundahl et al., 2013). Other top-down psychotherapies include hypnosis (Moene et al., 2003), retraining and control therapy (ReACT; Fobian et al., 2020), psychoeducation group interventions, psychodynamic psychotherapy, and mindfulness-based therapy (Myers et al., 2021). Most of these therapies engage in psychoeducation using the biopsychosocial approach, which in itself is a key intervention in FND (Karterud et al., 2015). Neuromodulation approaches are also showing promise.

In summary, FND is an unmapped clinical entity that mimics various conditions and may overlap with organic disorders. While we cannot identify one treatment approach to manage all the symptoms, the use of multimodal treatment approaches that target functional recovery while also addressing medical and psychiatric comorbidities appears to be the most effective way of supporting patients and families. As shown with Anna, novel approaches—in particular, noninvasive neuromodulating modalities that facilitate engagement in adaptive coping strategies—can have an important role in improving outcomes and should be further explored through clinical and research activities.

PART III

Monitoring and Stimulating the Vagus

8

Heart Rate Variability: A Personal Journey

Stephen W. Porges

Heart rate variability (HRV) has been a focal point throughout my academic history. To put this into perspective, I have published studies spanning 7 decades focusing on HRV (1969–2022). My interest in HRV started early in graduate school and continues to be an important portal informing my theoretical perspective. This chapter tracks some of this history, which started as an empirical observation and moved through several scientific stages including development of quantitative methods and investigations of neural mechanisms. Along this journey a variety of hypotheses were tested including the relative sensitivity of HRV metrics to neural mechanisms, psychological processes, and medical diagnoses. In addition, the research led to the identification of portals of intervention that have become strategies to optimize mental and physical health. These apparently disparate programs of inquiry have been tightly merged as the Polyvagal Theory (PVT) evolved. In the sections below, I have shared my personal journey through these stages of scientific inquiry and my attempts to integrate the new knowledge in an expansive theoretical model.

PERSONAL HISTORY

In the fall of 1966, I arrived at Michigan State University as an entering graduate student in a PhD program in psychology. At that time psychophysiology was emerging as a new discipline bridging psychology and physiology. It was a discipline with a scant literature. Few books and articles on the topic had been published. Only 2 years earlier, a new journal, *Psychophysiology*, was founded to provide a home for peer-reviewed research in this area. Previously psychophysiological research had been buried in journals such as *Experimental Psychology* and *Psychosomatic Medicine*. At the time, I did not appreciate my role as a pioneer, although the founding of the Society for Psychophysiological Research had only occurred 6 years earlier. Before we focus on the state of the emerging discipline of psychophysiology and my role in bringing interest in HRV research, it is important to see psychology and graduate training in psychology from a historical perspective.

On a personal level, my youth may have influenced my understanding of the history of psychology as an academic discipline. A student entering graduate school approaches novelty in ways that are like young children who are born into a preexisting family structure or are confronted with cultural institutions and expectations when they enter school and community. The child assumes that the context is stable and initially sets out to learn the rules without attempting to change them. Similarly, our intellectual perspective of a discipline is distorted by academic experience, and young initiates in a discipline see their field differently from the founders. Although it was clear to me that psychophysiology was new and an innovative approach to investigate historic brain–body or even mind–body questions, I had not fully appreciated that the entire field of psychology was a youthful discipline that only had emerged as an independent discipline during the academic careers of several of my mentors. At Michigan State University, psychology did not become an independent department until 1946, when it separated from the department of philosophy and psychology. A few of my professors started their academic careers in a department dominated by philosophers, not scientists.

As an entering graduate student, I assumed that psychology, as a discipline like biology, physics, and chemistry, was permanently etched into the structure of academics. I did not have a sense that psychology departments were relatively recent additions in many colleges and universities. Nor did I assume that academic disciplines would need to fluidly adapt to a rapidly changing scientific literature. Perhaps, when you are 21 years old, you are less interested in the past; events that occurred 20–50 years before do not appear relevant. Perhaps this was due my own experiences of being born at the end of World War II, a period of rapid change and forward thinking that emphasized the future and did not dwell on the past. As our culture becomes more trauma informed, we start to understand and appreciate the adaptive strategies of culture as it dynamically adjusted to the consequences of the collective trauma and devastation of war and the profound loss of agency felt by many during the Great Depression. Similar to personal trauma, reflection or rumination on societal trauma can numb our nervous system and interfere with our innate need to be social and our intellectual passions to create and discover and even a desire to uncover our roots.

Through the lens of our trauma-informed world, our optimistic dreams of equality and the opportunities to express our intellectual and ethical potential were, in part, an adaptive form of a societal dissociation. In any case, amid civil unrest and protests driven by the Vietnam War and civil rights movement, I was part of an optimistic subculture that was being driven by expansive opportunities for higher education and the rapid growth and accessibility of graduate programs. At the time I entered graduate school, a PhD from a respected program was usually sufficient to be hired without postdoctoral training or additional teaching experience as an assistant professor in a strong PhD-granting department.

This optimism was evident in my incoming classmates. Many came from uneducated families and were the first of their family to attend college. They shared a commitment to education, which several frequently verbalized as a firm desire to level the playing field of opportunities through education. Let's not forget, that in the mid-1960s misogyny was an accepted feature of graduate education. I recall the orientation meeting of all the incoming graduate students, which started with a faculty member looking at the class and inquiring why so many women (about 50%) were in the room. He continued to suggest that most would not complete degrees. All these cultural features were familiar to me as a 21-year-old.

When I elected to go to graduate school, I was enamored by the expansive questions that psychology encompassed. I was especially interested in the internal conflict between intentional behaviors and emotional state. Later, I would focus on the neurophysiological platform for emotion, autonomic state. My research would naturally flow from developing tools to monitor autonomic state (i.e., HRV) to link autonomic state with mental and behavioral processes, to identify mental and physical health vulnerabilities, and develop interventions that would optimize autonomic regulation.

However, when I arrived as an entering student in the broad area of experimental psychology, the available research that professors were studying did not seem to match my interests. At that time the research conducted by the Michigan State faculty in experimental psychology focused on verbal learning, operant learning, classical perception, physiological psychology, and child development. However, within experimental psychology, there were a couple of young faculty members who were interested in the emerging area of psychophysiology, an area that would enable empirical research of some of the historical mind–body questions linking feelings to performance by measuring physiological variables. By the fall of 1967, when I entered my second year of training, I had found a good match in being mentored by David Raskin. David was a young associate professor in his early 30s. He had been trained in physiological monitoring at UCLA by an established scientist, Irving Maltzman. Raskin's area focused on the bridge between learning and autonomic regulation that was a central topic in the scientists who followed Pavlov. These scientists were interested in classical conditioning and the unconditioned reactions to stimuli. In retrospect, the orienting and defensive responses may have been the intellectual trigger for the construct of neuroception in PVT, which functions as a reflexive detection of cues of being either safe or threatening.

I became David's mentee and teaching assistant for an undergraduate laboratory course in psychophysiology and he supervised my master's research (Porges & Raskin, 1969). David had a great influence on my research. He emphasized an empirical and quantitative perspective that effectively balanced my expansive thinking. He provided an opportunity for me to develop skills in monitoring and quantifying autonomic activity. David was a cautious scientist and thought like an engineer. He triggered my interests in designing and fabricating equipment. These interests continue as I have been awarded several patents related to monitoring and regulating autonomic function. A picture of the laboratory equipment used for my Masters' research is illustrated in Figure 8.1. The equipment on the left of the picture is the relay rack that was used to control the stimulus presentation of sounds and lights. This equipment was constructed by the technician in the psychology department from parts scavenged from a government salvage facility available to universities and other public institutions. On the right is a Beckman Dynograph, a physiological monitor with ink pens scrolling out in real time beat-to-beat heart rate changes from a cardiotachometer and electrodermal changes.

It was during the pilot phase of research for my master's thesis that I serendipitously observed systematic changes in heart rate variability during sustained attention. I was interested in identifying mental effort and intentionality from physiological signals. In a way, I was curious about what we could learn about human behavior from our bodily reactions without requiring a verbal response. As I watched the heart rate pattern being displayed on the polygraph paper, I noted that for several of the subjects the beat-to-beat heart rate pattern stabilized during the attention tasks and then returned to a baseline pattern that appeared to be systematically rhythmic at a frequency similar to spontaneous breathing. This was a new phenomenon; there was no literature of a respiratory pattern in beat-to-beat heart rate being sensitive to psychological demands linked to mental effort such as sustained attention. I immediately asked David what he thought. This started a discussion about potential mediating effects of breathing. Was the effect in heart rate being driven by a shift in breathing patterns or was there unique information in the heart rate pattern? We couldn't answer this question since we did not have a sensor to measure respiration. To solve this problem, we temporarily paused the experiment and David purchased a respiration sensor for the Dynograph. After a few weeks I returned to collecting data.

During the 1960s computers were not available in individual psychology laboratories. In fact, this was a time when the major computational tools in psychology departments were mechanical calculators (see Figure 8.2). As I was completing graduate school, this was replaced by a digital desktop calculator (see Figure 8.3). Most graduate students tediously conducted their analyses

FIGURE 8.1   David Raskin's laboratory circa 1967

FIGURE 8.2   1960s Supermetall mechanical calculator

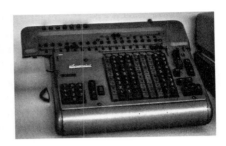

FIGURE 8.3   Early electronic calculator circa 1969   Courtesy Hans Bloemen

using these now archaic devices. However, those of us collecting large arrays of beat-to-beat data had several additional challenges. First, we had to quantify the beat-to-beat tracings from the Dynograph (see Figure 8.1). This was done with a millimeter ruler. Thanks to the innovation of the cardiotachometer heart rate was a calibrated deflection on the paper. Prior to the cardiotachometer, heart rate was derived by measuring the interval between R-waves on the paper. However, with this technique precision was dependent on paper speed. Thus, more precision required more paper and paper for the Dynogtraph was very expensive. Heart rate was sampled second-by-second within the experimental conditions. Similarly, respiration was analyzed by counting the frequency of inspirations and mean amplitude of completed inspirations within each experimental condition. As each value was scored, it was entered into a notebook. With this notebook, I would go to the computer center and create IBM punch cards via a machine like a typewriter that punched a hole in the card for every value I typed. Then I carried hundreds of data cards to the mainframe computer (CDC 3600/CDC 6400) to conduct the analyses of variance. Prior to the analyses, the data were subjected to a two-pass verification process during which the data were reentered and compared with the original card. If there were no differences, a verification notch was punched on the right edge of the card and the data could be submitted for analyses and placed in a queue. Often the delay between submitting data and analyses would be several days. Once analyzed, a large printout was placed in a bin that the user could retrieve. If a mistake was made on the format card, which instructed the computer what columns had specific data, a few days later you would pick up a very slim printout with the word ERROR prominently displayed. This type of error could cause major delays in completing the work and even scheduling thesis defenses.

Now back to the findings from this HRV study. Based on our intuitive scoring of the data, we calculated the variance of the second-by-second heart rate. First, the results documented that the traditional variables of heart rate, respiration amplitude, and respiration frequency exhibited a systematic reaction during attention and were not selectively sensitive to variations in attentional demands. Basically, during the attention tasks breathing became more rapid and shallow, while mean heart rate increased. Over repeated trials the task effect on heart rate dissipated. Interestingly, the HRV data uniquely documented differential task demands linking suppression of HRV with sustained attention. This finding documenting that mental effort resulted in a reduction of HRV was followed by my dissertation focused on linking HRV to reaction time performance and heart rate reactivity.

As I was finishing my masters' research, David moved from Michigan State University to the University of Utah. When he left, serendipitously I started to work with Hiram Fitzgerald, a young assistant professor in his late 20s. Hi was a developmental psychologist with an interest in infancy and early development. It was through Hi's benevolent mentorship that I was welcomed into the world of developmental psychology, which has greatly enriched my theoretical perspective. His influence led to my interest in neonatal and prenatal autonomic regulation. The dissertation uncovered another important finding in my HRV journey. It documented both the HRV level prior to the task and the suppression of HRV during the predicted reaction time. These findings set the stage for future research in individual differences and mental effort. The findings also influenced my research agenda by directing me into the interdependent challenges of understanding the neural mechanisms mediating HRV, developing methodologies to quantify HRV, and studying the maturation of the neural mechanisms.

The academic marketplace was far different from what it is now. When I finished my PhD at the age of 25 there was an expectation that I would have an academic job. This expectation was not atypical, and during my 4th year in graduate school I was offered attractive positions. I accepted a position at West Virginia University with an expectation that I would create a developmental psychophysiology research program. WVU had an optimistic perspective and the psychology department was expanding, hiring both a young cohort and also seasoned, established full professors. The department had a plan to become a visible program with a strength focusing on life-span developmental psychology. This seemed like a perfect place to start my academic career. At WVU I was given access to research space in the university hospital's newborn nursery, where I studied the heart rate patterns of newborns to visual and auditory stimuli and conducted a study on temporal conditioning. After 2 years, I left WVU to move to the University of Illinois at Urbana-Champaign, where I joined the department of psychology. Over the next 50 years I have been in several universities and affiliated with several academic programs; however, my research has continued to be focused on the autonomic nervous system and the important information that can be obtained through the quantification of HRV. Rather than elaborating on how my research bridged numerous disciplines and applications, the remaining part of the chapter provides a history of the antecedent science that preceded my work. It is an opportunity for me to honor those whose work provided the scholarly platform for mine.

WHERE DID HRV START?: A DEPENDENCE ON TECHNOLOGY

Although the research questions in psychophysiology are dependent on theory linking physiological responses to psychological and behavioral processes, these brain-body questions cannot be empirically investigated without devices that can measure bioelectrical potentials driven by the heart, brain, muscles, and skin as well as the physical changes associated with thoracic and abdominal activity during breathing. The history of the origin of these devices and their role in the study of HRV is described in this section. Astute students of psychophysiology will note that segments of this section reflect my contributions to a previously published guidelines paper (Berntson et al., 1997).

The ability to monitor, to conceptualize, and to interpret HRV is dependent upon both the technologies for observing the beating of the heart and the methodologies for quantifying heart rate parameters. These technologies and methodologies metaphorically provide windows of observation, resulting in either clear or blurred representations. Most of the research investigating HRV has occurred during the past 50 years. Clinical interpretations and applications have an even shorter history. However, before identifying the historical turning points in the study of HRV, I will provide a short sojourn into the prehistory of HRV.

Long before the invention of the electrocardiograph and the more recent emergence of the construct of HRV, physicians realized the importance of the heart and the rhythms of the beating heart. For several hundred years, physicians used auscultation to determine heart tones and heartbeat rhythms. Although the focus of auscultation is on listening to the closure of the heart valves, for centuries physicians have noted beat-to-beat rhythm shifts associated with aging, illness, and psychological states. The study of these rhythms became a central component of various medical diagnostic systems developed in India and China.

The scientific investigation of beat-to-beat heart rate rhythms was delayed until specific technological advances enabled accurate and reliable quantification of the electrical activity of the heart. This technology progressed through the development of four devices: the galvanometer, the kymograph, the ink-writing polygraph, and the ECG.

The work of Luigi Galvani and later that of Alessandro Volta, the discoverer of electrical current, led to the development of the galvanometer. The galvanometer is a device that measures the amount of electrical current by converting electrical energy into the physical displacement of a coil, which in turns moves a pointer. Through the application of Ohm's law, the galvanometer could be calibrated to accurately measure changes in voltage, even voltages in the range of biopotentials generated by the heart. Ludwig (1847) invented the smoked kymograph that allowed mechanical activity to be recorded on a smoked drum. MacKenzie (1910), after toiling with the cumbersome kymograph, developed an ink-writing polygraph. In the 1890s, Einthoven (see Erschler, 1988) integrated the galvanometer with photography to produce accurate and continuous tracings of the electrical activity of the heart.

Once the electrocardiograph was developed, it was possible to monitor normal and abnormal electrical conduction through the myocardia as well as to evaluate beat-to-beat changes in the heart rate pattern. Modern electrocardiographs are elaborations of the early Einthoven concept with the addition of paper recordings or computerized outputs.

The origins of the scientific study of HRV predate the ECG. The first documented observation of HRV may be credited to Hales (1733), who observed a respiratory pattern in the blood pressure and pulse in a horse. However, one might argue that the scientific investigation of HRV required quantification and started with Ludwig's report that, with the kymograph, he was able to observe a regular quickening of pulse rate with inspiration and a slowing with exhalation in the dog (Ludwig, 1847). This may be the first documented report of respiratory sinus arrhythmia (RSA), a provocative topic in contemporary research on HRV. In 1865, Traube (cited in Anrep et al., 1936a) speculated on the neurophysiological mechanisms mediating RSA and proposed that the brainstem nuclei controlling heart rate might be phase dependent and influence heart rate by direct neural pathways from the medullary respiratory centers. Interestingly, more recent foundational neuroanatomical and neurophysiological data support a contemporary version of this model. Specifically, Richter and Spyer (1990) proposed a common cardiopulmonary oscillator that was dependent on the interneuronal communication between brainstem structures involved in the vagal regulation of the heart and the bronchi (i.e., nucleus ambiguus and nucleus tractus solitarius) driving similar oscillations in heart rate (i.e., RSA) and the bronchi. The phase relationship between oscillations in heart rate and bronchi was proposed in PVT (Porges, 1995) and more recently documented (Giardino et al., 2003) to optimize diffusion of oxygen. Basically, the oscillatory rise in heart rate produces a transitory increase in blood pressure that is phase optimized with bronchial oscillations to literally push oxygen into the blood during inhalation.

In 1871, Hering (see Anrep et al., 1936a) proposed an alternative but not necessarily contradictive explanation. Hering proposed that reflex modulation of the cardioregulatory centers by pulmonary afferent feedback may be the physiological mechanisms underlying RSA. In addition, he reported that the systematic pattern of heart rate changes associated with breathing disappeared with advancing age. Consistent with this speculation, we confirmed an age related decrease in the amplitude of RSA (see Byrne et al., 1996). But perhaps most insightful and relevant to contemporary psychophysiology and RSA-focused biofeedback was Hering's observation (1910) that he could identify cardioinhibitory fibers traveling from the brainstem down to the heart through the vagus. As he so succinctly stated: "It is known with breathing that a demonstrable lowering of heart rate . . . is indicative of the function of the vagi." Hering's observation that breathing lowers our heart rate and that the vagus is behind this slowdown, was hugely foundational for the development of PVT. It also gave psychophysiologists and physiologists a neurophysiological basis to develop a noninvasive method for measuring vagal activity using the RSA component of HRV. In addition, it gave biofeedback researchers a validated neural portal to target and monitor. With the ability to easily measure vagal activity, various hypotheses derived from PVT could be objectively tested. This later point is critical in understanding the focus on quantitative methods to refine estimates of vagal activity in my research.

The history of the study of HRV is dependent upon the ability and strategy to quantify beat-to-beat activity. Accurate timing of beat-to-beat variability was dependent upon the detection of features of ECG (e.g., peak of the R-wave), and thus the era of scientific investigation of HRV was dependent upon the availability of the electrocardiograph for physiological and clinical research. As described above, specific electrophysiological devices were required to provide accurate measures of cardiac activity prior to the development of the research area. Research has been aided by techniques to detect and accurately time the onset of sequential heartbeats. Engineers developed electrical circuits to identify the peak of R-waves and timers that evolved into tachometers. With the advent of laboratory computers, timing became more precise and accurate and computer algorithms were able to detect R-waves and other components of the ECG.

Although not exhaustive, several historical studies highlight the emergence of HRV as a physiologically meaningful measure. Most of these early clinical and physiological studies have focused on RSA. In fact, in early research there is little distinction between a global concept of sinus arrhythmia and the more specific rhythmicity of RSA. However, from my perspective the descriptive statistics frequently used to quantify HRV are agnostic to neural mechanisms and have frequently diverted researchers from neural mechanisms, while RSA is implicitly a metric dependent on specific neural pathways embedded in the vagus (see section below on quantification).

From several scientific sources, references to RSA were made in the early 1900s. Even in the early psychology textbooks, there is mention of the phenomenon that later became known as RSA. For example, Wundt and Judd (1902) stated, "The movements of the lungs: their inflation accelerates, their collapse reduces the frequency of heartbeat. The respiratory movements are therefore regularly accompanied by fluctuations of the pulse, whose rapidity increases in inspiration and decreases in expiration."

Initially, research on HRV moved in two directions. First, there was a dominant trend toward understanding the physiological mechanisms mediating HRV. Second, clinical medicine identified specific relationships between HRV and clinical status. These two directions coexisted prior to the emergence of psychophysiology. However, in the 1960s with the availability of polygraphs in academic laboratories, a third trend appeared when psychophysiologists started to investigate the relationship between psychological processes and HRV. This trend also included the application of learning and conditioning strategies to modify HRV, which led to the emergence of biofeedback as a discipline focusing on clinical treatment strategies. As the third trend expanded research, HRV became an accepted variable capable of indexing resilience and vulnerability in medical and mental health. With this interest, researchers became intrigued with the possibility of enhancing HRV through biofeedback as a clinical technology to optimize health. This clinical and applied interest in modifying autonomic regulation led to the establishment in 1969 of the Biofeedback Research Society, which evolved into the Association for Applied Psychophysiology and Biofeedback.

Bainbridge (1920) provided an early example of physiological research on HRV when he attempted to explain RSA in terms of alterations in baroreceptor and volume receptor responses to changes in blood flow caused by changes in thoracic pressure associated with respiration. Anrep and colleagues (1936a, 1936b) pursued alternative explanations of the physiological mechanisms mediating RSA. They published what appears to be the first extensive study of RSA. Anrep and his colleagues investigated the influence of several physiological parameters on RSA including the influence of respiratory rate and amplitude, blood gas concentrations, and efferent cardioregulatory neural pathways.

Eppinger and Hess (1915) published a monograph in *Nervous and Mental Disease* entitled "Vagotonia." The publication illustrates the interest in the emerging area of psychiatry of the autonomic nervous system. The focus of their monograph was to emphasize that an apparent "hyperactivated" vagus was associated with mental disorders. Their monograph provided a starting point for the clinical trend. They stated that "clinical facts, such as respiratory arrhythmia, habitual bradycardia, etc., have furnished the means of drawing our attention to the variations in the tonus of the vagal system in man." Although Eppinger and Hess were interested in clinical medicine, their case studies described a relation between a clinical problem in the regulation of autonomic function that did not have a morphological correlate with the available technology. Their observations are relevant to contemporary psychophysiological investigation of HRV and the emerging discipline of functional medicine for several reasons including: (1) they alerted us to the importance of the autonomic nervous system in mediating atypical physiological responses; (2) they related individual differences in physiology to individual differences in psychiatric pathology (i.e., neuroses); (3) they recognized the pharmacological sensitivity of the vagus to cholinergic agents, thereby potentially identifying pharmacological treatments; and (4) they brought to the attention of the medical community the commonality of the vagal innervation of various peripheral organs and thus a possible common explanation for several clinical disorders.

Clinical research interests were rekindled in cardiology by the early research of Wolf (1967) and in obstetrics and gynecology by Hon (see Hon & Lee, 1963). Both Hon and Wolf emphasized the relationship between HRV and nervous system status. Hon treated HRV as a global index of clinical viability of the fetus and neonate. Wolf, with his focus on the contribution of central nervous system factors to sudden cardiac death, viewed HRV as representing brain-vagal-heart communication. Wolf's research with a theoretical interest in brain-heart relations provides an important bridge between clinical research and psychophysiology.

QUANTIFICATION

Heart rate patterns are complicated and often idiosyncratic time series. Although we now know that the beat-to-beat pattern is continuously influenced by the changing neural influence from the brainstem to the heart, within psychophysiology the focus on the neural component was often neglected in publications and presentations. The procedures selected to quantify HRV are critical both in extracting physiologically meaningful components and in building a plausible neurophysiological model relating physiological activity to behavior and psychological processes.

There are two basic approaches to the quantification of HRV: (1) the use of descriptive statistics (i.e., range, standard deviation, variance, etc.) and (2) the modeling of the heart rate pattern to extract variance components defined by amplitude and frequency determined by known physiological mechanisms (e.g., RSA). While both approaches produce descriptive statistics, the descriptive approach is influenced by the duration of the data sampled, the mean level and the complex interactions of various neural influences on the overall HRV. It is important to note that the two approaches are not convergent with the prevalent distinction of time domain versus frequency domain. Time domain methods can be used to model periodic processes and, if the data are statistically stationary, any frequency domain method can be transformed into a time domain method (Brillinger, 1975). However, time domain representations may have advantages when data are not statistically stationary (Bohrer & Porges, 1982; Porges & Bohrer, 1990). For example, since psychophysiologists are interested in the changing level of variables such as RSA, the data would be nonstationary. My work with Robert Bohrer, a mathematician, resulted in an innovative time domain method to study the changing amplitude of periodic components, even in dynamic situations (e.g., Bohrer & Porges, 1982; Porges, 1985, 1986a, 1986b; Porges & Bohrer, 1990).

The early history of psychophysiology focused on the use of descriptive statistics (e.g., Porges, 1972; Porges & Raskin, 1969). By the late 1970s there was interest in a different and perhaps more precise way of quantifying HRV via time-series analyses. Time-series analyses provided a method of modeling periodic components of the heart rate time series and in extracting periodic components that might have physiological and psychophysiological significance. With the support of my collaborator, Robert Bohrer, we organized a symposium and two workshops on the application of time-series analyses of HRV that were presented to the membership of the Society for Psychophysiological Research. In 1978 at the Madison, Wisconsin, meeting, we organized a preconference symposium on the potential applications of spectral and cross-spectral analyses for the quantification of HRV and heart rate–respiratory coupling. This was followed in 1983 when we conducted a full-day workshop on spectral analyses at the Asilomar meeting. In 1984 we conducted a second full-day workshop on HRV at the Milwaukee meeting. These well-attended workshops served to stimulate many investigators to apply spectral analyses and other time-series methods to the study of HRV.

The measurement of HRV also illustrates a historical trend. In early clinical research HRV was quantified as a descriptive statistic of range or standard deviation. For example, during the past 50 years clinicians in obstetrics and neonatology (e.g., Hon & Lee, 1963), have defined HRV in terms of the standard deviation of beat-to-beat values over short durations (i.e., short-term variability) or the range over longer periods (i.e., long-term variability). In basic research areas newer methods were introduced to extract periodic components from the heart rate pattern. Chess and colleagues (1975) introduced spectral analyses to the measurement of HRV. Porges and colleagues (1976, 1980) introduced cross-spectral analysis as a method of evaluating the linkage between respiration and HRV in humans and speculated that the sum of the spectral densities in the heart rate spectrum associated with the respiratory rhythms was an accurate estimate of vagal tone (1985b). Akselrod and colleagues (1981) applied spectral analysis to dog heart rate and demonstrated that the respiratory rhythm in the heart rate spectrum was related to vagal tone. In addition, they identified two slower frequency bands, which they presumed were related to an interaction between vagal and sympathetic influences. Although commonly assumed, there is no reliable evidence that the slower frequencies or the ratio between the slower frequencies and RSA reflect sympathetic influences or can be used as an index of sympathovagal balance (see Eckberg, 1997). In addition, research in my laboratory clearly documents that virtually all spontaneously periodic variability is determined via cholinergic pathways assumed to travel through the vagus (Grippo et al., 2007; Porges, 2007). These observations do not preclude potential interactions with sympathetic nervous system (SNS), but the lower frequency HRV components are certainly not a direct index of the SNS.

In the early 1980s my laboratory introduced a time-frequency methodology (Porges, 1985a; Porges & Bohrer, 1990). This methodology has been documented to be significantly more sensitive to vagal influences than the traditional time- and frequency-domain method (see Lewis et al., 2012). This time-frequency methodology, by enabling estimates of RSA during short epoch (e.g., 10–15 seconds), provided an opportunity to ask new questions. With short estimates the dynamic relationship between RSA and heart rate could be quantified. Functionally, the metric provides a measure of vagal efficiency operationally defined as the slope of the regression. The slope provides a metric that describes the millisecond change in heart period that would occur with a change of one log unit of RSA amplitude. The initial study documented that newborn sleep state could be reliably detected by this method (Porges et al., 1999). This finding recently has been replicated with high-risk preterm infants and expanded to index clinical course in this fragile group (Porges et al., 2019). Additional studies indicated that in response to alcohol, vagal efficiency decreased in humans (Reed, Porges, et al., 1999). As we became more familiar with the metric, systematic challenges were used. In a clinical study using a posture-challenge protocol, it was possible to detect a subset of patients in a pediatric gastroenterology clinic with joint hypermobility syndrome (Kolacz et al., 2021). In another study, an exercise bike challenge was used with college students, and vagal efficiency distinguished participants with and without a maltreatment history (see Dale, Kolacz, et al., 2022). On a clinical level, it appears that vagal efficiency may provide an objective metric related to the clinical features associated with a diagnosis of dysautonomia. Our current research is focusing on vagal efficiency as being an objective neurophysiological index that may be associated with a broad array of functional disorders.

DEPENDENCE ON THEORY AND THEORY AS FILTER

Psychophysiology has been the crossroads of different models and strategies for research. Unlike physiology with its interest in mechanism, or cardiology with its interest in clinical status, psychophysiology has often been driven by paradigms derived from psychology focusing on demonstrating that physiological parameters are correlated with psychological and behavioral states. The early history of the Society for Psychophysiological Research and the early issues of *Psychophysiology* echo this strategy with psychophysiologists expressing an aphysiological treatment of physiological parameters. Thus, although the measures of physiological activity were operationally defined and diligently quantified, the articles and presentations were virtually devoid of a reference to the neural mechanisms of the physiological response variables. In the early days of the society, psychophysiologists treated physiological parameters similarly to overt behavior or subjective reports with the exception that to study physiological activity it was first necessary to transform the physiological activity into an observable tracing on the polygraph.

At the time I first presented PVT, arousal theory was the prevalent theoretical perspective in psychophysiology. Although arousal theory had a long, influential history in science, it had a relatively simplistic underlying model. Basically, arousal theory emphasized that arousal was a linear construct indexing a dimension from low to high levels of activation that could be measured or inferred from observing behavior or physiology. The relationship between arousal and performance was often portrayed as an inverted U-shaped function in which optimal performance occurred within a mid-level range, while poor performance was observed at low and high levels of arousal. This relationship was known as the Yerkes-Dodson law (Yerkes & Dodson, 1908). Metaphorically, arousal represented the energy of the human nervous system. Arousal was easily understood, since when it was reflected behaviorally it could be quantified as greater activity and when reflected autonomically it could be observed as increases in sweating and heart rate.

Early psychophysiological research assumed that peripheral autonomic measures provided sensitive indicators of arousal. This view was based on a rudimentary understanding of the autonomic nervous system in which changes in electrodermal activity (e.g., sweating) and heart rate were assumed to be accurate indicators of sympathetic activity. As the activation arousal theory developed, a continuity between peripheral autonomic responses and central mechanisms was assumed (see Darrow et al., 1942), and sympathetic activity was assumed to parallel activation of the brain. According to this assumption, organs influenced by sympathetic efferent fibers, such as the sweat glands, blood vessels, or the heart, were potential indicators of limbic or cortical activity (Duffy, 1957; Lindsley, 1951; Malmo, 1959).

Although the specific pathways relating these various levels were never outlined and are still sketchy, electrodermal activity (e.g., galvanic skin resistance or GSR) and heart rate became the primary focus of research during the early history of the Society for Psychophysiological Research. This was due to their presumed sympathetic innervation and, in part, to their measurement availability. By default, this emphasis created a research environment that neglected several important factors: (a) parasympathetic (e.g., vagal) influences, (b) interactions between sympathetic and parasympathetic processes, (c) peripheral autonomic afferents, (d) central regulatory structures, (e) the adaptive and dynamic nature of the autonomic nervous system, and (f) phylogenetic and ontogenetic differences in structural organization and function.

In general, arousal theory was a top-down model that implicitly led to attempts to translate from psychological to physiological phenomena, a strategy that could be succinctly labeled as psychophysiological parallelism. As a research strategy, psychophysiological parallelism makes a strong assumption that it is possible to identify unique neurophysiological signatures of specific mental processes (e.g., feelings, emotions, thoughts, etc.).

In the 1960s, psychophysiology emerged as an interdisciplinary science with historic roots embedded in an assumed psychophysiological parallelism, which was consistent with arousal theory having parallel outputs in the brain, the autonomic nervous system, and behavior. Although PVT (Porges, 1995) emerged from traditional psychophysiology, it provided a theoretical demarcation from parallelism. In a sense, psychophysiological parallelism implicitly assumed that the constructs employed in different domains were valid (e.g., subjective, observable, physiological) and focused on establishing correlations across domains that optimistically would lead to an objectively quantifiable physiological signature of the construct explored in the psychological domain. In contrast, PVT underscores the interactive and integrative aspect of different levels of the nervous system.

PVT emphasizes a hierarchical organization that mirrors phylogenetic shifts among vertebrates. The evolutionary changes are also reflected in maturational trends. Thus, what appears to be more complex and related to higher brain structures, such as language and sensitivities to another's physiological state via intonation of voice and gesture, is reflecting the functional and structural changes mapped into the evolutionary history of vertebrates. Frequently missed with our cortico-centric and cognitive-centric orientation is the importance of lower brain mechanisms in managing our basic survival-oriented reactions. Although the less complex earlier evolved systems are often repurposed in mammals, they remain survival oriented and are efficiently available to support states of defense when survival is challenged.

Psychophysiological parallelism is functionally a scientific strategy that assumes an isomorphic representation of a process with the gradations being mapped with equivalent precision on all levels. An alternate and more parsimonious strategy would be to organize the nervous system into a hierarchical format in which neurophysiological processes related to basic biologically determined survival needs are required to be managed successfully before higher brain structures are functionally given access to be activated for problem solving, creativity, and even sociality. PVT postulates that our biology is hierarchically organized with the basic survival needs, such as managing homeostatic functions, residing in foundational brainstem structures; optimal access and utilization of higher neural circuits depend on success at the foundational level. PVT provides insights into what the hierarchy is and how it can be identified and potentially monitored. According to the theory, the hierarchy reflects the phylogenetic shifts in the nervous system (see Porges, 2021, 2022).

Against the backdrop of arousal theory, psychophysiological parallelism, a bias toward static metrics of autonomic function (e.g., resting heart rate, blood pressure), and a limited understanding of how the dynamic regulation of the autonomic nervous system could support or disrupt homeostasis, PVT emerged on an October morning in 1994 as the focus of my presidential address at the annual meeting of the Society for Psychophysiological Research in Atlanta, Georgia. The presentation was formalized into a manuscript and published in the society's journal, *Psychophysiology* (Porges, 1995). At that time, my objective was to archive the extracted principles from my previous 25 years of research and to challenge my discipline to explore autonomic reactivity from a new perspective. Although several of the principles were novel, the general questions were familiar to psychophysiologists, who were vested in exploring the utility of monitoring heart rate patterns to gain additional information about mental and health-related processes.

PVT did not fit well within the constraints of arousal theory, although PVT could provide a neural explanation of arousal theory. Arousal theory fit an outdated, but still taught, model of the autonomic nervous system that interpreted arousal as a competition between the sympathetic and parasympathetic nervous systems reflected in autonomic balance. However, it did not provide any explanation of how low arousal could occur with increases in parasympathetic nervous system activation.

In contrast to the top-down tenets of arousal theory, PVT approached the autonomic nervous system as a feedback system that functioned to optimize homeostatic processes of health, growth, and restoration. Through the lens of PVT, homeostasis has a more nuanced meaning involving the status of feedback circuits involving the bidirectional communication between organs and the brainstem. The traditional autonomic model assumed that homeostasis was relatively stable and was maintained by the competing inputs from the sympathetic and parasympathetic divisions of the autonomic nervous system, although the pathways involved in feedback circuits determining homeostasis were not elaborated. PVT, with its emphasis on bidirectional communication between brain structures and visceral organs, assumes that homeostasis is best described not solely by a static set point, but requires an additional assessment of the systematic perturbations around the set point. Strikingly, within physiology, psychophysiology, and even medicine, there is little acknowledgment of the important role of afferents (a defining feature of a feedback system) that travel primarily through the vagus from several visceral organs to a brainstem center, providing the relevant information to ensure that the output to the organs supports homeostatic functions.

PVT required a different quantification strategy. A new family of metrics (e.g., RSA as an index of vagal regulation of the heart and more recently vagal efficiency) needed to be developed to accurately monitor the dynamic regulation of the autonomic nervous system. The theory encouraged scientists to look beyond mean levels of variables and to study the periodicities in the physiological signal that represented the features of the feedback system that evolved to optimize homeostasis. Time-series methodologies complemented descriptive statistics, and new measures (e.g., RSA) described the systematic perturbations around the set point.

Conceptually, we can visualize the amplitude of RSA as an index of the degree that the autonomic nervous system is supporting either homeostasis or bodily movement, often in support of the mobilization of behavioral (i.e., fight-or-flight) reactions to threat. The vagal brake represents the actions of engaging and disengaging the vagal influences on the heart's pacemaker. If the vagus no longer influences the heart, heart rate spontaneously increases without any change in sympathetic excitation. The intrinsic heart rate of young healthy adults is about 90 beats per minute. However, baseline heart rate is noticeably slower due to the influence of the vagus functioning as a vagal brake. In addition, since the amplitude of RSA represents the strength of the vagal brake, by monitoring RSA we are functionally monitoring the homeostatic reserve of the autonomic nervous system to the challenges that we often label as stress. Thus, disruption of homeostasis, indexed by RSA and vagal efficiency, would be an accurate measurable indicator of the impact of challenges and might be a more functional definition of stress than levels of adrenal hormones (e.g., cortisol).

Without sensitive metrics to assess the neural regulation supporting visceral organs, clinical medicine is unable to detect the antecedent disruption in neural regulation that would precede organ damage. Although the sensory pathways of the vagus function as a surveillance system continuously updating brainstem regulatory centers on organ status, this conceptualization of dynamic feedback in the regulation of visceral organs has not been emphasized in the training of physicians. Although end-organ evaluation through biopsy and blood tests dominates the assessment models of visceral organs, tapping into the constant surveillance of visceral organs through vagal or other neural pathways has not been frequently acknowledged by physicians. If you are curious about this statement, just ask your internist what they have learned about the sensory fibers linking the brain with the organs they treat (e.g., heart, kidney, liver, lung).

The introduction of HRV within psychophysiology, and especially PVT, required a shift in theoretical orientation regarding heart rate to emphasize that neural influences via feedback produced oscillations in heart rate. In the early studies of HRV, HRV was treated as a descriptive variable without attributing any specific underlying physiological mechanism for the variability of the beat-to-beat variance. HRV was quantified as the variability of beat-to-beat or second-to-second patterns.

HRV cannot be studied without an understanding of the neural regulation of the heart and the construct of a feedback system. However, interest in neural regulation of the heart was **not** a major concern during the founding years of psychophysiology. Without an understanding of neural mechanisms, the prevalent theoretical perspective of psychophysiologists in the 1960s was that HRV was error caused by either poor experimental control or inaccurate measurement. When I presented my early studies on HRV, several senior colleagues argued that the findings were spurious and due to inadequate experimental control. Their perspective was consistent with an assumption that heart rate, similar to behavior, required an identifiable external stimulus to evoke a reliable response. This perspective highlights the inadequacy of a simplistic stimulus-response (S-R) or cause-and-effect model. An important tenet of PVT is the role of autonomic state as an intervening variable and placing indices of autonomic state (e.g., RSA, vagal efficiency) as the "O" in a more explanatory S-O-R model. Our research continues to document the important mediating influence of autonomic state on clinical outcome (see Dale, Cuffe, et al., 2022; Dale, Kolacz, et al., 2022; Kolacz et al., 2020), whether the metric used is autonomic (e.g., RSA, vagal efficiency) or subjective reports of autonomic state (e.g., Cabrera et al., 2018).

In closing, I have been informed by my personal journey studying HRV that certain strategies are beneficial. First, although we are attracted to psychological processes such as cognitions and emotions or mental health diagnoses, we need to respect that higher brain functions are dependent on brainstem foundational survival mechanisms not being triggered into states that support defense. Basically, the higher brain processes are dependent on circuits supporting homeostatic functions (see Porges, 2022). Similarly, when we focus on medical disorders, we need to acknowledge that the target organs expressing these disorders may be directly influenced by these brainstem foundational survival mechanisms; the symptoms may be a direct consequence of this system going into a state that supports defense and not homeostatic functions. Second, ANS states supporting homeostatic functions can be monitored through HRV metrics. However, the sensitivity of the HRV metric to neural influences varies by the methodology used. The predictive value of the HRV metric is dependent on its validity to track neural regulation. Specifically, we know most about the neural influences mediating RSA. When carefully quantified, RSA is an excellent index of vagal efferent activity regulated by the ventral vagal nucleus (i.e., nucleus ambiguus) (Lewis et al., 2011). Third, HRV metrics that have neural validity are more accurate indicators of the "O" in S-O-R models and hypothetically should be more sensitive to mental, behavioral, and health. Fourth, since biofeedback as a discipline is focused on optimizing the "O" in the "S-O-R" model, the implementation of more accurate indices of the "O" should result in a more efficient implementation of biofeedback protocols with more optimized outcomes.

Exploring Vagal Nerve Stimulation Through the Lens of the Polyvagal Theory

Stephen W. Porges

INTRODUCTION

Vagal nerve stimulation, viewed through the Polyvagal Theory (PVT), highlights three key aspects. First, it underscores the correlation between the ventral vagal complex's functions and the alleviation of symptoms achieved by vagal nerve stimulation, enhancing both mental and physical well-being. Second, it shifts the focus of vagal nerve stimulation from the entire nerve to specific afferent pathways communicating with brainstem regions regulating somatomotor and visceromotor efferent pathways originating in the ventral vagal complex. Third, it acknowledges that vagal nerve stimulation has a positive impact, counteracting the detrimental effects of trauma and chronic stress on autonomic function, disrupting the adaptive role of the ventral vagal complex in managing threat responses and optimizing sociality, health, growth, and restoration processes. As our understanding of the anatomical pathways within the vagus improves, the methods and clinical targets of vagal nerve stimulation will become more specific. As this new knowledge becomes integrated into technologies, new procedures may lead to a new class of vagal neuromodulators that act as neural exercises, fostering a more resilient autonomic nervous system without necessitating chronic usage.

EVOLUTION AND THE EMERGENCE
OF A VENTRAL VAGAL CIRCUIT

PVT highlights the evolutionary journey from the limited social behaviors of reptiles to the highly social face-to-face interactions of mammals. The theory emphasizes how the autonomic nervous system was repurposed and reorganized during this transition. In fact, there are unique structural and functional changes in the vagus that hypothetically would have distinguished the earliest mammals from their ancestral reptiles. These changes enabled mammals to suppress defensive strategies, allowing expression of signals of safety that both promote sociality and optimize homeostatic functions.

The product of this transition is an autonomic nervous system with a ventral vagal circuit that facilitates capacities to self-calm, to socially engage others, and to mitigate internal and external threat reactions in ourselves and others through social cues. When this uniquely mammalian ventral vagal pathway is chronically disrupted, mental and physical health problems arise.

Through a careful identification of these evolutionary changes in structure and function, contemporary interest in vagal nerve stimulation (VNS) is easily understood and justified. Moreover, by understanding how vagal activity is related to signals of safety and threat there is an opportunity to expand portals, effectively stimulating the vagus as a neuromodulatory intervention to support health-related functions (Porges, 2022).

The ventral vagus is part of a circuit that evolved, as a core mechanism, to mitigate threat, enhance sociality, and optimize visceral-organ regulation (i.e., homeostasis). The neuroanatomy and neurophysiology of important vagal pathways can be objectively monitored via noninvasive techniques (i.e., measuring components of heart rate variability) and potentially targeted for neuromodulation with vagal nerve stimulation techniques. By exploring new frontiers within neuroanatomy and neurophysiology, we gain insights into other portals that may functionally enhance vagal communication, through both direct and indirect neural pathways to support more optimal health and performance.

For mammals, survival is dependent on their sociality to cooperate, to connect, and to co-regulate. To enable these prosocial processes to occur, the primordial defense programs dependent on sympathetic activation to support fight-or-flight behaviors and vagal activation (via the dorsal motor nucleus of the vagus) to support immobilization (e.g., death feigning) had to be harnessed and repurposed. This transition in autonomic function was dependent on the ventral vagal circuit, which provided the neuroanatomical connections.

Ultimately, this evolutionary process resulted in a reorganized brainstem network known as the ventral vagal complex, from which a discrete branch of the vagus nerve enabled the expression of several uniquely mammalian features—such as the ability to calm and to signal safety to conspecifics. Consequently, sociality and feelings of safety became intrinsically linked with specific neurobiological processes capable of mitigating threats and supporting mental and physical health. The impact of this evolutionary transition on the adaptive biobehavioral repertoire of mammals cannot be underestimated. The ability to stimulate this component of vagal function contributes to the current interest in vagal nerve stimulation.

When this calming system is disrupted, markers of chronic stress and core features shared by several psychiatric conditions are expressed (e.g., flat facial affect, poor vocal prosody, hypervigilance, hyperreactivity, and hypersensitivities to auditory, visual, and tactile stimuli). These features are not unique to a specific diagnosis but rather reflect an adaptive adjustment of the autonomic nervous system to support strategies of defense. Moreover, not only are the psychological and behavioral features of calmness and sociality disrupted, but there are also frequent disruptions in the function of visceral organs reflected in cardiopulmonary and digestive disorders. The commonly observed parallel symptoms manifest in mental health challenges and end-organ disease are often misunderstood as unrelated comorbidities. From a polyvagal perspective, somatic and mental health conditions share a dependency on vagal regulation of the autonomic nervous system. Dampened vagal regulation specific to the ventral vagal pathway that is often detected as low heart rate variability or respiratory sinus arrhythmia (RSA) appears to be a common neurobiological marker of both mental health conditions (e.g., depression, PTSD) and visceral disorders (e.g., irritable bowel syndrome [IBS], heart disease, diabetes) (Arakaki et al., 2023; Mulcahy et al., 2019; Thayer et al., 2012). It is this common feature of an apparent diminished ventral vagal influence that has directed interest in remediating and optimizing vagal function via methods of vagal nerve stimulation.

Anatomically, the vagus is a mixed nerve containing both efferent and afferent fibers originating in three primary brainstem nuclei: the dorsal nucleus of the vagus, the nucleus of the solitary tract, and the nucleus ambiguus—often described as the ventral nucleus of the vagus. A fourth nucleus, the spinal trigeminal nucleus that receives primary input from the trigeminal nerve, has a minor input from the vagus nerve. The complexity of the neuronal activity traveling through the nerve can render concepts like vagal tone and vagus nerve stimulation confusing and ambiguous. Since the various vagal pathways evolved at different stages of vertebrate evolution and support distinct adaptive functions, metrics evaluating vagal activity and devices designed to stimulate activity need to indicate which pathways are being monitored or stimulated.

The dorsal vagal nucleus is a structure shared with virtually all vertebrate species. In mammals, the dorsal vagus is predominantly an unmyelinated motor pathway that exits the dorsal side of the brainstem and primarily regulates organs below the diaphragm. This does not preclude the observation that some dorsal vagal fibers influence organs above the diaphragm such as the heart. For example, dorsal vagal pathways are presumed to be responsible for the clinical bradycardia observed in high-risk newborns (Reed, Ohel, et al., 1999).

Developmentally, the vagal nuclei parallel evolution, with the dorsal vagus becoming functional prior to the ventral vagus. The nucleus of the solitary tract functions as the sensory portal for the organs regulated by the dorsal vagus, although there is reported afferent activity traveling through the solitary tract originating in organs regulated by the ventral vagus. The third vagal nucleus, nucleus ambiguus, serves as the source nucleus for the efferent pathways of the ventral vagus. The ventral vagal pathways are myelinated and originate in the brainstem ventral to both the dorsal vagal nucleus and the nucleus of the solitary tract. The three primary vagal nuclei (nucleus ambiguus, dorsal motor nucleus of the vagus, and nucleus of the solitary tract) have a viscerotropic representation in which different visceral organs are topographically linked to different portions of the nucleus.

Unlike other ancestral vertebrates, the cardioinhibitory ventral vagus originating in the nucleus ambiguus is uniquely mammalian and is a marker of a repurposed autonomic nervous system that integrates sociality as a portal for enhancing cardioinhibitory vagal function. Thus, sociality recruits the ventral vagus into an integrated biobehavioral calming circuit. Moreover, the chronotropic influence through ventral vagal pathways has a respiratory rhythm (Porges, 2011), while chronotropic influences through the dorsal vagal pathways do not (Gourine et al., 2016). This distinction enables the dynamic monitoring of the effect of vagal nerve stimulation on the ventral vagus via quantifying respiratory sinus arrhythmia.

Contemporary approaches to VNS are focused on afferents to enhance the efferent regulation of the **ventral** vagus. Functionally, this becomes obvious if we explore the impact of direct stimulation of the two primary vagal efferent pathways (i.e., the ventral vagus pathway originating in the nucleus ambiguus and the dorsal vagal pathway originating in the nucleus of the dorsal vagus). In general, increasing ventral vagal outflow is calming, supports sociality, and optimizes homeostatic function including the dorsal vagal regulation of organs below the diaphragm (Kolacz et al., 2019; Kolacz et al., 2021; Kovacic et al., 2020). In fact, extreme vagal influence through the dorsal vagus has been proposed as causal for severe gut problems including ulcers (Burge, 1970), and there are documented contraindications of diarrhea (Sanossian & Haut, 2002) when the intensity of an implantable vagal nerve stimulator is set to high.

A FUNCTIONAL SOCIAL ENGAGEMENT SYSTEM

The ventral vagus emerges from a brainstem area known as the ventral vagal complex. The ventral vagal complex contains the source nuclei of a subset of special visceral efferent pathways traveling through five cranial nerves (i.e., trigeminal, facial, glossopharyngeal, vagus, and accessory) that innervate the striated muscles of the face and head. These pathways regulate aspects of social engagement (e.g., intonation of voice, facial expression) and permit the coordination of sucking, swallowing, vocalizing, and breathing. Systematic recruitment of these systems as well as active listening may function as neural exercises to enhance the regulatory function of the ventral vagus.

As illustrated in Figure 9.1, the outputs of the social engagement system consist of motor pathways regulating striated muscles of the face and head (i.e., somatomotor) and smooth and cardiac muscles of the heart and bronchi (i.e., visceromotor). The somatomotor component involves a subset of special visceral efferent pathways that regulate the striated muscles of the face and head. The visceromotor component involves the myelinated supradiaphragmatic ventral vagal pathway that regulates the heart and bronchi. Functionally, the social engagement system emerges from a face-heart connection that coordinates the heart with the muscles of the face and head. An initial function of the system is to coordinate sucking, swallowing, breathing, and vocalizing. Atypical coordination of this system early in life may be life-threatening and may be a lead indicator of subsequent health-related difficulties including problems in eating, social behavior, and emotional regulation.

A functional social engagement system, based on the anatomical components of the ventral vagal complex, has been proposed (Porges, 1998). This system was operationally defined as consisting of the source nuclei of several special visceral efferent pathways and the ventral vagus (see Figure 9.1). Since the nerves regulating the striated muscles of the face and head included in the social engagement system are exclusively special visceral efferent, the exclusion of the hypoglossal nerve might be questioned. A deeper explanation notes that although the social engagement system is composed of special visceral efferent pathways, being classified as special visceral efferent is not the sole criterion for inclusion. Given that PVT has its roots in evolution and embryology, cranial nerves are viewed from an embryological and not solely from an anatomical perspective.

Incorporating an embryological perspective resulted in the selection of special visceral efferent pathways that arise only from the pharyngeal arches during embryonic development. These nerves innervate muscles involved in facial expression, mastication, and swallowing. The hypoglossal nerve originates from the occipital somites and migrates into the tongue. Since the tongue does not directly arise from the pharyngeal arches, the embryological origin of the hypoglossal nerve differs from that of other special visceral efferent pathways within the cranial nerves that were included in the social engagement system.

In structuring the functional social engagement system and its anatomical substrate, the ventral vagal complex, the inclusion of specific special visceral efferent nerves was based on two criteria: (1) the nerve arises from pharyngeal arches during embryonic development and (2) there is evidence of neural communication between the specific cranial nerve and the vagus. Applying these criteria resulted in clustering cranial nerves V, VII, IX, X, and XI, while excluding XII, the hypoglossal nerve. Consistent with these features,

FIGURE 9.1 The social engagement system consists of a somatomotor component (solid blocks) and a visceromotor component (dashed blocks). The somatomotor component involves special visceral efferent pathways that regulate the striated muscles of the face and head, while the visceromotor component involves myelinated ventral vagal pathways that regulate the heart and bronchi.

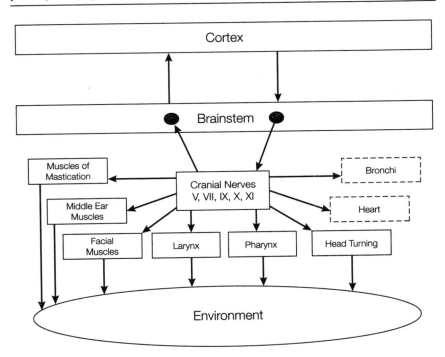

the sensory feedback into the motor centers regulating these specific special visceral pathways nerves may, via interneuronal connections, provide additional portals to regulate the ventral vagus and functionally may act as a vagal nerve stimulator.

Ingestion and social engagement share common underlying neural structures. Links between ingestion and sociality are observable through human development and within other social mammals. Both ingestion and sociality are essential for survival as evidenced by the profound consequences of malnutrition and social isolation (e.g., failure to thrive) on physical and mental well-being. Signs indicating dysfunction of the processes dependent on the ventral vagal complex appear in several clinical disorders in which patients commonly present with flat facial affect, low prosodic vocalizations, and an autonomic nervous system in a state of high sympathetic activation (e.g., autism spectrum disorders, PTSD, depression, anxiety).

When fully developed, this system expresses two important biobehavioral features. First, bodily state is efficiently regulated to promote growth and restoration (e.g., visceral homeostasis). Functionally, this is accomplished by increasing the influence of ventral vagal motor pathways on the cardiac pacemaker to calm bodily state by slowing heart rate, inhibiting the sympathetic nervous system support of fight-or-flight mechanisms, dampening the stress-response system of the hypothalamic-pituitary-adrenal axis (responsible for cortisol release), and reducing inflammation by modulating immune reactions (Porges, 2007). Second, the phylogenetically mammalian face-heart connection functions to convey a calm physiological state via facial expression and prosody (intonation of voice), as well as regulate the middle ear muscles to optimize species-specific listening within the frequency band used for social communication (Kolacz et al., 2018; Porges, 2007, 2009, 2011; Porges & Lewis, 2010).

The brainstem source nuclei of the social engagement system are influenced by higher brain structures (i.e., top-down influences) and by sensory pathways from visceral organs (i.e., bottom-up influences). Direct pathways from the cortex to the brainstem (i.e., corticobulbar pathways) reflect the influence of frontal areas of the cortex (i.e., upper motor neurons) on the medullary source nuclei of this system. Bottom-up influences occur via feedback through the sensory pathways of the vagus (e.g., tractus solitarius), conveying information from visceral organs to medullary areas (e.g., the nucleus of the solitary tract). In addition, these bottom-up pathways influence both the source nuclei of this system and the forebrain areas, via the insula, which are assumed to be involved in several psychiatric disorders, including depression and anxiety (Craig, 2005; Thayer & Lane, 2000). In addition, the anatomical structures involved in the social engagement system have neurophysiological interactions with the hypothalamic-pituitary-adrenal axis, the social neuropeptides (e.g., oxytocin and vasopressin), and the immune system (Carter, 2022; Porges, 2001).

SENSORY PATHWAYS OF THE SOCIAL ENGAGEMENT SYSTEM: POTENTIAL PORTALS TO STIMULATE VAGAL FUNCTION

The source nucleus of the facial nerve forms the border of the nucleus ambiguus, and sensory pathways from both the facial and trigeminal nerves provide sensory input to the nucleus ambiguus (Porges, 1995, 2007). Thus, the ventral vagal complex, consisting of the nucleus ambiguus and the nuclei of the trigeminal and facial nerves, is functionally related to the expression and experience of affective states and emotions. Activation of the somatomotor component (e.g., listening, ingestion, vocalizations, facial expressions) could trigger visceral changes that would support social engagement while modulating visceral state. Depending on whether there is an increase or decrease in the influence of the myelinated ventral vagal motor fibers on the sinoatrial node (i.e., increasing or decreasing the influence of the ventral vagus as a brake), social engagement behaviors would be either promoted or impeded (Porges, 1995, 2007). For example, stimulation of visceral states that promote mobilization (i.e., fight-or-flight behaviors) would impede the ability to express social engagement behaviors.

The face-heart connection enables mammals to detect whether a conspecific is in a calm physiological state and safe to approach, or in a highly mobilized and reactive physiological state during which engagement would be dangerous. The face-heart connection concurrently enables an individual to signal safety through patterns of facial expression and vocal intonation that could potentially calm an agitated conspecific to form a social relationship. When the ventral vagus is optimally functioning in social interactions, emotions are well-regulated, vocal prosody is rich, and the autonomic nervous system supports calm, spontaneous social engagement behaviors. The face-heart system is bidirectional, with the newer myelinated vagal circuit influencing social interactions and positive social interactions influencing vagal function. Thus, social interactions, similar to a vagal nerve stimulator, optimize health, dampen stress-related physiological states, and support growth and restoration. Social communication and the ability to co-regulate interactions via reciprocal social engagement systems lead to a sense of connectedness and are important defining features of the human experience.

VAGAL PATHWAYS

The ventral vagus provides the primary vagal regulation to the organs above the diaphragm. In addition, this efferent vagal pathway may inform all aspects of the autonomic nervous system, including the enteric system (Kolacz & Porges, 2018; Kolacz et al., 2019), to optimize homeostatic function. This is distinct from the vagal pathways originating in the dorsal vagal nucleus, which are unmyelinated and provide the primary vagal regulation of organs below the diaphragm. The ventral vagal complex also regulates the striated muscles of the face and head and is greatly influenced by **afferent pathways traveling through the vagus, trigeminal, and facial nerves**. This point informs us that stimulation of specific pathways of the trigeminal and facial nerves may function similarly to vago-vagal reflexes. In neurophysiological terms, there are functional trigeminal-vagal and potentially facial-vagal pathways that could efficiently and directly influence the cardioinhibitory actions of the ventral vagus on the heart, hypothetically (although not confirmed) without involving afferent pathways involving the nucleus of the solitary tract.

A functional ventral vagus, representing a restructuring of the autonomic nervous system in mammals, provides adaptive advantages that enable autonomic state to dynamically interface with the environment to down-regulate threat reactivity to optimize survival by supporting sociality and nurturance.

The dependence of survival on the ventral vagus is evident in the study of high-risk preterm infants, who may be born without a functional ventral vagus to support the coordination of suck-swallow-breath-vocalize processes.

In mammals, the brainstem areas regulating the heart and bronchi are interconnected with the areas regulating ingestion, facial expression, listening, breathing, and vocalizations, to form an integrated social engagement system. In fact, intonations of vocalizations are mediated by the vagus, enabling prosodic features of voice to convey a relatively accurate index of vagal regulation of the heart (Porges, 1995, 1998). Understanding the anatomy and neurophysiology of the ventral vagal complex informs strategies to retune autonomic function through vagal nerve stimulation and highlights the different neuroanatomical portals that may provide access to target specific functions through neuromodulation.

It is helpful to get an estimate of the distribution of different types of vagal fibers. Although the vagus is a mixed nerve, it is primarily a sensory nerve with approximately 80% of its fibers being afferent (Asala & Bower, 1986; Foley & DuBois, 1937). An estimated 80%–90% of vagal afferents are unmyelinated multimodal C-fibers, conveying mainly chemical information. The remaining 10%–20% are B- and A-fibers that convey mainly mechanical information (Jänig, 1996). Most efferent fibers involved in parasympathetic regulation are thinly myelinated or unmyelinated B- or C-fibers that arise from the dorsal vagal motor nucleus and the nucleus ambiguus (Berthoud & Neuhuber, 2000). In mammals, the current literature suggests that all myelinated vagal efferent fibers appear to originate in the nucleus ambiguus. Of the 20% of vagal fibers that are efferent, based on autopsy data with infants (Pereyra et al., 1992), approximately one-fifth are myelinated. In mammals, virtually all myelinated vagal efferent fibers appear to originate in the nucleus ambiguus. Thus, if we assume stability in the distribution ratio of myelinated to unmyelinated efferent fibers over the life span, then about 4% of all vagal fibers are myelinated efferent fibers with their primary targets being the heart and bronchi. It appears that **the activation of this small subset of vagal fibers provides the clinical focus and justification for VNS.**

VAGAL NERVE STIMULATION: ASSUMED MODE OF ACTION

Vagal nerve stimulation assumes that stimulation of vagal afferents has a direct effect on the regulation of both brainstem foundational structures regulating the autonomic nervous system and higher brain structures. The source nucleus of the vagal afferents is the nucleus of the solitary tract. This medullary nucleus plays an important role in the regulation of homeostatic functions (e.g., behavioral state, digestion, respiration, and blood pressure) and in conveying information to higher brain structures. The nucleus of the solitary tract relays the incoming sensory information via three primary pathways: (1) feedback to regulate the periphery; (2) direct projections to the nucleus ambiguus and dorsal nucleus of the vagus; and (3) ascending projections to the forebrain, primarily through the parabrachial nucleus and the locus coeruleus. The parabrachial nucleus and the locus coeruleus send direct connections to all levels of the forebrain (e.g., the hypothalamus, amygdala, thalamic regions that control the insula, orbitofrontal, and prefrontal cortices), areas that have been implicated in neuropsychiatric disorders. Thus, vagal afferent stimulation has direct input to both the lower motor neurons in the brainstem and the upper motor neurons in the cortex that regulate the social engagement system.

Early reviews provide a detailed description of the neurophysiologic basis for the intervention (George et al., 2000) and explain the neural mechanisms involved in treating depression with vagal nerve stimulation (Marangell et al., 2002). Missing from these explanations is an acknowledgment of the communication between ventral vagal efferents and the source nuclei of the nerves that regulate striated muscles of the face and head (i.e., special visceral efferent pathways), which collectively form the motor part of the social engagement system. It is this interaction that is emphasized in PVT, which may provide insights into identifying portals for vagal nerve stimulation in addition to the well-documented vago-vagal pathways via the nucleus of the solitary tract (Porges, 2001, 2007).

Extrapolating from an exogenous VNS model, one might speculate that other forms of vagal stimulation might have beneficial effects. In an earlier review (Porges, 2005) the link between vagal nerve stimulation and the reduction of autistic behaviors was described. Murphy and colleagues (2000) reported that vagal nerve stimulation reduced autistic-like behaviors. In their study, vagal stimulation was administered to six patients with hypothalamic hamartoma, a congenital brain malformation that is associated with medically refractory epilepsy and injurious autistic behavior. Four of the six patients had autistic behaviors that included poor communication, ritualisms, compulsions, poor social skills, and injury to self and others. The authors report that during vagal nerve stimulation all four participants showed impressive improvements in behavior. In one subject, the behavioral improvements were immediately reversed when the vagal nerve stimulation was temporarily discontinued without worsening of seizure frequency. Thus, as proposed by PVT, this documents a functional link between VNS and both biobehavioral state and the function of the muscles of the face and head.

Clues about the clinical effects of vagal nerve stimulation become more apparent when the neuroanatomy of the vagal pathways is understood. For example, vagal pathways from the dorsal nucleus of the vagus have powerful influences on the function of subdiaphragmatic organs. Spontaneous reactions to life threats, which may trigger a massive dorsal vagal surge associated with syncope or diarrhea, have often been experienced by individuals who have been diagnosed with PTSD or clinical disorders related to the gut or sexual function. Similar reactions have been reported in response to implantable vagal nerve stimulators.

Unlike the potential adverse direct effects of dorsal vagal pathways on visceral organs located below the diaphragm, the effects of stimulation of the ventral vagus tend to impact positively on a neurophysiological substrate that is involved in social communication, ingestion, and feelings of safety derived from a calmer autonomic nervous system (e.g., slower heart rate and optimized oxygen saturation). For example, auricular vagal nerve stimulation has been used to effectively treat acute asthma (Sandberg et al., 2000; Steyn et al., 2013), to increase peripheral blood oxygenation in diabetics (Kaniusas et al., 2015), and to reduce abdominal pain (Kovacic et al., 2017). It has been hypothesized that ventral vagal function is a mediator of dorsal vagal function, suggesting that compromises in ventral vagal regulation are lead indicators of dysfunctional dorsal vagal regulation of subdiaphragmatic organs (Kovacic et al., 2017; Kolacz et al., 2019, 2022).

VENTRAL VAGAL COMPLEX: A PORTAL FOR VAGAL NERVE STIMULATION

Neuroanatomical studies have demonstrated that visceromotor functions regulated by the ventral part of the nucleus ambiguus provide parasympathetic support for the somatomotor projections from the nucleus ambiguus as well as the trigeminal and facial nuclei. Neuroanatomical studies suggest that, unlike the dorsal vagal nucleus, which receives primary sensory input through the nucleus of the solitary tract, the nucleus ambiguus may also receive important sensory input from the trigeminal nerve. Moreover, the rostral region of the nucleus ambiguus may communicate directly with the facial nucleus. This potential coupling of nucleus ambiguus with facial and trigeminal nuclei provides a plausible anatomical substrate supporting the observed coordination between visceromotor (cardioinhibitory ventral vagal) and somatomotor (striated muscles of the face and head) pathways regulating observable behavioral functions such as swallowing (Brown, 1974), sucking (Humphrey, 1978; Porges & Lipsitt, 1993), vocal intonation (Kolacz et al., 2018; Porges & Lewis, 2010) and, perhaps, facial expressions.

The neuroanatomical mapping of the ventral vagal complex provides insight into potential portals of neuromodulation that would, by having a positive impact on autonomic regulation, produce an autonomic state that would promote calmness, sociality, and optimal mental and physical health. Specifically, PVT explains why engagement of the special visceral efferent pathways regulating the striated muscles of the face and head could function as a neural exercise dynamically influencing cardioinhibitory pathways originating in the nucleus ambiguus. Basically, these neural exercises would function as a vagal nerve stimulator. Moreover, the theory would suggest that there might be two synergistic pathways involving afferent input to enhance systemic autonomic regulation via ventral vagal efferent outflow.

ROLE OF AFFERENTS IN VAGAL NERVE STIMULATION

These two pathways, one via input from the nucleus of the solitary tract and the other via afferents providing feedback to the function of special visceral efferent pathways, travel through the vagus, accessory, trigeminal, and facial nerves that directly impact the nucleus ambiguus. Recall that the source nuclei of the facial and trigeminal nerves may provide sensory input to the nucleus ambiguus. The synergism of the functions of special visceral efferent pathways and the autonomic nervous system is observable in the complementary expression and experience of emotion and forms the basis of the social engagement system (Porges, 1998). Thus, the neuroanatomy provides two plausible routes for effect: (1) the well-documented neuroanatomical communication between the nucleus of the solitary tract and both vagal motor nuclei and (2) indirect and possibly direct communication between nucleus ambiguus and both the trigeminal and facial nuclei. In addition, the cranial portion of the accessory nerve arises directly from the nucleus ambiguus.

Noninvasive technologies that target the trigeminal afferents on the forehead have had positive effects. For example, the Monarch eTNS System has been approved for pediatric ADHD (Loo et al., 2021). Interestingly, the mode of action described on the website (https://www.monarch-etns.com/) does not acknowledge potential direct trigeminal-vagal connections. In the description, the company states, "The trigeminal nerve projects directly or indirectly to specific areas of the brain, such as the locus coeruleus, nucleus tractus solitarius, thalamus, and the cerebral cortex, which are involved in attention-deficit hyperactivity disorder (ADHD) and other disorders." Although this statement is consistent with the neuroanatomy literature, it may be incomplete. Another form of auricular neurostimulation via percutaneous electrical nerve-field stimulation reduced functional abdominal pain in adolescents (Kovacic et al., 2017). Interestingly, only participants who had poor vagal efficiency (the dynamic relationship between cardiac vagal tone, measured by respiration sinus arrhythmia, and heart rate) benefited from the stimulation. Vagal efficiency was quantified as the dynamic relationship between cardiac vagal tone (measured by respiratory sinus arrhythmia) and heart rate. Moreover, when the stimulation was terminated, the pain returned. These observations suggest we may identify a feature in vagal efficiency that would optimize the effectiveness of auricular neurostimulation (Kovacic et al., 2020).

It also appears that noninvasive technologies for vagal nerve stimulation have fewer side effects than invasive technologies. A plausible explanation of the fewer side effects is that stimulation through a select system of afferents avoids the profound possibility of directly stimulating the efferents—primarily the dorsal vagal nucleus. Functionally, a noninvasive approach of stimulating the auricular afferents of the vagus, facial, and trigeminal nerves provides an efficient means of targeting the ventral vagal pathways that neurophysiologically support homeostasis and not adaptive defense systems dependent on either access to or conservation of metabolic resources. This would be observed as an increase in sympathetic-adrenal activation to support fight-or-flight behavior or a conservation reaction of greatly reducing metabolic needs through a dorsal vagal reaction. Also, by stimulating the afferent limb, the endogenous neural regulation circuit may have endogenous constraints that hypothetically could evaluate the characteristics of the input stimulation and titrate the output to be more consistent with naturally occurring signaling. Thus, indirect vagal nerve stimulation through the afferent limb is likely not a simple pass-through circuit in which more input (i.e., stimulation) produces more outflow.

This focus on afferents that have direct and potentially indirect input, via the nucleus of the solitary tract, to the ventral vagal complex is consistent with PVT. It provides a theoretical conceptualization of exploring other portals to the ventral vagal complex that could potentially enhance and optimize the outflow of the 4% of vagal fibers that appear to be cardioinhibitory while providing an organizing signal to many attributes of the autonomic nervous system that support the homeostatic functions of health, growth, and restoration. These points support the conclusion that by refining our understanding of the component neural pathways within the vagus, we can refine the protocol to be more efficient and more directly targeted.

RECRUITING THE ACOUSTIC EFFERENT LIMB OF THE SOCIAL ENGAGEMENT SYSTEM: A PORTAL TO STIMULATE VAGAL EFFERENT ACTIVITY

The mechanisms mediating sound sensitivities, autonomic and behavioral state regulation, social engagement, and auditory processing are generally assumed to represent disparate response systems. From an empirical perspective, behavioral-state regulation and social engagement are manifested in observable behaviors. However, autonomic regulation is observed in peripheral physiology; sound sensitivities are manifested through subjective experiences; and auditory processing is manifested in expressive or receptive language skills. PVT leads us to think about a common brainstem mechanism regulating both autonomic state and the structures involved in listening. The theory proposes a strategy applying evolution as an organizing principle to understand a link between sound sensitivities, behavioral and autonomic state regulation, social engagement, and auditory processing.

According to PVT, the well-documented phylogenetic shift in neural regulation of the autonomic nervous system provided mammals with a neural circuit that promotes social interactions in safe contexts. Functionally, sociality evolved by the mechanisms that supported calm physiological states and an ability to broadcast physiological state through facial expressions and especially vocalizations within a frequency band distinct from the lower frequencies associated with reptilian predators. This mammalian circuit functions as the neural substrate for an integrated social engagement system that dampens the functional impact of sounds outside the frequency band of vocalizations employed for social communication and regulates the neural circuits that optimize autonomic regulation, behavioral state, social engagement, and auditory processing.

As illustrated in Figure 9.1, the social engagement system includes a somatomotor component with special visceral efferent pathways traveling through five cranial nerves (trigeminal nerve [V], facial nerve [VII], glossopharyngeal nerve [IX], vagus nerve [X] and accessory nerve [XI]) that regulate the striated muscles of the face and head (e.g., middle ear muscles, laryngeal muscles, muscles of mastication, facial muscles, pharyngeal muscles, and head-turning muscles). The somatomotor component regulates the pitch of vocalizations via pharyngeal and laryngeal vagal pathways, the tension on the middle ear muscles to enhance detection and processing of vocalizations, and facial expressions that supplement communicated messages and allow a listener to provide feedback to a vocalizer. But can this system be recruited to function as an acoustic simulator enhancing the function of the neural circuits dependent on the ventral vagal complex?

PVT proposes that the social engagement system is a portal to the ventral vagus, an important detail relevant to the field of vagal nerve stimulation. Specifically, the structures of the social engagement system include a visceromotor component that adjusts an individual's physiological state to complement facial and vocal signals of social communication. In effect, an individual functionally broadcasts their physiological state of calmness or defense through voice and face. Coincident with this projection of physiological state, the middle ear muscles change muscle tone to either facilitate the processing of vocalizations (e.g., by dampening the transfer of acoustic energy from low frequencies in the background) or enhance the processing of low-frequency acoustic energy at the expense of the ability to extract the acoustic information of vocalizations. This occurs because, via evolution, low-frequency acoustic information signals the proximity of predators or environmental danger.

Based on PVT, sound sensitivities and deficits in autonomic state regulation, social engagement, and auditory processing may be paralleled by reduced vagal influences on the heart and bronchi via myelinated vagal pathways. Such a reduction is an adaptive response strategy to support mobilization in dangerous environments (i.e., fight-or-flight behaviors). Since PVT articulates a hierarchy of neural circuits, the metabolic resources necessary for fight-or-flight behaviors are not efficiently available unless there is a retraction of the cardioinhibitory ventral vagal influences.

VAGAL BRAKE

The cardioinhibitory ventral vagal pathway functions as a powerful **vagal bake** on the heart's pacemaker. This pathway provides an efficient calming mechanism that functions to slow heart rate, optimize oxygenation of the blood, and down-regulate the sympathetic nervous system. This neurophysiological calming mechanism down-regulates defensive states and enables social engagement behaviors to spontaneously occur. Thus, the neural mechanisms defining the social engagement system provide a plausible model to explain why sound sensitivities and difficulties in both auditory processing and autonomic state regulation are prevalent in individuals with clinical symptoms that are due in part to an autonomic nervous system locked in a state of defense. Consistent with this model, features of the social engagement system may serve as efficient pathways to the ventral vagus. **Due to the integrated nature of the social engagement system, its structural components of the system may provide portals to stimulate vagal activity and function as a vagal nerve stimulator.**

In our research, we hypothesized that an accessible portal to the ventral vagus and the entire integrated social engagement system could be accessed by presenting acoustic stimulation that dynamically challenged the neural regulation of the middle ear muscles. The middle ear muscles facilitate the extraction of human speech by dampening the transmission of low-frequency noise from the external environment to the inner ear. Sound enters the outer ear and travels through the external auditory canal to the eardrum where it is transduced by the structures of the middle ear (i.e., small bones comprising the ossicular chain) that connect the eardrum with the cochlea. Complementing the ascending pathways are descending pathways that regulate the middle ear muscles. The descending pathways functionally adjust the transfer function of the middle ear structures to determine the energy (i.e., attenuate, pass, or amplify) of specific frequencies that reach the inner ear (Borg & Counter, 1989; Kolacz et al., 2018; Porges & Lewis, 2010).

Hypothetically, modulation of acoustic frequencies should dynamically adjust middle ear muscle tone by actively recruiting special visceral efferent pathways that travel through the trigeminal and facial nerves. Changes in middle ear muscle tone should, via feedback, through the sensory branches of the trigeminal and facial nerves, impact directly on the ventral vagal complex including influencing the cardioinhibitory ventral vagal pathways. The product of this feedback circuit could function as a neural exercise enhancing the regulation of both middle ear muscles and cardioinhibitory ventral vagal pathways (i.e., vagal brake).

PVT has led to the plausible hypothesis that the recruitment and exercise of the middle ear muscles can rehabilitate both visceromotor and somatomotor components of the integrated social engagement system. Thus, by engaging the descending auditory-processing limb (via facial and trigeminal special visceral efferent pathways) to enhance neural regulation of the middle ear muscles, one could also increase cardioinhibitory ventral vagal tone. Interestingly, there is convergent neuroanatomical evidence documenting that the lateral surface of the tympanic membrane (i.e., eardrum) receives innervation from cranial nerves V, VII, IX, and X (Widemar et al., 1985) that would complement the afferent pathways in optimizing listening to species-specific vocalizations (Kolacz et al., 2018; Porges & Lewis, 2010) via cranial nerves V and VII directly from the middle ear muscles.

The clinical outcome from this type of neuromodulation would reduce sound sensitivities, behavioral and autonomic state regulation deficiencies, auditory-processing and social engagement deficits, chronic pain and associated conditions, anxiety disorders, and other conditions for which vagal nerve stimulation treatment has demonstrated efficacy. Functionally, this technology would act as a noninvasive acoustic vagal nerve stimulator to increase cardioinhibitory vagal activity to the heart via an auditory pathway.

Our research has documented (Porges et al., 2013, Porges et al., 2014) that modulation of acoustic stimulation within the frequency band defined by the Speech Intelligibility Index (American National Standards Institute, 1997), a metric used to define the acoustic frequencies necessary to understand human speech, results in enhanced function of the social engagement system. These studies reported improved auditory processing, reduced auditory hypersensitivities, changes in autonomic state characterized by increased vagal regulation of the heart (e.g., increases in respiratory sinus arrhythmia), and increased spontaneous social behaviors (e.g., sharing). The research supports the theoretical expectations that variations in acoustic stimulation may trigger neural mechanisms that regulate the entire social engagement system, including enhanced vagal regulation of bodily organs. The use of modulated acoustic stimulation to optimize functions dependent on the social engagement system has been patented (Porges, 2018) and includes an approved claim for application for an acoustic vagal nerve stimulation.

CONCLUSION

Vagal nerve stimulation, when viewed through the lens of PVT, emphasizes three points. First, it emphasizes the link between the functions of the ventral vagal complex and symptoms reduced by vagal nerve stimulation that functionally enhance mental and physical health. Second, it shifts the emphasis of vagal nerve stimulation from the entire nerve to select afferent pathways that communicate with brainstem areas that regulate both somatomotor and visceromotor efferent pathways originating in the ventral vagal complex. Third, by documenting the positive impact of vagal nerve stimulation, it acknowledges that trauma and chronic stress can retune autonomic function and disrupt the adaptive function of the ventral vagal complex in mitigating threat reactions and optimizing homeostatic functions of health, growth, and restoration.

Understanding that the core neurophysiological mechanisms involved in brainstem structures regulated by the ventral vagal complex are expressed in a variety of clinical disorders provides an important neurophysiological justification for the application of vagal stimulation and identifies functions (e.g., voice, heart rate patterns, facial expression, ingestion) that can be quantified as objective-outcome variables. PVT, by defining an integrated social engagement system dependent on the ventral vagal complex, provides an organizing principle to understand how and why vagal nerve stimulation is effective in reducing apparently disparate symptoms. Through the lens of the theory, the observed disparate effects reflect processes dependent on the ventral vagal complex that are expressed through special visceral and ventral vagal pathways (see Figure 9.1). The theory leads to a shift in focus from higher brain structures to the foundational lower brainstem processes related to mammalian survival. This does not preclude upstream influences from the ventral vagal complex and communication with the nucleus of the solitary tract (Ellrich, 2011; Frangos et al., 2015). When these survival systems are disrupted by chronic illness and adversity history (e.g., trauma), the autonomic nervous system is retuned and frequently locked in a state that supports defense and threat reactions while disrupting homeostatic functions. The theory proposes that effective neuromodulation via vagal nerve stimulation enables a return to an autonomic state requiring the ventral vagus that supports more optimal mental and physical health.

Through the polyvagal lens, new questions about vagal nerve stimulation emerge. For example, if the positive effects are due to the processing of afferent information by brainstem structures regulating output systems mediated by the ventral vagal complex, then it is important to explore other potential afferent pathways that may form the basis for neuromodulation of vagal efferent pathways. In the future, there may be a category of vagal neuromodulators that function as neural exercises that would result in a more resilient autonomic nervous system and would not require chronic use. By emphasizing afferent limbs in vagal stimulation, numerous opportunities emerge. These may include strategies that systematically change vagal outflow through posture, movement, vocalization, behavior, active listening, and even mental effort. Functionally, any manipulation that reliably changes cardioinhibitory vagal regulation of the heart could be conceptualized as a vagal exercise. For example, the well-documented phenomenon of reduced ventral vagal tone during sustained attention (e.g., Aasman et al., 1987) provides the possibility that systematic variations in mental effort could function as a neural exercise promoting features similar to those produced via exogeneous vagal nerve stimulation.

It is anticipated that methods and clinical targets of vagal nerve stimulation will evolve as we become more informed about the specific anatomical pathways traveling through the vagus. As this knowledge becomes integrated into technologies and procedures, the science will lead to new forms and applications of vagal stimulation. The short history of clinical vagal nerve stimulation has already moved from placing an electrode around the vagus to a more functional portal leveraging an easily accessible afferent on the ear and face. There are two benefits in emphasizing the afferent limb as a target for vagal nerve stimulation: (1) there is no possibility of directly stimulating efferent pathways, especially those going to organs below the diaphragm resulting in adverse effects on digestive and sexual functions; and (2) stimulation of the afferent limb of a feedback system does not bypass the central regulatory functions of brainstem nuclei in the interpretation of the afferent input and may provide a neural signal that is more functional to the target organ.

PART IV

Brief Papers

Cardiac Vagal Tone: A Neurophysiological Mechanism That Evolved in Mammals to Dampen Threat Reactions and Promote Sociality

Stephen W. Porges

The evolutionary journey from asocial reptiles to social mammals is highlighted by a reorganized autonomic nervous system with unique structural and functional changes in the vagus. These changes enable mammals to suppress defensive strategies in order to support and express sociality. The product of this transition is an autonomic nervous system with capacities to self-calm, to socially engage others, and to mitigate threat reactions in ourselves and others through social cues.

For mammals, whose survival is dependent on their ability to cooperate, to connect, and to co-regulate, the ancient defense programs dependent on sympathetic activation supporting fight-or-flight behaviors and vagal activation supporting death feigning had to be harnessed and repurposed. This process resulted in a reorganized brainstem area, the ventral vagal complex, from which a unique branch of the vagus nerve enabled the expression of several uniquely mammalian features, including the ability to calm and to signal safety. Thus, sociality became embedded within specific neurobiological processes that had capabilities to mitigate threat and support mental and physical health. When this calming system is disrupted, prominent markers of chronic stress and core features shared by several psychiatric conditions are expressed (e.g., flat facial affect, poor vocal prosody, hypervigilance, hyperreactivity, auditory and visual hypersensitivities).

Anatomically, this vagal pathway is myelinated and originates in the brainstem structure called nucleus ambiguus. It provides the primary vagal regulation of organs above the diaphragm. This is distinct from the vagal pathways originating in the dorsal vagus nucleus, which are unmyelinated and provide the primary vagal regulation of organs below the diaphragm. The ventral vagal complex also regulates the striated muscles of the face and head and is greatly influenced by afferent pathways traveling through the vagus, trigeminal, and facial nerves. Thus, in mammals, the brainstem areas regulating the heart and bronchi are interconnected with the areas regulating ingestion, facial expression, listening, breathing, and vocalizations, to form an integrated social engagement system. In fact, intonations of vocalizations are mediated by the vagus, enabling prosodic features of voice to convey a relatively accurate index of vagal regulation of the heart (Porges & Lewis, 2010).

Following the work of Jackson (1884), the Polyvagal Theory (PVT) (Porges, 1995) assumes a phylogenetic hierarchy in which the newer circuits inhibit the older. Thus, when the ventral vagus and the social engagement system are dampened or go offline, which frequently is observed during chronic stress and in response to threat, the autonomic nervous system moves into a sympathetic state that supports mobilization (e.g., fight-or-flight). If this functional shift in state does not lead to a positive outcome, then the autonomic nervous system may abruptly shut down via the dorsal vagal circuit (e.g., syncope, death feigning).

Jackson described this process of sequentially disinhibiting older structures as dissolution or evolution in reverse. He used dissolution to explain the consequence of brain damage and disease, while PVT applies the principle to adaptive autonomic reactions to cues of threat, which may be reversible by cues of safety. In the realm of mental health, loss of access to the ventral vagus may be a product of chronic threat or a measurable core feature of several psychiatric disorders (e.g., post-traumatic stress disorder, PTSD), developmental disabilities (e.g., autism, Prader-Willi syndrome), and disabling chronic pain.

To survive, mammalian offspring must initially nurse as the primary mode of ingesting food. To nurse, the infant must suck, a process dependent on a brainstem circuit involving the ventral vagal complex. Survival is dependent on the infant's nervous system efficiently and effectively coordinating suck-swallow-breathe-vocalize behaviors with vagal regulation of the heart through the ventral vagal pathways originating in the nucleus ambiguus. Through maturation and socialization, this ingestive circuit provides the structural neural platform (i.e., social engagement system) for sociality and co-regulation as major mediators to optimize homeostatic function leading to health, growth, and restoration.

In mammals there is a dependency between reactions to contextual cues and the function of this circuit. Cues of threat may disrupt, while cues of safety may enhance function. The sensory branches of the facial and trigeminal nerves provide major input into the ventral vagal complex. Functionally, changes in the state of this circuit, through the process of dissolution, will either disinhibit phylogenetically older autonomic circuits to support defense (e.g., predator, disease, physical injury) or inform all aspects of the autonomic nervous system, including the enteric system (Kolacz & Porges, 2018), to optimize homeostatic function.

Polyvagal Theory introduces neuroception, a neural process that evaluates risk and safety and reflexively triggers shifts in autonomic state without requiring conscious awareness. This reflexive process, distinct from perception, detects environmental and visceral features that are safe, dangerous, or life-threatening (Porges, 2003). Although many vertebrates have a capacity to detect pain and threat, mammals repurposed the neuroception capacity of their reptilian ancestors not only to react instantaneously to threat, but also to calm instantaneously to cues of safety.

It is this latter feature that enables mammals to down-regulate defensive strategies to promote sociality by enabling psychological and physical proximity without the consequences of injury. It is this calming mechanism that adaptively adjusts the central regulation of autonomic function to dampen sympathetic activation and to protect the oxygen-dependent central nervous system, especially the cortex, from the metabolically conservative defensive reactions of the dorsal vagal complex (e.g., syncope, diarrhea).

This potential to calm autonomic state via the social engagement system is compromised in many psychiatric conditions, and leads to a variety of autonomic dependent comorbidities, including irritable bowel syndrome, migraine, and fibromyalgia. However, being a common feature of several disorders limits the potential utility of measures of ventral vagal function in differential diagnoses, although it would highlight the potential of recruiting the ventral vagal pathway as a portal for treatment via technologies (e.g., vagal nerve stimulation).

Our research documents that the quantification of the respiratory-related component of heart rate variability, known as respiratory sinus arrhythmia, provides a sensitive metric of the ventral vagus function (i.e., cardiac vagal tone; Lewis et al., 2012). Applications of our method confirmed that respiratory sinus arrhythmia was even more sensitive than the assumed gold standard of cardiac vagal tone (i.e., changes in heart rate in response to vagal blockade).

Respiratory sinus arrhythmia is a physiological phenomenon with an identifiable underlying neural mechanism reflecting ventral vagal control of the heart. With an accurate measure of ventral vagal function, there is the possibility to monitor autonomic adjustments to threat and safety. From a clinical perspective, the ability to monitor dampened vagal regulation would provide insight into understanding the mechanisms underlying clinical features. For example, chronic stress, clinical depression, or a life-threatening traumatic experience that may lead to PTSD could profoundly dampen ventral vagal regulation of the heart and the structures regulated by the ventral vagal complex constituting the social engagement system (Fanning et al., 2020; Hage et al., 2019).

Disrupting the brainstem locus of social engagement system would functionally impair social communication and co-regulation by reducing vocal prosody and facial affect, and, through the loss of neural tone to the middle ear muscles, influence auditory processing by inducing hypersensitivity to low-frequency background sounds and hyposensitivity to voice. In concert with these changes, brainstem communication with higher brain structures would impair cognitive function and affect regulation, while supporting the defense strategies of fight-or-flight or shutdown (e.g., syncope, dissociation).

Monitoring ventral vagal function may provide an objective neurophysiological marker of clinical improvement (Porges et al., 2013).

Ehlers-Danlos Syndrome Through the Lens of the Polyvagal Theory: A Preface to *Transforming Ehlers-Danlos Syndrome*

Stephen W. Porges

It is an honor and pleasure to write a preface for Dr. Stéphane Daens's volume, *Transforming Ehlers-Danlos Syndrome* (EDS). The volume provides an expansive review of cutting-edge research documenting the disparate symptoms associated with EDS. In this comprehensive, clinically oriented volume, expert clinical researchers effectively disentangle the plausible mechanisms underlying EDS. These clinical researchers share their compassionate attempt to identify common themes associated with the diagnosis and describe treatment strategies that are helpful in reducing the burden of pain and dysfunction.

Dr. Daens provides a long-needed resource that has the potential to inform medical practice that the symptoms associated with EDS are real and not psychogenic. The volume provides a broad tapestry of the clinical complexity of EDS and the history of inaccurate diagnoses and inappropriate treatments, which have led to suffering and uncertainty for many patients. The chapters, written by expert researchers and experienced clinicians in EDS, discuss symptoms associated with various subtypes, plausible underlying mechanisms, and optimistic management strategies that will enhance quality of life for those who are diagnosed with EDS.

Too many patients have been victimized by medicine in which uninformed physicians miss the defining symptoms of EDS and have inappropriately assumed their patients were feigning symptoms. Through well-documented clinical research, the chapters provide a perspective that EDS and the various subtypes of EDS have predictable symptom profiles. This information provides the physician with a new insight into the patient's experience that will move the physician-patient interaction toward helpful management of symptoms and a reduction of the patient's uncertainty.

The specific chapters that Dr. Daens has written highlight his personal journey with EDS. He describes his own diagnosis and the potential impact of his own personal trauma as a triggering event leading from vulnerability to disease. His experiences contribute to his deep personal and passionate commitment to develop a better understanding of the disorder and to contribute to compassionate treatments of EDS. Moreover, his experience highlights the frequently observed relationship between a trauma experience and the diagnosis. This observation suggests that there may be a larger subset of individuals with a vulnerability to being diagnosed as EDS who currently are not diagnosed or express severe symptoms. The observation also provides a clue that severity of symptoms might be a function of an interaction between a threat reaction to the trauma and a preexisting (genetic or epigenetic) vulnerability due to the disease.

It is only during the past decade that I have become aware of EDS. For several decades my research as a scientist has focused on the neural regulation of the autonomic nervous system and how the autonomic nervous system provides a neural platform for our emotional, cognitive, physiological, and behavioral reactivity. Little did I know that this background would provide an important lens that would contribute to a reconceptualization of EDS. Being invited into the world of EDS was an unexpected opportunity. My personal journey in this community is the product of my interactions with two dedicated physician scientists who are committed to understanding and treating patients with EDS. Working with them has provided me with opportunities to contribute to reorganizing the apparent disparate array of symptoms into a more predictable and understandable narrative.

I was introduced to EDS about 8 years ago, when an author in this book, Dr. Antonio Bulbena, contacted me. He was studying the prevalence of anxiety symptoms in EDS. He wanted to apply a scale that I developed to assess autonomic reactivity in his research with EDS. The scale, known as the Body Perception Questionnaire (BPQ), uses subjective methods to estimate autonomic reactivity. I was intrigued with Bulbena's interest in the link between anxiety and EDS. As a psychiatrist, he was interested in anxiety and other mental health comorbidities of EDS. As a neuroscientist, my interest focused on the neural mechanisms that supported anxiety. I viewed anxiety as an emergent property of a dysregulated autonomic nervous system (i.e., dysautonomia). From my perspective (e.g., Polyvagal Theory [PVT]) autonomic state provided a neural platform for anxiety and other features of emotional reactivity. I speculated that the autonomic regulation of an EDS patient would hypothetically be associated with a destabilized autonomic nervous system characterized by blunted neural regulation of the calming and homeostatic functions via the vagus and increased sympathetic excitation. Such an autonomic profile would support defensive strategies including fight-or-flight behaviors. The BPQ had subscales designed to capture the reactivity of the autonomic nervous system to enable inferences regarding neural pathways, vagal or sympathetic, influencing autonomic state. The BPQ data supported this speculation (Cabrera et al., 2018).

The BPQ data suggested that anxiety and other mental health morbidities frequently observed in EDS were psychological manifestations of an autonomic nervous system locked in a state of chronic threat. From my theoretical perspective the prevalence of anxiety and instability observed in EDS was a clue that these mental health vulnerabilities would have an autonomic substrate. As I read the chapters in the book, I realized that this speculation was consistent with the clinical observations of dysautonomia. However, to adequately test the hypothesis, the questionnaire data from the BPQ needed convergent objective measures of autonomic regulation. Fortuitously, this opportunity followed when I met Katja Kovacic (another contributor to this volume).

Dr. Kovacic is an extremely talented and inquisitive clinician-researcher who directs an active pediatric gastroenterology clinic. She was conducting research on the effectiveness of noninvasive vagal nerve stimulation on functional abdominal disorders in adolescents. Her mode of vagal stimulation applied electrical stimulation to the vagal afferents on the ear. She wanted to investigate whether reduction in abdominal pain was paralleled by a valid indicator of vagal regulation of the heart and whether the patient's autonomic profile prior to intervention was related to whether the vagal stimulation would effectively reduce pain. Since she was interested in learning methods to accurately monitor vagal regulation of the heart, she contacted me, and we initiated a fruitful collaboration. In our shared journey we learned that in her clinic approximately half the patients with functional abdominal disorders had Beighton scores of 4 or greater and about a third had Beighton scores of 5 or greater (Kolacz, Kovacic, et al., 2021). Many of the patients with high Beighton scores did not have an EDS diagnosis. We learned that the patients, who had noticeable pain reduction during vagal stimulation, were characterized by an atypical decoupling between heart rate and a measure of cardiac vagal tone (respiratory sinus arrhythmia) extracted from the beat-to-beat heart rate variability. This metric, known as vagal efficiency, evaluates the dynamic parallel changes between heart rate and cardiac vagal tone (measured via the respiratory sinus arrhythmia component of heart rate variability). Functionally, low vagal efficiency would reflect a decoupled feedback system, and a decoupled system may optimize the effectiveness of exogeneous vagal stimulation. Conceptually, the decoupled feedback system might result in the endogenous circuit not competing with the exogenous stimulation. Thus, hypothetically the stimulator would function more like a prosthetic source of vagal information that would not be competing with the ineffective endogenous feedback circuit. In support of this model, once the stimulator was turned off, pain returned.

Most relevant to understanding EDS, we observed a strong relationship between high Beighton scores and low vagal efficiency (Kolacz et al., 2021). The vagal efficiency metric appears to be providing a robust metric of dysautonomia, a feature that is mentioned in most chapters in this volume. The vagal efficiency metric is relatively easy to assess and in conjunction with measures of joint hypermobility might help refine the diagnosis of EDS. In our other research we have observed vagal efficiency to degrade with alcohol (Reed, Porges, et al., 1999), prematurity (Porges et al., 2019), trauma history, and the multisystem shutdown that precedes death in prairie voles (Williamson et al., 2010).

Through the lens of PVT, consistent with the views expressed in several of the chapters in this book, many of the features of EDS can be viewed as being dependent clinical features of dysautonomia. Dysautonomia is the clinical manifestation of an autonomic nervous system that is poorly regulated. Through the lens of PVT, the destabilized autonomic nervous system described by low vagal efficiency would provide the neural platform for many of the behavioral, psychological, and medical symptoms observed in patients with EDS.

Our initial documentation of a link between low vagal efficiency and severity of joint hypermobility provides another potential explanatory narrative. In this narrative, the observed poorly regulated autonomic nervous system is not a symptom of EDS but a component of a neural reaction that is locked in a chronic state to support threat. This state would be supported by sympathetic activation without access to the calming influence of a vagal circuit. In the terminology of PVT, the dynamic regulation of the calming vagal brake is unavailable, resulting in an autonomic state that would promote anxiety and dysregulated emotions. However, our research suggests that the prevalence of low vagal efficiency in EDS identifies an optimistic portal for treatment. It appears that low vagal efficiency enables exogeneous vagal nerve stimulation to be effective in reducing functional abdominal pain. Given the prevalence of dysautonomia in EDS, it is possible that with the reduction in functional abdominal pain other autonomic-dependent processes related to mental and physical health might also be improved.

In reading this volume, I have gained an appreciation for the progress that has been made in understanding and treating EDS. This volume provides an accessible portfolio of the pioneering work of clinical researchers at the forefront of research on EDS. These clinical researchers are actively reframing our understanding of the mechanisms underlying EDS and are developing and testing innovative treatments that will optimize the quality of life for their patients.

Addiction: A Polyvagal Perspective

Stephen W. Porges

The development of Polyvagal Theory (PVT) was not targeted toward explaining or treating addiction. Rather, the theory provided a general explanation of how the mammalian autonomic nervous system adaptively adjusts in complex environments to support survival. This perspective emphasizes two important points relevant to addiction: (1) context functionally defines what is appropriately adaptive and (2) behaviors are emergent properties of a neural platform mediated by autonomic states. Thus, the adaptive characteristics are dependent on the appropriateness of the behaviors within a specific context. Conceptualizing behavior (addiction) in these terms could change our understanding of behavioral pathologies. We might end up interpreting a behavioral pathology as a behavior that might have been adaptive in one setting and is now being elicited in a setting where it is maladaptive. For example, trauma survivors, who may be dissociating or shutting down through the use of addictive substances and behaviors, might be expressing a reaction that would be adaptive during a past traumatic event, but maladaptive in a current social setting.

As the principles of the theory as a science of feeling safe and sociality are outlined below, consider the quality of feelings and sociality of those who are addicted. Does addiction disrupt feelings of safety and sociality? Note that within the theory, autonomic state functions as an intervening variable biasing reactions to context. Reflecting on this latter point, consider addictive behavior as a valiant and yet failed strategy in regulating autonomic state, and as a poor substitute for the potent co-regulatory influences on calming autonomic state attributed to social behavior. As you read the sections on calming mechanisms and sociality, consider the limitations of the self-regulatory and co-regulatory repertoire of those who are addicted.

PVT emerged from the identification of the phylogeny of the vertebrate autonomic nervous system. The phylogenetic transition from asocial reptiles to social mammals required a repurposing the neural regulation of the autonomic nervous system, which had efficiently supported asocial reptiles. The repurposed system provided mammals with new pathways to down-regulate defensive states and to signal cues of safety. The title of the initial presentation of the theory (Porges, 1995) succinctly summarized its essence: *Orienting in a Defensive World: Mammalian Modifications of Our Evolutionary Heritage. A Polyvagal Theory.* The theory provided a neurophysiological understanding of how mammals were capable of sufficiently down-regulating the autonomic pathways that support defense to promote proximity, establish social bonds, and serve supportive roles in caring for their offspring and select others. This process of down-regulating defensive states provides insight into understanding the link between sociality and health. It also provides insights into the negative consequences of addictive behavior on relationships (i.e., co-regulation) and self-regulation. Consistent with this theme, PVT focuses on the evolved neural circuits that enabled mammals to down-regulate the sympathetic activation that could support mobilization to fight or flee, to reduce psychological and physical distance with conspecifics, and to functionally co-regulate physiological and behavioral states.

The core of the theory emerged through the identification of a phylogenetic transition in the regulation of vertebrate autonomic nervous systems that provided the neural resources for mammals to become social and to cooperate. The theory provides an innovative scientific-based perspective that incorporates an understanding of phylogenetic shifts in vertebrate neuroanatomy and neurophysiology. This perspective identifies neural circuits that down-regulate neural regulation of threat reactions and functionally neutralize defensive strategies via neural circuits communicating cues of safety. The theory proposes that feelings of safety are operationally the product of cues of safety, via neuroception, down-regulating autonomic states that support threat reactions and up-regulating autonomic states that support interpersonal accessibility and homeostatic functions. Basically, when a human feels safe, their nervous system supports the homeostatic functions of health, growth, and restoration, while they simultaneously become accessible to others without feelings of threat and vulnerability. In the optimal social context of humans, social interactions serve as the prominent mechanism to calm the autonomic nervous system. However, in the world of addiction, we learn that social interactions are displaced by drugs and behaviors to regulate the autonomic nervous system, and these strategies result in poor outcomes, disrupting homeostatic functions and potentially compromising mental and physical health.

The detection of threat appears to be common across all vertebrate species. However, mammals have an expanded capacity for neuroception by which they not only react instantaneously to threat, but also respond instantaneously to cues of safety. It is this latter feature that enables mammals to down-regulate defensive strategies to promote sociality by enabling psychological and physical proximity without anticipation of potential injury. It is this calming mechanism that adaptively adjusts the central regulation of autonomic function to dampen the metabolically costly fight-or-flight reactions dependent on sympathetic activation, and to protect the oxygen-dependent central nervous system, especially the cortex, from the metabolically conservative defensive reactions of the dorsal vagal complex (e.g., fainting, death feigning).

Is it possible that those most vulnerable to addiction are in an autonomic state that promotes feelings of threat and biases neuroception to detect cues of danger and adaptively be less sensitive to social cues of safety? Are those with addictions more likely to misinterpret positive social engagements via prosodic vocalizations, facial expressions, and gestures? If the addicted individual is chronically in an autonomic state that supports threat reactions and biases the detection of cues of threat, then these features would limit opportunities to co-regulate through the ventral vagal pathways and to successfully engage the social engagement system. The consequence of supporting an autonomic nervous system tuned for defense is to limit the functional neuromodulation benefit we derive from sociality and become more reliant on the use of addictive substances and behaviors to modulate state. Ironically, this strategy of state modulation will not produce the physiological calmness that supports homeostatic processes, although it might numb bodily feelings of distress and physical pain.

PVT provides the science to understand the profound role of feelings of safety in the expression of sociality. The theory leads to a reexamination of the roles that feelings of safety and social behavior play in understanding addictions and vulnerabilities to become addicted. PVT provides a perspective to understand addiction as a disruptor of the autonomic state that would support sociality and promote of feelings of safety.

Humans, as social mammals, are on an enduring lifelong quest to feel safe. This quest appears to be embedded in our DNA and serves as a profound motivator throughout our life. The need to feel safe is functionally our body speaking through our autonomic nervous system—influencing our mental and physical health, social relationships, cognitive processes, and behavioral repertoire and serving as a neurophysiological substrate upon which societal institutions dependent on cooperation and trust are based. While the optimal outcome occurs through fulfilling our biological imperative of connectedness, this is the product of individuals feeling safe through the co-regulatory properties of interactive social engagement systems. Even though the motivation to feel safe can be intense, the opportunity to feel safe may be difficult to achieve.

This may occur due to work schedule and location, in which proximity might limit availability of individuals who broadcast and are receptive to cues of safety. In addition, marginalized individuals experience barriers to the establishment of safe, trusting relationships even in their own community. Being marginalized through being identified by race, sex, ethnicity, religion, or disability frequency places an individual in a state of chronic threat and greatly limits opportunities to co-regulate in work, school, and community settings in which those who are not marginalized can feel safe and co-regulated. However, the motivation to feel safe remains high in those experiencing limited access to positive cues of safety, although the availability of appropriate individuals with whom to feel safe is low.

Although co-regulation and the use of sociality as a neuromodulator to regulate autonomic state is the neurobiological norm for our species to downregulate threat reactions, the norm is predicated on safe relationships. At times opportunities to co-regulate with a trusted other are not available, and feelings of safety are not easily accessible. This may occur through either physical or social isolation. It also can involve an inability to feel safe with others. For example, individuals with severe adversity histories often experience feelings of threat in the proximity of others and are unable to use sociality as a neuromodulator to calm autonomic state. Without access to sociality as a calming neuromodulator, individuals may be vulnerable to addiction, in which the biobehavioral richness of sociality is replaced with substances or behaviors. Unfortunately, the substitution of co-regulation with addictive substances and behaviors will fail and disrupt mental and physical health.

The literature confirms the strong link between trauma history and addiction. A survey conducted by SAMHSA confirmed that approximately 75% of women and men in substance-abuse treatment report histories of abuse and trauma (www.samhsa.gov/data/). From a polyvagal perspective, this link reflects an attempt to regulate autonomic state by numbing feelings of threat. This supports the proposed consequence of trauma history, especially in abuse experienced during childhood, as retuning the autonomic nervous system to be locked into states of defense that would lead to mental health vulnerabilities and attempts to ameliorate feelings of threat via addictive behaviors (e.g., Carliner et al., 2016; Enoch, 2011; Felitti, 2006). Unfortunately, those using these strategies mistakenly assume that numbing feelings of threat will lead to sociality.

The use of addictive substances and behaviors is effective in changing autonomic state, although the autonomic changes do not reliably support co-regulation and frequently lead to poor outcomes. Two important factors contribute to these changes in state disrupting both feelings of safety and sociality. First, addictive substances and behaviors often down-regulate the bidirectional feedback loops through which our nervous system communicates and regulates visceral organs. This numbing process may have short-term benefits, such as reduction of physical pain and mental distress, but it does not promote feelings of safety or positive social engagement behaviors. Moreover, by damping the neural regulation of visceral organs, it might lead to end-organ damage. Second, addictive substances and behaviors often recruit an autonomic state that supports defensive threat reactions, which may result in abusive and aggressive behaviors.

On the surface, addiction is related to difficulties in feeling safe and maintaining trusting relationships. Addiction from a polyvagal perspective reflects an unsuccessful strategy to reduce the impact of threat by numbing or mobilizing. Addiction can appear to successfully mask, distort, or numb feelings of threat. Interestingly, the strategy of numbing and masking seems to follow implicit strategies frequently employed to foster dissociation between feelings and actions and frequent attempts to prevent bodily feelings from disrupting intentional behaviors. However, unlike the neurobiological potency of sociality in generating feelings of safety, these strategies fail and over time exacerbate feelings of threat.

A polyvagal perspective of addiction focuses on the attempted use of addictive substances or behaviors to dampen underlying feelings of threat. This perspective frames the client's behavior within a quest to feel safe. Unfortunately, feeling safe is dependent on an autonomic state that can only efficiently be reached through sociality; recruiting ancient neurobiologically based survival strategies such as numbing that are insensitive to the intentions of higher brain circuits will fail in providing a biobehavioral state that would support or promote feelings of safety.

If the therapist's plan is to enable clients to feel safe, then it is important not to use evaluative phrases suggesting that their behavior is wrong or bad. By moving outside the moral veneer of societal norms, we need to explain to the client how their body responded in specific contexts. This exercise helps the client interpret their behavior not as an intentional violation of an expectancy, but as an adaptive feature of a nervous system that evolved to survive, and to explore potential pathways toward safety.

The client needs to appreciate this adaptive feature and to understand that this adaptive feature is flexible and can change in different contexts. The first step is to replace an evaluative focus with a curiosity about the adaptive survival-prioritized repertoire of the nervous system. This curiosity leads to an appreciation of the emergent behaviors, which are dependent on the flexibility of autonomic state regulation while adapting to the challenges of complex contexts. A product of this journey is the development of alternative perspectives and personal narratives that would lead to greater bodily awareness and an understanding of the difference between primitive neural pathways that support survival and higher brain structures detailing intentions. With this rich information, the client can develop a narrative that treats atypical behaviors not as bad, but as understandable in terms of adaptive functions that may often be heroic.

13

Autism Through the Lens of the Polyvagal Theory

Stephen W. Porges

During the 50 plus years that I have been an academic researcher, interest in autism has changed and so has public awareness. The domain of research in and treatment of autism has not followed a linear pattern in which research findings have led to advancements in treatments and optimized outcomes. Rather, from my perspective the trajectory has been one of misguided research priorities, based on faulty assumptions of causality, of a diverse phenotype that is greatly influenced by potentially transitory state changes. This sequence of academic biases has had a profound consequence on the autism community by limiting the development of alternative models of the disorder. Potentially, alternative strategies would lead to tools that would optimize quality of life for the individual with autism and lessen the burden of the diagnosis on the individual, family, caregivers, and schools.

Polyvagal Theory (PVT) presents an optimistic perspective for those with autism. The perspective emphasizes that many of the features of autism may not be locked to a genetic unfolding but are dependent on adaptive autonomic reactions to threat. By moving the causal model from genes to autonomic state, clinically relevant questions move from a genetic screening with an unfulfilled, promised remediation to neural exercises that would functionally rehabilitate autonomic state flexibility and resilience. Neural exercises that challenge autonomic regulation via withdrawing and reengaging the vagal brake could promote enhanced state regulation that would be observed in more optimal behavior, emotion, and physiology.

When I started my academic career in 1970, autism was considered a relatively rare disorder that was assumed to be characterized by two features: (1) permanence of the disorder and (2) genetic basis. These plausible assumptions biased and limited the research questions and the explanations that both researchers and clinicians could use to describe their observations in the laboratory and clinic. The scientific community, as well as my first publication mentioning autism (Porges, 1976), readily embraced these assumptions, which had consequences on research funding. Funding priorities within the National Institutes of Mental Health readily reflected this transition and prioritized funds to projects involving molecular genetics in a concerted effort to identify a genetic substrate. This resulted in funds being diverted from other more flexible and optimistic perspectives that might be conceptualized as neural exercises to optimize the life experiences of those with an autism diagnosis. The decision was costly to the science of understanding autism and supporting those with autism, their families, and their caregivers.

When clinicians and researchers observed that an individual, via maturation or intervention, no longer reached criteria for autism, they were confronted with the consensus view that the initial diagnosis was faulty. This perspective had great impact on intervention models, interpretations of research findings, and even the astute observations of clinicians who were effective in optimizing the function of their autistic clients. Explaining to colleagues or parents that an individual no longer reached diagnostic criteria following an intervention or with maturation placed clinical researchers in a quandary and challenged them in how to disseminate this information. If they proposed that the intervention functionally normalized the previously diagnosed autistic individual, then they would be vulnerable to being accused of curing autism. Such a label would be sufficient to exclude a researcher from opportunities to publish in peer-reviewed journals, obtain funding from the National Institutes of Health, and impede career advancement (e.g., tenure in a quality university). Yet, within the community of researchers and clinicians there were frequent discussions of possible explanations for shifts in the severity of autistic symptoms.

The first potential source of variation in clinical sequelae was diagnosis. Thus, it was assumed that if the community studying and treating autism used a common diagnostic tool, there would be more consistency in diagnosis. Consequently, it was anticipated that there would be both fewer false positives of reversing symptoms through maturation and intervention and the potential to systematically evaluate interventions reputed to normalize an autistic individual's behavior. In the 1990s, transformative research headed by Catherine Lord established a convergence between assessment tools and consensus of expert clinicians. These tools, the Autism Diagnostic Observation Schedule (ADOS and ADOS-2) and the Autism Diagnostic Interview (ADI and ADI-R), are considered the gold standard for the diagnosis of autism (Lord et al., 1993, 1999) and have led to a more inclusive diagnostic category to what is now called autism spectrum disorder (ASD).

The availability of these assessments framed peer-reviewed research on autism and became an important criterion to publish and be funded. However, it is important to acknowledge that this strategy assumed that the consensus judgment was sufficient to operationalize diagnosis. This is a powerful assumption, since it assumed the features that clinicians observed were sufficient to identify a disorder that the community had assumed was genetic or, at least, had a permanent neurobiological substrate. Unfortunately, the standardized diagnostic strategy has resulted in a phenomenological metric being used to infer a biological substrate. This assumption is functionally dependent on an acceptance of psychophysiological or psychobiological parallelism. This model of parallelism, which assumes continuity across neural, physiological, behavioral, and psychological domains, has led to faulty inference by assuming that the variations in expressed psychological and behavioral symptoms indexed by the ADOS and ADI would enable an accurate mapping of the variations in the underlying neurobiological mechanisms assumed to determine autism.

Research programs were initiated and funded that assumed that the standardized diagnostic tools would lead to a greater understanding of underlying mechanisms. However, this inferential inquiry made a powerful unsubstantiated assumption that defining a phenotype via phenomenological data (clinical observations) would lead to uncovering the mechanistic neurobiological pathways that would lead to the diagnosis. Although phenotype provides essential information about an individual's observable traits, it is not sufficient to accurately identify the underlying genotype, due to the complexities of genetics. For example, phenotype can be influenced by multiple genes, the environment, genetic variation, and epigenetic influences. At present, given the variations in phenotype, DNA sequencing has identified some genetic markers of an increased prevalence of diagnosis, but has not provided a more definitive model that would lead to genetic mapping of autism.

Although PVT (Porges, 1995) emerged from traditional psychophysiology, it provided a theoretical demarcation from parallelism. In a sense, psychophysiological parallelism implicitly assumed that the constructs employed in different domains were valid (e.g., subjective, observable, physiological) and focused on establishing correlations across domains that optimistically would lead to an objectively quantifiable physiological signature of the construct explored in the psychological domain. In the case of autism, in addition to the dedication to find a genetic basis, there also has been fervent interest in applying imaging technologies to monitor cortical processes and to identify a brain signature (e.g., connectivity pattern) that would lead to an objective metric of brain function that would support a functional diagnosis of autism.

In contrast, PVT emphasizes the interactive and integrative aspect of different levels of the nervous system that are expressed as autonomic states. The theory emphasizes a hierarchical organization that mirrors phylogenetic shifts among vertebrates. The evolutionary changes are also reflected in maturational trends. Thus, what appears to be more complex and related to higher brain structures, such as language and sensitivities to another's physiological state via intonation of voice and gesture, is reflecting the functional and structural changes mapped into the evolutionary history of vertebrates. Frequently missed in understanding autistic features with our cortico-centric and cognitive-centric orientation is the importance of lower brain mechanisms in managing our basic survival-oriented reactions. Although the less complex, earlier evolved systems are often repurposed in mammals, they remain survival oriented and are efficiently available to support states of defense when survival is challenged. Due to the hierarchical nature of the nervous system, when foundational survival systems are recruited in defense, as seen in autism as meltdowns and tantrums, the higher brain structures related to learning and sociality are compromised. From this perspective, an autonomic nervous system in a state of defense may reflect many features of autism as it would support hypersensitivities and tantrums while compromising sociality, state regulation, social communication, auditory processing, speech, and cognitive function. Implicit in this perspective is the possibility of the individual changing state and becoming calmer and spontaneously social when signals of threat are reduced and signals of safety are increased (see Porges, 2022).

Studies applying PVT's conceptualization of autonomic reactivity to autism have documented low ventral vagal influences on the heart measured via respiratory sinus arrhythmia (Bal et al., 2010; Patriquin et al., 2013, 2019; Van Hecke et al., 2009). According to the PVT, reduction of this vagal circuit, the removal of the vagal brake, potentiates the other components of the autonomic nervous system (i.e., sympathetic nervous system, dorsal vagal pathways) that support defense. These autonomic pathways, consistent with features commonly observed in those diagnosed with autism, support symptoms of anxiety and defensiveness. These observations highlight an autonomic substrate for behaviors often observed as tantrums and meltdowns (via the sympathetic nervous system) or immobilizations, social withdrawal, and total behavioral shutdown (via dorsal vagal pathways).

PVT (Porges, 1998) expanded its potential utility to understand the underlying mechanisms involved in expressed features of autism by introducing a social engagement system that linked the neural regulation of the face and head with the vagal pathways to the heart (i.e., vagal brake). In structuring this face-head connection as a social engagement system and linking it to the ventral vagus, several symptoms of autism (e.g., hypersensitivities, hyposensitivity to human voice, atypical vocal intonation, dampened facial expressivity, auditory processing deficits, language delay, selective eating, hypersensitivities, etc.) could now be explained by linking their expression to autonomic states of defense that would become efficiently available when the calming ventral vagal circuit (vagal brake) is withdrawn. PVT identified the functioning of the vagal brake, via measures of respiratory sinus arrhythmia (i.e., a respiratory pattern in the beat-to-beat heart rate pattern) as a physiological index that could be monitored to infer accessibility to the social engagement system that would promote physiological calmness and sociality. In the absence of a resilient vagal brake (i.e., vagal efficiency), the autonomic state could promote the primitive survival strategies that are frequently observed in autism. In addition to these obvious behavioral consequences, a loss of accessibility to the vagal brake (i.e., poor vagal efficiency) is also associated with a challenged digestive system locked in a pervasive defensiveness with symptoms frequently associated with autism including nausea, diarrhea, constipation, and general gut pain (Kolacz et al., 2019, 2022).

Through the process of neuroception, PVT describes neural mechanisms that reflexively detect safety or threat and reflexively shift autonomic state to promote adaptive behaviors. Although virtually all living organisms detect signals of threat, mammals seem to have a unique form of neuroception that enables them to down-regulate threat reactions through signals of safety. The classic example is the prosodic voice (range of intonation) of a mother in calming her infant. In fact, we have conducted research documenting that greater maternal vocal prosody was more effective in calming infants following a stressor (Kolacz et al., 2022). Consistent with PVT, understanding parameters of acoustic signals of safety have led to an innovative intervention that uses acoustic stimulation, similar to a mother's lullaby, that is capable of moving an infant from tantrum to calm. The intervention, known as the Safe and Sound Protocol™ (Heilman et al., 2023; Porges et al., 2013, 2014) has successfully been applied to autistic individuals with documented effects of calming, reducing hypersensitivities, improving auditory processing, and enhancing ventral vagal regulation of the heart.

When autism is viewed through the lens of PVT, several features associated with a diagnosis of autism can be explained as naturally occurring biobehavioral phenomena associated with an autonomic state of defense without being determined by genes, requiring a diagnosis, or being irreversibly permanent. Thus, many features associated with the diagnosis can be observed in neurotypical individuals when they are in states of chronic threat. Within this model, even other autonomic issues frequently associated with an autism diagnosis such as gut problems and inflammatory diseases could be explained. In addition, PVT provides insights into new intervention models including a deeper understanding of the inherent neural mechanisms that may be recruited to mitigate threat reaction. This has led to an emphasis on a neurophysiology of safety (Porges, 2022) that explains how signals of safety recruit the ventral vagus and promote calm autonomic states that support homeostatic functions (health, growth, restoration) and sociality.

PVT assumes that the autonomic nervous system provides the neural platform upon which different clusters of behaviors may spontaneously emerge. When the autonomic nervous system has access to the ventral vagal complex, the social engagement system is available to dynamically interact and co-regulate with others. This form of sociality involves signals of safety and social communication through facial expressions and vocal intonation. Functionally, when the nervous system detects safety, the ventral vagal circuit is preeminent, enabling the vagal brake to dynamically and efficiently regulate autonomic state to calm, support homeostatic functions, and promote sociality. However, if the nervous system detects threat, the vagal brake becomes unavailable. Under these conditions, the autonomic nervous system shifts from a state that is calm and social to defensive states that either support flight-or-flight behaviors or withdrawal and shutdown. Thus, PVT emphasizes that many of the features we assume are lifelong characteristics of autism may be the product of a nervous system being in a chronic state of threat. About 20 years ago several of these features were introduced to the autism research community (Porges, 2005) during a period of expanding interests in the neurobiology of autism (see Bauman & Kemper, 2005). However, at that time funding initiatives were heavily focused on genetic and imaging technologies and did not prioritize research focusing on the autonomic nervous system as a powerful intervening variable mediating diagnostic symptoms. Since the product of research focusing on genetic and cortical mapping has had limited impact on the welfare of individuals with autism, there is now an opportunity to support initiatives that focus on the role autonomic state plays in the expression of symptoms. Optimistically, research is beginning to document that interventions can be designed as neural exercises that have profound effects on social behavior and hypersensitivities by reengaging the vagal brake and enabling the social engagement system to become more accessible.

14

Empathy to Compassion: A Two-Step Physiological Process

Michael Allison and Stephen W. Porges

Like the immediate jolt we have to an unexpected rumble of thunder, empathy is our reflexive bodily reaction to the pain and suffering of another. We see the strain in their face, hear the hurt in their voice, and feel the discomfort in their body. These subconscious signals, which we may or may not be aware of, trigger an adaptive shift in our own physiology to prepare our body to attack, defend, protect, escape, or hunker down. This shift in our own bodily response is reflexive, immediate, autonomic, and initially beneath our conscious control. As an evolutionary strategy that is so important to our survival, autonomic changes occur rapidly and are regulated at the level of the brainstem through a very primitive brain detection system (i.e., neuroception) that reflexively shifts physiological state without awareness to prepare for the intentions beneath the facial expressions, bodily movements, and vocalizations coming at us from others. As social mammals, we need each other to survive throughout all stages of life, and we have a unique gift to detect and evaluate, without thinking, whether someone else is safe to come close to, cooperate with, bond with, and care for.

Compassion may or may not follow our initial empathic reaction to their hurt. We may get locked into an empathic state as we align our bodily response with theirs and remain stuck in our own defensive, reactive threat-oriented physiology. We may get upset, angry, frustrated or injured right alongside them. We might amp up and want to fix the problem, help them fight back, or encourage them to toughen up and get a move on. We might collapse with them, feel a deep wound arise in our own body, numb out, or even look away and get out of there altogether.

What happens or doesn't happen after our initial empathic response isn't necessarily a reflection of our intentions, character, values, and motivation to help. It might more accurately reflect our physiological resilience and our ability or inability to utilize the calming function of the vagus (a cranial nerve connecting the brain with the heart and other organs) as a brake to effectively and efficiently dampen threat reactions. We might have every intention and desire to express our compassion for someone we deeply care about; however, our physiology may be so massively triggered by their pain that we lose vagal control and erupt, spin out, run away, or implode. The more we care about and are connected with someone (e.g., children, partner, loved ones), the more massive our reflexive bodily responses and the more challenging it is to maintain and regain the calming vagal control of our physiology.

Compassion may only emerge when we are able to regain enough control of our physiology after the initial empathic shift to support our intentions, values, and goals of being a safe, accessible, and supportive witness to the other. This may occur in a two-step process. We may feel the reactive shift in our own body (i.e., interoception) as empathy, recognize that we've been triggered (i.e., self-awareness), and care for our bodily reactions in ways to realign our physiology to support our capacity for compassion (i.e., self-care).

This self-awareness, self-care, and self-compassion sequential process (i.e., neuroception, interoception, awareness) may occur rapidly in just a few seconds or it may take minutes, hours, or even days to reengage our calming vagal brake, bring our social engagement system back online, and recover back to safety, connection, and autonomic regulation (i.e., vagal control). The first step of experiencing a felt sense of empathy in our body as a reflexive response to the hurt of someone we care for is vital for the second step of feeling and expressing authentic compassion. If we don't experience this spontaneous and immediate jolt of empathic discomfort (i.e., autonomic shift in bodily state via neuroception), we will be neurophysiologically numb, unable to truly understand, be with, and connect to the injured other. It's as if we must tap directly into their hurt, feel it in our own body first, in order to be trusted by the other that we understand what they are going through.

At the same time, if we remain locked in an empathic state (i.e., angry, scared, sad, detached, etc.), the features we unintentionally broadcast to our loved ones will not be helpful, supportive, and what they truly need or want from us in their moment of hurt. This is where vagal resilience plays a key role, enabling the body to return to a physiology with enough vagal control of our heart, lungs, and internal bodily systems to authentically be a safe, supportive, and compassionate witness who no longer needs to correct, fix, fight, run, hide, or disappear.

When we discuss the need to establish self-compassion before we can express compassion for another, we are referring to this initial physiological act of recognizing, respecting, and caring for our own reflexive bodily reactions to the pain, suffering, and injury we are feeling in our own body.

When we look at compassion as an emerging property from a neurophysiological perspective consistent with Polyvagal Theory (PVT), we identify an underlying physiological state dependent on the vagus that supports feelings of safety and trust enabling supportive social connection. This neurophysiological perspective informs us that compassion is dependent on the vagus calming feelings of threat and discomfort. When we cultivate our capacity to foster compassion through daily practices that actually function as neural exercises, we actively improve the efficiency of the vagal brake to expand our capacity to rapidly recover from challenges over time.

More than sitting still, meditating, and then cultivating internal experiences of compassion, we might challenge our resilience (i.e., improve the efficiency of the vagal brake) in a context of safety through easily available practices such as through voluntary breathing patterns, playful social interactions, dancing and singing together, or even group movement classes that intermix intervals of higher intensity exercise with periods of recovery with interaction, high fives, laughter, or conversation.

Beyond our mindset, exercise, or intention, compassion co-exists with a physiology that can be seen in our faces, heard in our voices, and felt in our bodies. When we see compassion through the lens of our physiology, either promoting or interrupting our capacity to experience compassion, we can explore and play with far-reaching methods for training compassion that more appropriately match the many bodies locked in threat that would benefit most from both the giving and the receiving of compassion.

A DYNAMIC TWO-STEP PROCESS IN REAL TIME

Slowing the physiological process down in real time, we subconsciously see the pain in their face, hear the hurt in their voice, and feel the suffering in their body. This reflexive detection system triggers a cascade of bodily feelings and a shift in our physiology (e.g., breathing, heart rate, muscle tension, sensations, posture, etc.) that we may become aware of (i.e., interocept) and recognize as empathy. At this point, our bodily responses may be massive or subtle depending on how much we care about them or the severity of their pain, and we may or may not regain enough vagal control to realign our physiology to be a safe witness, to be with their pain and suffering without adding our own pain and suffering to the interaction. This is not a static situation, but more likely to be a dynamically changing process where we continually toggle between physiological states of empathy and compassion. This enables the person hurting to recognize subconsciously that we are actually with them—that they are seen, heard, and understood—and at the same time, they don't feel they are hurting us.

This is where an efficient and resilient vagal brake plays a vital role in our biobehavioral resilience, providing our capacity to be compassionate by enabling the vagal brake to dynamically engage and disengage, allowing us to move flexibly along with them but not get locked into our own threat response. We can rapidly amp up, calm down, and meet them where they are so they feel seen, understood, and validated. Just as quickly, we can return back to our own felt sense of safety and connection so that we do not add more hurt and pain back into the interaction.

BEGINNING THE PROCESS: VAGAL TONE AS A PERSONAL RESOURCE

We may begin by helping a body locked in a mobilized threat physiology (i.e., sympathetic mobilization) to find, feel, and trust having a felt sense of safety in combination with, or intermixed with, bodily movement or mobilized energy involving group or dyadic interactions such as play and support. This may actually be a safe and stealth approach to enabling a defensive body to begin to shift into a physiology that promotes an authentic experience of compassion for self and others. Over time, the mobilized body may become comfortable and accessible with less vigorous movements and/or within a shorter duration, ultimately enabling the physiology to engage in real-life experiences of compassion that require both adequate and adaptively resilient vagal tone.

For those in bodies retuned to be in a shutdown state of defense, who appear to be detached, numb, and immobilized, we may begin by helping the body to feel and to trust that it's safe to gently mobilize first and then skillfully integrate social engagement and connection with others over time. We may begin with diaphragmatic breathing exercises that gradually and progressively emphasize longer and deeper inhales, go for a walk, or link gentle bodily movements (e.g., yoga, body-weight exercises, dynamic stretching, etc.) with breathing or grounding practices. Over time, the immobilizing body may find comfort and accessibility as the body moves, elevates, and engages with life and others. These intuitive activities are functionally neural exercises that provide opportunities to improve regulation of autonomic state. With even minimal improvement, the individual's nervous system may become more available and even seek the benefits of co-regulation through more challenging exercises and practices that functionally enhance biobehavioral resilience. The product of this trajectory is a positive outcome expressed as greater behavioral flexibility, improved sociality, and more optimized mental and physical health.

TOGGLING BETWEEN EMPATHY AND COMPASSION: A NEURAL EXERCISE

Building a solid baseline characterized by a calm autonomic nervous system with an efficient vagal brake is the neurophysiological foundation for navigating challenging situations, conditions, and relationships. However, it's not enough to access physiological states that support compassion.

A healthy, resilient, and socially engaging body capable of expressing compassion and toggling effectively in real time between physiological states supporting empathy and compassion requires a second key component called vagal efficiency—the effectiveness of our vagal brake in dynamically regulating heart rate and metabolic output to match the demands of the environment, interaction, or situation.

We can explore a wide range of neural exercises to skillfully improve vagal efficiency within a context of safety and control. We do this through a series of transitory exercises of specific duration and intensity that progressively expand our capacity for challenge without exceeding our threshold for what we can manage or overwhelming our resources. For example, we could simulate the physiological demands of moving back and forth between empathy and compassion by engaging in a controlled breathing practice (e.g., Wim Hof) that intermixes cycles of breathing patterns that change the ratio of duration of inhale to exhale to deliberately release and reengage the vagal cardioinhibitory influences on the heart and shift metabolic output. We could also alternate between comfortable and hot or cold environments for brief periods of time while bringing awareness to our reflexive bodily responses to the environmental challenges, applying strategies and inner resources to care for our bodily feelings and realign our physiology to support our intentions to remain calm, present, and connected. We might also intermix Virtual Reality environments that reflexively trigger physiological states of calm, ease, and relaxation with those that mobilize a sympathetic threat response. This strategy would function as a neural exercise that simulates the physiological substrate necessary to support the empathy-to-compassion two-step process.

DOMAIN GENERAL TO DOMAIN SPECIFIC

Improving vagal tone and vagal efficiency becomes the neurophysiological foundation for our capacity to be self-compassionate; to build trusting, authentic relationships; and to express both empathy and compassion for those we care about so that we can meet them where they are and move along with them in a way that's helpful, not hurtful, to their recovery. However, in real life, we encounter dynamically changing and challenging conditions and relationships, and we enter into these unpredictable interactions in different physiological states of our own. We can't possibly prepare our physiology for all the variables we face over a lifetime and optimize our reflexive responses to the chaos of everyday life and uncertainty of everyday relationships. However, by improving our vagal tone and vagal efficiency, we would help our body to be less massively triggered, expand our capacity for how much we can be triggered before we lose vagal control altogether, and have a reliable tool kit of strategies, inner resources, and ways of relating to others that help to regain vagal control more quickly and effectively when we do lose control. These physiological enhancements would provide the neural platform for compassion and the autonomic resilience necessary for effectively shifting between states supporting empathy and compassion that build resilience and facilitate trusting, authentic, and supportive relationships vital for human thriving and surviving.

PART V

Blogs and Interviews

15

Our Nervous System Is Always Trying to Figure Out a Way for Us to Survive, to Be Safe

Kal Kseib and Stephen W. Porges

Kal Kseib meets Dr. Stephen Porges, founder of Polyvagal Theory
(PVT), to hear about his approach to trauma and more.

What has studying trauma taught you?

Trauma has taught me what it is to be human. You can see with such clarity what trauma takes away from the human experience. A person can be gregarious, co-regulatory, happy, and optimistic one day, and then something happens and you stop seeing these features. There's a shift in autonomic state, which is frequently accompanied with an array of medical comorbidities. The autonomic nervous system no longer appropriately manages the organs, becoming functionally dysautonomic. This is predictable when the nervous system is in a state of threat, a state in which it can't properly manage social relationships and it can't manage the healthy regulation of bodily organs. Priorities change from sociality and health, growth, and restoration to the here-and-now of survival.

What does a polyvagal-informed approach to trauma look like?

It begins with understanding that our nervous system is always trying to figure out a way for us to survive, meaning to be safe. It's negotiating and navigating within this world. Our body, more specifically our nervous system, has circuits that are geared to help us survive even without our awareness or intentions.

Sometimes survival requires a hypersensitivity to cues that may be dangerous or life-threatening, and sometimes it may require a numbing of one's own bodily feelings. We shut down, or we freeze, or we dissociate.

These strategies are adaptive. This means that they're not good or bad but serve, at least initially, a survival-related purpose. The body is enabling the person to not repeat the horrible events they once experienced. It's just taking good care of you. It's the body's way of saying "We're not going there again." Dissociation, for instance, is common among individuals who have severe trauma histories and can often be severely pathological, but we can also reframe it to be about the wisdom of the body. These strategies stay functional if they're used for short periods of time. But when they become chronic, mental health is challenged and often diagnostic features of both mental and physical illness are expressed because there's no differentiation between our mental state and our physiological state.

From a polyvagal perspective, what can we do to heal in the face of trauma?

We've come to think about trauma as being causal of other issues, whereas we need to think about it in terms of a retuning of the nervous system. Trauma is not the event itself, it's our body's reaction to the event. For individuals with trauma histories, it's not about "ooh, I have an insight, now I've figured it out." That's off the table. Because trauma gets in the body the real question becomes "How do I give my body a sense of meaning?" And that's what therapy is all about.

Treatment is about giving the nervous system the cues of safety so that it retunes itself to being more homeostatic. And when it does that you increase co-regulation with others. You start getting a more optimistic perspective on life and you start seeing the core of humanity expressing itself. Optimistically, that core of humanity is amazingly positive; even among those who are severely compromised by trauma histories, you find that they still have dreams. What are their dreams? To feel safe in the arms of another.

And so ultimately our nervous system needs safe and nurturing relationships.

Being connected is a biological imperative of our species. We can think of it in a very simple way. What is the worst punishment that you can do to a person? Isolation. Solitary confinement. Being buried alive. All of these metaphors evoke terror because our nervous system requires the co-regulation of another safe individual. Our social engagement system, the ventral vagal pathway, is the neural circuit that is involved in detecting and responding to cues of safety that empowers our body to immobilize without fear. We're such an adaptive and flexible species that we can survive severe life challenges, but we need to have the friendships, the love, the support and the care, that is, moments of co-regulation and safety, for at least some of the time. No one likes to feel marginalized.

It seems like those safe relationships may be in short supply at the moment.

The optimistic aspect is that the core of humanity is a core of empathy and compassion and co-regulation, but only if it's not in a state of threat. When you're not in states of threat you're open to dialogue and relationships with others. If our bodies move into states of threat, meaning our nervous system is in a state of threat, our ability to be compassionate, to be co-regulatory with others, just disappears. So does our ability to be appropriately future-oriented in the moment and in thinking about a helpful response.

People are also more prone to getting manipulated in states of threat. We think that arguments are easily accomplished by presentation of evidence but we forget that when people are angry or feel threatened, they're not even looking at the evidence. Critics, for instance, are not well co-regulated; they're angry. They react not because they're haters but because they're angry. And their anger basically impedes their understanding, learning, or listening.

Well, that explains a lot.

You saw it happening with the COVID-19 vaccinations. There was this degree of self-defeating stupidity through anger and threat. The vaccines were and are, if we can use the term, a godsend—they're a miracle. They're really effective, more so than any vaccinations that have ever been produced, and they're flexible, meaning they can be modified. There was a way out. Why weren't more people getting vaccinated? It's because there was this idea that someone was telling you what to do and that it's a violation of your personal rights. The messaging was "You're being abused and we need to fight back." In part the poor messaging of public health agencies created a vacuum since many people never processed a message that being vaccinated had to do with mutual responsibility, to others and our community.

How do society and culture influence our capacity to feel safe?

We know that the underlying phenotype of humanity is to be co-regulatory but in our culture we haven't respected that need, that biological imperative. We have functionally interfered with it by creating a hostile, competitive, survival-oriented world. The bottom line is that most cultures are traumatized, although it's not frequently acknowledged. The British culture, for instance, is known for the "stiff upper lip" where it's considered appropriate not to respond to your bodily feelings. But, of course, it's not just the British. My father, whose family came from central Europe, had some of these same features. To him it was about how you presented yourself, not about what's really going on inside of you. Survivors of war are another example. There's a great price to pay in terms of how people relate to each other when they return home and in terms of how they regulate their own bodies.

Why, as a society, do we tend to be so out of tune with our bodies?

The awareness of bodily state is something that we have kind of messed up in our culture because, if anything, we've taught the body, our nervous system to be numb, not to be aware of our bodily needs, to sit still. We tend to shame people who listen to their body. If you listened to the culture, it says "block your feelings" and teaches us that safety is resource-based rather than relationship-based, meaning that if you have more resources, you're safe. As you get older you realize that so-called accomplished individuals who have resources without relationships are frequently the least fulfilled people that you'll ever meet. I've been watching "Succession"—it's a reeducation for me to remind me that there are people for whom the laws don't matter and for whom money can solve everything, but who are the most miserable people in the world. They have nice jewelry, nice homes, private jets—all this stuff. And you've got to ask the question, what is it all for? What keeps them alive? And the answer is it's the need for power. It's not about relationships. They don't truly support each other or anyone. They're all, so to speak, "bad" people because they don't have trust.

So, what's the antidote? How can we shift the culture from one of threat to one of safety?

The solution is inclusion, but there's often a fear of inclusion. Once we understand that the nervous system can be optimistically and appropriately optimized or retuned with cues of safety then we realize the importance of social connectedness: sociality. We invest resources in giving people injections or electrical stimulation, but we forget that sociality is functionally a neural stimulator. And we have to elevate this part of our evolutionary history when our social interaction became nourishment for our nervous system.

And at an individual level, where do we start?

I talk a lot about co-regulation—regulating each other's physiology—but we also think about the co-regulation within our own body and, in a way, how we often try to sever that relationship. If you think about it, what is it to be angry at your body? When we have health concerns, for instance, being angry is to say "Don't do what you're doing." It's to turn yourself off. In contrast, personal mental and physical health requires our nervous system to foster communication between the brain and the body. Everything becomes about respecting what our own nervous system has been doing and about not supporting states of defense by being angry at your body. This enables us to self-witness and understand, respect, and honor the strategies that our nervous system is employing to keep us safe, at least in the short term.

The real critical point of being self-compassionate is how we support our capacity to be present to experience and functionally witness our emotional dimension. It's as if we are saying to ourselves "I'm here, I'm present, I'm listening." It's about respecting our body when our nervous system is conveying feelings to our consciousness. Several years ago, I had severe pneumonia and my illness resulted in chronic fatigue for many months. I had to listen to my body to manage my health while working, matching my limited energy with my workload. What most people tend to do is turn off the feedback loops and try to keep going; they numb out. Instead, we talk about developing ways to manipulate our bodily state. Ways that enable us to move into states of mobilization to work, and also into states of supporting sociality, calmness, and relaxation to recover.

Interestingly a similar sequence of dynamically moving from mobilization to sociality is the feature that defines play. Clinicians often note that people with trauma histories or chronic illness lose touch with their capacity for play. When we start to listen to and honor our nervous system, we lose feelings of shame; we respect the brilliance of our nervous system as successfully navigating through complex environments.

Losing feelings of shame seems like a critical point.

When we get into the mental health world, we tend to say "Oh, I would do fine under those situations," which translates as "it's your fault." And we can't make those judgments because we're not in the other person's skin; we don't have their nervous system and we don't have their history. Some people have an autonomic nervous system retuned to threat from experiences that many people wouldn't see as threatening. An event can have a high valence—a lot of power— meaning in retrospect you can talk about it and say "Well, that was really nothing" or even laugh about it, but that's not how the body remembers it. Someone, for instance, may experience public humiliation—a very visceral reaction that can change them. Feelings in these scenarios can be deep and powerful and can reflect multiple situations of loss of control and loss of agency. Others might experience the same scenario and say "Oh, that's a valid criticism" and they move on. Not that it's a cognitive decision; the body just didn't interpret it as a life-threatening situation. The issue is that due to the individual's specific personal history, their nervous system may have been retuned to be threat biased.

How can people feel safe within organizations and systems that demand much of them?

In the medical community self-care and self-compassion get put on the side. They're seen as voluntary or even irrelevant—certainly not obligatory. Without self-compassion and self-care what clinical staff end up doing is depleting their resources. When people ask me "How can you deal with this in the hospital setting?" my answer is peer group. You have to have time to sit together, you have to have breaks, you have to have the socialization process of the co-regulation among the team or clusters. It's also about asking self-reflective questions such as, "Am I nourished by my work as a caregiver or is it depleting me?" And if it's depleting, then respecting the need for self-care.

Difficult to model in demanding health care settings.

Well, it's because medicine has become a business and the staff have become a resource for that business. It's functionally a mechanical model where everyone is dispensable; you have one person and you replace them with another. Humans don't function well that way.

How can we improve the situation?

One project I'm involved in retrains physicians to become more polyvagal informed. It builds their understanding that the way they interact with their patients affects not only their patients' health, but also their own health. Essentially, it's about physicians helping their patients to develop strategies that recruit the nervous system as a collaborator in the journey of healing, rather than scaring them. I'm also part of a think tank with several frustrated physicians who have quit medicine and with research physicians in medical schools to try and help shift the educational model of physicians toward making it more polyvagal informed.

How would you guide someone who is struggling with a relationship?

I'm not a therapist but I try to give hints. I do things like say "Just listen. Just listen for a moment. Witness what the other person is saying. Don't create a justification. Just listen."

Then before you go and develop the narrative about what the other person is doing, ask questions like, "How is my body feeling?" "What do I feel inside my body?" And if your body is tensing up, ask "How can my body relax?" "Are there breath patterns or mental visualizations I can use?" "Can I venture out?" Honor your body's reaction, learn what your body is doing and don't create a reason for your body to react. If you can do that then you become more embodied and more respectful of what your body is doing.

So the key message, again, is about respecting the body's reaction.

The notion is to respect where you are and also to respect what the other person is doing before you take on a narrative that justifies whatever you do—your reactions. It's not easy. It requires both being an observer and a participant. The ability to understand that how we react to others affects how they feel and how we feel. In the case of partners or spouses sometimes they just start yelling at each other because their bodies have shifted state.

And it's very hard to tell another person, "Look, this is what you did, and it disrupted me" because part of that disengagement is their adaptive strategy and now, you're blaming them for their strategies, so it creates a cycle; to whom do you listen?

It's a lot to try and get right.

Look, we're humans which means we have great limitations. Simply knowing that we're all human and that this is the human response isn't the answer. We have vulnerabilities and we are going to be greatly affected by those around us who are in pain or who are disrupted. And the issue is what resource do we have to be present without being evaluative and defensive? It's not an easy journey. That's why I feel much more comfortable in talking about it than doing it. I can see the process and I use terms like "super co-regulators"—people whose presence is so special that you just give up your defenses. The best most of us can hope for is to be a "good enough" co-regulator.

What does success mean to you?

The real question of course is "What do you mean by success?" We make attributions that because people are financially successful or professionally successful, they are secure within themselves. I think it's a real fallacy because the world that we're in, whether we talk about academics, business, any form of educational model, or even in medicine, is not about nurturing the resource of the staff; it's all about bottom line, which means dollars.

Even universities are all about how much grant money you can bring in. In hospitals it's the same story; it's about dollars, insurance money, and grants. The majority aren't asking "What is the journey that we're all on?" From my perspective, the journey is about gaining an understanding of what it is to be a human and what it takes to make humanity a more comfortable, if not safe, place. To feel safer, to feel affinity and understanding—these are significant measures of success that aren't as valued because they don't pay.

What do you look forward to
postpandemic—if such a thing exists?

What I miss with this new world is the social interactions that come from proximity. It's nice to be accessible as a human being. One of the things that academics are not so good at is being accessible to other people. Typically, they are defensive and self-protected and that means that their accessibility becomes an impossibility, a vulnerability, or a distraction. And there is so much social nourishment in being accessible. So, if you can get that and feel it through giving talks, it can be extremely nourishing. That I missed during the pandemic.

16

An Interview with
Dr. Stephen W. Porges

Christina Devereaux and Stephen W. Porges

CD: To start, the Polyvagal Theory (PVT) emphasizes that "connectedness is a biological imperative" for all humans and that we are wired to connect to others and also to protect the self. Could you begin with a brief overview introducing what PVT says about the neural circuits that support social engagement behaviors and defensive strategies?

SP: To understand PVT you need a brief summary of the changes in the autonomic nervous system (ANS) that occurred during the evolution of vertebrates, the animals with backbones. The ANS includes the neural circuits that regulate the organs within our body. The neural regulation of our heart is a primary function of the ANS, since survival is dependent on the maintenance and distribution of oxygenated blood throughout the body. Through the process of evolution, the neural regulation of autonomic state was modified to enable social behavior to occur. To be social, a mammal had to turn off defenses. This process of inhibiting defenses included both a down-regulation of the autonomic state that supported aggressive behaviors and the emergence of spontaneous social behavior. This process illustrated two important features of the evolutionary transition from the ancient extinct reptiles to the early mammals. Mammals are social and need to interact with other conspecifics to reproduce and to nurture their young. In order to be social, mammals have to be accessible to others. Thus, we need to appreciate that the ANS that mammals inherited was a protective system. The ancient ANS system supported two behavioral defensive strategies: one, which was manifested as fight-or-flight or mobilization behaviors and a second, a phylogenetically old strategy, which was manifested as shutting down or immobilization behaviors. Mammals were dependent on each other and early in life couldn't survive as solitary creatures. To be social and to engage conspecifics, they had to turn down their defensive systems. This tuning down of the defensive system was linked in mammals to a myelinated vagal pathway that was integrated with the nerves that regulated the muscles of the face and the head. This integration of face and heart became the core of what I labeled as the social engagement system. The social engagement system enables engagement with others through facial expressivity, intonation of the voice, and head gesture. The neural mechanisms mediating these engagement behaviors are regulated in an area of the brainstem that also regulates the heart. The social engagement system is bidirectional. On one level we express our physiological state in our face and our voice, and on the other level the facial and vocal cues that we detect in others enable us to calm our physiological state.

CD: This is a great segue into the concept of neuroception. Can you talk about this further?

SP: Where does the intelligence come from that enables our nervous system to detect cues of safety, danger, or life threat? We can conceptualize this intelligence as a neural process involving higher brain structures that is not dependent on awareness or a conscious cognitive process. I needed a word to describe this process. Initially I wanted to use perception as the process involved in detecting risk in the environment. However, I realized that perception would be linked to conscious awareness. If I used the term perception of risk, it would imply a conscious evaluation of whether features in the environment were actually dangerous or innocuous. This internal evaluation would be difficult and slow to resolve and any delay in resolving the validity of risk might place the individual at risk. In contrast, we note that our responses to risk are often immediate and virtually reflexive. To be functionally adaptive this process evolved outside the realm of conscious awareness. Because neuroception can either turn on or turn off ancient evolutionary primitive defense systems, it needed to be dependent upon higher brain structures that were not constrained by conscious awareness. I needed a new word to describe the process, which emphasized that the nervous system was implementing the process of risk evaluation, but implementing the process independent of perception or any other process dependent on awareness. Thus, I coined the word neuroception.

Theoretically neuroception is dependent on neural circuits located in and near the temporal cortex. This area of our brain has the capacity to detect the intentionality of biological movement including body movements, gestures, facial expressions, and vocalizations. When we discuss dance and movement therapy, we focus on the physics and physiology of the movement. We also emphasize the intentionality of movement. Our nervous system, through neuroception, focuses on interpreting the intentionality of the movement. When neuroception interprets the movement as being safe, then the higher brain structures inhibit and down-regulate our defensiveness. But if neuroception interprets the movement as being unsafe, we immediately become defensive. Neuroception is like a high-level reflex that is unconscious and able to down-regulate defenses reflexively.

CD: The Polyvagal Theory discusses that individuals might struggle to successfully engage in voluntary social behaviors such as those with autism. Or those that experienced trauma may have "faulty neuroception"? Could you describe this concept further?

SP: Faulty neuroception detects risk when there is no risk. For the clients with faulty neuroception, their nervous systems may have been retuned to lower their threshold for detecting risk. If this occurs they detect risk when there is no risk and virtually all movements toward them may be interpreted, via neuroception, as dangerous. Faulty neuroception is associated with the client's history. For example, if a client experienced a traumatic event and was injured, the probability of the nervous system detecting movements toward them as dangerous is high. The nervous system has been retuned with a bias toward detecting cues of danger and not detecting cues of safety. This shift in bias toward detecting risk influences how neutral and often positive cues are interpreted. Frequently neutral cues and even positive cues may be interpreted via faulty neuroception as if they were dangerous or hurtful.

CD: You suggested that clients with difficulties with social engagement might manifest somatic disorders—specifically that this is a response to atypical neuroregulation becoming manifested in organs below the diaphragm. Could you talk more about this from the perspective of the Polyvagal Theory?

SP: Moving into autonomic states that support defensive behavioral strategies, it's not a free option. We pay a price in shifting neurophysiological state to support defense by interfering with our normal homeostatic processes. We interfere with the ability of the autonomic nervous system to support health, growth, and restoration. When we are in a state of chronic defensiveness our muscles are tense, our bodies are defensive and reactive, our voices are higher pitched and lack prosody, and our faces lack affect. Underlying these behavioral manifestations, our physiological state has changed, reflecting the dampened positive influences of the neural circuits that enable our body to heal, grow, and restore. These negative effects are due to the retraction of the evolutionarily newer mammalian vagal circuit.

Unfortunately, we live in a world in which environmental demands frequently require behaviors dependent upon a physiological state dominated by an activated sympathetic nervous system. For some people, sympathetic activation is not effective in regulating feelings of safety and they respond by shutting down through an older neural pathway traveling through the vagus. Immobilizing, defecating, and fainting may accompany the behavioral shutdown. The older vagal circuit is shared with the evolutionary ancestors of mammals and manifested in most vertebrate species. This older circuit, when not recruited in defense, is critical for supporting digestion and other functions of the organs located below our diaphragm. It's important not to recruit this vagal circuit for defense. However, if the older vagal circuit is recruited for defense, especially if chronically recruited, then disorders such as irritable bowel and fibromyalgia may be manifested.

When the older vagal circuit is recruited in defense, it may interfere with the enteric nervous system's function. In a way the vagus is like the gut's guard or sentry. When there is no threat, it tells the gut to do its job. If there is danger, it triggers that gut to stop functioning (e.g., constipation). If there is life threat, it triggers the gut to evacuate its content (e.g., diarrhea). The gut also sends signals back to the brain through the sensory pathways embedded in the vagus. The sensory signals confirm that the gut is being challenged.

If your clients have trauma histories, they may talk about a trauma gut, a situation in which their gut reacts to virtually everything they eat. Under these conditions, they might have to eat very bland foods. Behaviorally these same clients may also be emotionally labile and appear very temperamental. The emotions and the gut are parts of the same system, with the gut telling the brain it is having problems and the brain concurring to the gut and the entire body that the individual is not in a good place.

Polyvagal Theory provides a map to get out of this cycle. Polyvagal Theory emphasizes the hierarchical nature of how our ANS reacts to challenges and focuses on how signals of safety through the social engagement system can retune the ANS from a state that supports defensive reactions into physiological states that support health, growth, and restoration.

When cues of safety are detected, the newest circuit of the ANS (i.e., the myelinated mammalian vagus) buffers the evolutionarily older circuits and keeps them out of states of defense. Polyvagal Theory respects the role that the sympathetic nervous system and the older dorsal vagus have in maintaining physiological health, but proposes that those circuits optimally function only during states of safety. If the sympathetic nervous system or the dorsal vagal pathway is recruited for defense, all bets regarding a positive mental and physiological health outcome are off.

CD: You suggest that interventions that improve the neural regulation of the social engagement system hypothetically should enhance spontaneous social behavior and state and affect regulation. Staying in a state-supporting social engagement with the client through attuned-movement interactions is a focus in dance and movement therapy. You have referred to this as a "neural exercise." Could you talk more about what you mean by this and why this might be important?

SP: Movement and especially reciprocal movements with a partner are critical for dance and movement therapy. But it is not just movement. It is movement **with** social engagement. Dance and movement therapy integrates the power of the social engagement system with movement. In doing this it keeps the sympathetic nervous system contained, restricting it from going into defense. Movement coupled with social engagement is a feature of children's games, such as "Simon says" and "peek-a-boo." Within the context of play, immobilization without fear requires that the cues of immobilizing are associated with contextual feelings that do not trigger defense. For immobilization to occur without fear it needs not to be associated with restraint. For mobilization to occur without fear, it needs not to be associated with fight-or-flight behaviors. To enable mobilization and immobilization to occur without fear, these behavioral states need to be modulated or functionally contained by features of the social engagement system such as facial expressions, prosodic voices, and positive hand and head gestures.

What is dance? What is play? Both are neural exercises that shift affective states within a safe context. Once the context changes from cues of safety, there is a shift in physiological state. This may occur if the therapist moves too close to the client or if the client feels evaluated or threatened. In the therapeutic setting the therapist is also sending subtle cues to the client. For example, if your mind wanders, a client may feel threatened, because your face went flat and the client wasn't getting the reassuring cues. Your reaction to the client who yells at you will change as well. Your face would become sterner and more critical, and you might want to know why the client was being hurtful or angry. Hypothetically, as we watch a therapist-client dyad interacting, we can imagine parallels in how children play, spouses interact, and colleagues work. These interactions function as a dynamic dance, illustrating the reciprocal impact of cues outside our consciousness, although implicitly understood by our body.

CD: A dance and movement therapist might use music as a co-facilitator to some degree to support the tone of the session. Based on your work with the Listening Project and also what the Polyvagal Theory discusses about prosodic vocalizations through music, what suggestions might you make for dance and movement therapists in using music as an intentional tool to support social engagement and states of safety?

SP: Several features of music influence physiological state. These features include rhythm and the frequencies defining the acoustic stimulation that constitutes music. The Polyvagal Theory focuses on the modulation of frequencies that define the intonations associated with both vocal music and the acoustic features of vocalizations that convey information about content and intent. Based on the Polyvagal Theory, I developed an acoustic intervention that functionally amplifies the features of intonation that convey positive engaging cues of safety. This intervention initially known as the Listening Project Protocol was launched commercially through Integrated Listening Systems (iLs) as the Safe and Sound Protocol™. This was an important event for me, since it has taken more than 30 years to translate the ideas embedded in the intervention into an accessible product.

Therapists intuitively understand that a prosodic voice can support their clients and enable their clients to relax. They know when this strategy works, when the client orients toward the therapist and begins to make spontaneous eye contact.

The intervention leverages knowledge of our evolutionary history in understanding our biobehavioral responses to vocalizations. Our nervous system evolved to startle and become vigilant in response to the low-frequency bass sounds associated with an aggressive male's vocalizations. In contrast, our nervous system evolved to be comforted and to feel calm in response to melodic female voices. An infant's unlearned and spontaneous response to a mother's lullaby provides an example of this heritage. I suspect that many dance movement therapists intuitively use prosodic voices with their clients and use melodic music in their therapy sessions.

These positive calming effects of music function through a passive pathway and trigger a neuroception of safety. The passive pathway triggers the nervous system without any active demand on the client. This is contrasted by an active pathway, in which the client is involved in an activity in which reciprocal behaviors are required, such as dancing with a partner. The initial task in therapy is to make the client feel safe. Feeling safe shifts the ANS to a state that supports spontaneous social engagement behaviors. Once the client starts spontaneously engaging, then therapists can engage the client through the active pathway. In the active pathway the therapist involves the client in movement exercises such as dance involving reciprocal movements that are rhythmically organized.

Drum circles are powerful not just because of the acoustic frequencies generated while drumming, but because the participants emit spontaneous interactive social engagement behaviors through gaze and facial expressivity. Even if you do not know the other people in the drum circle, by the time the drumming session ends, the participants feel connected and familiar. These feelings are due to the spontaneous shifts in physiological state that dynamically occur due to the combined effects of the physical demands of drumming and the neurophysiological impact of social engagement behaviors on our ANS. Drum circles share two features common to several forms of movement therapy: reciprocity and synchronicity. These features form the constraints that create intersubjective moments in which the client has an opportunity to share a subjective state with another.

CD: What advice might you have to the profession of dance and movement therapy in developing evidence-based research?

SP: Therapists are intuitive. By delivering interventions, they provide important opportunities for clients to experience moments of safety and to rediscover personal resources that support resilience. Therapists frequently have outstanding outcomes while facilitating neural regulation of their client's ANS. Dance and movement therapists play an important role in the management of several disorders, but, in general, these therapists are not researchers. Conducting research to evaluate and to understand the mechanisms underlying clinical treatments is difficult and the treatment models applied by dance and movement therapists may not easily conform to the tight experimental designs used in clinical trials to document the effects of pharmaceuticals. While clinicians tailor their treatment model to the dynamically changing features of their clients, researchers attempt to determine cause-and-effect relationships by applying experimental designs that exert a systematic control of treatment parameters. In addition, researchers and therapists often ask different questions. Therapists want to know if their treatments work, while researchers are far more interested in the mechanisms and processes through which therapy may work.

This difference in perspective makes it difficult to apply research techniques to document efficacy. I would suggest two steps in developing a research program for dance and movement therapy. As an initial step, I would develop a theory statement that would propose a plausible explanation of the mechanisms through which dance and movement therapy works. I think Polyvagal Theory would be useful in developing explanations and mechanisms. Once a theoretical model is developed, plausible hypotheses can be tested. As an example, let's propose that dance and movement therapists want to test the efficacy of their therapies. From my perspective the test of efficacy cannot be evaluated in a tightly controlled study, because the treatment clients receive will vary; some will need more sessions than others and the content of the sessions will also vary both across sessions and among clients.

Researchers could take a pragmatic approach and focus on pre- and post-changes. For example, research might evaluate whether the underlying principles embedded in dance and movement therapy have specific neurophysiological effects. PVT provides a structure to develop these types of hypotheses. Specifically, research could evaluate whether there are changes in the features and function of the social engagement system following dance and movement therapy. I would hypothesize that dance and movement therapy implicitly incorporates methodologies that efficiently elicit and exercise the neurophysiological circuits involved in the social engagement system.

The evaluation of any intervention requires an agreement on the measures used to assess outcome. There are two strategies here that reflect the different biases of researchers and therapists. The first focuses on mechanisms. This is the path my research has been on for decades. This a path in which treatments are deconstructed into plausible mechanisms, which may be neurophysiological, behavioral, or psychological. The second focuses on clinical outcome and requires a consensus among dance and movement therapists to identify the features of their clients that improve due to their therapies. This step will be necessary before a research program can be established. Once there is documentation of specific improvements, then research evaluating mechanisms can be initiated.

CD: How do you see your work with the Polyvagal Theory influencing psychotherapy, mental health, or clinical practice?

SP: This is occurring on several levels. First, Polyvagal Theory is influencing clients by providing them with a plausible explanation of their experiences. The theory has helped clients understand the adaptive biobehavioral responses of shutting down in response to life threat. It provides a better understanding that their inability to mobilize and fight off a perpetrator is not equivalent to being complicit. This understanding of an involuntary immobilization reaction is having a major impact on the survivors of trauma. The theory provides a new understanding of why a person might not aggressively protect themselves. This knowledge provides an opportunity for a top-down healing process in which the personal narrative acknowledges the wisdom and heroic actions of the body. This change in self-understanding has positive effects.

Second, clinicians now have a better understanding of the adaptive biobehavioral reactions experienced by their clients and have hints of how to provide their clients with supportive cues of safety. We all require cues of safety to enable our nervous system to support our mental and physical health.

The third influence focuses on a better understanding that the mechanisms involved in optimal social behavior are disrupted by trauma. As I observed various clinical disorders I asked myself, "How can I trigger reversals? How can I optimize the mental and physical health of the individual?" My research with developing the acoustic intervention (Safe and Sound Protocol™) highlights one of those "ah-ha" moments, when I asked myself, "Can I tell the body unambiguously that it is in the place of safety?" At that moment many features of our evolutionary heritage started to make sense. I started to understand the power of a mother's voice, gesture, and cues in calming the tantrums of the baby. I also understood how the lower pitch and less prosodic voice of a father could be disruptive to the child. As I deconstructed how cues of safety calmed and cues of danger disrupted, I could visualize an active, dynamic biobehavioral dance between individuals as they try to co-regulate each other.

CD: Do you have anything more that you would like to add for our dance and movement therapy readers?

SP: I think the important point for dance and movement therapists is to understand the power of their treatment models and their intuition in manipulating cues of safety to manage the behavioral state of their clients during treatment. By implementing reciprocal movements with social engagement behaviors, dance and movement therapists support the neural mechanisms involved in optimizing mental and physical health. Please keep doing your good work!

17

The Anatomy of Calm

Stephen W. Porges

As a culture, we are endowed with the belief that anxiety, packed as it is with worry, is a condition that exists in our head. Decades of psychophysiological research have proved to me that, in fact, anxiety is in our body. It's even more accurate to say that it is in our nervous system. Like other animals, we humans have a unified nervous system. The body and the brain talk to each other—because they regulate each other. That system of regulation offers a whole new understanding of how we become anxious, how we perpetuate and even justify anxiety, and how we can release it.

Our physiologic state influences how we react to the world and how we make our way through it.

Unfortunately, it is nowhere accounted for in most models of mental health. My perspective differs from the prevailing model in psychology and psychiatry, which sees anxiety as a brain reaction, not a full-body phenomenon. Psychology holds that through cognitive and behavioral technologies, anxiety can be tamed with language. But the evidence demonstrates that certain physiologic states bias us to negativity and others to optimism and social experience, and we need a tool kit that grapples with that fact first.

Anxiety, like other emotions, arises from different bodily states as the neural signals they give off work their way up through the brainstem, where control of our basic states resides. That information also gets relayed to higher levels in the brain, where we make meaning of it—what we call emotions. Anxiety is the response of the body under threat.

One of the first obligations of all organisms is to maintain a means of defense. The ability to detect danger is critical to defense, and acute threat reactions, in which we quickly mobilize resources, are life-sustaining. Chronic threats, however, impose high costs on our physiology, disrupting the homeostatic mechanism that allows us to grow and flourish, not only imperiling our health but constricting our range of experience and, especially, our ability to relate to other human beings.

Every single one of us contends with states of threat, which are our responses to the uncertainty of survival. Threat can emanate from the external world or arise internally from memories. I devised the term neuroception to describe how, below the level of conscious awareness, neural circuits constantly monitor and assess internal and external risks, whether situations or people, as safe, dangerous, or life-threatening.

A potent mechanism that has the potential to down-regulate threat resides in the ventral portion of the brainstem, in an area known as the nucleus ambiguus, where the vagus nerve, the star player of the autonomic nervous system, originates. Vagus means wandering, and the vagus nerve begins at the base of the brain, branches down to the heart, the lungs, and the digestive tract, with stops along the way at the larynx, the pharynx, and the diaphragm, before descending into the abdomen.

The branches of the vagus nerve enable the organs to adjust instantly to the demands of a person's surroundings. It is the duty of the vagus nerve to orchestrate bodily responses to keep you safe or prepare your body for danger before you are even aware of it or have a chance to think about it. Most of the vagus is composed of sensory fibers that function as our surveillance system, informing the brain of the status of our visceral organs.

In our evolutionary journey to becoming social mammals, the basic reptilian structures underwent modification. In order for animals to become social, there had to be a way to turn off threat reactions; animals had to be able to cue one another that they were safe enough to come near. As distinct from reptiles, mammals have neuroception not only of threat but also of safety. The vagus nerve responds to cues of safety detected by higher brain structures, which bring on enough calm to open you up to socially engage with others.

Because information flows both to and from the brain via vagal pathways, the vagus nerve can be thought of as a major mind–body highway. Through the vagus nerve, you react to signals in your environment in ways that calm, alarm, or dysregulate the body, and these states in turn create emotional experience and play out in behavior. It has taken me decades to define how the vagal pathways operate and the control they exert—summed up in what I call Polyvagal Theory (PVT).

PVT explains the interconnectedness of body reactivity, cognitive and emotional function, and social behavior. It reveals that we humans are meant to regulate each other, that proximity, social interaction, and intonation of voice are all powerful neural signals.

As states of visceral calmness get transmitted up to the brainstem, the information is also relayed to more highly evolved brain structures, allowing full access to the brain's talents and means of expression and enabling social interaction, which has the effect of perpetuating a state of calmness. But in potential danger states such as completely novel environments, those higher systems turn off; we don't have access to problem-solving skills, to powers of creativity, to our full intelligence. We become vigilant and defensive. The vagal circuitry is down-regulated, narrowing our focus, mobilizing our resources, and preparing us to fight or flee, tripping the so-called stress response mediated by the sympathetic nervous system.

If the danger is so overwhelming that there is no escape or there is a feeling of being trapped, a third autonomic circuit utilizing different vagal pathways is involved in a biobehavioral shutdown. In this state of numbness, social contact becomes an intrusion and is aversive. None of the bodily responses are voluntary, and often people are not aware of what triggered them, although they are likely aware that their heart is pounding or their body is trembling.

As a social species, we evolved to use our nervous system to regulate and be regulated by those around us. Such co-regulation is perhaps most obvious in early life, when infant caregiving audibly modulates the baby's state. Think of a mother singing to her crying baby. Vocalizations are a way of broadcasting physiologic state. Universally, low-frequency growl sounds are understood as threat signals. Through evolution from reptiles to mammals, the middle ear bones broke off the jawbone and enabled the hearing of a frequency band that became the channel for social communication. Prosodic voices are on that bandwidth.

How much co-regulation people need varies significantly among individuals. But it is completely mistaken to think that we can manage threat states by ourselves. Sociality is a potent neurophysiological modulator, more potent than pharmaceuticals, more important than surgery. It's not just nice to be friendly; our nervous system requires it. We can quantify its impact, and we can apply it as an intervention.

People go a long way to make meaning of the agitated physiologic state we call anxiety. There's a package of negative emotions that get stirred by it. Using higher brain structures (e.g., memory, associations, previous learning, contextual learning) we create narratives of worry that attribute the driving force to something external and that literally keep us in this state. Most people find it difficult to separate the worry from the physical disturbance, but it's possible. Worry is a personal narrative we create in a state of threat to justify why we feel bad.

PVT not only explains anxiety as a physiologic state of threat, it also opens a portal of intervention. Applying specific maneuvers affecting vagal pathways, we can use the nervous system to reset physiologic state. Independent of the threshold of reactivity that pitches a person into alarm mode, it is possible to reeducate the nervous system with cues of safety. Removal of the threat isn't a bad tactic, but it is not sufficient and not what the nervous system demands; it needs cues of safety. Shift state and you change the character of experience.

The most direct way to access the neural pathway that turns off threat is through breathing: exhaling slowly. Our evolutionary journey endowed us with a gift, the ability to extend exhalation; this not only enables us to regulate our state, it also underlies the ability to speak. Neurophysiologically powerful, it acts on fibers of the ventral vagus nerve ferrying signals between visceral organs and the brainstem, where autonomic control of body organs originates. Extending the duration of phrases, even humming and gum-chewing, stimulates the nerve fibers of the muscles of the face, head, and oral cavity and opens the social engagement system, enabling people to respond reciprocally to the invitations of others.

Gaining control of physiologic state through breathing is why some people turn to yoga and meditation. Singing uses the same neurophysiological structures of breathing and facial muscles as the social engagement system. Playing a wind instrument gives you no choice but to exhale slowly. But most anxious people feed the physiologic state of threat by making slow inhalations and rapid exhalations.

Even cognitive behavioral therapy (CBT) has breathing components. Breathing sets the stage for the cognitive work. If you shift a person's state into calm, then cognitive and behavioral therapies can be extraordinarily efficient. But if physiology isn't supporting calmness, they can't work. A person is too tightly wrapped in a state of defense.

The job of therapist is to co-regulate a patient. An individual in a state of chronic threat is not capable of dialogue, not responsive to any form of co-regulation. The person expresses negativity, a reliable indicator of physiologic state. While breathing quickly shifts physiologic state from the bottom up, it is also possible to change state from the top down. The anxious person can be asked, "What puts a smile on your face? Was there a time when you felt safe, comfortable, secure? Was there a time you enjoyed getting up in the morning? Tell me about that." That exchange initiates a shift of physiologic state.

Once the internal neural dialogue is shifted from threat and defense to safety, physiology shifts, and many systems of the body are down-regulated. Cascades of chemical communication dampen down, including cortisol release. Cues of safety coming through the ventral vagus circuit (e.g., familiar faces, intonation of voice) shut off the defensive systems. The shift is immediate and global; no rewiring is required. The body goes into homeostatic mode, with use of resources for restoration and repair.

Shifting physiologic state restores access to your whole self. Memory and higher capacities are available. You become cognitively present to solve problems. The social engagement system becomes a portal to gaining back our human heritage.

How to Keep Your Cool in High-Stress Situations

Robert E. Quinn, David P. Fessell, and Stephen W. Porges

A CEO called one of us (Robert) for help. The company they were leading was on the cusp of a huge opportunity related to a new technology. But they were stymied and stuck.

One of the representatives for an investor in the project was extremely assertive and self-interested. They had intimidated several of the company's strong board members, who were now withdrawing the financial support they had already committed. The entire endeavor was at risk. It took 20 minutes for the CEO to describe all the complexities. As the CEO did, Robert felt a knot in his stomach. The CEO expected him to add value and yet he was struggling to even comprehend the issues. He worried that he wouldn't be able to help, and a part of him just wanted to end the call and distance himself from this mess. Rather than doing that, he understood that his anxiety was a signal to slow down. He began to self-regulate.

Recent research in the field of neuroscience, specifically Polyvagal Theory (PVT), offers insights into this process of self-regulation and how you can move from a fight-or-flight response to a higher state of openness that invites collaboration, creativity, and thriving. Studies have shown that specific tactics, which we'll explain below, can help us navigate our natural tendency to be defensive when confronted.

Another one of us (Stephen) developed Polyvagal Theory, which explains how our nervous system regulates our behavior, both collaborative and defensive, using the vagus nerve, the major parasympathetic nerve in the autonomic nervous system. This nerve provides bidirectional connections between the brain and the heart, gut, and other organs in our body and is part of a predictable response sequence that is activated when we are threatened. There are three levels to this response.

The first is immobilization, or what we call level one. Under dire threat, a reptile, mammal, or human may collapse and mimic death. This is a natural and adaptive reaction. For example, when a mouse is trapped by a cat, the mouse may reflexively shut down and appear to be dead. Consequently, the cat loses interest in the mouse and the mouse is able to escape. This is a rare reaction in humans but it does happen.

Level two is mobilization. Under threat, the heart begins to beat faster. The sympathetic nervous system is activated, the body produces cortisol and adrenaline and prepares for action. This is the fight-or-flight response. We become aggressive, or we flee.

The third level of response is engagement and connection. When we feel safe again, we begin to function differently. It is at this level that a uniquely mammalian vagal pathway becomes functional and quiets the defensive features of both the fight-or-flight and shutdown pathways. The body releases oxytocin. In this state, we are more open to others and experience a sense of connectedness that can lead to collaboration and learning.

Theodosius Dobzhansky (1962), a prominent evolutionary biologist, has refined Charles Darwin's famous quote about evolution being a "survival of the fittest," to add that, "The fittest may also be the gentlest because survival often requires mutual help and cooperation." In Dobzhansky's view, it is connectedness and collaboration that have enabled the evolutionary success of mammals and humans.

When we're able to reach level three, our vision, hearing, voice, and mind begin to work in concert with our heart. We are able to feel our bodies, as opposed to the numbness we may feel at levels one and two during a confrontation. We are not in the tunnel vision of fight-or-flight, so we can more accurately read the faces and the nonverbal signals of others. We see the bigger picture and connect with others around shared goals. In short, our relational and learning capacity increases.

As a leader, the more effectively you can self-regulate, particularly moving from the frequently occurring level two to level three, the better you can lead and help others. Based on our experience applying PVT to situations like the one Robert was in with the CEO, we've developed a five-step framework to help people make this shift.

> Step 1. *Understanding.* The first step is knowing the biology behind these reactions and accepting that being at level one, two, or three is normal. Knowing where you are on the hierarchy gives you choice and the power to shift.

Step 2. *Awareness*. When you feel challenged, notice the physical and emotional cues that signal you're experiencing anxiety. Do you feel a knot in your stomach? Or your heart racing? See these as signs of where you are in your reaction: likely level two.

Step 3. *Recall*. Bring to mind previous experiences where you've successfully moved through uncertainty in the past. You might even write down what you did to navigate a difficult situation and use your own success to give yourself hope that you can get through this one too.

Step 4. *Intention*. With hope in mind, let go of the need to serve your ego by clarifying your highest purpose. Focusing on your intention will release oxytocin and help you shift to level three.

Step 5. *Trusting the process*. When you're at level three, it's much easier to explore and develop ideas with the other person. The interaction is an emergent learning process; it will be challenging, but as long as you stay connected and don't move back to level one or two, you can get through it together. In fact, you can become skilled at making others safe and keep inviting them back into mutually beneficial conversations.

Robert used this framework when he was talking to the CEO and he noticed himself going into fight-or-flight, wanting to flee the conversation. To make sure he was in a state where he could think clearly, he consciously drew on his memory of past challenges and successes. He thought about prior experiences when he had felt uncertain and vulnerable yet managed to move forward. These memories increased his confidence in his ability to navigate this situation. He also thought about what he could bring to the conversation with the CEO—his higher purpose—which allowed him to consciously shift from fear to hope.

Energized by this purpose, he invited the CEO to continue speaking, rather than trying to end the call. He used oral signals of inclusion to support safety and trust. These included statements of authentic vulnerability and the use of genuine inquiry. When the CEO finished, for example, he said, "Your challenge is very difficult. I can barely understand it. So, let me repeat to you my flawed comprehension so you can correct me."

It was a vulnerable act to admit that he didn't fully comprehend what they were saying but being authentic signaled that he trusted the CEO, and his openness signaled they could trust him. The CEO spent another 7 minutes further clarifying and as they did, they and Robert entered into a state of co-regulation where ideas, emotions, and possibilities could be exchanged without hesitation, embarrassment, or fear.

Once Robert felt safe and deeply listened to the CEO's clarifications, oxytocin was metaphorically flowing and he felt more mentally open. Instead of orienting to the problem, he focused on possibility and called their attention to a larger vision. Instead of seeking to get the already promised resources, could the CEO take a new approach? Could they explore the original intentions of each actor? Why did the others care enough to sign up and invest? Were they committed enough to become more engaged? Could the CEO boldly ask for funding that would take the company, not a few months into the future, but years into the future? Could the CEO invite them to make a greater commitment? Could the CEO lead them in co-regulating their way to higher collaboration?

The CEO, intrigued, said they could try it out. A month later, the CEO called Robert to report that the strategy, with further modifications, had brought success. The board members were more committed and optimism was up.

Self-regulation opens the way to collaboration and change. Understanding our biological reactions in high-stress situations gives us a path to follow; it is then our choice if we walk this path or fight it. And the choice we make is often the difference between our success and failure.

What Putin's Physiological State Tells Us: How the Physiological State of a Leader Can Impact the World

Robert Legvold, Nancy Rubbico, and Stephen W. Porges

One man, angry and isolated, has upended the world, returned it to 1939, and set in motion untold suffering. Many are questioning his mental stability. James Clapper, a former U.S. intelligence chief, says he appears "unhinged" (2022). Former president Obama's secretary of defense, Robert Gates, suspects that "in some respects he's gone off the rails" (Zakaria, 2022). U.S. intelligence agencies are mobilizing resources to assess his mental health (Cohen et al., 2022).

One area of research may offer insights. Polyvagal Theory (PVT) (Porges, 2023), as part of the work applying neuroscience to mental health, suggests possible ways in which physiology is shaping Putin's mental state and behavior. The theory focuses on an individual's autonomic nervous system and the behaviors that it affects including how the foundational brainstem mechanisms regulating it influence and bias the cognitive processes dependent on higher brain structures.

This system is programmed to keep us safe and healthy by supporting the bodily functions of health, growth, and restoration. However, the system influences other processes intimately related to our survival and health. It has a direct effect on our sociality (Porges, 2021). When challenged by threat, the system shifts into a defensive state to deal with proximal illness and potential injury. This state change in the autonomic nervous system disrupts abilities to self-regulate, cooperate with others, and maintain balance within our larger environment. The primitive brainstem mechanisms controlling the autonomic nervous system do not have values or moral meanings, nor do they assign motivation. Our brain does that. It receives and assesses the signals sent by an environment not on a cognitive, but on a neural biological level. It is a survival-based detection process without awareness.

It is constantly surveilling three worlds: inside our body, outside our body (e.g., our immediate surroundings but also the larger world), and between the two, relationships at all levels. Polyvagal Theory addresses three neural circuits that, in hierarchical fashion, support different types of behavior. The first circuit is a state of safety (i.e., our social engagement system) involving five cranial nerves. The second circuit is a state of mobilization, the fight-or-flight impulse. The third circuit is a state of immobilization. When the first circuit is no longer available and the second circuit is overwhelmed, the body enters a conservation mode: blood flow to the brain and digestion slows; a disconnected sense of hopelessness and helplessness prevails; and the feeling is one of invisibility and abandonment, with safety and hope unreachable.

If the insights of PVT help to explain Putin's behavior (as opposed to his mental state) the relevant neural circuit would be the second. In the state of mobilization one no longer has access to the prefrontal lobe and the behaviors it supports: an ability to self-regulate, to connect with others, to receive support and offer support to others, and to be flexible and resilient. They are replaced by an overriding sense of danger and alarm, a feeling of anger and anxiety, and a preoccupying hypervigilance. It is called an **adaptive survival response**.

This appears to be where Putin is. His nervous system is now only looking for cues of danger. He is no longer able to listen. He cannot self-regulate or easily cooperate with others. And his behavior manifests a dominant sense of injustice and unfairness in what, for him, is a dangerous world. His mental state may be affected by his isolation, but his nervous system is producing the isolation.

The BBC's Russian correspondent, Farida Rustamova, quotes a source close to Putin as saying, "The Russian president has in his head that the rules of the game are destroyed and destroyed not by Russia, and if this is a fight without rules, then this is a fight without rules and the new reality in which we live. . . . He is in a state of resentfulness and insults. It's paranoia that has reached a point of absurdity" (2022). François Heisbourg, Special Advisor to the International Institute of Strategic Studies, draws the consequences: "When he is offered an off ramp, he doesn't know what is being mentioned. It's not a notion which he seems to understand" (Amanpour, 2022). Off ramps in his current physical state are not cues of safety but of danger.

The understandable outrage his decision to invade Ukraine has produced, the extraordinary worldwide support for Ukraine that it has generated, the vigorous U.S.-NATO effort to deny him a military victory in Ukraine, and their openly declared war on his country's economy will, if the insights from PVT apply, vastly intensify the cues to which he is responding. It is not clear who or what can alter the current dangerous and destructive state that his autonomic nervous system appears to be in, but as Washington and allied governments struggle to assess and then deal with his mental state, they also need to factor in the full range of biological factors shaping his behavior.

Appendix: The Polyvagal Perspective

POLYVAGAL THEORY: LIMITATIONS AND EXPANDING EXPLANATIONS

The Polyvagal Theory (PVT) provides neurophysiological organizing principles to interpret and to test hypotheses relating peripheral cardiovascular state to the psychological processes that have intrigued psychophysiologists (e.g., emotion, social engagement, fight-or-flight, face-to-face communication). The theory emphasizes that physiological state limits the range of social behavior and the ability to regulate emotion. Thus, creating states of calmness and exercising the neural regulation of the striated muscles of the face and head may potentiate positive social behavior by stimulating the neural regulation of the social engagement system.

PVT does not propose that the vagus is the ultimate cause of individual differences in social engagement behaviors or emotional regulation. The efferent vagal pathway originating in the nucleus ambiguus (i.e., manifested in RSA) is one of several output systems related to emotion and social engagement behaviors. In PVT, the source nuclei of the myelinated vagus are regulated by complex neural circuits, involving both visceral afferents and higher brain structures that influence the brainstem source nuclei controlling both the myelinated vagus and the striated muscles of the face and head (i.e., the social engagement system).

Specific central pathways from cortical and subcortical areas (e.g., the temporal cortex, central nucleus of the amygdala, and periaqueductal gray) are involved in the regulation of both the vagal component and somatomotor component of the social engagement system. Consistent with PVT, others have proposed direct neural pathways that integrate emotional activity with central structures that influence autonomic function (see Craig, 2005; Phillips et al., 2003a, 2003b; Thayer & Lane, 2000). The asymmetry of higher brain structures may also play a role in linking specific affective experiences with autonomic states. Consistent with the views that the right hemisphere appears to play a greater role in affect, especially the adaptive expression of negative affect (e.g., Canli et al., 1998; Fox, 1991; Noesselt et al., 2005; Simon-Thomas et al., 2005), the right hemisphere also appears to have a greater role in regulation of cardiac function, presumably via shifts in vagal regulation (Ahern et al., 2001; Porges et al., 1994). Although not the focus of this appendix, these central structures and their asymmetrical influence on autonomic function would be likely candidates to be involved in the hypothetical process of neuroception described above.

PVT leads to theory-driven research that will provide a plausible neurobiological foundation for the explanation and assessment of variants of social-emotional behavior and disorders, including the compromised social behavior observed during physical illness and psychiatric disorders. PVT supports research that breaks the tradition of single-variable psychophysiological research by identifying theoretically relevant variables involved in the regulation of social engagement behaviors. In addition, the theory provides a neurophysiological basis for understanding several relevant issues in health psychology, including the benefits of social support and face-to-face communication on visceral regulation and health. Perhaps most relevant to psychophysiology as a science, the theory leads to testable hypotheses that will, in turn, result in modifications to the theory.

Levels of Inquiry

Imbedded in PVT is a generalizable and expansive perspective of inquiry. What are the features of this perspective? How does this perspective influence the conceptualization of research questions and paradigms in psychophysiology? The polyvagal perspective reflects a level of inquiry that emphasizes neurophysiological mechanisms and neurobiological organizing principles to determine how heart rate measures, as noninvasive features of adaptive neural circuits, are related to psychological, behavioral, and health processes. The approach seeks to understand the "why" and "how" of the observed relations between heart rate variables and psychological, behavioral, and clinical processes. From this perspective, the Polyvagal Theory is pragmatically fluid as knowledge regarding the "why" and "how" of neurophysiological regulation of the autonomic nervous system expands.

Cardiovascular psychophysiology is influenced by theories, assumptions, and methodological biases. Often, clusters of ideas and traditions within a discipline form assumed, but untested, discipline myths that drive or limit a research agenda. Discipline myths often include information that, while accurate on a descriptive level, is naïve on other levels of inquiry. Levels of inquiry drive different questions. These questions lead to different paradigms. Embedded within each paradigm are implicit assumptions regarding the mechanisms mediating heart rate parameters and how these parameters are related to cognitive, affective, or health variables.

Within the discipline of psychophysiology, heart rate and HRV traditionally have been treated as operationally defined dependent variables, similar to behavior. Within the discipline of physiology, heart rate and HRV have been treated descriptively, and, through the use of stimulation and blockade paradigms, these variables have been used to infer the influence of heart rate on global neural regulation systems (i.e., vagal or sympathetic). However, the polyvagal perspective shifts the metaphor of inquiry by emphasizing neurophysiological mechanisms and adaptive functions. For example, the polyvagal perspective emphasizes the involvement of peripheral physiological activity in a system, how this system maintains bidirectional communication between central (e.g., brain) and peripheral (e.g., autonomic, behavioral) components, and how the adaptive functions of this system relate to various phylogenetic stages (e.g., Jackson, 1958). The polyvagal perspective attempts to dispel discipline myths by questioning assumptions that do not transcend levels of inquiry.

Four global levels of inquiry have been used in the psychophysiology literature. First, heart rate parameters have been used as either dependent or individual difference variables, without acknowledging the role of specific peripheral physiological mechanisms involved in the regulation of beat-to-beat heart rate. By excluding knowledge of peripheral physiology, explanations focus on statistical issues (e.g., reliability) and sensitivity to the experimental manipulation. Second, heart rate parameters have been used as a peripheral physiological response, without acknowledging the role of specific central structures and neural pathways and feedback circuits. By excluding this knowledge, constructs such as cardiac vagal tone emerge without an attribution to the vagal efferent pathways, the source nuclei, the influence of afferent feedback, and the profound effects that central circuits have on the selective modulation of specific vagal pathways to the heart. Third, heart rate parameters have been studied from a neurophysiological perspective. Fourth, heart rate response parameters have, as in the Polyvagal Theory, been studied from a neurobiological perspective that includes an understanding of phylogenetic and embryological contributions. Incorporation of phylogenetic information allows an understanding of the adaptive nature of the heart rate response.

PVT provides a perspective that encourages an appreciation of both underlying neurophysiological processes and neuroanatomical structures that express both developmental and adaptive phylogenetic transitions. The polyvagal perspective builds on the underlying neural structures, mechanisms, and processes related to adaptive autonomic reactions. This perspective guides research toward testing specific hypotheses, searching for specific neural mechanisms and mediators, asking fundamental questions regarding adaptive features of specific responses, and formulating specifications for methods and techniques. For example, the polyvagal perspective could address several contemporary issues including: (1) how RSA is quantified, (2) how HRV is decomposed and the components interpreted, and (3) how the mechanisms mediating HRV are related to the expression of emotion and the facilitation of social engagement (e.g., social engagement system).

Heart Rate and HRV: A Psychological Perspective

As psychophysiology grew as a discipline, it influenced several areas of psychology (e.g., developmental, clinical, social, health). Researchers in these subdisciplines embraced the use of physiological variables as an index or window into the psychological processes they studied (e.g., stress, attention, mental effort). Physiological variables were assumed to be objective measures of psychological processes, especially when the processes were difficult to infer from observable behavior (see psychophysiological parallelism described in Chapter 3). For example, in the late 1960s, heart rate deceleration was demonstrated to parallel the changes in stimulus parameters theoretically assumed to elicit an orienting response (Graham & Clifton, 1966). Heart rate deceleration, as a quantifiable physiological response, was rapidly transformed into a psychological construct, cardiac orienting (e.g., Jackson et al., 1971). As a construct, cardiac orienting emphasized the covariation between a psychological process (i.e., orienting) and a physiological response (i.e., heart rate deceleration). However, cardiac orienting implied that orienting occurred not only when an individual oriented and heart rate decelerated, but also when heart rate decelerated independent of intention to orient. This logic illustrates how, without an understanding of the neural regulation of the heart, a false assumption regarding a bidirectional covariation between psychological and physiological processes may be made.

The misunderstanding starts with the application of an experimental design and statistics to test hypotheses related to covariation (i.e., regression). Using this strategy, the literature illustrates a strong covariance between the occurrence of orienting and heart rate deceleration. However, the statistical model employed in the experimental design had an implicit directionality and, while focusing on the link from orienting to heart rate deceleration, did not test adequately whether there was a strong link from heart rate decelerations to orienting. The model neglects the possibility that the heart rate decelerates during conditions that are not related to orienting. However, an understanding of neural regulation of the heart would identify several neural mechanisms that produce rapid heart rate decelerations (e.g., heart rate reactions to movement, intention to move, posture shifts, breaths, and numerous well-documented vagal reflexes) that occur independently from the psychological process of orienting. Thus, a correlation between heart rate deceleration and orienting could approach zero when starting with the data domain of heart rate decelerations, or approach unity when starting with the data domain of orienting behaviors elicited by stimuli in the laboratory.

An extreme example of the successful acceptance of heart rate in psychological paradigms is found in research in which heart rate is treated as an observable behavior similar to the coding of behavior in videos. In this example, coders transcribe heart rate values from digital displays when testing infant responses to various stimuli (e.g., Blass & Watt, 1999). These quantification procedures follow the rules used to code observable behavior. These measures of heart rate, similar to the coding of behavioral data, had high inter-rater reliability. However, this strategy does not question the accuracy of the heart rate displayed on the monitor or the precision of the R-wave detection. Nor does it question the embedded algorithm found in the clinical device that may display a running average and dampen abrupt changes in heart rate. From a dependent variable perspective, the strategy focuses not on mechanism, but solely on reliability of the observer and sensitivity of the operationally defined variable to the experimental manipulation. Research that treated physiology as a behavior dominated the early history of psychophysiology and related areas that have applied physiological variables as correlates or indicators of psychological processes or psychiatric conditions. Unfortunately, a lack of knowledge in physiology, neurophysiology, phylogeny, and adaptive function has great impact on the questions, paradigms, methods, and interpretations available in psychophysiology.

In autonomic conditioning paradigms, heart rate measures have been treated as similar to observable behaviors. Although these studies are characterized by careful experimental procedures, there have been major failures. Some of these failures may be attributed to a misunderstanding of the neural mechanisms mediating the responses. In some cases, the failure might have been due to the experimental manipulations interacting with the neural regulation of the autonomic nervous system and confounding the ability to quantify the variables being studied.

In the late 1960s, Miller (see Miller, 1978 for review) and others attempted to extend the domain of instrumental learning to the autonomic nervous system. These studies provide an important example of this hypothetical problem. By the early 1960s, there were reliable reports of classical conditioning of heart rate in dogs (Black & Lang, 1964; Smith, 1967). In these studies, to insure that skeletal muscles did not confound or drive the heart rate responses, the dogs were completely paralyzed by curare. Consistent with their colleagues, who studied classical conditioning and were concerned that muscular activity might mediate visceral responses, Miller and others conducted experiments with rats paralyzed by curare and artificially ventilated. The initial studies demonstrated operant conditioning of heart rate and other autonomic variables. Miller (1978) stated that "these experiments were confirmed by results in three other laboratories, but later the results of apparently similar experiments progressively declined until it became impossible to repeat them in spite of extensive efforts in the author's laboratory and elsewhere."

The loss of this phenomenon perplexed the psychophysiological community and the researchers tried to find an explanation (for details, see Roberts, 1978). Experimental procedures were carefully manipulated by controlling for movement and respiration. Were the data from the early studies spurious? Were the studies testing a nonexistent phenomenon? Were the protocols inappropriate to study voluntary changes in heart rate and other visceral processes? The observed inability to reliably demonstrate instrumental heart rate conditioning in a curarized mammal is obvious, if the paradigm is deconstructed from the polyvagal perspective.

From a behavioral perspective, the first concern is to remove the potential influence of skeletal motor activity on autonomic reactivity. Curare is effective in blocking the nicotinic receptors on the postsynaptic membrane of the neuromuscular junction and results in paralysis. Thus, the scientists studying instrumental conditioning were effectively blocking the potential confounding influence of skeletal motor activity on the putatively conditioned heart rate responses. However, not only does curare block nicotinic receptors at the postsynaptic membrane of the neuromuscular junction to produce paralysis, but it also blocks nicotinic-preganglionic receptors in the sympathetic nervous system and in the sinoatrial node communicating with the myelinated vagus originating in the nucleus ambiguus and the unmyelinated vagus originating in the dorsal motor nucleus of the heart. Thus, functionally, curare, by blocking the efferent influence of the vagus, removes the primary mode of rapid neural regulation of the heart. This explains the inability to instrumentally condition heart rate in a curare preparation.

Heart Rate and HRV: A Physiological Perspective

The study of beat-to-beat heart rate patterns as a peripheral physiological response often involves the application of basic physiological tools (i.e., surgery, stimulation, and pharmacology manipulations) to determine neural function. For example, neural blockades can be used to determine whether vagal or sympathetic pathways regulate the heart rate response to a specific stimulus. Beta-blockers (e.g., propranolol or atenolol) can be used to determine sympathetic influences, and blocking the function of acetylcholine muscarinic receptors with atropine can be used to determine vagal influences.

Hypothetically, pharmacological blockade would be an effective method to evaluate cardiac vagal tone, if two restrictions were met: (1) the variable being measured is determined by vagal efferent action on the heart and (2) the vagal efferent action on the heart is mediated by a homogeneous neural pathway regulated by a single neurotransmitter via a common receptor. Under these constraints, a blockade would dampen or block vagal influences on the heart without influencing other structures or neural circuits. Unfortunately, such a restricted model seldom occurs in dynamically regulated neurophysiological systems. The vagal influences on the heart via myelinated and unmyelinated vagi constitute two efferent limbs of a complex feedback circuit regulating the heart. Not only are the two vagal pathways originating in different brainstem areas, but also the vagal efferent influences on the heart are conveyed through both myelinated and unmyelinated fibers. Since all vagal efferent fibers influence postganglionic muscarinic receptors, atropine is an effective blockade of total vagal efferent influence from both vagal pathways.

Standard methods of blockade or surgery, which have been used to identify vagal mechanisms mediating heart rate, cannot distinguish between the specific vagal pathways originating in either the nucleus ambiguus or the dorsal motor nucleus. Since vagal regulation of the heart is part of a complex feedback system, blockade could influence other features of the system regulating the heart. For example, a change in heart rate might, via afferent feedback, influence the heart directly, via neural mechanisms, or indirectly, through changes in vasomotor tone or blood pressure. Similarly, sympathetic blockade could influence vagal pathways indirectly by changing the state of the heart and altering afferent feedback to the central structures regulating cardiac vagal tone. Attempts to create total neural blockade by using more than one drug might, due to complex pharmacokinetics, result in interactions that cannot be explained as an additive model. Also, partial blockade manipulations with low doses are not reliable manipulations of neural tone, since with low doses there are large individual differences in sensitivity to the traditional blockade drugs. Current research in the neurophysiology of cardiovascular regulation is generating new knowledge regarding the selectivity and specificity of vagal pathways and pre- and postganglionic muscarinic and nicotinic receptors (e.g., Neff et al., 2003; Wang et al., 1995). Thus, our understanding of the neural mechanisms mediating heart rate patterns derived via old methods, even the trusted blockade strategy, need to be cautiously evaluated.

During the past few years, there has been a better understanding of vagal mechanisms and the neurophysiology of RSA. No longer is RSA defined solely by its covariation with peripheral respiratory activity. Neurophysiologists have established that RSA is the functional output of cardioinhibitory vagal efferent fibers that originate in the nucleus ambiguus (for review, see Neff et al., 2003; Porges, 1995) and that these pathways have a respiratory rhythm, are myelinated B-fibers, respond with short latencies, and function through nicotinic preganglionic receptors (Mendelowitz, 1996; Mendelowitz & Kunze, 1991). These vagal efferent pathways that originate in the nucleus ambiguus are inherently silent and require afferent feedback via the sensory vagus (i.e., tractus solitarius) and inputs from central structures (Neff, Humphrey, et al., 1998; Neff, Mihalevich, et al., 1998; Wang et al., 2001) to communicate with the sinoatrial node. Thus, the concept of a constant central vagal tone, independent of peripheral feedback and central modulation, is not neurophysiologically valid. Other cardioinhibitory fibers originate in the dorsal motor nucleus of the vagus. These pathways are unmyelinated C-fibers that respond with longer latencies (Cheng & Powley, 2000). B-fibers have a faster conduction velocity (3–15 m/s) than C-fibers (1–3 m/s). Stimulation of both vagal pathways produces bradycardia, although stimulation of B-fibers produces a shorter latency and larger magnitude heart rate response. Postganglionic vagal efferent pathways from both vagal sources function through muscarinic receptors. Thus, atropine is effective in blocking all sources of vagal activity, but does not allow the extraction of an accurate index of the function of either nucleus.

With this knowledge, a plausible model can be structured to relate RSA to cardiac vagal tone. Operationally, cardiac vagal tone (CVT) would be equivalent to the sum of the influences of the cardioinhibitory pathways originating in both the nucleus ambiguus (NA) and the dorsal motor nucleus of the vagus (DMX) or CVT = NA + DMX. Atropine blocks both vagal sources, which results in the monotonic relation between atropine dose and both the amplitudes of RSA and the lower frequencies in HRV (LF). However, although RSA appears to be a sensitive index of vagal pathways originating in the nucleus ambiguus, there is no apparent index of the other limb of this additive model (i.e., the influence of vagal pathways originating in DMX on the heart).

The Selection of Measurement Parameters: An Implicit Theory

Although less interested in physiological and neurophysiological mechanisms, psychophysiologists have set the standard for methodology by advocating greater precision and accuracy in heartbeat detection and expressing a concern for methods to deal with transitory disruptions in the beat-to-beat pattern due to arrhythmia and artifact (see Porges & Byrne, 1992). In contrast, publications in physiology often rely on global measures of HRV (e.g., range, standard deviation), with less precision (e.g., use of slow sampling rates for the ECG or use of pulse waves to detect heartbeat changes), and without setting a standard for editing transitory disruptions in the beat-to-beat pattern due to either arrhythmia or recording artifact.

If arrhythmias are true physiological processes, why should they be edited or adjusted in the time series of R–R intervals? Or, more specifically, which types of arrhythmias would confound the quantification of periodic rhythms in heart rate? The polyvagal perspective justifies solutions to specific problems of editing artifact and arrhythmias. From a neurophysiological perspective, RSA is linked to the vagal efferent influence on the sinoatrial node. RSA is an atrial rhythm. Thus, ventricular arrhythmias, such as ectopic ventricular complexes followed by a fully compensatory pause, would inflate the quantification of RSA by contributing additional variance due to ventricular activity, independent of the vagal modulation of the sinoatrial node. Therefore, these arrhythmias should be edited by summing the atypical short and compensatory long intervals. The mean of these two intervals will closely approximate the expected atrial rhythm and effectively remove the confounding ventricular source of variance. Not editing this type of arrhythmia will inflate the estimate of RSA, since the rate of heart rate change between these two beats will, via the statistical decomposition of the time series, attribute additional variance to a frequency band associated with breathing. This will occur regardless of the quantification strategy, including time domain methods (e.g., band-pass), frequency domain methods (e.g., spectral), and global descriptive statistics (e.g., peak-valley, range, variance).

The treatment of heart rate or RSA as a dependent variable similar to behavior requires only an atheoretical empirical perspective. Although this strategy may produce reliable findings, it will not lead to the development and application of methods necessary to investigate the mechanisms mediating the responses. For several years, it was assumed that ±8 ms was sufficient to quantify beat-to-beat heart rate, since many commercial clinical monitors in hospitals had this precision. Similar arguments were made with pulse measures (e.g., derived via plethysmography, phonography, or ultrasonography) as a surrogate metric for the ECG, such that these measures were sufficient for accurate calculation of heart rate in clinical settings. This, of course, was a truthful statement in estimating average heart rate over a few seconds. However, it imposed a fuzzy lens when researchers attempted to study beat-to-beat patterns and applied statistical methods to decompose HRV into periodic components. Although poor precision in the measurement of heart rate provided stable average values, it impeded the opportunity to study small-amplitude periodic components in the HRV.

Since cardiovascular psychophysiology is primarily conducted with commercial software and hardware, the researcher is a consumer who is seldom involved in the development and standardization of the parameters of R-wave detection and R–R quantification. Of course, precision is easily understood, and most scientists argue for a higher precision and follow guidelines of quantifying ECG at 500 Hz or 1 KHz. However, the information on R-wave detection is seldom provided. Both the amplitude of R-waves and the baseline ECG pattern influence detection of R-waves, and these parameters are not stable. To facilitate R-wave detection, electrode placement may be manipulated to maximize the R-waves relative to other components, and hardware filters can be used to stabilize the baseline ECG signal. Although filters stabilize the base level of ECG and provide a more easily observable R-wave, filters may distort the shape of the R-wave and may shift the temporal point of the peak by removing some of the higher frequency components that contribute to the R-wave.

The issue of precision and accuracy is imbedded in the polyvagal perspective. The polyvagal perspective motivates the researcher to study both the functional output and the peripheral and central mechanisms mediating the output of the two vagal systems. The polyvagal perspective directs the researcher to apply the best available technologies to measure low-amplitude periodic processes in the beat-to-beat pattern. Thus, this perspective enables the researcher to have a vested interest in applying the most accurate and precise methods to measure R–R intervals and to search for underlying mechanisms. These issues become more problematic when organisms with low-amplitude RSA are tested, such as anesthetized mammals, preterm infants, and other high-risk clinical populations. However, before resources can be directed toward developing new technologies, the research community must have an in-depth understanding of neural influences on the sinoatrial node.

Since the polyvagal perspective is vested in identifying underlying mechanisms, it encourages the researcher to question even the appropriateness of the R–R interval as the metric for the study of vagal influences on heart rate. This question arises through the convergence of several neurophysiological and physiological phenomena. First, cardioinhibitory vagal efferent fibers that originate in the nucleus ambiguus have a respiratory rhythm. Second, the vagal fibers synapse on the sinoatrial node. Third, the sinoatrial node is the heart's pacemaker and initiates the start of a heartbeat. Fourth, the heartbeat is initiated when depolarization spreads from the sinoatrial node through the atria and is manifested in the ECG as a p-wave. Fifth, the rhythmic cardioinhibitory vagal efferents functionally produce RSA in the heart rate pattern by inhibiting and releasing from inhibition the sinoatrial node.

Statistics May Be Misleading

Statistical techniques may mislead scientists to overestimate relationships describing the specificity between physiological responses and psychological processes. Interpretations of strong relations between physiological variables and psychological processes are dependent on observation constraints and an implicit directionality of the relationship. Strong correlations approaching unity can be observed between physiological variables and psychological processes in laboratory paradigms focusing on the psychophysiology of affect and cognition. Although a physiological response with predictable features may always occur during a specific psychological process, this does not provide information regarding the possibility that the same physiological response may occur independent of the psychological process. Scientists often use these strong findings of physiological-behavioral parallels to argue for the identification of a specific physiological, neural, or brain signature for a psychological process. This has occurred with cardiac orienting (see above), in which heart rate deceleration was used inappropriately as an interchangeable construct with orienting and attention. Similar issues are seen with various electrical potentials measured with scalp electrodes that monitor brain activity. For example, event-related potentials (ERPs) have been assumed only to occur during specific cognitive tasks. Most recently, fMRI imaging procedures have identified areas of the brain that are activated during affective states. These brain areas are often assumed to function solely as a source of affect without an understanding of the interconnectiveness of neural circuits and their potential functions. Other physiological variables that have been embraced by psychology, such as cortisol and oxytocin, have been used in the literature as physiological indices of psychological processes. Increases or high levels of salivary cortisol frequently have been used interchangeably with the construct of stress. This assumed isomorphism neglects the important adaptive functions of cortisol in converting norepinephrine to epinephrine, in breaking down lactate, and in regulating surfactant (e.g., see Porges, 2001b). Similarly, the important findings linking positive social experiences to oxytocin are often discussed independent of the important role that oxytocin has peripherally in regulating autonomic state (i.e., during nursing and parturition) and centrally in modulating the outflow of vagal efferent activity from the dorsal motor nucleus of the vagus (see Porges, 2001a).

A physiological state that covaries with a psychological process will generally be observed in settings independent of the context in which the psychological process occurs. This is, of course, the same problem that may be observed with measures of brain function, since the nervous system is not solely subservient to specific psychological processes, whether or not they require conscious awareness. Thus, physiological correlates of psychological processes are seldom unique and specific indicators of that process, although psychophysiology has not vested resources in investigating the covariation of psychological processes with physiological processes when selecting from a time series of physiological activity across contexts, demands, and behavioral states. Unfortunately, the assumption that there are cognitive and affective signatures in the brain and nervous system and that the search for these signatures constitutes valid scientific inquiry promotes an intellectual drift in our science toward the treatment of physiological or neurophysiological responses as specific (as contrasted with general states that promote a range of behaviors and psychological processes) attributes of the cognitive or affective process.

Extrapolations relating psychological processes to physiological variables are often overstated, because most neurophysiological and physiological systems reflect similar features during other contexts when the psychological process of interest is not occurring. The nervous system is constantly at work, and instances of physiological-behavioral covariation do not necessarily mean that the physiological parameters can be used to index specific psychological processes. The polyvagal perspective, which incorporates an emphasis on both neurophysiological mechanisms and adaptive functions, addresses this problem by proposing the plausibility that specific physiological states support or facilitate general domains of behavior such as social engagement behaviors or the defensive strategies of fight-or-flight or freeze. Thus, although the covariation between a physiological variable and a psychological process clearly implicates an important relationship, to better understand the neurobiology underlying specific psychological processes it is necessary to understand the broader range of functions in which these neural systems are involved.

Statistical techniques may mislead scientists to misinterpret constructs such as cardiac vagal tone. Regression models (i.e., either correlation or analysis of variance) may be problematic when attempts are made to validate the hypothesis that a physiological variable is mediated by a specific neural mechanism (i.e., cardiac vagal tone). Since these validation studies generally apply the physiologist's toolbox (consisting of blockade, surgery, and electrical stimulation), posttreatment measures have a restricted range of individual differences relative to pretreatment measures. Often the studies evaluating neural mechanisms are conducted while the organism is anesthetized. Anesthetics often make it difficult to study neural regulation of the heart, since several anesthetics have direct effects on vagal efferent tone to the heart.

Statistical techniques may mislead scientists to assume that highly correlated methods are interchangeable. Methods of quantifying RSA are not equivalent. Although statistics can be used to demonstrate high intervariable correlations, these high correlations do not provide evidence of equivalence (e.g., Grossman, van Beek, et al., 1990). If we return to questions of precision, we can see how this may occur. If we have a data set of measures of RSA calculated with 1 ms precision and smooth these data to a precision of 5 ms or even 10 ms, the correlation between the two measures will be very strong and approach unity (see Riniolo & Porges, 1997). Alternatively, we can reduce precision by assigning subjects into high- and low-RSA groups and correlate group assignment with individual values. With the dataset of 44 normal adults described in Denver et al. (2007), the correlation was .83. Similarly with a data set of 94 typically developing preschool children, the correlation was .82. When each sample was divided into quartiles, the quartile assignments correlated .94 with the individual measurements of RSA. Since both samples had a similar range of RSA, the correlations were similar. Even with the restricted range of RSA observed in these samples of healthy normal participants, the global estimate of RSA associated with group assignment (i.e., median split, quartile) was highly correlated with the individual scores. If our correlations included clinical samples with disorders such as hypertension, diabetes, and depression, then the range of RSA values would expand and the correlations would potentially increase. Thus, even when the precision and accuracy of the quantification strategy is greatly reduced by smoothing across individual differences, either by reducing sampling rate and decreasing trigger accuracy or by assigning into global groups, the correlations between the highly precise and accurate methodology and the smoothed one will be very high. Thus, methodologies can blur the range of individual differences (see Riniolo & Porges, 1997) and coax investigators into assuming equivalence of methods without testing whether there are differences in sensitivity to experimental manipulations or neural influences. Researchers must, therefore, be extremely cautious of justifications for methods that focus on correlations with other established techniques, because two highly correlated methods might be differentially sensitive to individual differences and to the underlying neurophysiological mechanisms.

Decomposition of HRV: A Polyvagal Perspective

The publication of the international guidelines for the quantification of HRV (Berntson et al., 1997; Task Force of the European Society of Cardiology and the North American Society of Pacing and Electrophysiology, 1996) influenced how researchers reported and interpreted HRV. The guidelines proposed an extraction of high- and low-frequency bands from the heart rate spectrum. The high-frequency band (HF) was assumed to represent vagal influences and to be statistically equivalent to the time domain methods frequently used to calculate RSA. The low-frequency band (LF) has been considered to be either a marker of sympathetic modulation (e.g., Malliani et al., 1991) or influenced by both sympathetic and vagal influences (Akselrod et al., 1981). Researchers also proposed a ratio measure as a potential index of sympathicovagal balance (Pagani et al., 1986). Many investigators assume that the frequency bands define variables that accurately assess vagal and sympathetic influences.

There are inherent problems with selecting frequency bands to quantify HRV without an understanding of neurophysiological mechanisms. These problems are exacerbated when the techniques are applied independent of an understanding that respiration parameters are age, species, and context dependent. In several experimental contexts, individual differences in spontaneous breathing rate are distributed across a broad range of frequencies, with individuals with faster breathing frequencies contributing to the HF band and individuals with slower breathing frequencies contributing to the LF band. Also problematic are manipulations that are assumed to control for variations in breathing, such as slow-paced breathing (i.e., outside the frequencies defining HF), which would be represented not in the HF band, but in the LF band. In both cases, HF would no longer accurately describe RSA. However, it is possible to use a frequency band in the heart rate spectrum to quantify RSA, when the distribution of breathing frequencies is spontaneous and confirmed to reside within a selected spectral band. As demonstrated in the Denver and colleagues (2007) study, the spectral decomposition of HRV provides a reliable method to estimate breathing frequency and to confirm (even if respiration is not monitored) that the selection of the frequency band to represent RSA is inclusive of individual differences in spontaneous breathing frequencies.

A disconnect between operationally defined objective measures and the physiological processes that mediate these measures has resulted in inappropriate analysis strategies. Studies have reported correlations between HF and RSA, as if these were different processes. In addition, researchers have used the frequency parameters for HF and LF developed for adult studies on human neonates (who breathe substantially faster than adults), without a consideration of what the frequency bands reflect in terms of neurophysiological processes.

The quantification of RSA is an important step toward the treatment of HRV as a defined physiological process with a specific identifiable neurophysiological mechanism. Traditional physiological techniques (i.e., cholinergic blockade with atropine) determined that RSA, as a physiological variable, is a vagal phenomenon. In our laboratory, we have focused on developing methods designed to extract accurate measures of RSA. Our methods modified time-series technologies to conform to the dynamic and often nonstationary characteristics of the beat-to-beat heart rate pattern (Porges & Bohrer, 1990; Porges & Byrne, 1992). These methods assume that HRV is a complex process in which components dynamically vary. Our methods provided new opportunities to measure how RSA interacts with behavior, psychological processes, and neurophysiological mechanisms. The methods, however, made no explicit assumption regarding potential influences on RSA from other variables, including pulmonary, movement, and the influence of special visceral efferent pathways such as nerves regulating laryngeal activity that also originate in the nucleus ambiguus. Rather, the availability of these methods provides an opportunity to evaluate and to study the dynamics of possible covariation and interaction between RSA and other physiological variables. From the polyvagal perspective, RSA is a direct measure of the vagal efferent outflow originating in the nucleus ambiguus that influences the nicotinic preganglionic receptors on the sinoatrial node. Thus, the measurement of RSA provides a unique opportunity for psychophysiologists to monitor central regulation via a peripheral measure of a neural circuit involved in the coordination of visceral state and the expression of emotion and social communication.

Consistent with the polyvagal perspective, our interest in RSA focuses on the established findings that the cardioinhibitory vagal fibers that originate in the nucleus ambiguus have a respiratory rhythm. The amplitude of RSA, which we as well as others (e.g., Grossman & Svebak, 1987) had assumed to be an index of cardiac vagal tone, was redefined to emphasize that RSA represented only the functional output of the vagal efferent pathways originating from the nucleus ambiguus that terminate on the sinoatrial node. In the past, we have not defined or speculated what would index vagal efferent pathways originating in the dorsal motor nucleus of the vagus.

Is RSA a Valid Measure of Cardiac Vagal Tone?

This question depends on how cardiac vagal tone is operationally defined. The literature reliably demonstrates that cholinergic blockade depresses RSA, while RSA is insensitive to B-adrenergic blockade. Thus, the argument is not whether RSA is mediated via vagal pathways, but whether RSA can be a surrogate measure of cardiac vagal tone. Following a physiological perspective, changes in heart rate in response to cholinergic blockade have served as a surrogate criterion variable for cardiac vagal tone. This surrogate variable can be correlated with either RSA or change in RSA to the blockade. When these variables are correlated, the relations are very strong, but not perfect. From a physiological perspective, this points to a weakness in RSA as an index of cardiac vagal tone and leads to strategies to correct RSA. However, from a neurophysiological perspective, this discrepancy is obvious. RSA is vagal, but it reflects only the vagal efferent pathways from the nucleus ambiguus. The vagal influence from the dorsal motor nucleus of the vagus is not included in the calculation of RSA, although it may contribute to heart rate (see Lewis et al., 2012).

Cardiac vagal tone, by definition, represents influences from both vagal nuclei to the sinoatrial node. This can be described by the following heuristic model: CVT = NA + DMX (CVT is cardiac vagal tone, NA is the vagal tone originating from the nucleus ambiguus, DMX is the vagal tone originating from the dorsal motor nucleus of the vagus). In this model, RSA can be substituted for NA (CVT = RSA + DMX). Thus, if atropine blockade affects the postganglionic transmission from both vagal pathways, the relation between changes in cardiac vagal tone and changes in RSA should be monotonic, but not unity.

Based on data obtained using the physiologist's toolbox, a strong argument could be made that RSA is a fine surrogate for cardiac vagal tone. However, this proposition is based on an assumption that the vagal influences originating in the dorsal motor nucleus of the vagus are constant or minimal. Without measuring this vagal component, the covariation between cardiac vagal tone and RSA would be dependent on the state of the dorsal vagal system. PVT has provided a perspective to study states in which the two systems deviate. For example, there are easily identified clinical conditions of severe and potentially lethal bradycardia that are mediated by the vagus in the absence of RSA (see Reed, Ohel, et al., 1999).

In a bold paper, Eckberg (1997) challenged the use of the LF component as an index of sympathico-vagal tone balance. The paper resulted in an interesting dialogue published in conjunction with Eckberg's article in the journal *Circulation*. Eckberg described the paradox in which LF was sensitive to atropine, although argued to be a sensitive indicator of sympathetic activity. Most interesting, this point was not refuted in any of the comments following the article. We observed the same effect. LF follows an atropine dose–response curve similar to both RSA and heart period. We noted that the effect sizes for LF were equivalent with RSA and about twice the size as heart period, thus demonstrating the dependence of the LF on vagal pathways. In other research, we demonstrated that variance within this frequency band was selectively sensitive to vagal blockade and that sympathetic blockade had no effect. Other researchers have argued similar points (Houle & Billman, 1999).

If the LF is not a direct index of sympathetic influences on the heart, could it reflect activity from the DMX? Knowledge regarding the influence of vagal fibers on the heart rate pattern is expanding. In 1995, when the Polyvagal Theory was published, little was known about the impact on the heart via the C-fibers originating in the DMX. It was assumed that the primary vagal influence on the heart was mediated via the B-fibers originating in the nucleus ambiguus. In addition, since few DMX fibers synapse on the sinoatrial node, it was thought that their impact on the regulation of heart rate would be minimal. Unlike global measures of heart rate or HRV, RSA is solely regulated via vagal fibers originating in the nucleus ambiguus. Thus, it appears that RSA would be an excellent criterion variable for cardiac vagal tone, especially if the definition of vagal tone were limited to the vagal efferent influences via ventral vagal pathways originating in the nucleus ambiguus. The polyvagal perspective approaches questions regarding mechanisms, adaptive function, and specific neural pathways. In dealing with investigations relating respiration to RSA, the strategy focuses on central neural regulation and does not focus on peripheral physiology. Based on our current interests, the polyvagal perspective directs research questions toward the involvement of the nucleus ambiguus in regulating heart rate (i.e., producing RSA) and whether this area of the brainstem is causal, interactive, or consequential to respiratory and pulmonary influences. From this perspective, several research questions would be of interest. Since afferents from the trigeminal and facial nerves provide input to the nucleus ambiguus, the polyvagal perspective would focus on the influence of respiratory resistance on RSA (e.g., Sargunaraj et al., 1996).

The concept of a common cardiopulmonary oscillator fits well within a polyvagal perspective. Researchers have documented the importance of a hypothetical respiratory gate on the vagal outflow (see Eckberg, 2003). Since the respiratory rhythm is selectively gating only the vagal outflow from the nucleus ambiguus, the Polyvagal Theory would encourage the speculation that inspiration/expiration (I/E) ratios would influence the amplitude of RSA. Based on this neurophysiological model, vagal outflow to the sinoatrial node increases during expiration, with higher amplitude of RSA being associated with relatively longer exhalation durations. Thus, the amplitude of RSA should be related to the ratio of inspiratory and expiratory durations. There are two ways of approaching this hypothesis: (1) manipulating inspiration and expiration ratios during paced breathing or (2) evaluating individual differences during spontaneous baseline breathing. The first strategy may confound the phenomenon, since task demands and the deviation from normal breathing patterns might trigger adaptive changes in autonomic state. The second strategy may also confound the phenomenon, since during baseline there is a restricted range of breathing patterns and the I/E ratio may covary with other variables such as weight, age, and health.

Strauss-Blache and colleagues (2000) approached this relation by manipulating breathing, while in my laboratory we investigated individual differences during spontaneous baseline breathing. Strauss-Blache and colleagues demonstrated that, during trials with short inspiration followed by long expiration, the amplitude of RSA was significantly greater than during trials with long inspiration followed by short expiration. These effects could not be accounted for by differences in breathing rate or amplitude. In our laboratory, we conducted a naturally occurring experiment relating individual differences in the *I/E* ratio to RSA. We monitored participants during a baseline condition with a Vivometrics LifeShirt. The LifeShirt monitors ECG and several ventilatory parameters including calibrated measures of tidal volume, inspiration and expiration duration, and breathing rate. Consistent with the Strauss-Blache and colleagues study, we observed that the *I/E* ratio was significantly related to the amplitude of RSA ($r(41) = -.50$, $p < .001$). However, the relations between RSA and both respiration frequency ($r = -.08$) and tidal volume ($r = -.11$) were not significant. (Denver et al., 2007).

CONCLUSION

The polyvagal perspective is an attempt to apply constructs derived from the Polyvagal Theory to understand the discrepancies in the literature related to method of measurement, neurophysiological and neuroanatomical mechanisms, and adaptive functions of vagal efferent pathways. The approach emphasizes that biases or discipline myths occur when investigations are limited to psychological or physiological levels of inquiry. The polyvagal perspective proposes that it is necessary not only to understand the vagal efferent actions on the heart from a neurophysiological level of inquiry, but also the adaptive function of neural regulation of the heart, interpreted within the context of the phylogeny of the autonomic nervous system. In the sections above, several discipline myths have been deconstructed and interpreted based on level of inquiry. These points are summarized below to provide targeted statements to stimulate further scientific investigations and challenges via well-designed experiments.

Discipline myth 1: Cardiac vagal tone is a useful construct in psychophysiological research.

Although tonic measures of cardiac vagal tone have an important role in understanding visceral states and in developing constructs related to autonomic balance, it is of limited use in describing and understanding response strategies to environmental and visceral stimuli. Cardiac vagal tone as a global construct provides limited information regarding specificity of the neural mechanisms through which heart rate patterns react to specific psychological stimuli, reflect health risk, and change with interventions or challenges. Measures of more specific vagal regulation, via either the nucleus ambiguus (i.e., RSA) or the dorsal motor nucleus (i.e., LF), may provide more meaningful information.

Discipline myth 2: To be a meaningful index of vagal influences, RSA must be adjusted by either paced breathing or by statistically adjusting for ventilatory parameters.

The motivation to adjust RSA is based on empirical reports of a divergence between surrogate measures of cardiac vagal tone and RSA. Adjustments are proposed to improve the relation between RSA and the surrogate measure for total cardiac vagal tone. Although RSA is not the equivalent of total cardiac vagal tone, as an index of total cardiac vagal tone it is at least as sensitive to blockade as traditional measures. Moreover, the validity of adjusted RSA variables as indices of cardiac vagal tone needs to be challenged by conducting dose–response blockade challenges. Even if RSA were not as sensitive as other indices of total cardiac vagal tone, RSA should be studied without adjustment. RSA is an important variable reflecting the functional output of specific vagal pathways originating in the nucleus ambiguus that are neurophysiologically and neuroanatomically linked to several processes of interest to psychophysiologists (e.g., emotion, social engagement, ingestion, health). Thus, there is no advantage in correcting RSA to map into a global surrogate variable for total cardiac vagal tone.

Discipline myth 3: The low frequency (LF) in the heart rate spectrum is related to sympathetic activity or sympathetic-vagal balance.

The low frequency in the heart rate spectrum is exquisitely sensitive to muscarinic blockade. LF can be totally blocked when the vagal efferent influences are blocked. In fact, LF is as sensitive to vagal blockade as RSA and more sensitive to vagal blockade than heart rate. Although sympathetic influences might be involved in triggering this neural circuit, the final common pathway is purely vagal. Since features of this periodicity respond differently than RSA to various challenges, the time course of LF may index vagal output from the dorsal motor nucleus.

Discipline myth 4: Methods to quantify RSA are equivalent if they are highly correlated.

High correlations, even those above 0.9, can be demonstrated between low- and high-resolution measures. Measures that smooth across a broad range of individual and intraindividual differences may be correlated with methods that provide high resolution and greater sensitivity to experimental manipulations or diagnostic features. Measures that have poor precision in timing, poor accuracy in detecting the peak of the R-wave, and may be influenced by other sources of variance including baseline trends may be highly correlated with more precise and accurate measures of RSA that incorporate statistically well-defined algorithms to extract accurately the amplitude of RSA. These high correlations are not arguments for equivalence. More appropriate tests would contrast size of effects in response to known methods of vagal blockade, including manipulations that would selectively block or increase the outflow from the source nuclei of vagal efferents.

The polyvagal perspective, with an emphasis on nervous system regulation, is a major shift for psychophysiological researchers, who historically have not attributed mechanism to heart rate or HRV. In addition, this perspective leads the researcher to ask new questions, including about such rudimentary issues as the establishment of data-collection parameters, the methods developed to quantify various components of the heart rate pattern, and even the strategies used to correct artifact. The polyvagal perspective encourages researchers interested in autonomic-behavioral relations to expand their research agenda to include questions related to: (1) features of the source nuclei in the nucleus ambiguus and the dorsal motor nucleus of the vagus, (2) influences of the afferent vagus via the nucleus tractus solitarius on the source nuclei of both vagi, (3) the influence of ascending pathways from the nucleus tractus solitarius on brain areas regulating cognition and affect, (4) the functional differences in the effect of myelinated and unmyelinated vagal efferent pathways on the sinoatrial node, (5) the interaction between the regulation of the special visceral efferent and myelinated vagal pathways, and (6) the influence of peripheral and central structures and circuits on modulating the output of the vagal efferent pathways.

By investigating the contradiction between methods used to measure RSA, we can see how different research questions and assumptions lead to different methods and paradigms. When research strategies are based on a peripheral physiological level of inquiry, then cardiac vagal tone is assumed to represent a unitary construct. However, when research strategies are based on a neurophysiological level of inquiry, then the quest for a measure of cardiac vagal tone is refined to focus on methods that selectively measure each of the two vagal systems. The latter strategy should be appealing to psychophysiologists, since the two vagal systems evolved to support different classes of behavior. Vagal activity originating in the nucleus ambiguus is neurophysiologically and neuroanatomically linked to the regulation of the striated muscles of the face and head, structures that are involved in social interaction and emotion. Theoretically, RSA should closely parallel individual and intraindividual variations in emotion expression, social communication, and behavioral state. In contrast, vagal activity originating in the DMX should reflect tonic influences to the visceral organs (i.e., primarily subdiaphragmatic). Rapid and massive increases in the output of the DMX that may produce bradycardia, apnea, or defecation would occur as a defense strategy to reduce metabolic demands. Perhaps the negative features of stress and health vulnerability being associated with the slower rhythms may have led scientists to assume that these rhythms were influenced by the sympathetic nervous system.

The polyvagal perspective shifts research from atheoretical strategies toward theory-driven paradigms dependent upon explicit neural mechanisms. Foremost, the polyvagal perspective emphasizes the importance of phylogenetic changes in the neural structures regulating the autonomic nervous system. The phylogenetic strategy provides insights into the adaptive function and the neural regulation of the two vagal systems (see Porges, 1995, 2001a). Without having constructs from PVT to describe adaptive functions and to determine the measurement specifications of the two vagal systems (one associated with calm states and social engagement behaviors and the other a vestigial defense system that is potentially lethal to mammals), it would not be possible to disentangle the mechanisms and functions of the components of cardiac vagal tone.

Sources

Chapter 1: The Vagal Paradox: A Polyvagal Solution
© 2023 Stephen W. Porges. Published by Elsevier Ltd.
Porges, S. W. (2023). The vagal paradox: A polyvagal solution. *Comprehensive Psychoneuroendocrinology*. https://doi.org/10.1016/j.cpnec.2023.100200.

Chapter 2: Polyvagal Theory: A Biobehavioral Journey to Sociality
© 2021 Stephen W. Porges. Published by Elsevier Ltd.
Porges, S. W. (2021). Polyvagal theory: A biobehavioral journey to sociality. *Comprehensive Psychoneuroendocrinology, 7*. doi: 10.1016/j.cpnec.2021.100069.

Chapter 3: Polyvagal Theory: A Science of Safety
© 2022 Stephen W. Porges
Porges, S. W. (2022). Polyvagal theory: A science of safety. *Frontiers in Integrative Neuroscience, 16*, 871227. doi: 10.3389/fnint.2022.871227.

Chapter 4: A Transdisciplinary Theory of Sociality: Polyvagal Theory
Stephen W. Porges's Keynote address © 2021 was originally prepared for the Third World Congress of Transdisciplinarity held virtually from Mexico City, on February 3, 2021.

Chapter 5: Appeasement: Replacing Stockholm Syndrome as a Definition of a Survival Strategy
© 2023 The Author(s), taken from *European Journal of Psychotraumatology*, © 2023 European Society of Traumatic Stress Studies (ESTSS), reprinted by permission of Informa UK Limited, trading as Taylor & Francis Group (www.tandfonline.com) on behalf of European Society of Traumatic Stress Studies (ESTSS).
Bailey, R., Dugard, J., Smith, S. F., & Porges, S. W. (2023). Appeasement: replacing Stockholm syndrome as a definition of a survival strategy. *European Journal of Psychotraumatology, 14*(1). doi: 10.1080/20008066.2022.2161038.

Chapter 7: Neuromodulation Using Computer-Altered Music to Treat a Ten-Year-Old Child Unresponsive to Standard Interventions for Functional Neurological Disorder
© 2022 The Authors. Published by Wolters Kluwer Health, Inc. on behalf of the President and Fellows of Harvard College. Reprinted with permission.

We thank Anna and her family for allowing us to share her story of her treatment process with other clinicians.

Rajabalee, N., Kozlowska, K., Lee, S. Y., Savage, B., Hawkes, C., Siciliano, D., . . . & Torbey, S. (2022). Neuromodulation using computer-altered music to treat a ten-year-old child unresponsive to standard interventions for functional neurological disorder. *Harvard Review of Psychiatry, 30*(5), 303–316.

Chapter 8: Heart Rate Variability: A Personal Journey

© 2022 Stephen W. Porges

Porges, S. W. (2022). Heart rate variability: A personal journey. *Applied Psychophysiology and Biofeedback, 47*(4), 259–271.

Chapter 9: Exploring Vagal Nerve Stimulation Through the Lens of the Polyvagal Theory

© 2024 Springer Science+Business Media, LLC, part of Springer Nature. Reprinted with permission.

Porges, S. W. (2024). Vagal nerve stimulation through the lens of the polyvagal theory: Recruiting neurophysiological mechanisms to dampen threat reactions and promote homeostatic functions. In M. G. Frasch & E. Porges (Eds.), *Vagus nerve stimulation* (pp. 31–49). Springer Nature. https://doi.org/10.1007/978-1-0716-3465-3_2.

Chapter 10: Cardiac Vagal Tone: A Neurophysiological Mechanism That Evolved in Mammals to Dampen Threat Reactions and Promote Sociality

© 2021 World Psychiatric Association. Reprinted with permission.

Porges, S. W. (2021). Cardiac vagal tone: A neurophysiological mechanism that evolved in mammals to dampen threat reactions and promote sociality. *World Psychiatry, 20*(2), 296–298. https://doi.org/10.1002/wps.20871.

Chapter 11: Ehlers-Danlos Syndrome Through the Lens of the Polyvagal Theory: A Preface to *Transforming Ehlers-Danlos Syndrome*

© 2022 Stéphane Daens. Reprinted with permission.

Porges, S. W. (2022). Preface. In S. Daens (Ed.), *Transforming Ehlers-Danos syndrome: A global vision of the disease.*

Chapter 12: Addiction: A Polyvagal Perspective

© 2022 Stephen W. Porges and USABP/EABP. Reprinted with permission.

Porges, S. W. (2022). Part I: Addiction: A polyvagal perspective (Revolutionizing addiction treatment with the Felt Sense Polyvagal Model™). *International Body Psychotherapy Journal, 21*(1), 13–31.

Chapter 13: Autism Through the Lens of the Polyvagal Theory

Porges, S. W. (in press). Foreword. In S. Inderbitzen, *Autism in polyvagal terms.* W. W. Norton.

Chapter 15: Our Nervous System Is Always Trying to Figure Out a Way for Us to Survive, to Be Safe

© 2022 The British Psychological Society. Reprinted with permission.

Kseib, K., & Porges, S. W. (2022, November 23). "Our nervous system is always trying to figure out a way for us to survive, to be safe": Kal Kseib meets Dr Stephen Porges, founder of Polyvagal Theory, to hear about his approach to trauma and more. *The Psychologist.* www.bps.org.uk/psychologist/our-nervous-system-always-trying-figure-out-way-us-survive-be-safe.

Chapter 16: An Interview with Dr. Stephen W. Porges
© 2017 American Dance Therapy Association. Reprinted with permission.
Devereaux, C. (2017). An interview with Dr. Stephen W. Porges. *American Journal of Dance Therapy*, 39(1), 27–35. Springer Nature. https://link.springer.com/article/10.1007/s10465-017-9252-6.

Chapter 17: The Anatomy of Calm
© 2021 Sussex Publishers, LLC. Reprinted with permission from *Psychology Today*.
Porges, S. W. (2021, September 7). The anatomy of calm. *Psychology Today*. www.psychologytoday.com/us/articles/202109/sigh-relief.

Chapter 18: How to Keep Your Cool in High-Stress Situations
Reprinted with permission from Harvard Business Publishing. © 2021 hbr.org.
Quinn, R. E., Fessell, D. P., & Porges, S. W. (2021, January 15). How to keep your cool in high-stress situations. *Harvard Business Review*. https://hbr.org/2021/01/how-to-keep-your-cool-in-high-stress-situations.

Chapter 19: What Putin's Physiological State Tells Us: How the Physiological State of a Leader Can Impact the World
© 2022 Robert Legvold, Nancy Rubbico, and Stephen W. Porges
Legvold, R., Rubbico, N., & Porges, S. W. (2022, April 5). What Putin's physiological state tells us: How the physiological state of a leader can impact the world. *Psychology Today*. www.psychologytoday.com/us/blog/polyvagal-perspectives/202204/what-putin-s-physiological-state-tells-us.

References

PREFACE

Porges, S. W. (1995). Orienting in a defensive world: Mammalian modifications of our evolutionary heritage. A polyvagal theory. *Psychophysiology*, 32, 301–318.

Porges, S. W. (2007). The polyvagal perspective. *Biological Psychology*, 74, 116–143.

Porges, S. W. (2011). *The polyvagal theory: Neurophysiological foundations of emotions, attachment, communication, and self-regulation* (Norton series on interpersonal neurobiology). W. W. Norton.

Porges, S. W. (2021). *Polyvagal safety: Attachment, communication, self-regulation (IPNB)*. W. W. Norton.

1. THE VAGAL PARADOX: A POLYVAGAL SOLUTION

Becker, L. E., Zhang, W., & Pereyra, P. M. (1993). Delayed maturation of the vagus nerve in sudden infant death syndrome, *Acta. Neuropathologica*, 86, 617–622. https://doi.org/10.1007/BF00294301.

Burge, H. (1970). A vagal paradox, *British Medical Journal*, 4, 302.

Cabrera, A., Kolacz, J., Pailhez, G., Bulbena-Cabre, A., Bulbena, A., & Porges, S. W. (2018). Assessing body awareness and autonomic reactivity: Factor structure and psychometric properties of the Body Perception Questionnaire-Short Form (BPQ-SF), *International Journal of Methods in Psychiatric Research*, 27, e1596.

Calaresu, F. R., & Pearce, J. W. (1965). Effects on heart rate of electrical stimulation of medullary vagal structures in the cat. *Physiology*, 176, 241. https://doi.org/10.1113/jphysiol.1965.sp007547.

Caldeyro-Barcia, R., Casacuberta, C., Bustos, R., Giussi, G., Gulin, L., Escarcena, L., & Méndez-Bauer, C. (1967). Correlation of intrapartum changes in fetal heart rate with fetal blood oxygen and acid-base state. In *Diagnosis and treatment of fetal disorders* (pp. 205–225). Proceedings of the International Symposium on Diagnosis and Treatment of Disorders Affecting the Intrauterine Patient Dorado, Springer, Puerto Rico.

Campbell, H. A., Leite, C. A., Wang, T., Skals, M., Abe, A. S., Egginton, S., Rantin, F. T., Bishop, C. M., & Taylor, E. W. (2006). Evidence for a respiratory component, similar to mammalian respiratory sinus arrhythmia, in the heart rate variability signal from the rattlesnake, Crotalus durissus terrificus. *Experimental Biology, 209,* 2628–2636. https://doi.org/10.1242/jeb.02278

Campbell, H. A., Taylor, E. W., & Egginton, S. (2005). Does respiratory sinus arrhythmia occur in fishes? *Biology Letters, 1,* 484–487. https://doi.org/10.1098/rsbl.2005.0365

Cerritelli, F., Frasch, M. G., Antonelli, M. C., Viglione, C., Vecchi, S., Chiera, M., & Manzotti, A. (2021). A review on the vagus nerve and autonomic nervous system during fetal development: Searching for critical windows, *Frontiers in Neuroscience, 15,* 721605. https://doi.org/10.3389/fnins.2021.721605

Cohen, J., & Cohen, P. (1983). *Applied multiple regression/correlations analysis for the behavioral sciences.* Lawrence Erlbaum Associates.

Dale, L. P., Kolacz, J., Mazmanyan, J., Leon, K. G., Johonnot, K., Bossemeyer Biernacki, N., & Porges. S. W. (2022). Childhood maltreatment influences autonomic regulation and mental health in college students, *Frontiers in Psychiatry, 13,* 1130. https://doi.org/10.3389/fpsyt.2022.841749

Dobzhansky, T. (1962). *Mankind evolving.* Yale University Press, JSTOR.

Donchin, Y., Caton, D., & Porges, S. W. (1984). Spectral analysis of fetal heart rate in sheep: The occurrence of respiratory sinus arrhythmia, *American Journal of Obstetrics and Gynecology, 148,* 1130–1135. https://doi.org/10.1016/0002-9378(84)90641-0

Doody, J. S., Burghardt, G., & Dinets, V. (2023). The evolution of sociality and the polyvagal theory. *Biological Psychology, 180,* 108569. https://doi: 10.1016/j.biopsycho.2023.108569

Doussard-Roosevelt, J. A., Porges, S. W., Scanlon, J. W., Alemi, B., & Scanlon, K. B. (1997). Vagal regulation of heart rate in the prediction of developmental outcome for very low birth weight preterm infants. *Child Development, 68,* 173–186. https://doi.org/10.2307/1131844

Gabora, L. (2018). The neural basis and evolution of divergent and convergent thought. In R. E. Jung & O. Vartanian (Eds.), *The Cambridge handbook of the neuroscience of creativity* (pp. 58–70). Cambridge University Press. https://doi.org/10.1017/9781316556238.005

Geggel, L. (2016). Meet the ancient reptile that gave rise to mammals. *Scientific American.* www.scientificamerican.com/article/meet-the-ancient-reptile-that-gave-rise-to-mammals/

Geis, G. S., & Wurster, R. D. (1980). Cardiac responses during stimulation of the dorsal motor nucleus and nucleus ambiguus in the cat. *Circulation Research, 46*, 606–611. https://doi.org/10.1161/01.res.46.5.606

Gellhorn, E. (1957). *Autonomic imbalance and the hypothalamus: Implications for physiology, medicine, psychology, and neuropsychiatry*. University of Minnesota Press.

Gourine, A. V., Machhada, A., Trapp, S., & Spyer, K. M. (2016). Cardiac vagal preganglionic neurones: An update. *Autonomic Neuroscience, 199*, 24–28. https://doi.org/10.1016/j.autneu.2016.06.003

Grossman, P. (2023). Fundamental challenges and likely refutations of the five basic premises of the polyvagal theory. *Biological Psychology, 180*, 108589. https://doi.org/10.1016/j.biopsycho.2023.108589

Grossman, P., & Taylor, E. W. (2007). Toward understanding respiratory sinus arrhythmia: Relations to cardiac vagal tone, evolution and biobehavioral functions. *Biological Psychology, 74*, 263–285. https://doi.org/10.1016/j .biopsycho.2005.11.014

Gunn, C. G., Sevelius, G., Puiggari, J., & Myers, F. K. (1968). Vagal cardiomotor mechanisms in the hindbrain of the dog and cat. *American Journal of Physiology, 214*, 258–262. https://doi.org/10.1152/ajplegacy.1968.214.2.258

Hage, B., Sinacore, J., Heilman, K., Porges, S. W., & Halaris, A. (2017). Heart rate variability predicts treatment outcome in major depression. *Psychiatry and Brain Science, 2*, 1. https://doi.org/10.20900/jpbs.20170017

Heilman, K. J., Heinrich, S., Ackermann, M., Nix, E. J., & Kyuchukov, H. (2023). Effects of the Safe and Sound Protocol™ (SSP) on sensory processing, digestive function, and selective eating in children and adults with autism: A prospective single-arm study. *Developmental Disabilities, 28*(1).

Hering, H. E. (1910). A functional test of heart vagi in man. *Menschen Munchen Medizinische Wochenschrift. 57*, 1931–1933.

Hon, E. H. (1960). The diagnosis of fetal distress. *Clinical Obstetrics and Gynecology, 3*, 860–873.

Hopkins, D. A., & Armour, J. A. (1982). Medullary cells of origin of physiologically identified cardiac nerves in the dog. *Brain Research Bulletin, 8*, 359–365. https://doi.org/10.1016/0361-9230(82)90073-9

Jackson, J. H. (1884). The Croonian lectures on evolution and dissolution of the nervous system. *British Medical Journal, 1*, 703. https://doi.org /10.1136/bmj.1.1215.703

Jänig, W. (2022). *The integrative action of the autonomic nervous system: Neurobiology of homeostasis*. Cambridge University Press.

Kolacz, J., Chen, X., Nix, E. J., Roath, O. K., Holmes, L. G., Tokash, C., . . . & Lewis, G. F. (2023). Association of self-reported autonomic symptoms with sensor-based physiological measures. *Psychosomatic Medicine*, 10–1097.

Kolacz, J., Dale, L. P., Nix, E. J., Roath, O. K., Lewis, G. F., & Porges, S. W. (2020). Adversity history predicts self-reported autonomic reactivity and mental health in US residents during the COVID-19 pandemic. *Frontiers in Psychiatry, 11,* 1119.

Kolacz, J., daSilva, E. B., Lewis, G. F., Bertenthal, B. I., & Porges, S. W. (2022). Associations between acoustic features of maternal speech and infants' emotion regulation following a social stressor. *Infancy, 27,* 135–158. https://doi.org/10.1111/infa.12440

Kolacz, J., Holmes, L. G., & Porges, S. W. (2018). *Body Perception Questionnaire (BPQ) manual.* Bloomington, IN.

Kolacz, J., Hu, Y., Gesselman, A. N., Garcia, L., Lewis, G. F., & Porges, S. W. (2020). Sexual function in adults with a history of childhood maltreatment: Mediating effects of self-reported autonomic reactivity. *Psychological Trauma: Theory, Research, Practice, and Policy, 12,* 281–290.

Kolacz, J., Kovacic, K., Dang, L., Li, B. U., Lewis, G. F., & Porges, S. W. (2023). Cardiac vagal regulation is impeded in children with cyclic vomiting syndrome. *American Journal of Gastroenterology, 118,* 1268–1275. https:/doi.org/10.14309/ajg.0000000000002207

Kolacz, J., Kovacic, K., Lewis, G. F., Sood, M. R., Aziz, Q., Roath, O. R., & Porges, S. W. (2021). Cardiac autonomic regulation and joint hypermobility in adolescents with functional abdominal pain disorders. *Neurogastroenterology and Motility, 33,* e14165.

Kolacz, J., Kovacic, K. K., & Porges, S. W. (2019). Traumatic stress and the autonomic brain-gut connection in development: Polyvagal theory as an integrative framework for psychosocial and gastrointestinal pathology. *Developmental Psychobiology, 61,* 796–809. https://doi.org/10.1002/dev.21852

Kolacz, J., Lewis, G. F., & Porges, S. W. (2018). The integration of vocal communication and biobehavioral state regulation in mammals: A polyvagal hypothesis. *Handbook of Behavioral Neuroscience, 25,* 23–34. https://doi.org/10.1016/B978-0-12-809600-0.00003-2

Kovacic, K., Kolacz, J., Lewis, G. F., & Porges, S. W. (2020). Impaired vagal efficiency predicts auricular neurostimulation response in adolescent functional abdominal pain disorders. *American Journal of Gastroenterology, 115,* 1534–1538. https://doi.org/10.14309/ajg.0000000000000753

Kumar, S., & Hedges, S. B. (1998). A molecular timescale for vertebrate evolution. *Nature, 392,* 917–920. https://doi.org/10.1038/31927

Larson, S. K., & Porges, S. W. (1992). The ontogeny of heart period patterning in the rat. *Developmental Psychobiology, 15,* 519–528. https://doi.org/10.1002/dev.420150604

Lewis, G. F., Furman, S. A., McCool, M. F., & Porges, S. W. (2012). Statistical strategies to quantify respiratory sinus arrhythmia: Are commonly used metrics equivalent? *Biological Psychology, 89,* 349–364. https://doi.org/10.1016/j.biopsycho.2011.11.009

Machhada, A., Ang, R., Ackland, G. L., Ninkina, N., Buchman, V. L., Lythgoe, M. F., Trapp, S., Tinker, A., Marina, N., & Gourine, A. V. (2015). Control of ventricular excitability by neurons of the dorsal motor nucleus of the vagus nerve. *Heart Rhythm, 12,* 2285–2293. https://doi.org/10.1016/j.hrthm.2015.06.005

Machhada, A., Hosford, P. S., Dyson, A., Ackland, G. L., Mastitskaya, S., & Gourine, A. V. (2020). Optogenetic stimulation of vagal efferent activity preserves left ventricular function in experimental heart failure. JACC *Basic to Translational Science, 5,* 799–810.

Machhada, A., Marina, N., Korsak, A., Stuckey, D. J., Lythgoe, M. F. & Gourine, A. V. (2016). Origins of the vagal drive controlling left ventricular contractility. *Physiology, 594,* 4017–4030.

Machhada, A., Trapp, S., Marina, N., Stephens, R. C., Whittle, J., Lythgoe, M. F., Kasparov, S., Ackland, G. L., & Gourine, A. V. (2017). Vagal determinants of exercise capacity. *Nature Communications, 8,* 15097. https://doi.org/10.1038/ncomms15097

Meny, R. G., Carroll, J. L., Carbone, M. T., & Kelly, D. H. (1994). Cardiorespiratory recordings from infants dying suddenly and unexpectedly at home. *Pediatrics, 93,* 44–49.

Monteiro, D. A., Taylor, E. W., Sartori, M. R., Cruz, A. L., Rantin, F. T., & Leite, C. A. (2018). Cardiorespiratory interactions previously identified as mammalian are present in the primitive lungfish. *Science Advances,* 4(2). https://doi.org/10.1126/sciadv.aaq0800

Neuhuber, W. L., & Berthoud, H. R. (2022). Functional anatomy of the vagus system: How does the polyvagal theory comply? *Biological Psychology, 174,* 108425. https://doi.org/10.1016/j.biopsycho.2022.108425

Nosaka, S., Yamamoto, T., & Yasunaga, K. (1979). Localization of vagal cardioinhibitory preganglionic neurons within rat brain stem. *Comparative Neurology, 186,* 79–92. https://doi.org/10.1002/cne.901860106

Pereyra, P. M., Zhang, W., Schmidt, M., & Becker, L. E. (1992). Development of myelinated and unmyelinated fibers of human vagus nerve during the first year of life. *Neurological Sciences, 110,* 107–113. https://doi.org/10.1016/0022-510x(92)90016-e

Poli, A., Gemignani, A., Soldani, F., & Miccoli, M. (2021). A systematic review of a polyvagal perspective on embodied contemplative practices as promoters of cardiorespiratory coupling and traumatic stress recovery for PTSD and OCD: Research methodologies and state of the art. *International Journal of Environmental Research and Public Health,* 18(22), 117.

Porges, S. W. (1976). Peripheral and neurochemical parallels of psychopathology: A psychophysiological model relating autonomic imbalance to hyperactivity, psychopathy, and autism. *Advances in Child Development and Behavior, 11,* 35–65. https://doi.org/10.1016/s0065-2407(08)60094-4

Porges, S. W. (1985). Method and apparatus for evaluating rhythmic oscillations in aperiodic physiological response systems. US4510944A. [Patent.]

Porges, S. W. (1992). Vagal tone: A physiologic marker of stress vulnerability. *Pediatrics, 90,* 498–504.

Porges, S. W. (1993). *Body Perception Questionnaire*. Laboratory of Developmental Assessment, University of Maryland.

Porges, S. W. (1995). Orienting in a defensive world: Mammalian modifications of our evolutionary heritage. A polyvagal theory. *Psychophysiology, 32*, 301–318. https://doi.org/10.1111/j.1469-8986.1995.tb01213.x

Porges, S. W. (2001). The polyvagal theory: Phylogenetic substrates of a social nervous system, *International Journal of Psychophysiology, 42*, 123–146. https://doi.org/10.1016/S0167-8760(01)00162-3

Porges, S. W. (2003). Social engagement and attachment: A phylogenetic perspective, *Annals of the New York Academy of Sciences, 1008*, 31–47. https://doi.org/10.1196/annals.1301.004

Porges, S. W. (2004). Neuroception: A subconscious system for detecting threats and safety. *Zero to Three (J.), 24*, 19–24.

Porges, S. W. (2007a). A phylogenetic journey through the vague and ambiguous Xth cranial nerve: A commentary on contemporary heart rate variability research. *Biological Psychology, 74*, 301–307. https://doi.org/10.1016/j.biopsycho.2006.08.007

Porges, S. W. (2007b). The polyvagal perspective. *Biological Psychology, 74*, 116–143. https://doi.org/10.1016/j.biopsycho.2006.06.009.

Porges, S. W. (2011). *The polyvagal theory: Neurophysiological foundations of emotions, attachment, communication, and self-regulation.* (Norton series on interpersonal neurobiology.) W. W. Norton.

Porges, S. W. (2021). Polyvagal theory: A biobehavioral journey to sociality. *Comprehensive Psychoneuroendocrinology, 7*, 100069. https://doi.org/10.1016/j.cpnec.2021.100069

Porges, S. W. (2022). Polyvagal theory: A science of safety. *Frontiers in Integrative Neuroscience, 16*, 27. https://doi.org/10.3389/fnint.2022.871227

Porges, S. W., Bazhenova, O. V., Bal, E., Carlson, N., Sorokin, Y., Heilman, K. J., Cook, E. H., & Lewis, G. F. (2014). Reducing auditory hypersensitivities in autistic spectrum disorder: Preliminary findings evaluating the listening project protocol. *Frontiers in Pediatrics*, 80. https://doi.org/10.3389/fped.2014.00080

Porges, S. W., & Bohrer, R. E. (1990). The analysis of periodic processes in psychophysiological research. In J. T. Cacioppo & L. G. Tassinary (Eds.), *Principles of psychophysiology: Physical, social, and inferential elements* (pp. 708–753). Cambridge University Press.

Porges, S. W., Davila, M. I., Lewis, G. F., Kolacz, J., Okonmah-Obazee, S., Hane, A. A., Kwon, K. Y., Ludwig, R. J., Myers, M. M. & Welch, M. G. (2019). Autonomic regulation of preterm infants is enhanced by Family Nurture Intervention. *Developmental Psychobiology, 61*, 942–952.

Porges, S. W., Doussard-Roosevelt, J. A., Portales, A. L., Greenspan, S. I. (1996). Infant regulation of the vagal "brake" predicts child behavior problems: A psychobiological model of social behavior. *Developmental Psychobiology, 29*, 697–712. https://doi.org/10.1002/(SICI)1098-2302(199612)29:8

Porges, S. W., Doussard-Roosevelt, J. A., Stifter, C. A., McClenny, B. D., & Riniolo, T. C. (1999). Sleep state and vagal regulation of heart period patterns in the human newborn: An extension of the polyvagal theory. *Psychophysiology, 36*, 14–21.

Porges, S. W., & Furman, S. A. (2011). The early development of the autonomic nervous system provides a neural platform for social behaviour: A polyvagal perspective. *Infant Child Development, 20*, 106–118. https://doi.org/10.1002/icd.688

Porges, S. W., & Kolacz, J. (2021). Neurocardiology through the lens of the polyvagal theory. In S. W. Porges, *Polyvagal safety*. W. W. Norton.

Porges, S. W., & Lewis, G. F. (2010). The polyvagal hypothesis: Common mechanisms mediating autonomic regulation, vocalizations and listening. *Handbook of Behavioral Neuroscience, 19*, 255–264. https://doi.org/10.1016/B978-0-12-374593-4.00025-5

Porges, S. W., Macellaio, M., Stanfill, S. D., McCue, K., Lewis, G. F., Harden, E. R., Handelman, M., Denver, J., Bazhenova, O. V., & Heilman, K. J. (2013). Respiratory sinus arrhythmia and auditory processing in autism: Modifiable deficits of an integrated social engagement system? *International Journal of Psychophysiology, 88*, 261–270. https://doi.org/10.1016/j.ijpsycho.2012.11.009

Portales, A. L., Porges, S. W., Doussard-Roosevelt, J. A., Abedin, M., Lopez, R., Young, M. A., Beeram, M. R., & Baker, M. (1997). Vagal regulation during bottle feeding in low-birthweight neonates: Support for the gustatory-vagal hypothesis. *Developmental Psychobiology, 30*, 225–233.

Rajabalee, N., Kozlowska, K., Lee, S. Y., Savage, B., Hawkes, C., Siciliano, D., Porges, S. W., Pick, S., & Torbey, S. (2022). Neuromodulation using computer-altered music to treat a ten-year-old child unresponsive to standard interventions for functional neurological disorder. *Harvard Review of Psychiatry, 30*, 303–316. https://doi.org/10.1097/HRP.0000000000000341

Reed, S. F., Ohel, G., David, R., & Porges, S. W. (1999). A neural explanation of fetal heart rate patterns: A test of the polyvagal theory, *Developmental Psychobiology, 35*, 108–118. https://doi.org/10.1002/(SICI)1098-2302(199909)35:23.0.CO;2-N

Reed, S. F., Porges, S. W., & Newlin, D. B. (1999). Effect of alcohol on vagal regulation of cardiovascular function: Contributions of the polyvagal theory to the psychophysiology of alcohol. *Experimental and Clinical Psychopharmacology, 7*, 484.

Richter, C. A. (1957). On the phenomenon of sudden death in animals and man. *Psychosom. Med., 19*, 191–198. https://doi.org/10.1097/00006842-195705000-00004

Richter, D. W., & Spyer, K. M. (1990). Cardiorespiratory control. In A. D. Loewy & K. M. Spyer (Eds.) *Central regulation of autonomic function*. Oxford University Press.

Sachis, P. N., Armstrong, D. L., Becker, L. E., & Bryan, A. C. (1982). Myelination of the human vagus nerve from 24 weeks postconceptional age to adolescence. *Neuropathology and Experimental Neurology, 41*, 466–472. https://doi .org/10.1097/00005072-198207000-00009

Sanches, P. V., Taylor, E. W., Duran, L. M., Cruz, A. L., Dias, D. P., & Leite, C. A. (2019). Respiratory sinus arrhythmia is a major component of heart rate variability in undisturbed, remotely monitored rattlesnakes, Crotalus Durissus. *Experimental Biology, 222.* https://doi.org/10.1242/jeb.197954

Sholapurkar, S. L. (2015). Categorization of fetal heart rate decelerations in American and European practice: Importance and imperative of avoiding framing and confirmation biases. *Clinical Medicine Research, 7*, 672. https://doi.org/10.14740/jocmr2166w

Suess, P. E., Alpan, G., Dulkerian, S. J., Doussard-Roosevelt, J., Porges, S. W., & Gewolb, I. H. (2000). Respiratory sinus arrhythmia during feeding: A measure of vagal regulation of metabolism, ingestion, and digestion in preterm infants. *Developmental Medicine and Child Neurology, 42*(5), 353.

Taylor, E., Campbell, H. A., Levings, J. J., Young, M. J., Butler, P. J., & Egginton, S. (2006). Coupling of the respiratory rhythm in fish with activity in hypobranchial nerves and with heartbeat. *Physiological and Biochemical Zoology, 79*, 1000–1009. https://doi.org/10.1086/507663

Taylor, E. W., Wang, T., & Leite, C. A. (2022). An overview of the phylogeny of cardiorespiratory control in vertebrates with some reflections on the "Polyvagal Theory." *Biological Psychology, 172*, 108382. https://doi.org/10.1016/j.biopsycho.2022.108382

Vogel, G. (2018). Got milk? Even the first mammals knew how to suckle. *Science.* www.science.org/content/article/got-milk-even-first-mammals-knew -how-suckle

Wenger, M. (1966). Studies of autonomic balance: A summary. *Psychophysiology, 2*, 173–186. https://doi.org/10.1111/j.1469-8986.1966.tb02641.x

Williamson, J. B., Lewis, G., Grippo, A. J., Lamb, D., Harden, E., Handleman, M., Lebow, J., Carter, C. S., & Porges, S. W. (2010). Autonomic predictors of recovery following surgery: A comparative study. *Autonomic Neuroscience, 156*, 60–66. https://doi.org/10.1016/j.autneu.2010.03.009

Windle, W., O'Donnell, J., & Glasshagle, E. (1933). The early development of spontaneous and reflex behavior in cat embryos and fetuses. *Physiological Zoology, 6*, 521–541.

Wolf, S. (1965). The bradycardia of the dive reflex—A possible mechanism of sudden death. *Transactions of the American Clinical and Climatological Association, 76*, 192.

2. POLYVAGAL THEORY: A BIOBEHAVIORAL JOURNEY TO SOCIALITY

Borg, E., Counter, S. A. (1989). The middle-ear muscles. *Scientific American, 261*(2), 74–81.

Darrow, C. W., Jost, H., Solomon, A. P., & Mergener, J. C. (1942). Autonomic indicators of excitatory and homeostatic effects on the electroencephalogram. *Psychology, 14*, 115–130.

Doussard-Roosevelt, J. A., Porges, S. W., Scanlon, J. W., Alemi, B., & Scanlon, K. B. (1997). Vagal regulation of heart rate in the prediction of developmental outcome for very low birth weight preterm infants. *Child Development, 68*(2), 173–186.

Duffy, E. (1957). The psychological significance of the concept of "arousal" or "activation. *Psychological Review, 64*, 265–275.

Hess, W. R. (1954). *Diencephalon, autonomic and extrapyramidal functions.* Grune and Stratton.

Huxley, J. (1962). Mankind evolving. The evolution of the human species by Theodosius Dobzhansky. *Perspectives in Biology and Medicine, 6*(1), 144–148. https://doi.org/10.1353/pbm.1963.0002

Jackson, J. H. (1884). The Croonian lectures on evolution and dissolution of the nervous system. *British Medical Journal, 1*(1215), 703–707.

Kolacz, J., Kovacic, K. K., & Porges, S. W. (2019). Traumatic stress and the autonomic brain-gut connection in development: Polyvagal theory as an integrative framework for psychosocial and gastrointestinal pathology. *Developmental Psychobiology, 61*(5), 796–809.

Kolacz, J., Lewis, G. F., & Porges, S. W. (2018). The integration of vocal communication and biobehavioral state regulation in mammals: A polyvagal hypothesis. *Handbook of Behavioral Neuroscience, 25*, 23–34.

Kolacz, J., & Porges, S. W. (2018). Chronic diffuse pain and functional gastrointestinal disorders after traumatic stress: Pathophysiology through a polyvagal perspective. *Frontiers in Medicine, 5*, 145.

Lewis, G. F., Furman, S. A., McCool, M. F., & Porges, S. W. (2012). Statistical strategies to quantify respiratory sinus arrhythmia: are commonly used metrics equivalent? *Biological psychology, 89*(2), 349–364.

Lindsley, D. (1951). Emotion. In S. S. Stevens (Ed.), *Handbook of experimental psychology* (pp. 473–516). Wiley.

Malmo, R. B. (1959). Activation: A neurophysiological dimension. *Psychological Review, 66*, 367–386.

Porges, S. W. (1992). Vagal tone: A physiologic marker of stress vulnerability. *Pediatrics, 90*(3Pt 2), 498–504.

Porges, S. W. (1995). Orienting in a defensive world: Mammalian modifications of our evolutionary heritage. Polyvagal theory. *Psychophysiology, 32*(4), 301–318.

Porges, S. W. (1998). Love: An emergent property of the mammalian autonomic nervous system. *Psychoneuroendocrinology, 23*(8), 837–861.

Porges, S. W. (2001). The polyvagal theory: Phylogenetic substrates of a social nervous system. *International Journal of Psychophysiology, 42*(2), 123–146.

Porges, S. W. (2007). The polyvagal perspective. *Biological Psychology, 74*(2), 116–143.

Porges, S. W. (2018). Methods and systems for reducing sound sensitivities and improving auditory processing, behavioral state regulation and social engagement behaviors. U.S. Patent 10,029,068 issued July 24, 2018.

Porges, S. W., Bazhenova, O. V., Bal, E., Carlson, N., Sorokin, Y., Heilman, K. J., & Lewis, G. F. (2014). Reducing auditory hypersensitivities in autistic spectrum disorder: Preliminary findings evaluating the listening project protocol. *Frontiers in Pediatrics, 2*, 80.

Porges, S. W., Davila, M. I., Lewis, G. F., Kolacz, J., Okonmah-Obazee, S., Hane, A. A., Kwon, K. Y., Ludwig, R. J., Myers, M. M., & Welch, M. G. (2019). Autonomic regulation of preterm infants is enhanced by Family Nurture Intervention. *Developmental Psychobiology, 61*(6), 942–952.

Porges, S. W., Doussard-Roosevelt, J. A., Stifter, C. A., McClenny, B. D., & Riniolo, T. C. (1999). Sleep state and vagal regulation of heart period patterns in the human newborn: An extension of the polyvagal theory. *Psychophysiology, 36*(1), 14–21.

Porges, S. W., & Furman, S. A. (2011). The early development of the autonomic nervous system provides a neural platform for social behaviour: A polyvagal perspective. *Infant Child Development, 20*(1), 106–118.

Porges, S. W., & Lewis, G. F. (2010). The polyvagal hypothesis: Common mechanisms mediating autonomic regulation, vocalizations and listening. *Handbook of Behavioral Neurobiology, 19*, 255–264.

Porges, S. W., Macellaio, M., Stanfill, S. D., McCue, K., Lewis, G. F., Harden, E. R., & Heilman, K. J. (2013). Respiratory sinus arrhythmia and auditory processing in autism: Modifiable deficits of an integrated social engagement system? *International Journal of Psychophysiology, 88*(3), 261–270.

Portales, A. L., Porges, S. W., Doussard-Roosevelt, J. A., Abedin, M., Lopez, R., Young, M. A., & Baker, M. (1997). Vagal regulation during bottle feeding in low-birthweight neonates: Support for the gustatory-vagal hypothesis. *Developmental Psychobiology, 30*(3), 225–233.

Reed, S. F., Ohel, G., David, R., & Porges, S. W. (1999). A neural explanation of fetal heart rate patterns: A test of the polyvagal theory. *Developmental Psychobiology, 35*(2), 108–118.

Reed, S. F., Porges, S. W., & Newlin, D. B. (1999). Effect of alcohol on vagal regulation of cardiovascular function: Contributions of the polyvagal theory to the psychophysiology of alcohol. *Experimental and Clinical Psychopharmacology, 7*(4), 484.

Richter, D. W., & Spyer, K. M. (1990). Cardiorespiratory control. In A. D. Loewy & K. M. Spyer (Eds.), *Central regulation of autonomic function* (pp. 189–207). Oxford University Press.

Taylor, E. W., Leite, C. A., Sartori, M. R., Wang, T., Abe, A. S., & Crossley, D. A. (2014). The phylogeny and ontogeny of autonomic control of the heart and cardiorespiratory interactions in vertebrates. *Experimental Biology*, 217(5), 690–703.

van der Kolk, B. A. (2015). *The body keeps the score: Brain, mind, and body in the healing of trauma*. Penguin Books.

Wozñiak, W., & O'Rahilly, R. (1981). Fine structure and myelination of the human vagus nerve. *Acta Anatomica*, 109, 118–130.

Yerkes, R. M., & Dodson, J. D. (1908). The relation of strength of stimulus to rapidity of habit-formation. *Comparative Neurology and Psychology*, 18(5), 459–482.

3. POLYVAGAL THEORY: A SCIENCE OF SAFETY

Ahnert, L., Eckstein-Madry, T., Piskernik, B., Porges, S. W., & Lamb, M. E. (2021). Infants' stress responses and protest behaviors at childcare entry and the role of care providers. *Developmental Psychobiology*, 63(6), e22156.

Bond, S. A., Tuckey, M. R., & Dollard, M. F. (2010). Psychosocial safety climate, workplace bullying, and symptoms of posttraumatic stress. *Organization Development*, 28(1), 37.

Borg, E., & Counter, S. A. (1989). The middle-ear muscles. *Scientific American*, 261, 74–81.

Bowlby, J. (1988). *A secure base: Parent-child attachment and healthy human development*. Basic Books.

Brosschot, J. F., Verkuil, B., & Thayer, J. F. (2017). Exposed to events that never happen: Generalized unsafety, the default stress response, and prolonged autonomic activity. *Neurosci. Biobehav. Rev.* 74, 287–296. doi: 10.1016/j. neubiorev.2016.07.019

Cacioppo, J. T., Berntson, G. G., Sheridan, J. F., & McClintock, M. K. (2000). Multilevel integrative analyses of human behavior: Social neuroscience and the complementing nature of social and biological approaches. *Psychological Bulletin*, 126, 829–843. doi: 10.1037//0033-2909.126.6.829

Dale, L. P., Kolacz, J., Sambuco, N., Majdick, J., Johonnot, K., & Porges, S. W. (2022). Vagal efficiency: An autonomic metric mediating the impact of maltreatment history, exercise, and psychiatric and physical health in college students. *Frontiers in Psychiatry*, 13.

Damásio, A. R. (1994). Descartes' error: Emotion, reason, and the human brain. http://ci.nii.ac.jp/ncid/BA81390277

Dana, D. (2018). The polyvagal theory in therapy: Engaging the rhythm of regulation. (Norton series on interpersonal neurobiology.) W. W. Norton.

Descartes, René, 1596–1650. (1986). *Discourse on method*. Macmillan Collier Macmillan. (Original work published 1637)

Dobzhansky, T. (1962). *Mankind evolving*. Yale University Press.

Dollard, M. F., & McTernan, W. (2011). Psychosocial safety climate: A multi-level theory of work stress in the health and community service sector. *Epidemiology and Psychiatric Sciences, 20*(4), 287–293.

Fanning, J., Silfer, J. L., Liu, H., Gauvin, L., Heilman, K. J., Porges, S. W., & Rejeski, W. J. (2020). Relationships between respiratory sinus arrhythmia and stress in college students. *Behavioral Medicine, 43*(2), 308–317.

Folkman, S., & Lazarus, R. S. (1984). Stress, appraisal, and coping (vol. 2). Springer.

Gendlin, E. (2017). *A process model*. Northwestern University Press.

Jackson, J. H. (1884). The Croonian lectures on evolution and dissolution of the nervous system. *British Medical Journal, 1*, 703.

Kolacz, J., Dale, L. P., Nix, E. J., Roath, O. K., Lewis, G. F., & Porges, S. W. (2020a). Adversity history predicts self-reported autonomic reactivity and mental health in US residents during the COVID-19 pandemic. *Frontiers in Psychiatry*, 1119.

Kolacz, J., daSilva, E. B., Lewis, G. F., Bertenthal, B. I., & Porges, S. W. (2022). Associations between acoustic features of maternal speech and infants' emotion regulation following a social stressor. *Infancy, 27*, 135–158. https://doi.org/10.1111/infa.12440

Kolacz, J., Hu, Y., Gesselman, A. N., Garcia, J. R., Lewis, G. F., & Porges, S. W. (2020b). Sexual function in adults with a history of childhood maltreatment: Mediating effects of self-reported autonomic reactivity. *Psychological Trauma: Theory, Research, Practice, and Policy, 12*(3), 281.

Kolacz, J., Kovacic, K., Lewis, G. F., Sood, M. R., Aziz, Q., Roath, O. R., & Porges, S. W. (2021). Cardiac autonomic regulation and joint hypermobility in adolescents with functional abdominal pain disorders. *Neurogastroenterology and Motility, 33*, e14165. https://doi.org/10.1111/nmo.14165

Kolacz, J., Kovacic, K. K., & Porges, S. W. (2019). Traumatic stress and the autonomic brain-gut connection in development: Polyvagal theory as an integrative framework for psychosocial and gastrointestinal pathology. *Developmental Psychobiology, 61*, 796–809. https://doi.org/10.1002/dev.21852

Kolacz, J., Lewis, G. F., & Porges, S. W. (2018). The integration of vocal communication and biobehavioral state regulation in mammals: A polyvagal hypothesis. *Handbook of Behavioral Neuroscience, 25*, 23–34. https://doi.org/10.1016/B978-0-12-809600-0.00003-2

Kolacz, J., & Porges, S. W. (2018). Chronic diffuse pain and functional gastrointestinal disorders after traumatic stress: Pathophysiology through a polyvagal perspective. *Frontiers in Medicine, 5*, 145. https://doi.org /10.3389/fmed.2018.00145

Kovacic, K., Kolacz, J., Lewis, G. F., & Porges, S. W. (2020). Impaired vagal efficiency predicts auricular neurostimulation response in adolescent functional abdominal pain disorders. *American College of Gastroenterology*, 115(9), 1534–1538.

Levenson, R. W. (2003). Autonomic specificity and emotion. *Handbook of Affective Sciences*, 2, 212–224.

Lewis, G. F., Furman, S. A., McCool, M. F., & Porges, S. W. (2012). Statistical strategies to quantify respiratory sinus arrhythmia: Are commonly used metrics equivalent? *Biological Psychology*, 89, 349–364. https://doi.org/10.1016/j .biopsycho.2011.11.009

McEwen, B. S. (2013). The brain on stress: Toward an integrative approach to brain, body, and behavior. *Perspectives on Psychological Science*, 8(6), 673–675.

Porges, S. W. (1985). Spontaneous oscillations in heart rate: Potential index of stress. In G. P. Moberg (Ed.), *Animal stress* (pp. 97–111). Springer. https://doi.org/10.1007/978-1-4614-7544-6_7

Porges, S. W. (1995). Orienting in a defensive world: Mammalian modifications of our evolutionary heritage. A polyvagal theory. *Psychophysiology*, 32, 301–318.

Porges, S. W. (1996). Physiological regulation in high-risk infants: A model for assessment and potential intervention. *Development and Psychopathology*, 8, 43–58.

Porges, S. W. (2004). Neuroception: A subconscious system for detecting threats and safety. *Zero to Three (J.)*, 24, 19–24.

Porges, S. W. (2003). Social engagement and attachment: A phylogenetic perspective. Annals of the New York Academy of Sciences. 1008, 31–47. https://doi.org/10.1196/annals.1301.004

Porges, S. W. (2009). The polyvagal theory: New insights into adaptive reactions of the autonomic nervous system. *Cleveland Clinic Journal of Medicine*, 76, S86. https://doi.org/10.3949/ccjm.76.s2.17

Porges, S. W. (2021a). *Polyvagal safety: Attachment, communication, self-regulation*. W. W. Norton.

Porges, S. W. (2021b). Polyvagal theory: A biobehavioral journey to sociality. *Comprehensive Psychoneuroendocrinology*, 7, 100069. https://doi.org/10.1016/j .cpnec.2021.100069

Porges, S. W., & Furman, S. A. (2011). The early development of the autonomic nervous system provides a neural platform for social behaviour: A polyvagal perspective. *Infant and Child Development*, 20, 106–118. https://doi.org/10.1002/icd.688

Porges, S. W., & Lewis, G. F. (2010). The polyvagal hypothesis: Common mechanisms mediating autonomic regulation, vocalizations and listening. In *Handbook of Behavioral Neuroscience*, 19, 255–264. https://doi.org/10.1016/B978-0-12-374593-4.00025-5

Porges, S. W., & Lipsitt, L. P. (1993). Neonatal responsivity to gustatory stimulation: The gustatory-vagal hypothesis. *Infant Behavior and Development*, 16(4), 487–494.

Porges, S. W., Macellaio, M., Stanfill, S. D., McCue, K., Lewis, G. F., Harden, E. R., Handelman, M., Denver, J., Bazhenova, O. V., & Heilman, K. J. (2013). Respiratory sinus arrhythmia and auditory processing in autism: Modifiable deficits of an integrated social engagement system? *International Journal of Psychophysiology*, 88, 261–270. https://doi.org/10.1016/j.ijpsycho.2012.11.009, *Developmental Psychobiology*, 61, 942–952. https://doi.org/10.1002/dev.21841

Reed, S. F., Porges, S. W., & Newlin, D. B. (1999). Effect of alcohol on vagal regulation of cardiovascular function: Contributions of the polyvagal theory to the psychophysiology of alcohol. *Experimental and Clinical Psychopharmacology*, 7, 484–492. https://doi.org/10.1037/1064-1297.7.4.484

Slavich, G. M. (2020). Social safety theory: A biologically based evolutionary perspective on life stress, health, and behavior. *Annual Review of Clinical Psychology*, 16, 265–295.

Tronick, E., Als, H., Adamson, L., Wise, S., & Brazelton, T. B. (1978). The infant's response to entrapment between contradictory messages in face-to-face interaction. *American Academy of Child Psychiatry*, 17, 1–13.

Williamson, J. B., Porges, E. C., Lamb, D. G., & Porges, S. W. (2015). Maladaptive autonomic regulation in PTSD accelerates physiological aging. *Frontiers in Psychology*, 5, 1571.

Wundt, W. M., & Judd, C. H. (1902). *Outlines of psychology*. W. Engelmann.

4. A TRANSDISCIPLINARY THEORY OF SOCIALITY: POLYVAGAL THEORY

Dobzhansky, T. (1973). *American biology teacher*, 35(3), 125–129.

Hess, W. R. (1949). *Nobel lecture*. Nobel Lectures, Physiology or Medicine (1942–62). www.nobelprize.org/prizes/medicine/1949/hess/lecture/

Jackson, J. H. (1884). The Croonian lectures on evolution and dissolution of the nervous system. *British Medical Journal*, 1(1215), 703.

Porges, S. W. (1994). Orienting in a defensive world: Mammalian modifications of our evolutionary heritage. *Psychophysiology*, 32(4), 301–318.

Porges, S. W. (2004). Neuroception: A subconscious system for detecting threats and safety. *Zero to Three (J.)*, 24(5), 19–24.

Porges, S. W. (2007). The polyvagal perspective. *Biological Psychology*, 74(2), 116–143.

Porges, S. W. (2011). *The polyvagal theory: Neurophysiological foundations of emotions, attachment, communication, and self-regulation.* (Norton series on interpersonal neurobiology.) W. W. Norton.

Porges, S. W. (2020). The COVID-19 pandemic is a paradoxical challenge to our nervous system: A polyvagal perspective. *Clinical Neuropsychiatry, 1* 7(2),135–138.

Snow, C. P. (1959). *The Rede Lecture: The Two Cultures.* Cambridge Press.

5. APPEASEMENT: REPLACING STOCKHOLM SYNDROME AS A DEFINITION OF A SURVIVAL STRATEGY

Bailey, R., Dana, D., Bailey, E., & Davis, F. (2020). The application of the polyvagal theory to high conflict co-parenting cases. *Family Court Review, 58*(2), 525–543. https://doi.org/10.1111/fcre.12485

Bonanno, G. A. (2004). Loss, trauma, and human resilience: Have we underestimated the human capacity to thrive after extremely aversive events? *American Psychologist, 59*(1), 20–28. https://doi.org/10.1037/0003-066X.59.1.20

Bonanno, G. A. (2021). The resilience paradox. *European Journal of Psychotraumatology, 12*(1), 1942642. https://doi.org/10.1080/20008198.2021.1942642

Bonanno, G. A., & Burton, C. L. (2013). Regulatory flexibility: An individual differences perspective on coping and emotion regulation. *Perspectives on Psychological Science, 8*(6), 591–612. https://doi.org/10.1177/1745691613504116

Bonanno, G. A., Romero, S. A., & Klein, S. I. (2015). The temporal elements of psychological resilience: An integrative framework for the study of individuals, families, and communities. *Psychological Inquiry, 26*(2), 139–169. https://doi.org/10.1080/1047840X.2015.992677

Cannon, W. B. (1942). "Voodoo" death. *American Anthropologist, 44*(2), 169–181.

Cantor, C., & Price, J. (2007). Traumatic entrapment, appeasement and complex post-traumatic stress disorder: Evolutionary perspectives of hostage reactions, domestic abuse and the Stockholm syndrome. *Australian & New Zealand Journal of Psychiatry, 41*(5), 377–384. https://doi.org/10.1080/00048670701261178

Chemtob, C., Hatfield, E., & Hsee, C. K. (1992). Assessments of the emotional states of others: Conscious judgments versus emotional contagion. *Social and Clinical Psychology, 11*(2), 119–128. https://doi.org/10.1521/jscp.1992.11.2.119

Chen, S., & Bonanno, G. A. (2020). Psychological adjustment during the global outbreak of COVID-19: A resilience perspective. *Psychological Trauma: Theory, Research, Practice, and Policy, 12*(S1), S51–S54. https://doi.org/10.1037/tra0000685

Etchison, M., & Kleist, D. M. (2000). Review of narrative therapy: Research and utility. *The Family Journal, 8*(1), 61–66.

Geisler, F. C. M., Kubiak, T., Siewert, K., & Weber, H. (2013). Cardiac vagal tone is associated with social engagement and self-regulation. *Biological Psychology, 93*(2), 279–286. https://doi.org/10.1016/j.biopsycho.2013.02.013

Geller, S. M., & Porges, S. W. (2014). Therapeutic presence: Neurophysio
logical mechanisms mediating feeling safe in therapeutic relationships.
Psychotherapy Integration, 24(3), 178–192. https://doi.org/10.1037/a0037511

Graham, D. L. R., Rawlings, E., & Rimini, N. (1988). Survivors of terror: Battered
women, hostages, and the Stockholm Syndrome. In K. Yllö & M. Bograd
(Eds.), *Feminist perspectives on wife abuse* (pp. 217–233). Sage Publications.

Han, H. R., Miller, H. N., Nkimbeng, M., Budhathoki, C., Mikhael, T., Rivers,
E., Gray, J., Trimble, K., Chow, S., & Wilson, P. (2021). Trauma informed
interventions: A systematic review. *PloS One, 16*(6), e0252747. https://doi
.org/10.1371/journal.pone.0252747

Jaeger, J., Lindblom, K. M., Parker-Guilbert, K., & Zoellner, L. A.
(2014). Trauma narratives: It's what you say, not how you say it. *Psychological Trauma: Theory, Research, Practice, and Policy, 6*(5),
473–481. https://doi.org/10.1037/a0035239

Jiang, X., Topps, A. K., & Suzuki, R. (2021). A systematic review of self-care
measures for professionals and trainees. *Training and Education in Professional Psychology, 15*(2), 126–139. https://doi.org/10.1037/tep0000318

Jordan, J. (2013). From victim to survivor - and from survivor to victim:
Reconceptualising the survivor journey. *Sexual Abuse in Australia and New
Zealand, 5*(2), 48–56. https://doi.org/10.3316/informit.832896370790754

Jülich, S. (2005). Stockholm syndrome and child sexual abuse. *Child
Sexual Abuse, 14*(3), 107–129. https://doi.org/10.1300/J070v14n03_06

Lex, B. W. (1974). Voodoo death: New thoughts on an Old Explanation.
American Anthropologist,76(4), 818–823. https://doi.org/10.1525/aa.1974.76
.4.02a00060

López-Castro, T., Saraiya, T., Zumberg-Smith, K., & Dambreville, N.
(2019). Association between shame and posttraumatic stress disorder: A
meta-analysis. *Traumatic Stress,* 32(4),484–495. https://doi.org/10.1002/jts.22411

McFarlane, C. A., & Kaplan, I. (2012). Evidence-based psychological interventions for adult survivors of torture and trauma: A 30-year review.
Transcultural Psychiatry, 49(3–4), 539–567. https://doi.org/10.1177/1363461512
447608

Mohandie, K. (2002). Human captivity experiences. *Threat Assessment,*
2(1), 3–41. https://doi.org/10.1300/J177v02n01_02

Namnyak, M., Tufton, N., Szekely, R., Toal, M., Worboys, S., & Sampson,
E. L. (2008). "Stockholm syndrome": Psychiatric diagnosis or urban myth?
Acta Psychiatrica Scandinavica, 117(1), 4–11. https://doi.org/10.1111/j.1600
-0447.2007.01112.x

Ogden, R. M. (1907). Wundt's doctrine of psychical analysis and the psychical
elements, and some recent criticism. I. The criteria of the elements and attributes; II. Feeling and feeling analysis. *Psychological Bulletin, 4*(2), 47–49. https:/
/doi.org/10.1037/h0065062

Owca, J. (2020). The association between a psychotherapist's theoretical orientation and perception of complex trauma and repressed anger in the fawn response [Doctoral dissertation]. The Chicago School of Professional Psychology. www.proquest.com/openview/83faad71347dae7bba4d3b130d083 e88/1?pq-origsite=gscholar&cbl=18750&diss=y

Painter, S. L., & Dutton, D. G. (1985). Patterns of emotional bonding in battered women: Traumatic bonding. *International Journal of Women's Studies*, 8(4), 363–375.

Porges, S. W. (2004). Neuroception: A subconscious system for detecting threats and safety. *Zero to Three (J.)*, 24(5), 19–24.

Porges, S. W. (2011). The polyvagal theory: Neurophysiological foundations of emotions, attachment, communication, and self-regulation. (Norton series on interpersonal neurobiology.) W. W. Norton.

Porges, S. W. (2021). Polyvagal theory: A biobehavioral journey to sociality. *Comprehensive Psychoneuroendocrinology, 7*, 100069. https://doi.org/10.1016/j.cpnec.2021.100069

Porges, S. W. (2022). Polyvagal theory: A science of safety. *Frontiers in Integrative Neuroscience, 16*, 871227. https://doi.org/10.3389/fnint.2022.871227

Porges, S. W., & Dana, D. (2018). Clinical applications of the polyvagal theory: The emergence of polyvagal-informed therapies (Norton series on interpersonal neurobiology.) W. W. Norton.

Pyszczynski, T., Greenberg, J., & Solomon, S. (1999). A dual-process model of defense against conscious and unconscious death-related thoughts: An extension of terror management theory. *Psychological Review, 106*(4), 835–845. https://doi.org/10.1037/0033-295X.106.4.835

Reid, J., Haskell, R., Dillahunt-Aspillaga, C., & Thor, J. (2013). Trauma bonding and interpersonal violence. *Psychology of Trauma*. https://digitalcommons.usf.edu/fac_publications/198

Saraiya, T., & Lopez-Castro, T. (2016). Ashamed and afraid: A scoping review of the role of shame in post-traumatic stress disorder (PTSD). *Clinical Medicine, 5*(11), 94. https://doi.org/10.3390/jcm5110094

Sarrate-Costa, C., Lila, M., Comes-Fayos, J., Moya-Albiol, L., & Romero-Martínez, Á. (2022, November 22). Reduced vagal tone in intimate partner violence perpetrators is partly explained by anger rumination. *Current Psychology*. https://doi.org/10.1007/s12144-022-03994-z

Treisman, D. (2004). Rational appeasement. *International Organization, 58*(2), 345–373. https://doi.org/10.1017/S002081830458205X

Warshaw, C., Sullivan, C., & Rivera, E. (2013). A systematic review of trauma-focused interventions for domestic violence survivors. Retrieved October 11, 2022, from http://www.nationalcenterdvtraumamh.org/wp-content/uploads/2013/03/NCDVTMH_EBPLitReview2013.pdf

Williamson, E., Dutch, N., & Clawson, H. C. (2010). Evidence-based mental health treatment for victims of human trafficking. Office of the Assistant Secretary for Planning and Evaluation, U.S. Department of Health and Human Services.

6. THE SENSITIVE PATIENT THROUGH THE LENS OF THE POLYVAGAL THEORY: A NEUROSCIENCE OF THREAT AND SAFETY

Bernard, C. (1865). Introduction à l'étude de la médecine expérimentale. [Introduction to the Study of Experimental Medicine]. J. B. Ballierre.

Burton, C., Fink, P., Henningsen, P., Löwe, B., & Rief, W. (2020). Functional somatic disorders: Discussion paper for a new common classification for research and clinical use. *BMC Medicine, 18*(1), 1–7.

Cannon, W. B. (1927). The James-Lange theory of emotions: A critical examination and an alternative theory. *American Journal of Psychology,* 39(1/4):106–124.

Carter, C. S. (2022). Oxytocin and love: Myths, metaphors and mysteries. *Comprehensive Psychoneuroendocrinology, 9,* 100107.

Carter, C. S., Kenkel, W. M., MacLean, E. L., Wilson, S. R., Perkeybile, A. M., Yee, J. R., . . . & Kingsbury, M. A. (2020). Is oxytocin "nature's medicine"? *Pharmacological Reviews, 72*(4), 829–861.

Craig, A. D. (2002). How do you feel? Interoception: The sense of the physiological condition of the body. *Nature Reviews Neuroscience, 3*(8), 655–666.

Craig, A. D. (2003). A new view of pain as a homeostatic emotion. *Trends in Neurosciences, 26*(6), 303–307.

Critchley, H. D., Wiens, S., Rotshtein, P., Öhman, A., & Dolan, R. J. (2004). Neural systems supporting interoceptive awareness. *Nature Neuroscience,* 7(2), 189–195.

Darwin C. (1872). *The expression of emotions in man and animals.* D. Appleton.

Gendlin, E. (2017). *A process model.* Northwestern University Press.

Henningsen, P., Zipfel, S., & Herzog, W. (2007). Management of functional somatic syndromes. *The Lancet, 369,* 946–955.

Hess W. (1949). The central control of the activity of internal organs [Internet]. Nobelprize.org, 1949/2014 [cited 5 June 2017]. www.nobelprize .org/prizes/medicine/1949/hess/lecture/

Hyams, J. S., Di Lorenzo, C., Saps, M., Shulman, R. J., Staiano, A., & van Tilburg, M. (2016). Childhood functional gastrointestinal disorders: child/ adolescent. *Gastroenterology, 150*(6), 1456–1468.

Jackson, J. H. (1884). The Croonian lectures on evolution and dissolution of the nervous system. *British Medical Journal, 1,* 703.

James, W. (1884). What is an emotion? *Mind, 9,* 188–204.

Kleckner, I. R., Zhang, J., Touroutoglou, A., Chanes, L., Xia, C., Simmons, W. K., Quigley, K. S., Dickerson, B. C. & Feldman Barrett, L. (2017). Evidence for a large-scale brain system supporting allostasis and interoception in humans. *Nature Human Behaviour, 1*(5), 1–14.

Kovacic, K., Kolacz, J., Lewis, G. F., & Porges, S. W. (2020). Impaired vagal efficiency predicts auricular neurostimulation response in adolescent functional abdominal pain disorders. *Official Journal of the American College of Gastroenterology, 115*(9), 1534–1538.

Kozlowska, K., Scher, S., & Helgeland, H. (2020). *Functional somatic symptoms in children and adolescents: A stress-system approach to assessment and treatment* (p. 383). Springer Nature.

Langley, J. N. (1898). On the union of cranial autonomic (visceral) fibres with the nerve cells of the superior cervical ganglion. *Physiology, 23*, 240–270.

Marks, E. M., & Hunter, M. S. (2015). Medically unexplained symptoms: An acceptable term? *British Journal of Pain, 9*(2), 109–114. https://doi.org/10.1177/2049463714535372

Porges, S. W. (1993). The infant's sixth sense: Awareness and regulation of bodily processes. *Zero to Three (J.), 14*(2), 12–16.

Porges, S. W. (1995). Orienting in a defensive world: Mammalian modifications of our evolutionary heritage. A polyvagal theory. *Psychophysiology, 32*, 301–318.

Porges, S. W. (1998). Love and the evolution of the autonomic nervous system: The polyvagal theory of intimacy. *Psychoneuroendocrinology, 23*, 837–861.

Porges, S. W. (2001). The polyvagal theory: Phylogenetic substrates of a social nervous system. *International Journal of Psychophysiology, 42*, 123–146.

Porges, S. W. (2004). Neuroception: A subconscious system for detecting threats and safety. *Zero to Three (J.), 24*, 19–24.

Porges, S. W. (2007). The polyvagal perspective. *Biological Psychology, 74*, 116–143.

Porges, S. W. (2009). The polyvagal theory: New insights into adaptive reactions of the autonomic nervous system. *Cleveland Clinic Journal of Medicine, 76*, S86. https://doi.org/10.3949/ccjm.76. s2.17

Porges, S. W. (2011). *The polyvagal theory: Neurophysiological foundations of emotions, attachment, communication, and self-regulation.* W. W. Norton.

Porges, S. W. (2021a). *Polyvagal safety: Attachment, communication, self-regulation.* W. W. Norton.

Porges, S. W. (2021b). Polyvagal theory: A biobehavioral journey to sociality. *Comprehensive Psychoneuroendocrinology, 7*, 100069. https://doi.org/10.1016/j.cpnec.2021.100069

Porges, S. W. (2022). Polyvagal theory: A science of safety. *Frontiers in Integrative Neuroscience, 16.* https://doi.org/10.3389/fnint.2022.871227

Rajabalee, N., Kozlowska, K., Lee, S. Y., Savage, B., Hawkes, C., Siciliano, D., Porges, S. W., Pick, S., & Torbey, S. (2022 s). Neuromodulation using computer altered music to treat a ten-year-old child unresponsive to standard interventions for functional neurological disorder. *Harvard Review of Psychiatry, 30*(5), 303.

Selye, H. (1936). A syndrome produced by diverse nocuous agents. *Nature, 138*, 32.

Selye H. (1956). *The stress of life.* McGraw-Hill.

Stone, J. (2016). Functional neurological disorders: The neurological assessment as treatment. *Practical Neurology, 16*(1), 7–17.

van der Kolk, B. A. (2015). *The body keeps the score: Brain, mind, and body in the healing of trauma.* Penguin Books.

7. NEUROMODULATION USING COMPUTER-ALTERED MUSIC TO TREAT A TEN-YEAR-OLD CHILD UNRESPONSIVE TO STANDARD INTERVENTIONS FOR FUNCTIONAL NEUROLOGICAL DISORDER

Ahearn, E. P., Juergens, T., Cordes, T., Becker, T., & Krahn, D. (2011). A review of atypical antipsychotic medications for posttraumatic stress disorder. *International Clinical Psychopharmacology, 26*, 193–200.

Benarroch, E. E. (2007). Brainstem respiratory chemosensitivity: New insights and clinical implications. *Neurology, 68*, 2140–2143.

Bouton, M. E. (2002). Context, ambiguity, and unlearning: Sources of relapse after behavioral extinction. *Biological Psychiatry, 52*, 976–986.

Bowman, E. S., & Markland, O. N. (2005). Diagnosis and treatment of pseudoseizures. *Psychiatric Annals, 35*, 306–316.

Broersma, M., Koops, E. A., Vroomen, P. C., Van der Hoeven, J. H., Aleman, A., Leenders, K. L., Maurits, N. M., & van Beilen, M. (2015). Can repetitive transcranial magnetic stimulation increase muscle strength in functional neurological paresis? A proof-of-principle study. *European Journal of Neurology, 22*, 866–873.

Brown, R. P., & Gerbarg, P. L. (2005). Sudarshan Kriya yogic breathing in the treatment of stress, anxiety, and depression: Part I–neurophysiologic model. *Alternative and Complementary Medicine, 11*, 189–201.

Carsley, D., & Heath, N. L. (2018). Effectiveness of mindfulness-based colouring for test anxiety in adolescents. *School Psychology International, 39*, 251–272.

Carson, A., Ludwig, L., & Welch, K. (2016). Psychologic theories in functional neurologic disorders. *Handbook of Clinical Neurology, 139*, 105–120.

Chudleigh, C., Savage, B., Cruz, C., Lim, M., McClure, G., Palmer, D. M., Spooner, C. J., & Kozlowska, K. (2019). Use of respiratory rates and heart rate variability in the assessment and treatment of children and adolescents with functional somatic symptoms. *Clinical Child Psychology and Psychiatry, 24*, 29–39.

Craig, A. D. (2005). Forebrain emotional asymmetry: A neuroanatomical basis? *Trends in Cognitive Sciences, 9*, 566–571.

Craig, A. D. (2016). Interoception and emotion: A neuroanatomical perspective. In L. F. Barrett, M. Lewis, & J. M. Haviland-Jones (Eds.), *Handbook of emotions* (4th ed., pp. 215–234). Guilford.

Cristea, I. A., Vecchi, T., & Cuijpers, P. (2021). Top-down and bottom-up pathways to developing psychological interventions. *JAMA Psychiatry, 78,* 593–594.

Dale, R., & Stacey, B. (2016). Multimodal treatment of chronic pain. *Medical Clinics of North America, 100,* 55–64.

Ezra, Y., Hammerman, O., & Shahar, G. (2019). The four-cluster spectrum of mind-body interrelationships: An integrative model. *Frontiers in Psychiatry, 10,* 39.

FDA [U.S. Food & Drug Administration]. (2021). FDA Authorizes marketing of device to improve gait in multiple sclerosis patients. www.fda.gov/news -events/press-announcements/fda-authorizes-marketing-device-improve -gait-multiple-sclerosis-patients

Fleming, S., Thompson, M., Stevens, R., Heneghan, C., Plüddemann, A., Maconochie, I., Tarassenko, L. & Mant, D. (2011). Normal ranges of heart rate and respiratory rate in children from birth to 18 years of age: A systematic review of observational studies. *The Lancet, 377,* 1011–1018.

Fobian, A. D., & Elliott, L. (2018). A review of functional neurological symptom disorder etiology and the integrated etiological summary model. *Psychiatry and Neuroscience., 43,* 170190.

Fobian, A. D., Long, D. M., & Szaflarski, J. P. (2020). Retraining and control therapy for pediatric psychogenic non-epileptic seizures. *Annals of Clinical and Translational Neurology, 7,* 1410–1419.

Frangos, E., Ellrich, J., & Komisaruk, B. R. (2015). Non-invasive access to the vagus nerve central projections via electrical stimulation of the external ear: fMRI evidence in humans. *Brain Stimulation, 8,* 624–636.

Garcin, B., Mesrati, F., Hubsch, C., Mauras, T., Iliescu, I., Naccache, L., Vidailhet, M., Roze, E., & Degos, B. (2017). Impact of transcranial magnetic stimulation on functional movement disorders: Cortical modulation or a behavioral effect? *Frontiers in Neurology, 8,* 338.

Gasparini, S., Beghi, E., Ferlazzo, E., Gasparini, S., Beghi, E., Ferlazzo, E., Beghi, M., Belcastro, V., Biermann, K. P., Bottini, G., Capovilla, G., Cervellione, R. A., Cianci, V., Coppola, G., Cornaggia, C. M., De Fazio, P., De Masi, S., De Sarro, G., Elia, M., Erba, G., Fusco, L., Gambardella, A . . . Aguglia, A. (2019). Management of psychogenic non-epileptic seizures: A multidisciplinary approach. *European Journal of Neurology, 26,* 205–e15.

Gevirtz, R. (2000). Resonant frequency training to restore homeostasis for treatment of psychophysiological disorders. *Biofeedback, 27,* 7–9.

Harbourne, R, Becker, K., Arpin, D. J., Wilson, T. W., & Kurz, M. J. (2014). Improving the motor skill of children with posterior fossa syndrome: A case series. *Pediatric Physical Therapy, 26,* 462–468.

Hilton, M. N., Boulton, K. A., Kozlowska, K., McClure, G., & Guastella, A. J. (2022). The co-occurrence of neurodevelopmental disorders in gender dysphoria: Characteristics within a paediatric treatment-seeking cohort and factors that predict gender distress pertaining to gender. *Psychiatric Research, 149*, 281–286.

Hou, J., Kulkarni, A., Tellapragada, N., Nair, V., Danilov, Y., Kaczmarek, K., Meyerand, B., Tyler, M., & Prabhakaran, V. (2020). Translingual neural stimulation with the Portable Neuromodulation Stimulator (PoNS®) induces structural changes leading to functional recovery in patients with mild-to-moderate traumatic brain injury. *European Medical Journal Radiology, 1*, 64–71. IB-Stim. Important information for IB-Stim patients. https://ibstim .com/important-information/

Janet, P. (1907). *The major symptoms of hysteria: Fifteen lectures given in the Medical School of Harvard University*. Macmillan.

Jung, W., Jang, K. I., & Lee, S. H. (2019). Heart and brain interaction of psychiatric illness: A review focused on heart rate variability, cognitive function, and quantitative electroencephalography. *Clinical Psychopharmacology and Neuroscience, 17*, 459–474.

Kaczmarek, K. A. (2017). The Portable Neuromodulation Stimulator (PoNS) for neurorehabilitation. [*Sci. Iran D Comput. Sci. Eng. Electr. Eng., 24*, 3171–3180.] *Scientia Iranica 24*(6). https://doi.org/10.24200/sci.2017.4489

Karterud, H. N., Risor, M. B., & Haavet, O. R. (2015). The impact of conveying the diagnosis when using a biopsychosocial approach: A qualitative study among adolescents and young adults with NES (non-epileptic seizures). *Seizure, 24*, 107–113.

Kolacz, J., daSilva, E. B., Lewis, G. F., Bertenthal, B. I., & Porges, S. W. (2019). Using acoustic features of mothers' infant-directed speech to predict changes in infant biobehavioral state. *Acoustical Society of America, 145*, 1764–1765.

Kolacz, J., daSilva, E. B., Lewis, G. F., Bertenthal, B. I., & Porges, S. W. (2022). Associations between acoustic features of maternal speech and infants' emotion regulation following a social stressor. *Infancy, 27*, 135–158.

Kolacz, J., Lewis, G. F., & Porges, S. W. (2018). The integration of vocal communication and biobehavioral state regulation in mammals: A polyvagal hypothesis. *Handbook of Behavioral Neuroscience, 25*, 23–34.

Kolacz, J., Porges, S. W. (2018). Chronic diffuse pain and functional gastrointestinal disorders after traumatic stress: Pathophysiology through a polyvagal perspective. *Frontiers in Medicine (Lausanne), 5*, 145.

Kovacic, K., Hainsworth, K., Sood, M., Chelimsky, G., Unteutsch, R., Nugent, M., Simpson, P., & Miranda, A. (2017). Neurostimulation for abdominal pain-related functional gastrointestinal disorders in adolescents: A randomised, double-blind, sham-controlled trial. *The Lancet Gastroenterol and Hepatology, 2*, 727–737.

Kovacic, K., Kolacz, J., Lewis, G. F., & Porges, S. W. (2020). Impaired vagal efficiency predicts auricular neurostimulation response in adolescent functional abdominal pain disorders. *American Journal of Gastroenterology, 115*, 1534–1538.

Kozlowska, K. (2017). A stress-system model for functional neurological symptoms. *Neurological Sciences, 383*, 151–152.

Kozlowska, K., Chudleigh, C., Cruz, C., Lim, M., McClure, G., Savage, B., Shah, U., Cook, A., Scher, S., Carrive, P., & Gill, D. (2018a). Psychogenic non-epileptic seizures in children and adolescents: Part I–diagnostic formulations. *Clinical Child Psychology and Psychiatry, 23*, 140–159.

Kozlowska, K., Chudleigh, C., Cruz, C., Lim, M., McClure, G., Savage, B., Shah, U., Cook, A., Scher, S., Carrive, P., & Gill, D. (2018b). Psychogenic non-epileptic seizures in children and adolescents: Part II–explanations to families, treatment, and group outcomes. *Clinical Child Psychology and Psychiatry, 23*, 160–176.

Kozlowska, K., English, M., Savage, B., & Chudleigh, C. (2012). Multimodal rehabilitation: A mind-body, family-based intervention for children and adolescents impaired by medically unexplained symptoms. Part 1: The program. *American Journal of Family Therapy, 40*, 399–419.

Kozlowska, K., Gray, N., Scher, S., & Savage, B. (2021). Psychologically informed physiotherapy as part of a multidisciplinary rehabilitation program for children and adolescents with functional neurological disorder: Physical and mental health outcomes. *Paediatric Child Health, 57*, 73–79.

Kozlowska, K., & Mohammad, S. (2023). Functional neurological disorder in children and adolescents: Assessment and treatment. In: L. Sivaswamy &D. Kamat (Eds). *Symptom based approach to pediatric neurology* (pp. 699–724). Springer Nature.

Kozlowska, K., Palmer, D. M., Brown, K. J., Scher, S., Chudleigh, C., Davies, F., & Williams, L. M. (2015). Conversion disorder in children and adolescents: A disorder of cognitive control. *Neuropsychology, 9*, 87–108.

Kozlowska, K., Rampersad, R., Cruz, C., Shah, U., Chudleigh, C., Soe, S., Gill, D., Scher, S. & Carrive, P. (2017). The respiratory control of carbon dioxide in children and adolescents referred for treatment of psychogenic non-epileptic seizures. *European Child and Adolescent Psychiatry, 26*, 1207–1217.

Kozlowska, K., Scher, S., & Helgeland, H. (2020). Functional somatic symptoms in children and adolescents: A stress-system approach to assessment and treatment. Palgrave Macmillan.

Krasaelap, A., Sood, M. R., Li, B. U. K., Unteutsch, R., Yan, K., Nugent, M., Simpson, P., & Kovacic, K. (1987). Efficacy of auricular neurostimulation in adolescents with irritable bowel syndrome in a randomized, double-blind trial. *Clinical Gastroenterology and Hepatology, 18*, 1987–1994.e2.

LaFrance, W. C. Jr., Baird, G. L., Barry, J. J., Blum, A. S., Frank Webb, A., Keitner, G. I., Machan, J. T., Miller, I., J. P.; & NES Treatment Trial (NEST-T) Consortium. (2014). Multicenter pilot treatment trial for psychogenic nonepileptic seizures: A randomized clinical trial. *JAMA Psychiatry, 71*, 997–1005.

Lefaucheur, J. P., Andre-Obadia, N., Antal, A., Ayache, S. S., Baeken, C., Benninger, D. H., Cantello, R. M., Cincotta, M., de Carvalho, M., De Ridder, D., Devanne, H., Di Lazzaro, V., Filipović, S. R., Hummel, F. C., Jääskeläinen, S. K., Kimiskidis, V. K., Koch, G., Langguth, B., Nyffeler, T., . . . Garcia-Larrea, L. (2014). Evidence-based guidelines on the therapeutic use of repetitive transcranial magnetic stimulation (rTMS). *Clinical Neurophysiology 125*, 2150–2206.

Leonard, G., Lapierre, Y., Chen, J. K., Wardini, R., Crane, J., & Ptito, A. (2017). Noninvasive tongue stimulation combined with intensive cognitive and physical rehabilitation induces neuroplastic changes in patients with multiple sclerosis: A multimodal neuroimaging study. *Multiple Sclerosis Journal Experimental, Translational and Clinical, 3*, 2055217317690561.

Lewis, P. M., Thomson, R. H., Rosenfeld, J. V., & Fitzgerald, P. B. (2016). Brain neuromodulation techniques: A review. *Neuroscientist, 22*, 406–421.

Loo, S. K., Salgari, G. C., Ellis, A., Cowen, J., Dillon, A., & McGough, J. J. (2021). Trigeminal nerve stimulation for attention-deficit/hyperactivity disorder: Cognitive and electroencephalographic predictors of treatment response. *American Academy of Child and Adolescent Psychiatry, 60*, 856–864.e1.

Lundahl, B., Moleni, T., Burke, B. L., Butters, R., Tollefson, D., Butler, C., & Rollnick, S. (2013). Motivational interviewing in medical care settings: A systematic review and meta-analysis of randomized controlled trials. *Patient Education and Counseling, 93*, 157–168.

McCraty, R., & Childre, D. (2010). Coherence: Bridging personal, social, and global health. *Alternative Therapies in Health and Medicine, 16*, 10–24.

McGough, J. J., Loo, S. K., Sturm, A., Cowen, J., Leuchter, A. F., & Cook, I. A. (2015). An eight-week, open-trial, pilot feasibility study of trigeminal nerve stimulation in youth with attention-deficit/hyperactivity disorder. *Brain Stimulation, 8*, 299–304.

McGough, J. J., Sturm, A., Cowen, J., Tung, K., Salgari, G. C., Leuchter, A. F., Cook, I. A., Sugar, C. A., & Loo, S. K.. (2019). Double-blind, sham-controlled, pilot study of trigeminal nerve stimulation for attention-deficit/hyperactivity disorder. *American Academy of Child and Adolescent Psychiatry, 58*, 403–411.

Moene, F. C., Spinhoven, P., Hoogduin, K. A., & van Dyck, R. (2003). A randomized controlled clinical trial of a hypnosis-based treatment for patients with conversion disorder, motor type. *International Journal of Clinical and Experimental Hypnosis, 51*, 29–50.

Myers, L., Sarudiansky, M., Korman, G., & Baslet, G. (2021). Using evidence-based psychotherapy to tailor treatment for patients with functional neurological disorders. *Epilepsy and Behavior Reports,16*, 100478.

NeuroSigma. Monarch eTNS System® for pediatric ADHD. 2020. www.monarch-etns.com/.

Nicholson, T. R., Carson, A., Edwards, M. J., Goldstein, L. H., Hallett, M., Mildon, B., Nielsen, G., Nicholson, C., Perez, D. L., Pick, S., Stone, J., & the FND-COM (Functional Neurological Disorders Core Outcome Measures) Group. (2020). Outcome measures for functional neurological disorder: A review of the theoretical complexities. *Neuropsychiatry and Clinical Neurosciences, 32,* 33–42.

Nielsen, G., Stone, J., Matthews, A., Brown, M., Sparkes, C., Farmer, R., Masterton, L., Duncan, L., Winters, A., Daniell, L., Lumsden, C., Carson, A., David, A. S., Edwards, M. (2015). Physiotherapy for functional motor disorders: A consensus recommendation. *Neurology, Neurosurgery, and Psychiatry, 86,* 1113–1119.

Patriquin, M. A., Hartwig, E. M., Friedman, B. H., Porges, S. W., & Scarpa, A. (2019). Autonomic response in autism spectrum disorder: Relationship to social and cognitive functioning. *Biological Psychology, 145,* 185–197.

Peake, J. M., Kerr, G., Sullivan, J. P. (2018). A critical review of consumer wearables, mobile applications, and equipment for providing biofeedback, monitoring stress, and sleep in physically active populations. *Frontiers in Physiology, 9,* 743.

Perez, D. L., Aybek, S., Popkirov, S., Kozlowska, K., Stephen, C. D., Anderson, J., Shura, R., Ducharme, S., Carson, A., Hallett, M., Nicholson, T. R., Stone, J., LaFrance Jr., W. C., & Voon, V. (2021). A review and expert opinion on the neuropsychiatric assessment of motor functional neurological disorders. *Neuropsychiatry and Clinical Neurosciences, 33,* 14–26.

Perez, D. L., Nicholson, T. R., Asadi-Pooya, A. A., Bègue, I., Butler, M., Carson, A. J., David, A. S., Deeley, Q., Diez, I., Edwards, M. J., Espay, A. J., Gelauff, J. M., Hallett, M., Horovitz, S. G., Jungilligens, J., Kanaan, R. A. A., Tijssen, M. A. J., Kozlowska, K., LaFaver, K., . . . Aybek, S. (2021). Neuroimaging in functional neurological disorder: State of the field and research agenda. *Neuroimage Clinical, 30,* 102623.

Pick, S., Goldstein, L. H., Perez, D. L., & Nicholson, T. R. (2019). Emotional processing in functional neurological disorder: A review, biopsychosocial model and research agenda. *Neurol Neurosurg Psychiatry, 90,* 704–711.

Pick, S., Hodsoll, J., Stanton, B., Eskander, A., Stavropoulos, I., Samra, K., Bottini, J., Ahmad, H., David, A. S., Purves, A., & Nicholson, T. R. (2020). Trial of neurostimulation in conversion symptoms (TONICS): A feasibility randomised controlled trial of transcranial magnetic stimulation for functional limb weakness. *British Medical Journal Open, 10,* e037198.

Pintor, L., Bailles, E., Matrai, S., Carreño, M., Donaire, A., Boget, T., Setoain, X., Rumia, J. & Bargalló, N. (2010). Efficiency of venlafaxine in patients with psychogenic nonepileptic seizures and anxiety and/or depressive disorders. *Neuropsychiatry and Clinical Neurosciences, 22,* 401–408.

Pollak, T. A., Nicholson, T. R., Edwards, M. J., & David, A. S. (2014). A systematic review of transcranial magnetic stimulation in the treatment of functional (conversion) neurological symptoms. *Neurology, Neurosurgery, and Psychiatry, 85*, 191–197.

Porges, S. W. (1995). Orienting in a defensive world: Mammalian modifications of our evolutionary heritage. A polyvagal theory. *Psychophysiology, 32*, 301–318.

Porges, S. W. (2007). The polyvagal perspective. *Biological Psychology, 74*, 116–143.

Porges, S. W. (2009). The polyvagal theory: New insights into adaptive reactions of the autonomic nervous system. *Cleveland Clinic Journal of Medicine, 76*(suppl 2), S86–90.

Porges, S. W. (2011). *The polyvagal theory: Neurophysiological foundations of emotions, attachment, communication, and self-regulation.* W. W. Norton.

Porges, S. W. (2017). *The pocket guide to polyvagal theory: The transformative power of feeling safe.* W. W. Norton.

Porges, S. W. (2018). Methods and systems for reducing sound sensitivities and improving auditory processing, behavioral state regulation and social engagement behaviors. Patent no. US 10,029, 068 B2.

Porges, S. W., Bazhenova, O. V., Bal, E., Carlson, N., Sorokin, Y., Heilman, K. J., Cook, E. H., & Lewis, G. F. (2014). Reducing auditory hypersensitivities in autistic spectrum disorder: Preliminary findings evaluating the Listening Project Protocol. *Frontiers in Pediatrics, 2*, 80.

Porges, S. W., Lewis, G. F. (2010). The polyvagal hypothesis: Common mechanisms mediating autonomic regulation, vocalizations and listening. *Handbook of Behavioral Neuroscience, 19*, 255–264.

Porges, S. W., Macellaio, M., Stanfill, S. D., McCue, K., Lewis, G. F., Harden, E. R., Handelman, M., Denver, J., Bazhenova, O. V., & Heilman, K. J. (2013). Respiratory sinus arrhythmia and auditory processing in autism: Modifiable deficits of an integrated social engagement system? *International Journal of Psychophysiology, 88*, 261–270.

Reuber, M. (2009). The etiology of psychogenic non-epileptic seizures: Toward a biopsychosocial model. *Neurologic Clinics, 27*, 909–924.

Rice, T., Grasso, J., Dembar, A., Caplan, O., Cohen, A., & Coffey, B. (2018). Guanfacine as a facilitator of recovery from conversion disorder in a young girl. *Child and Adolescent Psychopharmacology, 28*, 571–575.

Richter, D. W., Spyer, K. M. (1990). Cardiorespiratory control. In A. D. Loewy & K. M. Spyer (Eds.). *Central regulation of autonomic function* (pp. 189–207). Oxford University Press.

Slotema, C. W., Blom, J. D., Hoek, H. W., & Sommer, I. E. (2010). Should we expand the toolbox of psychiatric treatment methods to include repetitive transcranial magnetic stimulation (rTMS)? A meta-analysis of the efficacy of rTMS in psychiatric disorders. *Clinical Psychiatry, 71*, 873–884.

Stahl, S. M. (2021). *Essential psychopharmacology neuroscientific basis and practical applications* (5th ed.). Cambridge University Press.

Sullivan, C. R. P., Olsen, S., & Widge, A. S. (2021). Deep brain stimulation for psychiatric disorders: From focal brain targets to cognitive networks. *Neuroimage, 225*, 117515.

Sutherland, A. M., Nicholls, J., Bao, J., & Clarke, H. (2018). Overlaps in pharmacology for the treatment of chronic pain and mental health disorders. *Progress in Neuropsychopharmacol and Biological Psychiatry, 87*, 290–297.

Taib, S., Ory-Magne, F., Brefel-Courbon, C., Moreau, Y., Thalamas, C., Arbus, C., & Simonetta-Moreau, M. (2019). Repetitive transcranial magnetic stimulation for functional tremor: A randomized, double-blind, controlled study. *Movement Disorders, 34*, 1210–1219.

Velani, H., & Gledhill, J. (2021). The effectiveness of psychological interventions for children and adolescents with non-epileptic seizures. *Seizure, 93*, 20–31.

Vuilleumier, P., & Trost, W. (2015). Music and emotions: From enchantment to entrainment. *Annals of the New York Academy of Sciences, 1337*, 212–222.

Weiss, K. E., Steinman, K. J., Kodish, I., Sim, L., Yurs, S., Steggall, C., & Fobian, A. D. (2021). Functional neurological symptom disorder in children and adolescents within medical settings. *Clinical Psychology in Medical Settings, 28*, 90–101.

Wildenberg, J. C., Tyler, M. E., Danilov, Y. P., Kaczmarek, K. A., & Meyerand, M. E. (2011). Electrical tongue stimulation normalizes activity within the motion-sensitive brain network in balance-impaired subjects as revealed by group independent component analysis. *Brain Connectivity, 1*, 255–265.

Wildenberg, J. C., Tyler, M. E., Danilov, Y. P., Kaczmarek, K. A., & Meyerand, M. E. (2013). Altered connectivity of the balance processing network after tongue stimulation in balance-impaired individuals. *Brain Connectivity, 3*, 87–97.

Yap, J. Y. Y., Keatch, C., Lambert, E., Woods, W., Stoddart, P. R., & Kameneva, T. (2020). Critical review of transcutaneous vagus nerve stimulation: Challenges for translation to clinical practice. *Frontiers in Neuroscience, 14*, 284.

Yu, B., Funk, M., Hu, J., Wang, Q., & Feijs, L. (2018). Biofeedback for everyday stress management: A systematic review. *Frontiers in ICT, 5*, 23.

8. HEART RATE VARIABILITY: A PERSONAL JOURNEY

Akselrod, S., Gordon, D., Ubel, F. A., Shannon, D. C., Berger, A. C., & Cohen, R. J. (1981). Power spectrum analysis of heart rate fluctuation: A quantitative probe of beat-to-beat cardiovascular control. *Science, 213*(4504), 220–222.

Anrep, G., Pascual, W., & Rössler, R. (1936a). Respiratory variations of the heart rate-I—The reflex mechanism of the respiratory arrhythmia. Proceedings of the Royal Society of London. Series B-Biological Sciences, *119*(813), 191–217.

Anrep, G., Pascual, W., & Rössler, R. (1936b). Respiratory variations of the heart rate-II—the central mechanism of the respiratory arrhythmia and the inter-relations between the central and the reflex mechanisms. Proceedings of the Royal Society of London. Series B-Biological Sciences, *119*(813), 218–230.

Bainbridge, F. A. (1920). The relation between respiration and the pulse-rate. *Physiology, 54*(3), 192–202. https://doi.org/10.1113/jphysiol.1920.sp001918

Berntson, G. G., Bigger J. T., Eckberg, D. L., Grossman, P., Kaufmann, P. G., Malik, M., Haikady, N. N., Porges, S. W., Saul, J. P., Stone, P. H., & Van der Molen, M. W. (1997). Heart rate variability: Origins, methods, and inter-pretive caveats. *Psychophysiology, 34*, 623–648. https://doi.org/10.1111/j.1469-8986.1997.tb02140.x

Bohrer, R. E., & Porges, S. W. (1982). The application of time-series statistics to psychological research: An introduction. *Psychological statistics* (pp. 309–345). Lawrence Erlbaum Associates.

Brillinger, D. R. (1975). *Time series: Data analysis and theory.* Holt, Reinhart, and Winston.

Byrne, E. A., Fleg, J. L., Vaitkevicius, P. V., Wright, J., & Porges, S. W. (1996). Role of aerobic capacity and body mass index in the age-associated decline in heart rate variability. *Applied Physiology, 81*(2), 743–750. https://doi.org/10.1152/jappl.1996.81.2.743

Cabrera, A., Kolacz, J., Pailhez, G., Bulbena-Cabre, A., Bulbena, A., & Porges, S. W. (2017). Assessing body awareness and autonomic reactivity: Factor struc-ture and psychometric properties of the Body Perception Questionnaire-Short Form (BPQ-SF). *Int. J. Methods in Psychiatric Research, 27*(2), e1596. https://doi.org/10.1002/mpr.1596

Cabrera, A., Kolacz, J., Pailhez, G., Bulbena-Cabre, A., Bulbena, A., & Porges, S. W. (2018). Assessing body awareness and autonomic reactivity: Factor struc-ture and psychometric properties of the Body Perception Questionnaire-Short Form (BPQ-SF). *International Journal of Methods in Psychiatric Research, 27*(2), e1596.

Chess, G. F., Tam, R. M., & Calaresu, F. R. (1975). Influence of cardiac neural inputs on rhythmic variations of heart period in the cat. *American Journal of Physiology-Legacy Content, 228*(3), 775–780.

Dale, L. P., Cuffe, S. P., Kolacz, J., Leon, K. G., Bossemeyer Biernacki, N., Bhu-llar, A., Nix, E. J., & Porges, S. W. (2022). Increased autonomic reactivity and mental health difficulties in COVID-19 survivors: Implications for medical providers. *Frontiers in Psychiatry, 13.* https://doi.org/10.3389/fpsyt.2022.830926

Dale, L. P., Kolacz, J., Mazmanyan, J., Leon, K. G., Johonnot, K., Bossemeyer Biernacki, N., & Porges, S. W. (2022). Childhood maltreatment influences autonomic regulation and mental health in college students. *Frontiers in Psychiatry, 13.* https://doi.org/10.3389/fpsyt.2022.841749

Darrow, C. W., Jost, H., Solomon, A. P., & Mergener, J. C. (1942). Autonomic indications of excitatory and homeostatic effects on the electroencephalogram. *Psychology, 14*(1), 115–130. https://doi.org/10.1080/00223980.1942.9917115

Duffy, E. (1957). The psychological significance of the concept of "arousal" or "activation." *Psychological Review, 64*(5), 265–275. https://doi.org/10.1037/h0048837

Eckberg, D. L. (1997). Sympathovagal balance. *Circulation, 96*(9), 3224–3232. https://doi.org/10.1161/01.cir.96.9.3224

Eppinger, H., & Hess, L. (1915). VAGOTONIA. *Nervous and Mental Disease, 42*(4), 247–250. https://doi.org/10.1097/00005053-191504000-00004

Ershler, I. (1988). Willem Einthoven—the man. The string galvanometer electrocardiograph. *Archives of Internal Medicine, 148*(2), 453–455. https://doi.org/10.1001/archinte.148.2.453

Giardino, N. D., Glenny, R. W., Borson, S., & Chan, L. (2003). Respiratory sinus arrhythmia is associated with efficiency of pulmonary gas exchange in healthy humans. *American Journal of Physiology-Heart and Circulatory Physiology, 284*(5), H1585–H1591. https://doi.org/10.1152/ajpheart.00893.2002

Grippo, A. J., Lamb, D. G., Carter, C. S., & Porges, S. W. (2007). Cardiac regulation in the socially monogamous prairie vole. *Physiology & Behavior, 90*(2–3), 386–393. https://doi.org/10.1016/j.physbeh.2006.09.037

Hales, S. (1733). *Statical essays: Containing haemastaticks; or, An account of some hydraulick and hydrostatical experiments made on the blood and blood-vessels of animals.* W. Innys, R. Manby, and T. Woodward.

Hering, H. E. (1910). A functional test of heart vagi in man. *Menschen Munchen Medizinische Wochenschrift, 57,* 1931–1933.

Hon, E. H., & Lee, S. T. (1963). The electronic evaluation of the fetal heart rate. VIII. Patterns of preceding fetal death; further observations. *American Journal of Obstetrics and Gynecology, 87,* 814.

Kolacz, J., Dale, L. P., Nix, E. J., Roath, O. K., Lewis, G. F., & Porges, S. W. (2020). Adversity history predicts self-reported autonomic reactivity and mental health in US residents during the COVID-19 pandemic. *Frontiers in Psychiatry, 11.* https://doi.org/10.3389/fpsyt.2020.577728

Kolacz, J., Kovacic, K., Lewis, G. F., Sood, M. R., Aziz, Q., Roath, O. R., & Porges, S. W. (2021). Cardiac autonomic regulation and joint hypermobility in adolescents with functional abdominal pain disorders. *Neurogastroenterology & Motility, 33*(12). https://doi.org/10.1111/nmo.14165

Lewis, G. F., Furman, S. A., McCool, M. F., & Porges, S. W. (2012). Statistical strategies to quantify respiratory sinus arrhythmia: Are commonly used metrics equivalent? *Biological Psychology, 89*(2), 349–364. https://doi.org/10.1016/j.biopsycho.2011.11.009

Lindsley, D. B. (1951). Emotion. In S. S. Stevens (Ed.), *Handbook of experimental psychology* (pp. 473–516). Wiley.

Ludwig, C. (1847). Beitrage zur Kenntniss des Einflusses der Respiration sbewegungen auf den Blutlauf im Aortensysteme. *Muller's Archiv für Anatomie, Physiologie, und Wissenschaftliche Medicin,* 242–302.

MacKenzie, J. (1910). *Diseases of the heart* (2nd ed.). Oxford Medical Publications.

Malmo, R. B. (1959). Activation: A neuropsychological dimension. *Psychological Review, 66*(6), 367–386. https://doi.org/10.1037/h0047858

Porges, S. W. (1972). Heart rate variability and deceleration as indexes of reaction time. *Experimental Psychology, 92*(1), 103–110. https://doi.org/10.1037/h0032181

Porges, S. W. (1985a) Method and apparatus for evaluating rhythmic oscillations in aperiodic physiological response systems. Patent Number: US4,510,944. April 16, 1985.

Porges, S. W. (1985b). Respiratory sinus arrhythmia: An index of vagal tone. *Psychophysiology of Cardiovascular Control: Models, Methods, and Data,* 437–450.

Porges, S. W. (1986a). Data analysis in the frequency domain. In M. G. H. Coles, E. Donchin, & S. W. Porges (Eds.), *Psychophysiology: Systems, processes, and applications* (pp. 206–211). Guilford.

Porges, S. W. (1986b). Respiratory sinus arrhythmia: Physiological basis, quantitative methods, and clinical implications. In P. Grossman, K. H. L. Janssen, & D. Vaitl (Eds.), *Cardiorespiratory and cardiosomatic psychophysiology. NATO ASI Series* (vol. 114, pp. 101–115). Springer.

Porges, S. W. (1995). Orienting in a defensive world: Mammalian modifications of our evolutionary heritage. A polyvagal theory. *Psychophysiology, 32*(4), 301–318. https://doi.org/10.1111/j.1469-8986.1995.tb01213.x

Porges, S. W. (2007). The polyvagal perspective. *Biological Psychology, 74*(2), 116–143. https://doi.org/10.1016/j.biopsycho.2006.06.009

Porges, S. W. (2021). Polyvagal theory: A biobehavioral journey to sociality. *Comprehensive Psychoneuroendocrinology, 7,* 100069. https://doi.org/10.1016/j.cpnec.2021.100069

Porges, S. W. (2022). Polyvagal theory: A science of safety. *Frontiers in Integrative Neuroscience, 16.* https://doi.org/10.3389/fnint.2022.871227

Porges, S. W., & Bohrer, R. E. (1990). The analysis of periodic processes in psychophysiological research. In J. T. Cacioppo & L. G. Tassinary (Eds.), *Principles of psychophysiology: Physical, social, and inferential elements* (pp. 708–753). Cambridge University Press.

Porges, S. W., & Raskin, D. C. (1969). Respiratory and heart rate components of attention. *Experimental Psychology, 81*(3), 497–503. https://doi.org/10.1037/h0027921

Reed, S. F., Porges, S. W., & Newlin, D. B. (1999). Effect of alcohol on vagal regulation of cardiovascular function: Contributions of the polyvagal theory to the psychophysiology of alcohol. *Experimental and Clinical Psychopharmacology*, 7(4), 484–492. https://doi.org/10.1037/1064-1297.7.4.484

Richter, D. W., & Spyer, K. M. (1990). Cardiorespiratory control. In A. D. Loewy & K. M. Spyer (Eds.), *Central regulation of autonomic function* (pp. 189–207). Oxford University Press.

Wolf, S. (1967). The end of the rope: The role of the brain in cardiac death. *Canadian Medical Association Journal*, 97, 1022–1025.

Wundt, W. M., & Judd, C. H. (1902). Outlines of psychology. W. Engelmann.

Yerkes, R. M., & Dodson, J. D. (1908). The relation of strength of stimulus to rapidity of habit-formation. *Comparative Neurology and Psychology*, 18(5), 459–482. https://doi.org/10.1002/cne.920180503

9. EXPLORING VAGAL NERVE STIMULATION THROUGH THE LENS OF THE POLYVAGAL THEORY

Aasman, J., Mulder, G., & Mulder, L. (1987). Operator effort and the measurement of heart-rate variability. *Human Factors*, 29(2), 161–170. https://doi.org/10.1177/001872088702900204

American National Standards Institute. (1997). *American National Standard: Methods for calculation of the Speech Intelligibility Index*. Acoustical Society of America.

Arakaki, X., Arechavala, R. J., Choy, E. H., Bautista, J., Bliss, B., Molloy, C., & Kloner, R. A. (2023). The connection between heart rate variability (HRV), neurological health, and cognition: A literature review. *Frontiers in Neuroscience*, 17, 1055445.

Asala, S., & Bower, A. J. (1986). An electron microscope study of vagus nerve composition in the ferret. *Anatomy and Embryology*, 175(2), 247–253. https://doi.org/10.1007/bf00389602

Berthoud, H., & Neuhuber, W. (2000). Functional and chemical anatomy of the afferent vagal system. *Autonomic Neuroscience: Basic and Clinical*, 85(1–3), 1–17. https://doi.org/10.1016/s1566-0702(00)00215-0

Borg, E., & Sa, C. (1989). The middle-ear muscles. *Scientific American*, 261(2), 74–80. https://doi.org/10.1038/scientificamerican0889-74

Brown, J. W. (1974). Prenatal development of the human chief sensory trigeminal nucleus. *Comparative Neurology*, 156(3), 307–335. https://doi.org/10.1002/cne.901560304

Burge, H. (1970). A vagal paradox. *British Medical Journal*, 4(5730), 302–303. https://doi.org/10.1136/bmj.4.5730.302-a

Carter, C. S. (2022). Oxytocin and love: Myths, metaphors and mysteries. *Comprehensive Psychoneuroendocrinology*, 9, 100107. https://doi.org/10.1016/j.cpnec.2021.100107

Craig, A. D. (2005). Forebrain emotional asymmetry: A neuroanatomical basis? *Trends in Cognitive Sciences*, 9(12), 566–571. https://doi.org/10.1016/j.tics.2005.10.005

Ellrich, J. (2011). Transcutaneous vagus nerve stimulation. *European Neurological Review*, 6(4), 254. https://doi.org/10.17925/enr.2011.06.04.254

Foley, J. O., & DuBois, F. S. (1937). Quantitative studies of the vagus nerve in the cat. I. The ratio of sensory to motor fibers. *Comparative Neurology*, 67(1), 49–67. https://doi.org/10.1002/cne.900670104

Frangos, E., Ellrich, J., & Komisaruk, B. R. (2015). Non-invasive access to the vagus nerve central projections via electrical stimulation of the external ear: FMRI evidence in humans. *Brain Stimulation*, 8(3), 624–636. https://doi.org/10.1016/j.brs.2014.11.018

George, M. S., Sackeim, H. A., Rush, A. J., Marangell, L. B., Nahas, Z., Husain, M. M., Lisanby, S. H., Burt, T., Goldman, J., & Ballenger, J. C. (2000). Vagus nerve stimulation: A new tool for brain research and therapy. *Biological Psychiatry*, 47(4), 287–295. https://doi.org/10.1016/s0006-3223(99)00308-x

Gourine, A. V., Machhada, A., Trapp, S., & Spyer, K. M. (2016). Cardiac vagal preganglionic neurones: An update. *Autonomic Neuroscience: Basic and Clinical*, 199, 24–28. https://doi.org/10.1016/j.autneu.2016.06.003

Humphrey, T. (1978). Function of the nervous system during prenatal life. In U. Stave (Ed.), *Peritnatal physiology*. Springer eBooks (pp. 651–683). https://doi.org/10.1007/978-1-4684-2316-7_30

Jänig, W. (1996). Neurobiology of visceral afferent neurons: Neuroanatomy, functions, organ regulations and sensations. *Biological Psychology*, 42(1–2), 29–51. https://doi.org/10.1016/0301-0511(95)05145-7

Kaniusas, E., Kampusch, S., & Szeles, J. C. (2015, April). Depth profiles of the peripheral blood oxygenation in diabetics and healthy subjects in response to auricular electrical stimulation: Auricular vagus nerve stimulation as a potential treatment for chronic wounds. In *2015 IEEE Sensors Applications Symposium (SAS)* (pp. 1–6). IEEE.

Kolacz, J., Kovacic, K., Dang, L. C., Li, B. U., Lewis, G. F., & Porges, S. W. (2023). Cardiac vagal regulation is impeded in children with cyclic vomiting syndrome. *American Journal of Gastroenterology*, 118(7), 1268–1275. https://doi.org/10.14309/ajg.0000000000002207

Kolacz, J., Kovacic, K., Lewis, G. F., Sood, M. R., Aziz, Q., Roath, O. R., & Porges, S. W. (2021). Cardiac autonomic regulation and joint hypermobility in adolescents with functional abdominal pain disorders. *Neurogastroenterology and Motility*, 33(12). https://doi.org/10.1111/nmo.14165

Kolacz, J., Lewis, G. F., & Porges, S. W. (2018). The integration of vocal communication and biobehavioral state regulation in mammals: A polyvagal hypothesis. In *Handbook of Behavioral Neuroscience*, 25 (pp. 23–34). https://doi.org/10.1016/b978-0-12-809600-0.00003-2

Kolacz, J., & Porges, S. W. (2018). Chronic diffuse pain and functional gastrointestinal disorders after traumatic stress: Pathophysiology through a polyvagal perspective. *Frontiers in Medicine, 5.* https://doi.org/10.3389/fmed.2018.00145

Kolacz, J., Kovacic, K., & Porges, S. W. (2019). Traumatic stress and the autonomic brain-gut connection in development: Polyvagal theory as an integrative framework for psychosocial and gastrointestinal pathology. *Developmental Psychobiology. 61*(5). https://doi.org/10.1002/dev.21852

Kovacic, K., Hainsworth, K. R., Sood, M. R., Chelimsky, G., Unteutsch, R., Nugent, M., Simpson, P., & Miranda, A. (2017). Neurostimulation for abdominal pain-related functional gastrointestinal disorders in adolescents: A randomised, double-blind, sham-controlled trial. *The Lancet Gastroenterology & Hepatology, 2*(10), 727–737. https://doi.org/10.1016/s2468-1253(17)30253-4

Kovacic, K., Kolacz, J., Lewis, G. F., & Porges, S. W. (2020). Impaired vagal efficiency predicts auricular neurostimulation response in adolescent functional abdominal pain disorders. *The American Journal of Gastroenterology, 115*(9), 1534–1538. https://doi.org/10.14309/ajg.0000000000000753

Loo, S. K., Salgari, G. C., Ellis, A. J., Cowen, J., Dillon, A., & McGough, J. J. (2021). Trigeminal nerve stimulation for attention-deficit/hyperactivity disorder: Cognitive and electroencephalographic predictors of treatment response. *American Academy of Child and Adolescent Psychiatry, 60*(7), 856–864.e1. https://doi.org/10.1016/j.jaac.2020.09.021

Marangell, L. B., Rush, A. J., George, M. S., Sackeim, H. A., Johnson, C. R., Husain, M. M., Nahas, Z., & Lisanby, S. H. (2002). Vagus nerve stimulation (VNS) for major depressive episodes: One year outcomes. *Biological Psychiatry, 51*(4), 280–287. https://doi.org/10.1016/s0006-3223(01)01343-9

Murphy, J. V., Wheless, J. W., & Schmoll, C. (2000). Left vagal nerve stimulation in six patients with hypothalamic hamartomas. *Pediatric Neurology, 23*(2), 167–168. https://doi.org/10.1016/s0887-8994(00)00170-3

Mulcahy, J. S., Larsson, D. E. O., Garfinkel, S. N., & Critchley, H. (2019). Heart rate variability as a biomarker in health and affective disorders: A perspective on neuroimaging studies. *NeuroImage, 202,* 116072. https://doi.org/10.1016/j.neuroimage.2019.116072

Pereyra, P. M., Zhang, W., Schmidt, M., & Becker, L. E. (1992). Development of myelinated and unmyelinated fibers of human vagus nerve during the first year of life. *Neurological Sciences, 110*(1–2), 107–113. https://doi.org/10.1016/0022-510x(92)90016-e

Porges, S. W. (1995). Orienting in a defensive world: Mammalian modifications of our evolutionary heritage. A polyvagal theory. *Psychophysiology, 32*(4), 301–318. https://doi.org/10.1111/j.1469-8986.1995.tb01213.x

Porges, S. W. (1998). Love: An emergent property of the mammalian autonomic nervous system. *Psychoneuroendocrinology, 23*(8), 837–861. https://doi.org/10.1016/s0306-4530(98)00057-2

Porges, S. W. (2001). The polyvagal theory: Phylogenetic substrates of a social nervous system. *International Journal of Psychophysiology*, 42(2), 123–146. https://doi.org/10.1016/s0167-8760(01)00162-3

Porges, S. W. (2005). The vagus: A mediator of behavioral and physiologic features associated with autism. In M. L. Bauman & T. L. Kemper (Eds.), *The neurobiology of autism* (pp. 65–78). Johns Hopkins University Press. https://psycnet.apa.org/record/2014-19910-006

Porges, S. W. (2007). The polyvagal perspective. *Biological Psychology*, 74(2), 116–143. https://doi.org/10.1016/j.biopsycho.2006.06.009

Porges, S. W. (2009). The polyvagal theory: New insights into adaptive reactions of the autonomic nervous system. *Cleveland Clinic Journal of Medicine*, 76(4 suppl 2), S86–S90. https://doi.org/10.3949/ccjm.76.s2.17

Porges, S. W. (2011). *The polyvagal theory: Neurophysiological foundations of emotions, attachment, communication, and self-regulation*. W. W. Norton.

Porges, S. W., Bazhenova, O. V., Bal, E., Carlson, N. N., Sorokin, Y., Heilman, K. J., Cook, E. H., & Lewis, G. F. (2014). Reducing auditory hypersensitivities in autistic spectrum disorder: Preliminary findings evaluating the listening project protocol. *Frontiers in Pediatrics*, 2. https://doi.org/10.3389/fped.2014.00080

Porges, S. W., & Lewis, G. F. (2010). The polyvagal hypothesis: Common mechanisms mediating autonomic regulation, vocalizations and listening. *Handbook of Behavioral Neuroscience*, 19, 255–264. https://doi.org/10.1016/b978-0-12-374593-4.00025-5

Porges, S. W., & Lipsitt, L. P. (1993). Neonatal responsivity to gustatory stimulation: The gustatory-vagal hypothesis. *Infant Behavior & Development*, 16(4), 487–494. https://doi.org/10.1016/0163-6383(93)80006-t

Porges, S. W., Macellaio, M., Stanfill, S. D., McCue, K., Lewis, G. F., Harden, E., Handelman, M., Denver, J. W., Bazhenova, O. V., & Heilman, K. J. (2013). Respiratory sinus arrhythmia and auditory processing in autism: Modifiable deficits of an integrated social engagement system? *International Journal of Psychophysiology*, 88(3), 261–270. https://doi.org/10.1016/j.ijpsycho.2012.11.009

Porges, S. W. (2018). *U.S. Patent No. 10,029,068*. Washington, DC: U.S. Patent and Trademark Office.

Porges, S. W. (2022). Polyvagal theory: A science of safety. *Frontiers in Integrative Neuroscience*, 16. https://doi.org/10.3389/fnint.2022.871227

Reed, S. F., Ohel, G., David, R., & Porges, S. W. (1999). A neural explanation of fetal heart rate patterns: A test of the polyvagal theory. *Developmental Psychobiology*, 35(2), 108–118. https://doi.org/10.1002/(sici)1098-2302(199909)35:2

Sandberg, S., Paton, J. Y., Ahola, S., McCann, D. C., McGuinness, D., Hillary, C., & Oja, H. (2000). The role of acute and chronic stress in asthma attacks in children. *The Lancet*, 356(9234), 982–987. https://doi.org/10.1016/s0140-6736(00)02715-x

Sanossian, N., & Haut, S. R. (2002). Chronic diarrhea associated with vagal nerve stimulation. *Neurology*, 58(2), 330. https://doi.org/10.1212/wnl.58.2 .330

Steyn, E., Mohamed, Z., & Husselman, C. (2013). Non-invasive vagus nerve stimulation for the treatment of acute asthma exacerbations—results from an initial case series. *International Journal of Emergency Medicine*, 6(1). https://doi.org/10.1186/1865-1380-6-7

Thayer, J. F., & Lane, R. D. (2000). A model of neurovisceral integration in emotion regulation and dysregulation. *Affective Disorders*, 61(3), 201–216. https://doi.org/10.1016/s0165-0327(00)00338-4

Widemar, L., Hellström, S., Schultzberg, M., & Le, S. (1985). Autonomic innervation of the tympanic membrane an immunocytochemical and histofluorescence study. *Acta Oto-laryngologica*, 58–65. https://doi.org/10.3109 /00016488509108588

10. CARDIAC VAGAL TONE: A NEUROPHYSIOLOGICAL MECHANISM THAT EVOLVED IN MAMMALS TO DAMPEN THREAT REACTIONS AND PROMOTE SOCIALITY

Fanning, J., Silfer, J. L., Liu, H., Gauvin, L., Heilman, K. J., Porges, S. W., & Rejeski, W. J. (2020). Relationships between respiratory sinus arrhythmia and stress in college students. *Behavioral Medicine*, 43, 308–317.

Hage, B., Britton, B., Daniels, D., Heilman, K., Porges, S. W., & Halaris, A. (2019). Low cardiac vagal tone index by heart rate variability differentiates bipolar from major depression. *World Journal of Biological Psychiatry*, 20, 359–367.

Jackson, J. H. (1884). The Croonian lectures on evolution and dissolution of the nervous system. *British Medical Journal*, 1, 703–707.

Kolacz, J., & Porges, S. W. (2018). Chronic diffuse pain and functional gastrointestinal disorders after traumatic stress: Pathophysiology through a polyvagal perspective. *Frontiers in Medicine*, 5, 145.

Lewis, G. F., Furman, S. A., McCool, M. F., & Porges, S. W. (2012). Statistical strategies to quantify respiratory sinus arrhythmia: Are commonly used metrics equivalent? *Biological Psychology*, 89, 349–364.

Porges, S. W. (1995). Orienting in a defensive world: Mammalian modifications of our evolutionary heritage. A polyvagal theory. *Psychophysiology*, 32, 301–318.

Porges, S. W. (2003). Social engagement and attachment: A phylogenetic perspective. *Annals of the New York Academy of Sciences*, 1008, 31–47.

Porges, S. W., Lewis, G. F. (2010). The polyvagal hypothesis: Common mechanisms mediating autonomic regulation, vocalizations and listening. *Handbook of Behavioral Neuroscience*, 19, 255–264.

Porges, S. W., Macellaio, M., Stanfill, S. D., McCue, K., Lewis, G. F., Harden,

E. R., Handelman, M., Denver, J., Bazhenova, O. V., & Heilman, K. J. (2013). Respiratory sinus arrhythmia and auditory processing in autism: Modifiable deficits of an integrated social engagement system? *International Journal of Psychophysiology*, 88, 261–270.

11. EHLERS–DANLOS SYNDROME THROUGH THE LENS OF THE POLYVAGAL THEORY: A PREFACE TO *TRANSFORMING EHLERS-DANLOS SYNDROME*

Cabrera, A., Kolacz, J., Pailhez, G., Bulbena-Cabre, A., Bulbena, A., & Porges, S. W. (2018). Assessing body awareness and autonomic reactivity: Factor structure and psychometric properties of the Body Perception Questionnaire-Short Form (BPQ-SF). *International journal of methods in psychiatric research*, 27(2), e1596

Kolacz, J., Kovacic, K., Lewis, G. F., Sood, M. R., Aziz, Q., Roath, O. R., & Porges, S. W. (2021). Cardiac autonomic regulation and joint hypermobility in adolescents with functional abdominal pain disorders. *Neurogastroenterology & Motility*, 33(12), e14165.

Porges, S. W., Davila, M. I., Lewis, G. F., Kolacz, J., Okonmah-Obazee, S., Hane, A. A., Kwon, K. Y., Ludwig, R. J., Myers, M. M., & Welch, M. G. (2019). Autonomic regulation of preterm infants is enhanced by Family Nurture Intervention. *Developmental Psychobiology*, 61(6), 942–952.

Reed, S. F., Porges, S. W., & Newlin, D. B. (1999). Effect of alcohol on vagal regulation of cardiovascular function: Contributions of the polyvagal theory to the psychophysiology of alcohol. *Experimental and Clinical Psychopharmacology*, 7(4), 484.

Williamson, J. B., Lewis, G., Grippo, A. J., Lamb, D., Harden, E., Handleman, M., Lebow, J., Carter, C. S., & Porges, S. W. (2010). Autonomic predictors of recovery following surgery: A comparative study. *Autonomic Neuroscience*, 156(1–2), 60–66.

12. ADDICTION: A POLYVAGAL PERSPECTIVE

Carliner, H., Keyes, K. M., McLaughlin, K. A., Meyers, J. L., Dunn, E. C., & Martins, S. S. (2016). Childhood trauma and illicit drug use in adolescence: A population-based national comorbidity survey replication- adolescent supplement study.*American Academy of Child and Adolescent Psychiatry*, 55(8), 701–708.

Enoch, M. A. (2011). The role of early life stress as a predictor for alcohol and drug dependence. *Psychopharmacology*, 214(1), 17–31.

Felitti, V. J. (2006). The origins of addiction. *Evidence from adverse childhood experiences.* [https://nijc.org/pdfs/Subject%20Matter%20Articles/Drugs%20and %20Alc/ACE%20Study%20-%20OriginsofAddiction.pdf]

Porges, S. W. (1995). Orienting in a defensive world: Mammalian modifications of our evolutionary heritage. A polyvagal theory. *Psychophysiology*, 32(4), 301–318.

13. AUTISM THROUGH THE LENS OF THE POLYVAGAL THEORY

Bal, E., Harden, E., Lamb, D., Van Hecke, A. V., Denver, J. W., & Porges, S. W. (2010). Emotion recognition in children with autism spectrum disorders: Relations to eye gaze and autonomic state. *Autism and Developmental Disorders*, 40, 358–370.

Bauman, M. L., & Kemper, T. L. (Eds.). (2005). *The neurobiology of autism*. Johns Hopkins University Press.

Heilman, K. J., Heinrich, S., Achermann, M., Nix, E., & Kyuchukov, H. (2023). Effects of the Safe and Sound Protocol (SSP) on sensory processing, digestive function and selective eating in children and adults with autism: A prospective single-arm study. *Developmental Disabilities*, 28(1).

Kolacz, J., Kovacic, K. K., & Porges, S. W. (2019). Traumatic stress and the autonomic brain-gut connection in development: Polyvagal theory as an integrative framework for psychosocial and gastrointestinal pathology. *Developmental Psychobiology*, 61(5), 796–809.

Lord, C., Storoschuk, S., Rutter, M., & Pickles, A. (1993). Using the ADI-R to diagnose autism in preschool children. *Infant Mental Health*, 14(3), 234–252.

Patriquin, M. A., Scarpa, A., Friedman, B. H., & Porges, S. W. (2013). Respiratory sinus arrhythmia: A marker for positive social functioning and receptive language skills in children with autism spectrum disorders. *Developmental Psychobiology*, 55(2), 101–112.

Porges, S. W. (1976). Peripheral and neurochemical parallels of psychopathology: A psychophysiological model relating autonomic imbalance to hyperactivity, psychopathy, and autism. *Advances in Child Development and Behavior*, 11, 35–65.

Porges, S. W. (1995). Orienting in a defensive world: Mammalian modifications of our evolutionary heritage. A polyvagal theory. *Psychophysiology*, 32(4), 301–318.

Porges, S. W. (1998). Love: An emergent property of the mammalian autonomic nervous system. *Psychoneuroendocrinology*, 23(8), 837–861.

Porges, S. W. (2005). *The vagus: A mediator of behavioral and physiologic features associated with autism*. In M. L. Bauman & T. L. Kemper (Eds.), *The neurobiology of autism* (pp. 65–78). Johns Hopkins University Press.

Porges, S. W. (2022). Polyvagal theory: A science of safety. *Frontiers in Integrative Neuroscience*, 16, 27.

Porges, S. W., Bazhenova, O. V., Bal, E., Carlson, N., Sorokin, Y., Heilman, K. J., Cook, E. H., & Lewis, G. F. (2014). Reducing auditory hypersensitivities in autistic spectrum disorder: Preliminary findings evaluating the listening project protocol. *Frontiers in Pediatrics*, 2, 80.

Porges, S. W., Macellaio, M., Stanfill, S. D., McCue, K., Lewis, G. F., Harden, E. R., Handelman, M., Denver, J., Bazhenova, O. V., & Heilman, K. J. (2013). Respiratory sinus arrhythmia and auditory processing in autism: Modifiable deficits of an integrated social engagement system? *Int. J. Psychophysiology*, 88(3), 261–270.

Van Hecke, A. V., Lebow, J., Bal, E., Lamb, D., Harden, E., Kramer, A., Denver, J., Bazhenova, O. V., & Porges, S. W. (2009). Electroencephalogram and heart rate regulation to familiar and unfamiliar people in children with autism spectrum disorders. *Child Development*, 80(4), 1118–1133.

19. WHAT PUTIN'S PHYSIOLOGICAL STATE TELLS US: HOW THE PHYSIOLOGICAL STATE OF A LEADER CAN IMPACT THE WORLD

Amanpour, C. (2022, February 28). Interview with former campaign adviser to Emmanuel Macron Francois Heisbourg. CNN. https://transcripts.cnn.com/show/ampr/date/2022-02-28/segment/01

CNN. (2022, February 27). Clapper: Putin is "unhinged" and has finger on nuclear trigger. CNN. www.cnn.com/videos/politics/2022/02/27/9a-panel-full.cnn

Cohen, Z., Lillis, K. B., & Perez, E. (2022, March 1). US intelligence agencies make understanding Vladimir Putin's state of mind a top priority. CNN. www.cnn.com/2022/03/01/politics/us-intelligence-putin-state-of-mind/index.html

Porges, S. W. (2021). Polyvagal theory: A biobehavioral journey to sociality. *Comprehensive Psychoneuroendocrinology*, 7, 100069.

Porges, S. W. (2023, February). *Polyvagal theory: Summary, premises & current status*. Polyvagal Institute. www.polyvagalinstitute.org/background

Rustamova, F. (2022, March 6). "They're carefully enunciating the word cluster-f*ck." *Faridaily*. https://faridaily.substack.com/p/theyre-carefully-enunciating-the

Zakaria, F. [@FareedZakaria]. (2022, February 27). *Putin seems to have "gone off the rails," says fmr US Defense Sec. & CIA Dir. Robert Gates*. [Tweet]. Twitter. https://twitter.com/FareedZakaria/status/1498001342320812037

APPENDIX: THE POLYVAGAL PERSPECTIVE

Ahern, G. L., Sollers, J. J., Lane, R. D., Labiner, D. M., Herring, A. M., Weinand, M. E., Hutzler, R., & Thayer, J. F. (2001). Heart rate and heart rate variability changes in the intracarotid sodium amobarbital test. *Epilepsia*, 42(7), 912–921.

Akselrod, S., Gordon, D., Ubel, F. A., Shannon, D. C., Barger, A. C., & Cohen, R. J. (1981). Power spectrum analysis of heart rate fluction: A quantitative probe of beat to beat cardiovascular control. *Science*, 213, 220–222.

Berntson, G. G., Cacioppo, J. T., & Quigley, K. S. (1994). Autonomic cardiac control. I. Estimation and validation from pharmacological blockades. *Psychophysiology*, 31, 572–585.

Berntson, G. G., Bigger, J. T., Eckberg, D. L., Grossman, P. G., Kaufmann, M., Malik, H. N., Nagaraja, H. N., Porges, S. W., Saul, J. P., Stone, P. H., & van der Molen, M. W. (1997). Heart rate variability: Origins, methods, and interpretive caveats. *Psychophysiology, 34,* 623–648.

Black, A. H., & Lang, W. M. (1964). Cardiac conditioning and skeletal responding in curarized dogs. *Psychological Review, 71,* 80–95.

Blass, E. M., & Watt, L. B., 1999. Suckling and sucrose-induced analgesia in human newborns. *Pain, 83,* 611–623.

Canli, T., Desmond, J. E., Zhao, Z., Glover, G., & Gabrieli, J. D. E. (1998). Hemispheric asymmetry for emotional stimuli detected with fMRI. *Neuroreport, 9,* 3233–3239.

Cheng, Z., & Powley, T. L. (2000). Nucleus ambiguus projections to cardiac ganglia of rat atria: An anterograde tracing study. *Comparative Neurology, 424,* 588–606.

Craig, A. D. (2005). Forebrain emotional asymmetry: A neuroanatomical basis? *Trends in Cognitive Sciences, 9,* 566–571.

Denver, J. W., Reed, S. F., & Porges, S. W. (2007). Methodological issues in the quantification of respiratory sinus arrhythmia. *Biological Psychology, 74*(2), 286–294.

Eckberg, D. L. (1997). Sympathovagal balance: A critical appraisal. *Circulation, 96,* 3224–3232.

Eckberg, D. L. (2003). The human respiratory gate. *Physiology, 548,* 339–352.

Fox, N. A. (1991). If it's not left, it's right: Electroencephalography asymmetry and the development of emotion. *American Psychologist, 46,* 863–872.

Graham, F. K., & Clifton, R. K. (1966). Heart rate change as a component of the orienting response. *Psychological Bulletin, 65,* 305–320.

Grossman, P., & Svebak, S. (1987). Respiratory sinus arrhythmia as an index of parasympathetic cardiac control during active coping. *Psychophysiology, 24,* 228–235.

Grossman, P., Van Beek, J., & Wientjes, C. (1990). A comparison of three quantification methods for estimation of respiratory sinus arrhythmia. *Psychophysiology, 27*(6), 702–714.

Houle, M. S., & Billman, G. E. (1999). Low-frequency component of the heart rate variability spectrum: A poor marker of sympathetic activity. *American Journal of Physiology, 276,* H215–H223.

Jackson, J. C., Kantowitz, S. R., & Graham, F. K. (1971). Can newborns show cardiac orienting? *Child Development, 42,* 107–121.

Lewis, G. F., Furman, S. A., McCool, M. F., & Porges, S. W. (2012). Statistical strategies to quantify respiratory sinus arrhythmia: are commonly used metrics equivalent? *Biological Psychology, 89*(2), 349–364.

Malliani, A., Pagani, M., Lombardi, F., & Cerutti, S. (1991). Cardiovascular neural regulation explored in the frequency domain. *Circulation, 84,* 1482–1492.

Mendelowitz, D. (1996). Firing properties of identified parasympathetic cardiac neurons in nucleus ambiguus. *American Journal of Physiology, 271,* H2609–H2614.

Mendelowitz, D., & Kunze, D. L. (1991). Identification and dissociation of cardiovascular neurons from the medulla for patch clamp analysis. *Neuroscience Letters, 132,* 217–221.

Miller, N. E. (1978). Biofeedback and visceral learning. *Annual Review of Psychology, 29,* 373–404.

Neff, R. A., Humphrey, J., Mihalevich, M., & Mendelowitz, D. (1998). Nicotine enhances presynaptic and postsynaptic glutamatergic neurotransmission to activate cardiac parasympathetic neurons. *Circulation Research,* 83, 1241–1247.

Neff, R. A., Mihalevich, M., & Mendelowitz, D. (1998). Stimulation of NTS activates NMDA and non-NMDA receptors in rat cardiac vagal neurons in the nucleus ambiguus. *Brain Research, 792,* 277–282.

Neff, R. A., Wang, J., Baxi, S., Evans, C., & Mendelowitz, D. (2003). Respiratory sinus arrhythmia: Endogenous activation of nicotinic receptors mediates respiratory modulation of brainstem cardioinhibitory parasympathetic neurons. *Circulation Research, 93,* 565–572.

Noesselt, T., Driver, J., Heinze, H. J., & Dolan, R. (2005). Asymmetrical activation in the human brain during processing of fearful faces. *Current Biology,* 15, 424–429.

Obrist, P. A. (1981). *Cardiovascular sychophysiology.* Plenum Press.

Pagani, M., Lombardi, F., Guzzetti, S., Rimoldi, O., Furlan, R., Pizzinelli, P., Sandrone, G., Malfatto, G., Dell'Orto, S., & Piccaluga, E. (1986). Power spectral analysis of heart rate and arterial pressure variabilities as a marker of sympathovagal interaction in man and conscious dog. *Circulation Research, 59,* 178–193.

Phillips, M. L., Drevets, W. C., Rauch, S. L., & Lane, R. (2003a). Neurobiology of emotion perception. I. The neural basis of normal emotion perception. *Biological Psychiatry, 54,* 504–514.

Phillips, M.L., Drevets, W. C., Rauch, S. L., & Lane, R. (2003b). Neurobiology of emotion perception. II. Implications for major psychiatric disorders. *Biological Psychiatry, 54,* 515–528.

Porges, S. W. (1995). Orienting in a defensive world: Mammalian modifications of our evolutionary heritage: A polyvagal theory. *Psychophysiology,* 32, 301–318.

Porges, S. W. (2001a). The polyvagal theory: Phylogenetic substrates of a social nervous system. *International Journal of Psychophysiology, 42,* 123–146.

Porges, S. W. (2001b). Is there a major stress system at the periphery other than the adrenals? In D. M. Broom (Ed.), *Dahlem workshop on coping with challenge: Welfare in animals including humans* (pp. 135–149). Dahlem University Press.

Porges, S. W., & Bohrer, R. E. (1990). Analyses of periodic processes in psychophysiological research. In J. T. Cacioppo & L. G. Tassinary (Eds.), *Principles of psychophysiology: Physical, social, and inferential elements* (pp. 708–753). Cambridge University Press.

Porges, S. W., & Byrne, E.A. (1992). Research methods for measurement of heart rate and respiration. *Biological Psychology, 34,* 93–130.

Porges, S. W., Doussard-Roosevelt, J. A., & Maiti, A. K. (1994). Vagal tone and the physiological regulation of emotion. In N. A. Fox (Ed.), *Emotion regulation: Behavioral and biological considerations* [vol. 59 (2–3, Serial no. 240), pp. 167–186]. Monograph of the Society for Research in Child Development.

Reed, S. F., Ohel, G., David, R., & Porges, S. W. (1999). A neural explanation of fetal heart rate patterns: A test of the polyvagal theory. *Developmental Psychobiology, 35,* 108–118.

Riniolo, T. C., & Porges, S. W. (1997). Inferential and descriptive influences on measures of respiratory sinus arrhythmia: Sampling rate, r-wave trigger accuracy, and variance estimates. *Psychophysiology, 34,* 613–621.

Roberts, L. E. (1978). Operant conditioning of autonomic responses: One perspective on the curare experiments. In G. E. Schwartz & D. Shapiro (Eds.), *Consciousness and self-regulation: Advances in research and theory* (vol. 2). Plenum Press.

Sargunaraj, D., Lehrer, P. M., Hochron, S. M., Rausch, L., Edelberg, R., & Porges, S. W. (1996). Cardiac rhythm effects of .125 Hz paced breathing through a resistive load: Implications for paced breathing therapy and the polyvagal theory. *Biofeedback and Self-Regulation, 21,* 131–147.

Smith, K. (1967). Conditioning as an artifact. In G. A. Kimble (Ed.), *Hilgard and Marquis's foundation of conditioning and learning.* Appleton-Century-Crofts.

Strauss-Blache, G., Moser, M., Voica, M., McLeod, Klammer, N., & Marktl, W. (2000). Relative timing of inspiration and expiration affects respiratory sinus arrhythmia. *Clinical and Experimental Pharmacology and Physiology, 27,* 601–606.

Task Force of the European Society of Cardiology and the North American Society of Pacing and Electrophysiology, 1996. Heart rate variability: Standards of measurement, physiological interpretation, and clinical use. *Circulation, 93,* 1043–1065.

Thayer, J. F., & Lane, R. D. (2000). A model of neurovisceral integration in emotion regulation and dysregulation. *Affective Disorders, 61,* 201–216.

Wang, F. B., Holst, M. C., & Powley, T. L. (1995). The ratio of pre- to postganglionic neurons and related issues in the autonomic nervous system. *Brain Research, Brain Research Reviews, 21,* 93–115.

Wang, J., Irnaten, M., Neff, R. A., Venkatean, P., Evans, C., Loewy, A. D., Mettenleiter, T. C., & Mendelowitz, D. (2001). Synaptic and neurotransmitter activation of cardiac vagal neurons in the nucleus ambiguus. *Annals of the New York Academy of Sciences, 940,* 237–246.

Index

autonomic nervous system (ANS) *(continued)*
limited, 118–19
PVT in linking sociality to, 51–52
regulation of. *see* autonomic nervous system (ANS) regulation
autonomic nervous system (ANS) regulation
antagonistic vs. hierarchical, 7–8
BPQ-SF in measuring, 25
evolution in repurposing, 45–48
from phylogenetic perspective, 67–69
sociality dependence on, 43
in supporting sociality, 45–48
autonomic reactivity
autism, 204
hierarchy, 8
self-reported, 24–25
autonomic state
addictive substances and behaviors in changing, 198–99
feelings of safety related to, 63–65
impact of COVID-19 pandemic on mental health influenced by, 63
as intervening variable, 27t, 29, 52
neural regulation of, 223–24
sociality related to, 64–65
autonomic state of defense
sensitive patients locked in, 114

B
Bailey, R., 103
Bainbridge, F. A., 156
Beckman Dynograph, 150–51, 151f
behavior(s)
autonomic state impact on, 198–99
feelings vs., 64
Beighton scores
Ehlers-Danlos Syndrome (EDS) and, 193
Bernard, C., 118, 119
B-fibers, 174
Biofeedback Research Society, 156
biological imperative(s)
connectedness as, 90–91
defined, 90
described, 89–90
Biological Psychology, xiv, 37
biology
understanding, 86–87
blogs, 213–42
Body Perception Questionnaire (BPQ), 192–93

Body Perception Questionnaire Short Form (BPQ-SF), 25
Bohrer, R. E., 158
Bonanno, G. A., 109–11
Bonanno's theory, 109
bottom-up mechanisms
neuroception and, 26
BPQ. *see* Body Perception Questionnaire (BPQ)
BPQ-SF. *see* Body Perception Questionnaire Short Form (BPQ-SF)
bradycardia
life-threatening, 19
brain
conscious, 114–15
brainstem source nuclei
of social engagement system, 171f, 172
Brosschot, J. F., 75
Bulbena-Cabré, A., 192
Burge, H., 7

C
calm
anatomy of, 232–35
Cannon, W.B., 111, 119
Cantor, C., 104–5
cardiac vagal tone (CVT), 187–90, 250
defined, 257
described, 259
RSA as measure of, 256–59
cardioinhibitory neurons, 27t, 32
ventral migration of, 13–15, 16f
"Cardiorespiratory Interactions Previously Identified as Mammalian Are Present in the Primitive Lungfish," 36
cardiotachometer, 151
Cartesian dualism, 72–73, 86–87
cause-and-effect model, 164
CBT. *see* cognitive behavioral therapy (CBT)
C-fibers, 174
Chess, G.F., 158
chronic stress
dissolution in explaining response to, 48–49
Circulation, 257
Clapper, J., 240
cognitive behavioral therapy (CBT)
breathing components of, 235
comparative neuroanatomy
in evolutionary transitions, 11–13
compassion
described, 207–8

About the Author

Stephen W. Porges, PhD, holds positions as a Distinguished University Scientist at Indiana University, professor of psychiatry at the University of North Carolina, and professor emeritus at the University of Illinois at Chicago and the University of Maryland. He has published more than 400 peer-reviewed scientific papers that have been cited in more than 55,000 peer-reviewed papers. He holds several patents involved in monitoring and regulating autonomic state. He is the creator of Polyvagal Theory and the Safe and Sound Protocol™, an innovative acoustic intervention. In collaboration with Anthony Gorry, he cocreated Polyvagal Music™ and the Rest and Restore Protocol™. He has authored *The Polyvagal Theory, The Pocket Guide to the Polyvagal Theory,* and *Polyvagal Safety.* He has coauthored *Our Polyvagal World: How Safety and Trauma Change Us* with his son Seth and coedited *Clinical Applications of the Polyvagal Theory* with Deb Dana. He is a cofounder of the Polyvagal Institute.